MW00860749

THE DIVINE LUMINOUS WISDOM

THAT DISPELS THE DARKNESS

EXPLANATORY NOTE BY THE AUTHOR

If we wish to understand the mystery of human existence, we should reflect with our Wisdom (Arivu) the explanatory note given below.

Human birth is a mystery. This mystery originated from a crevice in the hard mysterious rock of Maya which is harder than the hardest of rocks. From within the mystery of the crevice through which man originated, there grew a tree of mystery. The tree germinated from the fertile seed of Egoism, Action (Karma) and Illusion (Maya). This tree grew up with six main branches without any leaves. In this tree without leaves are found enticing elusive fruits amounting to 400 billion hypnotic fascinations of Maya, such as mental delusion caused by the hypnotic effect of Maya, darkness, illusion, sex urge, craving, intoxication, lust, theft, murder, falsehood, etc.

The mind and desire of man, whose origin is a mystery, embrace that tree of Maya which grew from the mysterious crevice and try to pluck and eat the elusive fruits of the tree of Maya. Since they are the elusive fruits of mystery and since they glimmer and appear like fruits in the darkness, his mind and desire are unable to eat the fruits, and are unable to know the nature of the tree. As a result of their vain attempts, his mind and desire get fatigued. As a result, this man, whose origin is a mystery, embraces that tree of mystery, sitting on the mysterious rock of Maya which arose from the crevice and wails: "Oh, My Fate! Oh, My Intellect! How can I leave you and go away? The tree has no shadow to shelter me from the sun and the rain. The tree has no leaves for me to eat. Even though I desire to eat the fruits, my hands are unable to reach them. This birth is a mystery. The crevice from which I originated is a mystery. The tree which grew out of that crevice is a mystery. The fruits in the tree are a mystery. When can I unravel these mysteries? When will my desire be fulfilled? When will my mind feel satisfied?"

This being who has been born as man, the rarest of creations, caught within the mysterious crevice, wails: "Alas! My Fate! My Intellect! Do you not know the suffering I am undergoing? Sitting under this tree of mystery, I am being scorched by the sun which scorches without scorching; I am being drenched by the rain and water which drench without drenching; I am being pushed about by the wind and whirl-wind which push me about without pushing. I am killed without being killed by egoism, hypnotic stupor, craving and Karma (evil action), all of which cause me to take several births. I am wailing because of all these. Alas! My Fate! O, tree of mystery which causes a hypnotic stupor in me to kill me! I have not been able to get fruit from you to satisfy my hunger. You do not have a shadow to protect me from the heat of the scorching sun. I do not find any paths to lead me elsewhere from this mysterious crevice. Tell me how I can get free from births, remove my obsessions, obtain clarity of Wisdom, get hold of the Ultimate One and obtain Bliss. Is there none who can save me from the stranglehold of this mystery? Is this then fate? Is this then my end?"

One should know the reality of the mystery of man's birth. If man, who is potential Man-God, is to escape from these five mysteries, he should cross the dark forest of this mystery guided by the Light of the Radiance of his Divine Wisdom (Pahuth-Arivu). When the mind and

i

craving are active, numberless Illusions will appear in that forest and make his Divine Wisdom (Pahuth-Arivu) succumb to their hypnotic fascinations and thereby detract his attention from the mysterious crevices on the path and make him fall into them. If he does not use the Light of Wisdom in the proper manner he is liable to fall into the mysterious pits which are found everywhere in that forest of Maya. If he falls into those pits it is not possible to save him or take him out. It will not be possible to remove himself from the hordes of demons and animals in that mysterious forest.

Oh! Man being born as the rarest and noblest of creations! You are born with Wisdom of the Divine Grace (Arul-Arivu). Your mission is to solve the mystery of human birth and know the Creator of Man. To unravel the mystery of your birth, you need the help of Wisdom (Arivu). Know the mystery of life with that Wisdom (Arivu). When you know the mystery, the mystery will disappear. When the mystery disappears, the mind also will disappear. Where the mind disappears, Craving will disappear. Where Craving disappears, Man becomes God. That state will be you. You will become the Soul (Atma). The Light of this Soul is God. God is Eternal. If you know this mystery, you will become Man-God (Manu Eesan).

THE DIVINE LUMINOUS WISDOM

THAT DISPELS THE DARKNESS

GOD~MAN

MAN~GOD

M. R.
BAWA MUHAIYADDEEN

REVISED EDITION

THE FELLOWSHIP PRESS   PHILADELPHIA

Acknowledgments

Muhammad Raheem Bawa Muhaiyaddeen ☙, a Sufi mystic from Sri Lanka, was a man of extraordinary wisdom and compassion. For over seventy years he shared his knowledge and experience with people of every race and religion and from all walks of life until his passing in 1986.

The discourses and illustrations presented here were given by M. R. Bawa Muhaiyaddeen in Sri Lanka (Ceylon) during 1970-71, prior to his first arrival in the United States. Spoken in Tamil, Bawa Muhaiyaddeen's words were written down verbatim by the scribe, Mr. Thajudeen, and then later translated into English by Mr. M. Nadarajah, D.R.O., and by Mr. T. Sabaratnam. The written material was organized and edited for publication in America by Professor Ajwad Macan-Markar with Mrs. Elizabeth Fenske and Mr. Paul Fenske.

Now in its fifth printing, *The Divine Luminous Wisdom That Dispels the Darkness* has introduced thousands of western readers to the uniquely original teachings of M. R. Bawa Muhaiyaddeen, and the many stories and parables, which faithfully retain the flavor of the Ceylonese landscape where they were narrated, continue to delight and inspire seekers both old and young.

Library of Congress Cataloging-in-Publication Data
Muhaiyaddeen, M. R. Bawa.
   The divine luminous wisdom that dispels the darkness; God-man, man-God, by M. R. Shaikh Muhaiyaddeen Guru Bawa.
     viii, 308 p. illus. 22 cm.
   Includes index.
   ISBN 0-914390-11-2 (pbk.) ISBN 0-914390-26-0 (hc.)
   1. Spiritual life

BL624 .G87 2004
294   721883357

Copyright ©1972 by The Bawa Muhaiyaddeen Fellowship
5820 Overbrook Avenue, Philadelphia, Pennsylvania 19131
All rights reserved. No portion of this book may be reproduced in any manner without written permission from the publisher.

Printed in the United States of America by
THE FELLOWSHIP PRESS
Bawa Muhaiyaddeen Fellowship

First Printing 1972   Second Printing 1977
Third Printing 1992   Fourth Printing 1997
Fifth Printing 2004

CONTENTS

Section II

ILLUSTRATIONS

FOREWORD

A quiver, a vibration, a series of vibrations, then an utterance, and at last a word—speech! Through speech man has communicated and handed down more knowledge and revelation than the written tradition will ever boast.

We who are alive at this time have to cope with a strange combination. We have printed whatever we could of that which has been spoken, as if it had been written! Since we now come of a literary tradition, we do not have all the understanding (which people once had) that relates to spoken tradition. This understanding is very important because it sets forth knowledge in subtle ways.

We literate people put great value in memorizing particulars, and we expect them to be accurate because we expect to draw our conclusions based upon their accuracy. Spoken wisdom has other priorities. For example the details of any story can be changed. It is the point of the story that counts, that has value, that opens the listener to something he never before knew. It is for this reason that we find in the Bible several different versions of the same happening. A different scribe in another time slot could write down the story as told by yet another story teller; but the point of the story would be the same.

When wisdom is spoken, the level of understanding of those in the audience is an important factor. A wise man does not speak over the heads of his listeners. If the point is to be made, he must reach into the seeker's existing frame of reference. This ability to penetrate, to take the genuine measure of another person's depth, to be able to read his whole life 'reels' as if they were a movie, is given to only the truly wise. Without the sure evaluation of the depth of the seeker of knowledge, there can be no real progress.

So it is that in a room full of people with many levels of acquired and real knowledge, the sage may address the group in the simplest language to tell a childlike story. Someone in that group is sitting there waiting to be brought to a higher station, and the point that has to be made in order to help him can be understood only through that simple story of the teacher. There is no place here for the specialized language of the academic world. All the great ones throughout the ages have given the nourishment of the highest wisdom to the people of their times in easily digested language.

Another characteristic of spoken wisdom is repetition. On a written page the reader may go back again and again to re-read the information which led to a certain conclusion. But in listening, the circumstances are different. Inner distraction, outer distraction, and other obstacles can cause the listener to miss the point. For this reason the teacher will hit the point from different angles, sometimes more than three times; but he will say it at least three times.

In truth, the vibration that exists between a genuine teacher and his students has the dynamics of music. The harmonies are played on the instruments which are assembled at the time. On the following day the instruments may be different. The music composed for those instruments will have to accommodate their special qualities and combinations, in order to bring about realization.

A teacher who can communicate with babies and aged professors, with artists and farmers, with mechanics and psychologists, with householders and wanderers is very rare. Those who gather to receive knowledge from Bawa Muhaiyaddeen are as varied as God's creation. Their ages, forms, and styles, their religious backgrounds, educations, and proclivities are not alike. Only the spoken wisdom, with its ability to move quickly through all levels of consciousness, can accommodate this group. What is necessary in the listeners is the kindness and patience that permits the teacher to at one time address a person with no education and at another time to address persons with very specialized training. Each one allows the work to be done for the other because he knows that the wealth of a wise man has to be shared among all. Still, in each person there will be the fullness, the completion, the wholeness, and the holiness—as if it all came to that one person alone.

When we read a 'spoken book' such as this—one which has originated in the spoken word of the teacher—we should impose upon ourselves an important condition in order to gain the most meaning from it. We must imagine ourselves as one of that group that sat at the feet of the teacher. The words we read must also be heard, listened to. They must vibrate through our dense material form into our own inner formless space, which will then vibrate in response and cause an awakening. As we grow in knowledge, more and more meanings are gleaned from the very same stories. Years from now, the life within the spoken story told by Bawa will still be teaching us new things.

Because thousands of people have already appreciated this 'spoken book' in its first edition and because so many have requested a reprinting of it, **The Divine Luminous Wisdom** is presented here with slight revisions and with the inclusion of fourteen new illustrations.

The place of this book on the path to Wisdom is an interesting and special one.

Bawa's Child, Sonia Leon Klein

INTRODUCING THE AUTHOR

The author of this wonderful book of illustrations, His Holiness Sheik Muhaiyaddeen Guru Bawa, is a living Sage of the twentieth century. Sufi, Master, Saint, and the Living Guide of the Mystics, he is indeed the Spiritual Light of the Universe. His is a state that rises above caste, color, creed, religions, and religious dogmas. The Wisdom that keeps gushing forth from this Fountain of Life—to give life, strength, and Wisdom through the illustrations mirrored in this book—is indeed a boon for all seekers after Truth, whatever religions or faiths they may belong to. These illustrations are facets of Wisdom shimmering with a Light that penetrates deep into the hearts of their devoted readers.

> Fathomless is thy Wisdom, wondrously told
> In sweet parables as in the era of the old;
> Priceless in thy Spirit, the Aroma of Love,
> Bird of the other sphere, perched on His Bough.

In the preface to this book, His Holiness says that the purpose of his illustrations is to serve as a guide—to open the eyes and hearts of those immersed in this world of maya and covered by the veils of lust and ignorance which belittle man, whose purpose in life is to reach ethereal heights by comprehending the meaning of his birth, existence, and death. His Holiness says that in this world of maya, man is surrounded by four billion hypnotic fascinations which make him a prisoner of himself, unable to know himself or his Divine State. Living in this state of blind ignorance, at the moment his heart clings to the worldly dust of fame and name, pomp and power, possessiveness, greed, and lust, man perishes with the world. Man thus becomes poorer than he was when he came into this world.

His Holiness beseeches all readers and devoted seekers in the Path of Truth to digest the substance of this book with patience and understanding, so that they may taste the sweetness of the Wisdom of Man that radiates through these descriptive illustrations and unveils the Truth which should be the goal of Man.

The purpose of man's birth and existence, his ultimate return to the Divine Source, the Path of self analysis and self unfoldment which all seekers must discover through the proper use of their Divine Intellect and Wisdom, and the Path leading to the Divine Secrets that unveil the Ultimate Truth between Man and God are clearly indicated through these wonderful illustrations, which are rare jewels that keep dazzling the hearts of all those devoted to the Path of the One Truth concealed within Man.

May all who read this book, presented to man by a Selfless Heart radiating Divine Luminous Wisdom, attain Peace, Contentment, Wisdom, and Understanding.

Fuard Uduman
Wattala, Ceylon

PREFACE

O children, you who have emerged as the rarest creation of God's Love and who have come to understand the Wisdom within His Grace, I shall explain God's Grace, Love, and Wisdom. Please reflect upon this.

Man's birth is of the highest order, rare and dear, emerging from God's Grace, begetting His Divine Light and Radiance. Man continually remains as God's Mystery. Within the human form lies the Grace of God as the mystery within the mystery. Within this Grace lies the Divine Luminous Wisdom as the mystery within the mystery. Within this mystery also lies the deceptive darkness of man's birth, which is also a mystery. The elements and the senses, which are part and parcel of his physical form, are also a mysterious illusion.

The forms of these elements and the senses comprise the four hundred billion hypnotic fascinations of maya. The deception, darkness, and desires lying within these consist of: the sixty-four types of hypnotic allurements; the one hundred million deceptive powers and forms of maya; those contained within the 4,448 tissues of the body; the eighty-four types of air; water, fire, air, and ether; the nine different kinds of gems (diamond, emerald, pearl, ruby, cat's eye, sapphire, coral, lapis lazuli, and gomada) which are the nine openings of the human body; the cry, the smile, joy, and sorrow; the desire to possess all that is seen and unseen; and the desires of the mind which is like a baby that keeps jumping and dancing around, singing, yelling, shouting and falling. Within this baby-mind exists the power to take all types of forms, shapes, and desires. These include: the characteristics of the monkey; the five elements, symbolized by the bear; the ten hands of the ten deadly sins which have the ability to suck the blood of devotees, perfect souls, scholars, seekers after Truth, and kings, and thereby weaken the nerves and extract the marrow from the bones, squeezing the muscles, drying its essence, torturing the body, reducing Wisdom, fostering ignorance, veiling the Truth, and increasing sins. Using wickedness as their weapon, the ten hands of the ten deadly sins try to take revenge against the lives of others. This is the mysterious role played by the five elements.

If man, (whose birth is so extremely rare) wishes to know and understand the one thousand and eight forms of desires which are taken and performed by the five elements, he must possess Wisdom. With this Wisdom, he must overcome the evil forces described above. Then, with the Light of this Wisdom, the following can be experienced, understood, and realized: the Truth and that which is in the Truth, the Grace within this, the Love within this Grace, the Compassion within this Love, the Equality within this Compassion, the Unity of Life in this Equality, the Radiance within this Unity, the Wisdom within the Radiance, the Light within this Wisdom, the God within this Light, Man within God, and God within Man.

In the morals of the following illustrations, one can understand the Truth and God. The emergence of Wisdom in man, the Omnipotent God within that Wisdom, and the Wisdom within this Wisdom is the Ultimate Truth. This book also illustrates the reality of man's Wisdom and the Truth of God's Grace. If one is born as a man and ponders with his Wisdom, he can comprehend this book. Therefore, my beloved and learned children, I beseech you to understand the contents of this book by studying, contemplating, and exploring the substance contained herein.

The creation of man and the Universe, the play of the senses, the roaming of the mind-monkey, the many explanations of birth, poverty, disease, old age, and death are clearly indicated and explained in these illustrations. Man, who is possessed of a deathless soul, brings upon himself through ignorance the repetition of several births. Therefore, by obtaining the help of his real Wisdom, man must understand the Truth that will show the Omnipotent God. Realizing the Truth by understanding this book entitled **The Divine Luminous Wisdom That Dispells the Darkness: God-Man, Man-God**, Man can become Man-God. He thus becomes the Perfect Man and becomes One with God.

Through their Wisdom, lovers of Truth and Wisdom must reflect upon and learn the Love, Compassion, and all the Qualities of God. They must strive to live in a God-like state.

M.R. Bawa Muhaiyaddeen
Jaffna, Ceylon

xviii

INTRODUCTION

O my God, You who are the Plenitude, the Omnipresent One who is found in everything and spread everywhere, the One who is resonating, manifesting, and appearing always; O my God, to me and to my children, grant us Your Divine Grace, Your Divine Wisdom, Your Divine Truth, Your Divine Patience, Your Tolerance, Peacefulness, Justice, Truthfulness, Forbearance, and Tranquility. Your Duty, Your 3,000 Good Thoughts and Divine Qualities, Your Perfect Conscience, the qualities of the 124,000 Prophets, their beauty, and Your Beauty. Grant these to me and to my children and protect and sustain us. I request this with my open heart and with my truthful Wisdom. I implore You, O God. Ameen. Ameen. Alhamdulillah. All Praise is to You, O God. It is Your Duty, as well as Your Debt, to protect and sustain us. I say this with absolute certainty and with sincere trust that You will grant our prayer.

My children, who are the light within my eyes, the light of my pupils, the perfection of my Love, my beloved children who are within my perfect Wisdom, I address this to your hearts and to your compassion. I am preaching this Truth through my Love and Wisdom, to the Wisdom of your hearts. You must analyze and reflect upon this.

This book, **The Divine Luminous Wisdom That Dispels The Darkness: God-Man, Man-God,** has been written to expound the Truth and Wisdom of man. What we have learned is equivalent to a handful, and what we have not learned is equivalent to the dimensions of the world. Like this, God's Beauty, His Grace, His Truth, and the Beauty of the eighty-four hundred thousand different creations of God—the reptiles, the animals, the beauty and the colors of the birds, the creations of the sea and their beauties; the jinns, fairies, angels, malaks, devas, and all other heavenly beings; the Prophets and the saints, their beauties, their nature, and their qualities; and the Qutb; the Gnanis, their overwhelming forbearance and tolerance and their Divine Wisdom; the four hundred trillion illusory forces and energies of the glitters of this earth, the earthly qualities, their colors, good and evil, the precious gems, gold, and other metals found in the earth; the element fire and its 1,008 forces and energies; the element water and its 1,008 illusory forces and energies; the element air and its 2,000 illusory forces and energies; the colors of ether, the stars, the sun, the moon, the lightning, and their forces and energies—have all been created by God.

Of His 3,000 beautiful Qualities, God took one atom of this and divided it into four hundred trillion portions and gave one minute portion of this to all His creations. And within this minute portion of this atom is contained all the beauties and all the forces and energies of His entire creation. And then He took another minute portion of this atom and divided that into 3,000 parts and divided that 3,000 into four divisions. He gave three hundred of these to the religion of Zaboor (Hinduism), three hundred to the religion of Hanal (Fire Worship), three hundred to the religion of Injeel (Christianity), ninety-nine to the religion of Furkhan (Islam), one thousand to the angels and one thousand to the Prophets. And He kept one of these attributes for Himself within Himself. And in that other minute portion are the qualities of creation, nourishment, sustenance, protection, judgment, and inquiry of good and evil; the power to open the hearts of all beings and to understand them; the protection of the Soul, which is Jesus; the Wisdom which appears in the Prophets and saints and in the Qutb as Moses; the protection of the Noor which is the Gnostic Effulgence manifested at the time of awwal (the primal beginning); and, like this, countless other protections. He lodged all this within a particle and kept it within Himself. In addition to this, He has within Himself 2,999 other beautiful Qualities.

What we are revealing in this book is a particle within a particle, which is equivalent to one of His particles divided into a billion finer particles. To the extent of our Wisdom we have revealed an infinitesimal quantum of knowledge in many other books, writings, and tape recordings. Yet, however much of His Divine Grace has been revealed in all these materials, it would not be equivalent to even one drop of water in all the seven oceans. Even if all these oceans were converted into ink and all the trees in this earth were made into pens, it would not be possible to express or write about His Divine Beauty, His Miraculous Nature, and everything else about Him. That we must understand through our true Divine Wisdom and from a true Gnostic Guru.

After He created all His creations and created their wisdoms of feeling, awareness, intellect, judgment, and wisdom, and lodged these wisdoms within His creations, and created four hundred trillion creatures (formless and with forms), and gave them their appropriate lives, God kept them in His Presence and asked them to look at Him. But none of these creations nor their lives nor their bodies were able to understand God. After this He sifted the essence from these four hundred trillion creatures and made that essence His Secret, and He made this Secret into His Grace. He gave this Grace seven forms of Beauty: feeling, awareness, intellect, judgment, wisdom, Divine Analytic Wisdom, and Divine Luminous Wisdom. He gave these His Light. Then He made this Light into a Secret and divided this Secret into four. One was made the physical body, one the Soul, one the Wisdom, and one the Perfection of God. Then He made it radiant within Him and made that Radiance His Heart and His Countenance. He kept this State within Himself as His Secret and told this Secret to look at His Effulgent Form.

This Secret addressed God: "My God, my Protector, my Ocean of Compassion. Bismillahirahmaniraheem. My Creator, my Nourisher, my Sustainer, the One who does these three Duties, the First One. I have not seen anyone as great as You." It then paid obeisance to God and worshipped Him.

Then God transformed this Secret Thing that witnessed His Secrets into His Divine Life and addressed it as follows: "I am going to create you in the form of three mysteries. I will be a Secret, My Gracious Soul will be a Secret, and the form of man that I am going to create will also be a Secret. In this mysterious way I am going to make you manifest. To understand these mysteries you will have to know Me and I will have to know you. And within this I shall lodge all the universes and all the earlier creations. I will reduce it to an invisible particle and will lodge it within your Secret. You must return to Me only after you have solved the mysteries of all My creations: the secret of your form and the mind within that form, the 18,000 universes contained within the mind, and the Form of that Light which is shadowless and which exists as a Secret within a Secret; the Secrets of the Soul, the Prophets and the saints who are contained within that Secret; and the mystery of who you are and who I am. Only after you transform these three Secrets (the Soul, the Wisdom, and the Noor) into One, and after you are transformed into your original state of Purity in which you are contained within Me and I am contained within you, can We converse with one another as in the present state. You are I and I am you. You are My Beauty and I am your beauty. I am the King and you are the Prince. You must know all these. It is in this most beautiful Form that I am going to create the human form. This is a secret between you and Me. This is a mystery between you and Me—mystery beyond the understanding of all beings.

"Although this man may be created as a mystery of all mysteries, he will not be able to see Me and My Beauty with the visions of his eyes, with his mind, with his desire, with the four hundred trillion aspects of his physical body, nor with religions. He must go beyond all these barriers and come to realize the three Secrets within each person. One who has attained this station will exist in this world as the Qutb and as the Son of God. This is very rare. Since the Qutb is within Me and I am within the Qutb, he will not create any equal to Me. He will not accept magics or mantras or any of the four hundred trillion deities, nor will he equate them with Me. He will not keep as My equal nor worship any of the forces or energies of the earth, the forces of fire, the forces of water, the forces of air, or the forces and energies of ether (such as the sun and moon). He will not keep any of these as My equal or worship them.

"He will unravel the mystery of 'La illaha, il Allahu—Nothing other than God exists. Only God exists. Everything else is nothing. Only God is God.' The completion of this mystery is the Mystery of God, and that Secret is Man. His body is a Secret, his Soul is a Secret, and the God within him is a Secret. One who fails to understand this mystery of man will never come to know God, his Self, and God's Grace. This mystery is one that has not been seen by the visions of the eyes, the visions of the mind, or the visions of desires."

My children must understand this. With all the learnings you have learned and with all the actions you have acquired, you will never be able to realize the Truth. What the eye sees, the monkey-mind pictures. What the monkey-mind pictures, the desire grabs. What the desire grabs, the elements see. What the elements see is projected as dreams. And to accept what your elements perceive is a degradation of Wisdom. It is the six sins. These six sins are the world that the mind created.

You must understand the inner Heart that lies within. If you know this inner Heart, you will know that Mystery. That Secret has two manifestations: one is the body that is formed of the physical elements, the other is the Body of Light. Of these two bodies, the body of the elements has been made into the world and into a stage. The actors on this stage are the creations of the mind. They will act out all the illusory forces that are contained in the six sins and that are seen by vision, by mind, and by desire. These actors can be divided into seventy-two main groups.

There is another group, a single group, a 'secret' group. For that group the whole world is stretched out as a prayer mat on which each man worships. He worships God in the world of Divine Wisdom, the Divine Soul, and the Divine Light spread out in the form of a mat. He recites the Kalima: La illaha (Nothing other than God exists); il Allahu (Only You are God). And on this mat of Divine Plenitude he worships that One God from all positions. This is the Divine Mystery. If you try to understand this Divine Mystery from the things that your eyes have shown you or that the mind has revealed to you or that the desires have grabbed, you will never be able to understand this Mystery. The only way to realize this Mystery is through the knowledge of the Perfect Guru and through the Wisdom of the Perfect Guru. You can then understand the mysteries of this book. My children must reflect upon this and use the Wisdom of the Guru to analyze, to understand, and to comprehend the writings in this book. The mind contains within it the four hundred trillion glitters of this earth, both good and evil, the dirt and the filth. Through these glitters you will not be able to understand the Mystery of this shadowless Light.

My children! If you wish to get on to the ship that is awaiting in the harbor near the shore, do not carry with you the sea shores on which you stand. It is not possible to take the shore with you on this ship. You will never be able to lift this shore, nor will you be able to get into the ship. Like this, if you see God through the glitters of your mind, you will never be able to get into the boat of His Wisdom with the weight of your mind. So please cast aside all these glitters of the mind and come alone with your wisdom, your faith, your certitude, and your determination. If you get into the boat in this manner, the boat will take you to the mysteries of God, the Wisdom, and the Soul. So please remember, my children—when you go to the Guru, go with your mind completely empty of all the things you have gathered within it. Then only will the Guru be able to show you these Divine Mysteries: the mystery of the Soul, the mystery of Wisdom, and the mystery of God.

I humbly request you, my children, to appreciate what I have said in order that you may fully comprehend the wisdom and the Truth that is contained in this book. Do not try to understand it through your intelligence or through the four hundred trillion intelligences of the gurus and their worships and meditations. You will never be able to understand this mystery through these things. This is the Commandment of God and this is His Judgment. One who fully grasps the Wisdom and the Truth in this book will become the Son and the Prince of God.

I pray to the Almighty God that He may bestow upon my children the Truth and Wisdom. Ameen. May God protect us and sustain us and give us His Grace and all His Qualities. Ameen.

M.R. Bawa Muhaiyaddeen
Philadelphia,
Pennsylvania
April, 1972

SECTION I

DISCOURSES

THE SEVEN STATES OF CONSCIOUSNESS

In every discourse of the Teacher, one cannot fail to grasp the emphasis which he places on Man's conscious state as the determinant of his destiny. Therefore, in order to avoid any confusion, it becomes necessary to set out below, the Seven States of Consciousness, in ascending order of importance, in so far as they constitute the mechanism of understanding or of realisation, whether it be a simple cause and effect relationship, or the more significant Reality. These states are described by their Tamil equivalent, and one would be tempted to resort to the Tamil Dictionary to ascertain their meaning. But such dictionary meanings have no relevance, whatsoever, to the connotations placed upon them by the Teacher in the light of his own experiences and attainments. There terms therefore take upon themselves an entirely different meaning, far wider, deeper and more poignant than their dictionary definitions. The Teacher thus proceeds to explain these states or processes of consciousness on two levels, (A) the ordinary cause and effect relationship, as for example, when a man experiences pain caused by fire touching his leg, and (B) on the spiritual level, as when he is compelled to ask himself, "why was I born?" Thus the seven states or processes of consciousness are:

1. UNARVU Sensory Feeling, Perception
2. UNARCHI Sensory Awareness, Cognition
3. PUTHTHI Lower Mind, Intellect
4. MADTHI Practical Understanding, Knowledge
5. ARIVU Conscience within Reason, Wisdom
6. PAHUTH-ARIVU Intuitive Spiritual Wisdom in association with purity of heart, Divine Wisdom
7. PERR-ARIVU Divine Intelligence, Divine Luminous Wisdom

(1) UNARVU

(A) "It is the first state of consciousness, when the feeling of pain strikes the mind of the man."

(B) "A man begins to feel that all is not well with life and he asks himself, 'Why was I born?' 'Where did I come from?' " This state of consciousness, UNARVU, is the starting point of the spiritual inquiry into himself.

Therefore, the suggested English equivalents are: (A) Feeling Sensation, the consciousness of perceiving or seeming to perceive some state or affection of one's body or (B) Perception.

(2) UNARCHI

(A) "Then he becomes aware of the location of pain in the body, that is centered in the leg."

(B) The man makes a scrutiny of himself, asking himself, "What is it that constitutes my body, and with what did I first appear on earth? How did I come into the world?" This is the second state of consciousness.

Therefore, the suggested English equivalents are: (A) Awareness, Sense Awareness. (B) Cognition.

(3) PUTHTHI

(A) "Then he tries to find out how the pain was caused, whether it was injury caused by contact with fire or by the pricking of a thorn or the cutting by a sharp knife."

(B) When the man reflects on the causality of his origins, posed by the states of Unarchi, the third state of consciousness, PUTHTHI, provides the answers as when it purports to say 'your body is constituted of five elements, Earth, Fire, Water, Air and Ether. You come into this world because you were fascinated, hypnotised by its Illusion (Maya).' "

The suggested English equivalents, therefore, are: Lower Mind; Intellect; Lower Intelligence; Ascertainment; the Ascertainment of Causality, the action by which the mind refers its sensations to external objects as cuase, or in spiritual sense, the ascertainment of the cause of existence, causality: (Per His Holiness: —"Intellect is limited in comprehensive power, by the inherent attributes of the five elements".)

(4) MADTHI

(A) "Then he assesses the nature, the extent and the gravity of the injury."

(B) When he reflects further on what his Puththi has revealed, then MADTHI, the fourth state of consciousness, takes over to reveal to him the consequences or the effects of his existence, or when it purports to say "your period of life in this state is short; The world has thrown on to your consciousness, millions of fascinating Illusions which overpower your life; your life on earth is a business venture undertaken by five virtual enemies, sworn to destroy each other, but presently working together as partners. This partnership is not permanent, it is temporary. If one partner breaks away, the partnership is at an end, upon which you must certainly depart from this world. When you appeared in this world you came with a debt owed to your Creator. How else then are you going to repay this debt before you leave? There is no question that you must leave when your time should come. Therefore, break away from the stranglehold of these five enemies before you depart, so that when you do, you may take away the wealth called Perfection. Gather it soon because you may tarry but only for a week."

Accordingly, the suggested English equivalents of MADTHI are: Knowledge (per His Holiness: —"He applies the searchlight of knowledge on the fortress of his intellect."); and Ascertainment of the Consequence. This state of consciousness, Madthi, marks the highest mental attainment in man, sometimes called the apex of "Cerebral" activity, on the plane of mundane existence. It marks the highest level of intellectual achievement founded on observed phenomena, on knowledge concerned with every day living. In the spiritual sense, the causality of life, etc., having been determined by Puththi, Madthi reveals the consequence of earthly existence, such as its illusive character, its impermanence, the fleeting or temporary pleasures associated with it, its inevitable termination, its imbalance and unreality, and proclaiming, therefore, the need to achieve Perfection and Realisation.

2

(5) ARIVU

(A) "Then he thinks of the various remedies that can be used to heal the wound."

(B) "When the subject contemplates deeply on what Madthi has revealed, then the fifth state of consciousness, ARIVU, begins to function. In the silence of his contemplative state, the fifth state of consciousness purports to reveal the inner state of his being beyond the frontiers of birth or death; the seeds of his past which had fashioned his present, and the future that shall be determined by the present. Arivu identifies the innumerable seeds of life and death carried by him. It is an Inner Reason which compels the individual to divert his attention from the several attractions of the world to the contemplation of his inner state of being. Moreover, Arivu satisfies him, and convinces him that Reality cannot be found outside him in the world of Illusion, but rather that it is within him, and that, he may achieve it only by his Certitude, his convictions and his determination, and his Will. To this end it compels him to seek Perfection; a state of being which it prescribes for the present and for the future, and the several modes to achieve it." In the light of these explanations, therefore, it is not possible to render into English by appropriate English terminology the precise meaning of this Tamil word which the Teacher uses in explaining the knowledge gathered from his own experiences. Ordinarily, the term "Arivu" means Wisdom, Reason, Understanding.

But the Teacher uses the term in an entirely different way because it has a far deeper meaning in relation to the spiritual understanding of oneself. In this regard the following additional explanation by His Holiness might also be helpful.

(1) "Arivu" is of a higher plane, of a higher order than ordinary Intellect.

(2) It may most approximately be defined as "Reason" or "the Conscience within Reason."

(3) This state of consciousness, when relevant to one's spiritual state, becomes evident only on the cessation of one's satanic traits, e.g., Egoism, Envy, Jealousy, Hatred, Desire and Lust, as well as one's capacity to be attracted by the phenomenal world.

(4) It becomes pronounced on one's mastery over the physical body, that is, on the death of all desires for worldly attachment, on the shunning of the illusory aspects of worldly existence, and conversely, when worldly attractions are rendered powerless to corrode one's conscience.

It is only on this achievement that this consciousness is activated.

(5) It is innate in the state of development immediately after Madthi. It is self-revealing.

(6) It is seated in the Deeper Conscience.

(7) It is not dependent or governed by any book learning or observed scientific phenomena. Therefore, this state of consciousness is evident even in the unlettered provided he has caused the cessation of worldly attachments.

(8) It is a state of consciousness, spiritually speaking; which is remedial or curative in its objective.

The suggested English equivalents are Wisdom (as when Purified Intellect now becomes Discriminating Wisdom, immanent in the "Heart" transcending the practical understanding), Illumined Intellect, Reason and Conscience within Reason.

(6) PAHUTH-ARIVU

(A) "Then he considers and analyses the efficacy of various remedies and comes to a decision that a particular remedy is the best."

(B) "When the subject examines the variety of modes ascertained by his Arivu to achieve Perfection and Reality, he is called upon to rely on the next state of consciousness, called Pahuth-Arivu, to select from among them, one particular mode. The selection of this one mode, this one way, calls for a prior analytical assessment of all other modes of attainment. And in this analytical assessment, this state of consciousness, Pahuth-Arivu, purports to tell him thus, 'You know why you were born here. If you know the cause of your birth, I shall tell you how you may remove that cause, so that it will be non-existent in the future in order that it will preserve that causeless purified state without in any way befouling it.' Therefore: —

"Spread then this state on the table (of your Sense of Duty).
And account it in your book of Compassion,
Writing upon it with the pen of Forebearance,
Which has as its point, Certitude of the highest,
And fill that pen with the ink of Contentment,
And holding it with the hand of Compassion,
Direct with your eyes called Reason,
To adorn the pages with Truth"

Then the Teacher says "From within the recesses of Knowledge emerges Wisdom which investigates Truth." Thus Pahuth-Arivu, quite apart from its ordinary Tamil meaning is regarded by the Teacher as the highest form of Reasoning Wisdom (or Enlightening Reason), resulting from Deep Spiritual Contemplative Wisdom of the highest order, which the power and capacity of the higher human consciousness in association with the purity of heart can achieve. We may, even on the explanation offered by the Teacher, say that it is an innate and immanent power which is activated by a penetrating, incisive, reasoning insight. Its purpose is to reveal the two poles of human endeavour and their respective merits from the spiritual standpoint. These are first the pole of worldly attachment, governed by the 5 senses, with its utter Illusion, transitoriness, triviality, and futility, the only advantage of such attachment being temporary pleasures and mundane stimuli. The other pole is the identification of the Supreme Reality (Haq) as the purpose in life; Pahuth-Arivu, therefore, reaches the point of perfection upon the rejection of the former for the latter. Therefore it is introspective in content, analytical in its approach, contemplative and meditative in form. For these reasons, it may be regarded as an inner spiritual guide or menthor (Quthb or Quthubiyat or Guru) inborn in man. This supra-mundane Wisdom is by some called the Soul, which impels him to seek the Divine source of his origin.

Such Wisdom induces a reasoned self assessment, self analysis, self-criticism, and an all-revealing self estimation permitted by the limits of the Conscience and the Sense of Justice, which, incidentally, are Divine Attributes innate in man. This Spiritual Wisdom is the stimuli to such self realisation. Conversely, Pahuth-Arivu or the Quthubiyat compels the acceptance of that which is right, that which is good, that which is correct, and that which is real; and the unrepentent rejection of that which is wrong, that which is evil, and that which is incorrect. So that in this light Pahuth-Arivu, or the Quthubiyat (Quthb or Guru), is man's sixth state of consciousness leading to the restoration of the original and unblemished state of purity.

The suggested English equivalents are: Divine Wisdom, Intuitive Spiritual Wisdom, the Light of Wisdom, Enlightenment and Illumined Wisdom, occurring in association with a purified heart.

(7) PERR-ARIVU

(A) "Then he applies the remedy ultimately selected by the Pahuth-Arivu as the most suitable and uses it in a manner that would give him the quickest relief."

(B) "Perr-Arivu, the Seventh state of consciousness becomes manifest upon the enlightening analysis of the Pahuth-Arivu."

Perr-Arivu or the "Noor", is the consciousness that is liberated from the bonds of matter, from every trace of the human ego, from the mundane experiences of joy and sorrow, pleasure and pain, the selfish and self-centered divisive tendencies of "mine" and "thine". Above all, since every temptation inclining towards the hypnotic pull of Illusion, the fascination for the stimuli preferred by the world at large, has ceased, Perr-Arivu is the very essence of Enlightened Reason, a unique state of consciousness upon which no limit can be placed. It is the most perfect, the purest Perception (or shall we say) Enlightened Wisdom. It encompasses the Totality of Truth or Reality (Haq)."

Further when all other states of consciousness are put away the concept of "I the individual" departs, leaving only the 7th state of consciousness, the consciousness of the highest which brings to an end, the duality of man and God, while identifying Reality within man as God. Perr-Arivu then eliminates every trace in the individual of the "I" consciousness (Fana) while merging with the Reality (Truth, God) (Baq'aa). The objective, then, of the Perr-Arivu is truly the merging, as when "he becomes Him and He becomes him".

Therefore, Perr-Arivu or Noor may be called the Light of God, Divine Luminous Wisdom, the Illuminated Intelligence and the Divine Intelligence, if God, Himself, is Light. In Sufistic terminology it is called "Noor" or "Noor Muhammad", the Effulgence which reflects the Omniscience of God, His Wisdom, His Supreme Intelligence. Therefore until such time as it is activated, it is immanent in man, if man is looked upon as an expression of God's Essence (Zat). It is self-revealing through the medium of the Pahuth-Arivu, as the Truth, and as such, it is the Divine Truth which will illumine his soul.

5

It also represents the final attainment of the unity expressed in the Kalima, "There is no god but God (La-illaha-ill-Allah Allahu)", whereby the microcosmic is identified with the macrocosmic. It may also be regarded as a Conscious State of Being, when the individual and physical personality of man has ceased to exist in preference to God in man. It is the source of Revelation and the Light of an all encompassing knowledge, marking the individual as a Luminant Being, and as a window to the Divine Omniscience which embraces the Divine Plan or Scheme and renders man an heir to all knowledge, whether presently known or unknown. Conversely, it is that indiscernible faculty innate in man which makes him seek, sometimes involuntarily, sometimes consciously, sometimes unknowingly, the source of his origin, namely God. It is the state of consciousness which has as its objective, Perfection in Purity, and Purity in Perfection. But Certitude is its very foundation, while Forebearance, Conviction, Belief, Contentment, Compassion, and Wisdom, are its most sacred attributes. It is the stamp of the Perfect Man (Insan Kamil) or (Manu-Eesan) and has as its objective, the discovery of Reality, immanent in all things both seen and unseen. That man should be invested with such a supreme consciousness designed to identify the reality that is within himself is but only one of the myriad mysteries of his being.

The suggested English terminology is Divine Luminous Wisdom, Divine Intelligence, (or the Sufistic definition) "Noor Muhammad" or "Noor Muhammadia".

NOTE on—Thiru Marai—Literally, it means Holy Scripture and as such it refers, to the Scriptures and words of every Religion. In a narrow sense it is used to describe the Quran. But in that context in which the Teacher uses it, the term Thiru Marai takes on an entirely different complexion. In the Sufistic analysis, as explained by the Teacher it is the manifestation of the Conscience of God from time to time, in every age to every nation, revealing to mankind the mode of attaining Him, in the form of Divine Exhortation. For this reason, it may be called the Primeval Quran or the Primeval Scripture, which becomes manifest from time to time, setting out the guidelines of human conduct in relation to Spiritual evolution. If God is Reality, immanent in man, the voice of God, the Revelation that proceeds from the "Noor", the Perr-Arivu, is called the "Thiru Marai".

WHERE IS GOD?

Down the centuries, seekers after truth have posed the question, "Where is God?"

Throughout the centuries, religious leaders of the four religions, very learned in their respective theological lore and each of them wearing an attire appropriate to his particular religion, took up the onerous mission of expounding to their followers as to where is God.

Each of these religious leaders is possessed with reputedly high academic attainments of his particular theological doctrine. Their manner of approach to this very important question is bound to be sectional, narrow, and rigidly confined, within the latitude permitted and enjoined by the doctrines of their particular religions.

This approach, on the face of it, is incorrect, because the Creator Allah is Omnipotent, Omnipresent and Omniscient. He is not the exclusive monopoly of any particular segment of humanity professing certain sets of dogmatic beliefs.

When a man with Divine Luminous Wisdom sees the spectacle of humanity engaged in the search for their Creator under conditions permitted by their particular doctrines, he sighs at the utter futility of their quest. For a person engaged in searching for his Creator he must, as a prerequisite, be permeated with the Glorious Attributes and Qualities of the Supreme Creator, Allah.

Within the innermost recesses of the Heart (Qalb) of a Man (Insan) is present the latent Divine Effulgence of Allah. The physical composition of man is made of the five elements.

Among these elements the Earth radiates over 400 crores of hypnotic fascinations.

Each of these hypnotic fascinations is endowed with Power (Sakti) capable, when fully developed, of enormous destructive potential.

Then there is the element of Air in the physical composition of man. This element of Air is capable of being disintegrated into 84,000 different varieties of Air, one different from the other. Each variety has a particular Power (Sakti) capable, when fully developed, of highly destructive potential.

Then there is the element of Water in the body of man which can be disintegrated into 70,000 varieties of water, each with its own Power (Sakti) capable of immense destructive potential.

Then there is the element of Fire in the bodily composition of man. This Fire disintegrates into 10½ crores (one crore is 10 million) of different varieties of Fire, each exuding a particular variety of warmth and heat.

Each of these varieties of Fire is endowed with a particular Power (Sakti) of stupendous consuming potential.

Then there is the element of Ether within which is potentially enshrined crores of radiant colours, varieties of smells and qualities, one different from the other.

Within the vast spectrum of Ether is also potentially present all the infinite range of qualities and attributes of a being who is subject to 3½ crores of births.

All these qualities and attributes of the physical body assail man, who is bereft of Wisdom and who is saturated in the darkness stemming from Mayic Ignorance and Delusion.

7

All these attributes and qualities permeate, envelop, and engulf the life of man in the form of crores of enticing entities, each endowed with a particular Power (Sakti).

It is within this vast spectrum of power stemming from the darkness of Illusion (Maya) that a person bereft of Wisdom and deeply caught within the tentacles of Illusion (Maya) encounters very enticing hypnotic fascinations which he erroneously imagines as Divine Luminosities radiating from the Effulgence of the Creator.

Within the Heart (Qalb) of this person, the hypnotic fascinations arising from the Earth are preponderantly active. This person, himself, is hypnotically entranced in the misbelief that these enticing fascinations bear an affinity and relationship with the Divine Luminosities radiating from the Divine Effulgence of Allah.

Still further this person lavishes an unstinted devotion to these influences.

This devotional state to these objects of devotion is construed as Faith (Bakti).

The net result of his conduct is that he is firmly bound to the hypnotic fascinations of the Earth. And the Divine Luminous Wisdom potentially present within his Heart (Qalb) is smothered and scotched.

Such people are guilty of three heinous crimes against the Supreme Creator.

The first crime is when certain people pay devotion to Allah through an intermediary. This attitude is incorrect, for Allah is Supreme, without an equal and needs no intermediary.

The second crime is when devotion is bound and circumscribed by religious dogmas.

For the Creator Allah is beyond all creeds, sects and dogmas: He is Omnipresent.

The third crime is when their devotion to their Creator is limited by various names of the Creator. For Allah Himself is without a name, country, wife or children. He is without beginning or end and is Omnipresent. When the Creator bears the description detailed above it is very wrong to label Him with names and then search for Him by this name.

The true way is for man to know and understand why he was ushered into this world of Illusion (Maya). Thereafter, he should endeavour to know the attributes and qualities of all other created beings.

Then he should come to know the qualities and attributes of the five elements of his physical body namely Earth, Fire, Water, Air and Ether and also come to know the varied manifestations in the whole range of God's Creation. Such a person would certainly come to know and realise all that has been detailed above when his entire being is lit with the Resplendence of Divine Luminous Wisdom.

A person in this state would have successfully passed the test of realising the purpose of his existence on earth.

Such a person, endowed with the Overpowering Grace of Allah, will place himself in a state of complete and utter surrender to Allah and would become integrated within the Effulgence of Allah. This is the highest point of man's existence on earth.

The Divine Luminous Wisdom now opens up the innermost recesses of the Heart (Qalb).

Man is manifestly in error in thinking that he is an insignificant entity in the wide range of Creation. On the contrary, man is the rarest and the noblest of Allah's Creation, and within him is present his Creator in the form of Divine Effulgence.

Within the Heart (Qalb) of Man is enshrined crores of characteristics, qualities and attributes acquired from the world of Illusion (Maya) and crores of attributes and qualities inherent in the five elements in his physical composition.

In addition there are crores of allurements radiating from the sense world of Illusion (Maya) which tend to attach themselves to his Heart.

In any person the distance between Allah and himself is the vast terrain occupied by the crores of attachments arising from the world of Illusion (Maya).

The Divine Luminous Wisdom in man is the seat and citadel of the Effulgence of Allah. This is potentially present within the inner-most recesses of the Heart (Qalb) of man. Between man and his Creator lie the crores of hypnotic fascinations which have to be over-powered before he is integrated within the Effulgence of Allah.

This process has to begin by rooting out these hypnotic evil illusions from his Heart (Qalb) and make his Heart (Qalb) spotlessly pure.

When this metamorphosis occurs in the personality of the man, Divine Luminous Wisdom will emerge from within his Heart (Qalb). Such a person will come to know himself and his Creator.

He would also come to know that within the seat of his Divine Luminous Wisdom is found the Effulgence of Allah, the Resplendence of the Light of God (Noor) and the Radiance of his own Soul (Ruh), all integrated in one Supremely Lustrous Radiant Splendour.

9

MAN SEEKS HIS CREATOR

Man is the highest and noblest being in the entire range of Creation and it should be his endeavour to discover the limitless potentialities embedded within his Heart (Qalb). To do so and realise them, he must absorb the attributes of Allah, his Creator within his very being, through inner awareness and direct realization.

Only those who stamp out egoism, realise their Divine Heritage and develop love and compassion for their fellow beings can impregnate themselves with these Divine Attributes.

A person saturated with the attributes of Allah would realize within himself the gradual unfoldment of Divine Luminous Wisdom (Noor) which when it illumines his entire being reveals to him the causes which generate hunger, disease, old age and eventually death. He would also come to know through the penetrating power of his inner Illumined Wisdom the remedy for hunger, disease, old age and eventually death. He would also come to know through the penetrating power of his inner Illumined Wisdom the remedy for hunger, disease, old age and death to which mankind as a whole is vulnerable.

Man in his Devotion and Prayer to God should place himself in a state of complete and utter surrender. But many believe that they can obtain the favour of their Creator by giving offerings to Him. Some Hindus offer a number of coconuts to God asking for rain, while another group of Hindus offer a number of coconuts to God to stop the rain so they can cultivate their crops. Only those in ignorance and darkness act in this way. But the Grace of Allah which envelopes the entire Creation, like the rain, falls on every object within its orbit, making no distinction whatsoever in its distribution. It is like the rain water which, falling on steep and stony places, does not collect but gets washed away, while that which falls in crevices, cavities and receptive soils collects in volume relative to their size and the area.

Similarly, Allah's Grace which envelopes every human being can penetrate and permeate only those with receptive hearts. People wedded to false doctrines and erroneous doctrines are completely impervious and non-receptive to Divine Grace.

Many people spend their lives wandering about in search of their Creator. This is like the fish in the vast ocean searching for water. They, like the fish, do not realize that once they leave the expanse of water in the ocean and come to land, life itself would be come extinct. They cannot exist outside the Creator. Man should realize that in his Heart (Qalb) are present all potentialities found in the entire Creation itself and in the fifteen other worlds.

Man should try to awaken the Divine Luminous Wisdom latent within himself. Once his Luminous Wisdom becomes fully Resplendent he would come to know the seat and citadel of the Divine Effulgence of Allah within himself; and in this glorious state, Man would come to know himself and thereafter he would come to know his Creator.

There are 10½ crores (one crore is 10 million) of evil propensities of Illusion (Maya) which assail mankind with their hypnotically enticing temptations.

It should forever be the main endeavour of man to root out these evil propensities of Illusion (Maya).

10

Detachment

Man in his upward Divine ascent, although living in this world, should for all practical purposes concentrate his consciousness in his higher self.

Like an aluminum pot and spoon, for example, provide the means towards the preparation of say 32 different kinds of food dishes, each of them with a particular and peculiar taste. People who taste these delicacies relish the particular taste of each delicacy according to their likes and dislikes, but the aluminum pot and spoon, although they conjointly provide the means and preparation of the 32 dishes, did not register any particular reaction in respect of any particular dish or for that matter even the 32 dishes cumulatively provided no reaction whatever on the aluminum pot and spoon.

Similarly, Man treading on the path of righteousness should react exactly like the aluminum pot and spoon to things of joy and sorrow in this world.

It is also inevitable for Man in the course of his existence on this earth to be involved in innumerable manifestations generated in the world of Illusion (Maya) in the discharge of his duties and obligations.

But he should perform his duties in the same spirit of detachment evidenced in the illustration of the aluminum pot and spoon.

Such a person would find his ascent on the path of Divine Wisdom, free from the encumbrances generated by the world of Illusion (Maya).

Vigilance

A snake charmer who entices a snake from its pit through various techniques and stratagems gets hold of the snake and brings it under his full mastery and control. This snake, trained with great effort, reaches a point when it becomes absolutely docile and obedient to the snake-charmer, who communicates with the snake by playing a particular strain of music to which the snake is receptive.

The snake is all aglow, vigilant, and active to obey the slightest command of the snake-charmer for fear lest it invokes his anger in not carrying out a particular command. An important fact to be noticed during this performance is that the eyes of the snake are fixed intently on the eyes of the snake-charmer, its master.

The snake-charmer in turn is also alert, active and ever vigilant in noticing the slightest deviation in the behaviour of the snake. The moment the snake deviates in its behaviour, the ever-vigilant snake-charmer brings the snake under control within a split second.

There is this danger, however, if the snake deviates in its behaviour and if during this time, the snake-charmer himself is off his guard, the situation becomes wrought with danger. The snake emboldened by the relaxation shown by the snake-charmer would display its inherent attributes by pouncing on the snake-charmer and thrusting its venomous fangs into his flesh with fatal results.

Man and Maya

Similarly Man in his relationship with the world of Illusion (Maya) should utilize his Wisdom (Arivu) in his dealings with the numerous mani-

11

festations of Illusion (Maya). He should be ever alert and vigilant, meticulously wedded to the Divine Truths, in thought and deed and never deviate from them, even an iota. In this situation the person concerned keeps the manifestations from the world of Illusion (Maya) under his proper control; and such a man is indeed in the right process of awakening his Divine Luminous Wisdom (Perr-Arivu).

On the contrary, if this person relaxes his vigilance and deviates from the meticulous adherence to Divine Truths during his encounter with the manifestations of Illusion (Maya), then most assuredly these manifestations of Illusion (Maya) would exercise their fascination and enticement on him.

Such a person, meshed and entangled within the tentacles of Illusion (Maya) would inevitably slide deeper and deeper into Illusion (Maya) and his eventual fate would be a state of utter demoralization and degradation.

Religious Knowledge

A frog in the well once asked the frog from the ocean as to whether the extent of the ocean would be about the distance it jumped within the well, namely 3 feet. The answer from the frog in the ocean was in the negative. The frog in the well jumped one foot more than the original distance and wanted to know as to whether the ocean can be that long. The frog from the ocean again replied in the negative.

The frog in the well had no means of knowing the vast nature of the ocean when compared to its own well.

There are likewise vast segments of humanity divided rigidly into four divisions which we call religions which have a very considerable following wedded to their particular dogmas and doctrines. They believe that they alone possess exclusively the keys to unlock the innermost citadel of Divine Wisdom leading towards Knowledge and Realization of the Supreme Creator. On the contrary, by their rigid exclusiveness and fanatical adherence to certain doctrinary beliefs, they have erected tremendous barriers which shut them off from the reservoir of the Divine Truth in the ocean of Ilm (Knowledge).

It is only those who enter this ocean of Divine Knowledge and realize the Divine Truth who can emulate the lofty attributes of Allah and come to know their Creator.

The followers of the four Religious Authorities forget the fact that in the beginning man had his origin in a principle of duality within a unity. They also forget the fact that there is one Supreme Creator who does not make any invidious distinction among His created beings.

They also forget the fact that Allah is Omnipotent, Omnipresent and His Perennial Grace envelops and engulfs the entire Creation.

Followers of the four divisions of religions, have erected stupendous barriers which bar them from the vast reservoir of the Divine Truth gleaming in Divine Splendour within the Divine Effulgence of Allah. Their predicament is analogous to the symbolic frog in the well which does not know and in view of the physical limitations of its well, it cannot possibly know the vast expanse of the ocean.

God The Source of Power

How tragic would it be if man, forgetting his Divine Heritage, elevates the propensities of Illusion (Maya) which are perishable, to the position of Divinity. It should be the endeavour and central aim of man to know and understand That One which is imperishable. Therefore, it is incumbent that man should be aware of his Divine Heritage. Here is an illustration on electric current to amplify this point of view.

The electric current emanates from a certain power station positioned at some point. A person looking at the electric light manifested in a bulb, cannot possibly determine from the light itself, the place and source of power from which the electric current comes. Neither can this person describe the colour of the current which is invisible. Sometimes one sees numerous different coloured bulbs, shedding different coloured lights. The light these bulbs shed is identical to the colour of the particular bulb.

But it must be remembered, that although there are different coloured bulbs shedding different coloured lights, the current which is the central source of power remains the same. The only constant factor here is the current, the source of power, invisible to normal vision and is symbolic of the Creator who is the Source of all life.

The bulbs with their diverse colours, each bulb shedding light according to its colour, symbolically represent the various religions, creeds and sects. Each of them represents a particular set of dogmas and doctrines, but all of them declare that realisation of Divinity is their central and basic purpose in life.

Some of the adherents of these doctrinal beliefs proclaim their adherence to a particular religion or creed not out of conviction, but purely because of their material advantage.

But persons truly wedded to the path of rectitude would find the Divine Wisdom within themselves active and emergent. This Divine Wisdom would annihilate from the Heart (Qalb) of these persons all erroneous beliefs which form the bedrock of misguided religions. It is only persons of this nobility and Wisdom who are just and truly entitled to the name of Man (Insan).

It is only a person of such calibre who would be able to reject and discard the bulbs of different colours and the symbolic bulbs which are false manifestations of the real electric current and the colourless light.

Thereafter, this person would direct all his endeavours and efforts with enthusiasm to know and realise that the current, which is the Source of power, is symbolic of that imperishable, eternal and everlasting object, namely the Creator, Allah. This Man (Insan) in whom the Divine Wisdom is emergent and active is possessed of Divinely Resplendent Certitude of Faith (Iman).

Such a person would exhibit at all times Magnanimity, Forbearance, Love, Compassion and Charity to all. This Man, lofty and noble, is indeed a person of Divine Excellence and places himself for ever in complete surrender to Allah.

Ameen.

WHO IS AN INSAN (MAN)

In the Creation of Allah, every single human being ushered into existence, is endowed with the eternal, everlasting and imperishable attribute of Ruh (Soul) which is spotless Effulgence and Impeccable Purity.

This Ruh (Soul), is the supremely Majestic Effulgence of Allah and has been in existence from the beginningless beginning.

This fact should be realised and understood by all persons of Wisdom wedded to the path of Divine Rectitude.

In the beginningless beginning, the Creator Allah was in a state of Spotless Effulgence, radiating Divine Luminescence of Majestic Lustrous Splendour.

Within this limitless orbit of Divine Luminescence also burgeoned Ruh (Soul), Self-Luminous, Lustrous, and reflecting the Majestic Splendour of Allah Himself. This Ruh (Soul) is perennially in this august state of Divine Splendour.

It reflects the Majesty, Glory and Splendour of Allah. Therefore an Insan (Man) in his fullest resplendent state reflects the Effulgence of Allah.

The crowning achievement of an Insan (Man) during his sojourn on this Earth is to get himself integrated within the Limitless Effulgence of Allah.

This Ruh (Soul) of an Insan (Man) is absolutely pure and does not possess within it the remotest possible trace of an evil attribute or even the most infinitesimal particle of an evil propensity.

This Ruh is formless and within its Lustrous Radiance there gleams in Majestic Splendour the Effulgence of Allah.

Therefore, if a person knows and understands his Ruh (Soul) he would also come to know the Divine Effulgence of Allah.

If the limitless Divine Effulgence of Allah stops radiating even for a moment there would immediately occur an astonishingly tremendous phenomenon.

The Ruh (Soul), which in itself is a reflection of the Divine Effulgence of Allah, present in each of the crores and crores of human beings in every nook and corner and crevice of Creation, would also with unerring precision stop radiating.

Some people blame the Creator for the sufferings that engulf the existence of man during his sojourn on Earth.

It is a fact that in the vast spectrum of humanity there are some who are lame, some bereft of an arm, some dumb, some blind and some deaf. Further, it is also a fact that all mankind is vulnerable to diseases of infinite variety and diversity, old age and death.

In addition to the above, man is subject to the influence of ten and a half crores of evil propensities, stemming from the world of Maya, each of which in the form of hypnotic fascination is capable of deviating man from the path of Divine Rectitude.

A person of Wisdom should first ponder and reflect what has been detailed above in order to understand and evaluate the meaning and significance of the exposition which follows.

As stated earlier, this Ruh (Soul), which is the real source center and pivot of man's existence on Earth, is the Luminous Reflection of the limitlessly Radiant Luminescence of Allah.

But man during his sojourn on Earth develops certain insatiable desires which he satisfies by mobilizing in his service all manner of resources at his command.

The Ruh (Soul) of man is of infinitesimal size. It is smaller than the smallest possible particle conceivable by the mind of man.

If this Ruh (Soul) develops naturally to the state of fullest Divine Resplendence then the Insan (Man) becomes lit with the Radiantly Lustrous Splendour of Divine Luminous Wisdom, and in this Glorious State he is integrated with the limitless Divine Effulgence of Allah.

Let us ponder over the following illustration.

A gardener plants a mango seed, waters it and allows it to germinate.

The mango seed is allowed to germinate. The mango seed if allowed to grow to its fullest would produce fruits bearing the same characteristics as the fruit from which the seed was taken.

If, however, the gardener decides within a year to cut off this plant at a certain height and on its trunk to graft the tender shoots of an older mango tree, he can do so. Having grafted this alien shoot onto the trunk of the young mango tree, he would use proper manure to facilitate the graft to take on the trunk of this young mango tree. Until the alien shoot is fully grafted within the young mango tree, the gardener would support the alien shoot with artificial props.

After a certain span of time, the alien shoot becomes firmly grafted on the trunk of the young mango tree and this shoot grows without hinderance, nourished on the manure regularly supplied by the gardener.

If the gardener notices the growth of tender leaves shooting out from the trunk of the original mango plant, he removes these tiny tender leaves and stems completely and allows only the shoots on the graft to thrive.

Within a couple of years the grafted portion of the mango tree flowers as a prelude to the bearing of fruits; about the same time as the seasonal flowering of the mother mango tree from which the graft was taken.

The grafted mango tree exhibits characteristics similar to the original Mango tree from which the graft was taken, but are alien to the characteristics of the original mango tree on which the graft was made to take.

This transformation so radical and fundamental has taken place within two years where the intrinsic qualities of the original mango tree have been replaced by the qualities immanent in the grafted portion of the alien mango tree.

The above illustration clearly illustrates how natural characteristics, intrinsic and immanent in the natural object, can be replaced by the acquired characteristics particular and peculiar to the alien object, when the latter becomes an integral part of the former.

His Holiness further said: The moment when the resplendence of Ruh (Soul) was ushered by Allah for the Creation of Insan (Man) there were six distinct and separate constituents in man.

Of these constituents five are of the five elements; namely, Earth, Fire, Water, Air and Ether which constitute the physical composition of man, while the solitary remaining constituent was the most Luminous Lustrously Resplendent and Imperishable Element of Ruh (Soul) itself. It is this last constituent element which in the beginningless beginning arose within the Limitless Divine Effulgence of Allah.

Continuing, His Holiness said: When a child is ushered into existence to this world, it grows up from infancy towards adolescence in the traditional way.

During this crucial period of growth, the parents of the child exercise complete sway, power and authority over the growing child and modify its Divine Nature.

The parents of this child are already engulfed, enveloped, and interpenetrated with ten and a half crores of evil propensities from the world of Maya.

These evil propensities are in the form of tempting and alluring hypnotic fascinations such as love of gold, of wealth, of lands, and property. Further these parents are saturated in the darkness of Ignorance and are vulnerable as the greater segment of humanity is to hunger, disease, age and death.

These parents are subject to the extremes of joy and sorrow and are fanatically wedded to their creed and caste.

These parents are conceited, arrogant, and immersed in self aggrandisement.

These parents are deeply afflicted with material glory and earthly renown and take immense pride in titles conferred by society.

The parents while living and moving in these conditions subtly and surely inculcate their evil attributes and propensities to the child until its adolescence.

The growing child, subject to a continuous and continued pressure by the parents, gradually succumbs to the ways of existence of its own parents.

This indoctrination of the child by the parents is similar to the cutting off of the trunk of the first mango tree and the grafting on it the shoots of an alien mango tree.

The parents, by their influence, cut off within the Qalb (Heart) of their own child the emergence of the inherent Divine Radiance of the Ruh (Soul), which is also the seat and citadel of his Noor (Divine Luminous Wisdom) and thus prevent it from developing into its full and natural splendour within the child.

As stated earlier, of the six constituent elements ushered in by Allah towards the Creation of Man, only the five elements; namely, Earth, Fire, Water, Air and Ether are allowed free and unhampered development within the child by the parents. This leads to the superimposition of crores and crores of evil propensities and attributes of Maya within the Qalb (Heart) of the child and results in the remaining constituent element, the Divine Ruh (Soul), being smothered and scotched. In consequence, the Ruh (Soul), is prevented from manifesting its Divine, Majestic, Lustrous and Resplendent qualities within the Qalb (Heart) of the child.

As the gardener had cut off, at a certain height, the young mango plant and on its trunk grafted the shoots of an alien plant, the parents have succeeded in scotching and smothering the imperishable constituent element, the Ruh (Soul), the fountain of Divine Luminous Wisdom, and in its place grafted crores and crores of hypnotic fascinations from the world of Maya (the love of the material world).

Like the first mango tree where natural growth was nullified by the grafting of the shoots of an alien mango tree, the child growing into adolescence loses its natural Divine Heritage and instead is grafted into the Ocean of Maya resulting in his demoralisation, degradation and death.

His Holiness continues: The natural trunk of the young mango tree, which was prevented by the gardener from shooting out its tender leaves by cutting them out as soon as they appear, is still not dead and is potentially capable of developing its natural shoots if the grafted portion is cut off. Likewise, though the Ruh (Soul), the imperishable element in man, has been smothered by the super-imposition of evil propensities, its potential Divine Power is always present without an iota of diminution and this can still become manifest if the artificial tree of Maya is cut off.

What exactly happens to the indoctrinated child is that as it grows into adolescence it is fully enveloped and engulfed with crores of evil propensities generated by Maya. This child moving up towards maturity and manhood is now vulnerable to hunger, disease, age and death as well as crores of troubles, travail and tribulation to which the generality of mankind is vulnerable.

If the child grows into adolescence with the free, full and unhampered emergence of the imperishable element, the Ruh (Soul), developing naturally to its full state of Divine Lustrous Splendour, then this child growing into maturity and manhood becomes possessed with a fully resplendent Ruh.

Such a person would be perennially engulfed within the Effulgence of the Divine Luminous Wisdom which would free him from hunger, disease and age and death forever.

What has been detailed about the indoctrination of the child by the parents in the earlier portion of this exposition is the pattern of existence in which the generality of mankind is exposed.

This being the actual position, it is certainly erroneous on the part of any man to apportion the blame on the Creator for the ills that engulf and afflict humanity.

Rather than blame the Creator for the ills of mankind it should be the Principal Endeavour of a person born in the noble heritage of an Insan (Man) to assiduously work towards the emergence of Wisdom potentially present within himself.

Such an enlightened person, when he focuses the searchlight of his Wisdom within himself, would know that a person puts the blame on the Creator for the ills of mankind because the eye of Wisdom is blind.

Further, this enlightened person would realise the limitless Divine potential power embedded within the imperishable element, the Ruh (Soul), and having known this, it would be his supreme purpose of existence to work towards its full resplendence.

In the full realisation of its Divine Resplendence, this person would have achieved the crowning purpose of his existence on Earth.

Such a person would be forever freed from the crores of ills which afflict and engulf mankind at large.

This person now Divinely Resplendent would come to know himself and would thereafter come to know his Creator.

The above discourse vividly portrays how utterly bereft of Truth is the blame for the ills of mankind, hurled by some, in their ignorance, at their Creator.

SEVEN STEPS TO MYSTIC UNION

A seeker after Truth came to a Kamil Sheik (Gnana Guru) and humbly beseeched him for a remedy to eliminate hunger, disease, age and death. The Kamil Sheik stated that he could administer the remedy sought for by the seeker if the seeker brings it to him.

The Kamil Sheik confirmed that there is a glorious remedy available for eliminating hunger, disease, age and death. The person who successfully obtains this remedy will reach a state of Divine Resplendence and when administered, he would come to know himself as well as his Creator, Allah.

The Kamil Sheik cited an illustration to explain the difficulties that would assail, engulf, and envelop the aspirant while seeking this remedy.

He said that there was a patient who was suffering from an incurable disease. He went to a doctor of very great repute and distinction for medical treatment.

The doctor examined the patient and in diagnosing the nature of the disease realised that the resources of medical science would be unable to effect a permanent cure for the disease.

However, the doctor in addition to his powers and renown in the realm of medicine also possessed considerable Divine Insight.

He advised the patient that there was only one way to effect a permanent cure of the deadly disease from which the patient was suffering. The patient had to procure the cure himself. He had to go and obtain the brightest lime fruit from the lime tree which was positioned within the Royal Garden overhanging the Royal Palace and the Royal Bed. The fruit referred to above is the elixir of life.

The patient was determined and enthusiastic to effect a cure for his ailment, and embarked on his journey to the Royal Palace. The Royal Palace was guarded by seven guards each of whom were under strict orders not to let anyone into the Palace. On approaching the Royal Palace, the patient confronted the first guard who was firm and unrelenting in his refusal to allow admission.

However, the patient was not taken aback, but used his Insight and Wisdom to win the guard over.

The patient told the guard that the King had specifically sent for him to give him a very valuable and rare present.

The patient, bargaining with the first guard, said that if he allowed him to enter the Palace, he would, on his return, give him half of the valuable present.

As the offer was very tempting, the first guard agreed, with one provision, that the half share of the present should be an exact half, nor more, not less.

The patient agreed and moved on into the Palace grounds and confronted the second guard.

The same discussion took place with this guard who enjoined the same conditions regarding the division of the present and this was accepted by the patient.

Contracting this same agreement with each of the five remaining guards, the patient eventually made his way to the lime tree in the Royal Gardens overhanging the Royal Palace.

The patient saw the lime tree clustered with numerous lime fruits of which only one was Luminously Radiant.

Here the patient paused, pondered and reflected as to how many fruits he needed to satisfy the seven guards and have the one Luminously Radiant Fruit for himself. His problem was to satisfy the guards and make his exit from the palace with that one Radiant Fruit for himself.

He calculated and found that he needed 128 fruits including the one for himself.

According to his agreement with each of the seven guards, the patient gave the first guard 64 fruits; the second guard 32 fruits; the third guard 16 fruits; the fourth guard 8 fruits; the fifth guard 4 fruits; and the sixth guard 2 fruits; the seventh guard 1 fruit; and the remaining one he kept with him was the one and only Luminously Radiant Fruit.

With this priceless Everlasting Imperishable, Eternal and Ever-Luminous, Ever-Radiant Fruit, the patient returned to his doctor who administered the juice of this fruit and cured him completely so that not even the remotest possible trace of his ailment remained.

The illustration cited above concerned what the seeker after Truth has to pursue in order to eliminate hunger, disease, age and death. A seeker of Truth is a person whose Heart (Qalb) is aglow with Luminous Wisdom.

This person, already in the path of Divine Rectitude, goes to a Kamil Sheik (Gnana Guru) and beseeches him very reverentially, to show the way to eliminate hunger, disease, age and death to which the body of Man, structured of the five elements namely, Earth, Fire, Water, Air and Ether, is vulnerable. The seven guards in the illustration represents the Seven Evil Souls (Nafs).

Through his Luminous Wisdom, he sees with utmost clearly and precision what the 128 fruits in the illustration represents.

100 fruits represent the 99 names of Allah (God) and the name Allah making a total of 100. The other 28 fruits represent the 28 Arabic letters in the structural composition of a Man (Insan). Further, he sees that out of the 100 names of Allah, 99 names represent the infinitely diverse manifestations extant in the whole range of Creation.

And the One name, Allah, is the Omnipotent, Omnipresent, Omniscient God who envelops the whole Creation. This overpowering name Allah is supreme and majestic without an equal.

The seeker further sees through his Luminous Wisdom that the 28 letters in the body of man have a close affinity and relationship to the Earth. The physical body, he is aware, was made to be the seat and citadel of His Divine Luminous Wisdom.

Endowed with the above clarity and vision, the seeker realises what the lime fruits from the lime tree, including the One Solitary Radiant Fruit, mean. In his outward journey, he encounters the seven guards or Nafs and gives the first guard or Nafs 64 fruits. By this act, the seeker had given up half of the worldly attachments he had gathered, nursed and nourished since he was born.

On meeting the second guard or Nafs the seeker gives up 32 fruits. By this act the seeker had given up half of his attachment to the various hypnotic fascinations of the world of Maya.

On meeting the third guard or Nafs he gives up 16 fruits. By this act he exhibits the emergence of Divine Luminous Wisdom and assumes the mantle of a 16-year-old boy, robust, resolute, alert and virile, free from the tentacles of passion to which older people are addicted.

A 16-year-old boy finds the passage to Divine Resplendence considerably accelerated since he is completely free from earthly ties and entanglements.

To the fourth guard or Nafs he gives up 8 fruits. By this act, he has reached a Divine Stature of such surpassing excellence that he is utterly indifferent and immune to praise or blame from people who are engulfed in the materialistic way of life.

To the fifth guard or Nafs he gives up 4 fruits. This act signals his renunciation of the four religions, each of which are wedded to a particular code of conduct, rites, rituals and ceremonies.

He is fully convinced, assured and certain within the innermost recesses of his Heart (Qalb), the seat and citadel of his Divine Luminous Wisdom, that the 4 religions have nothing whatsoever to offer to the realisation of the One and Only Creator, the Supreme Majestic Allah.

To the sixth guard or Nafs he gives up two fruits. By this act, the seeker after truth reaches the very exalted state of Divinity when his personal identity is submerged well and truly in the universal and becomes ego-less. Now, he does not see any difference amongst the creatures of Allah and treats them all alike.

To the seventh guard or Nafs he gives up one fruit. By this act the seeker gives up his body consciousness.

In this glorious state of Divine Resplendence, he is left with the one and only solitary Luminously Radiant fruit, imperishable and everlasting, and that is the Divine Luminous Wisdom (Noor). He brings this supremely priceless fruit to his very revered Kamil Sheik (Gnana Guru) who administers it to him.

Thereafter, this seeker becomes Divinely Resplendent, and merges within Allah. In this supremely glorious state he is Ever-Radiant, Ever-Lustrous and Immortal in both the worlds.

Such a seeker who has reached this very exalted state has indeed found an everlasting remedy to hunger, disease, age and death to which humanity at large is vulnerable.

GURU AND DISCIPLE

There once lived a Guru of exemplary character, nobility and honesty who was loved, respected and revered by all those who had occasion to meet him.

During the day, this Guru used to retire to the deep recesses of the forest, where undisturbed by any human being, he used to engage himself quite assiduously in very regular devotions to his Creator. He had been engaged in this pursuit, day after day, week after week, month after month, and year after year, so much so, that he won the regard and reverence of people around as a person of spotless purity and holiness.

During these long years, the Guru had a very devoted disciple, who was of noble disposition, and at all times constant in his unsurpassing devotion to his Guru, carrying out his orders, with the utmost promptitude and enthusiasm.

This disciple, never for a passing moment considered any work assigned to him as menial, degrading or not in keeping with his status.

During these long years, this great Guru, on occasion admitted disciples to the Ashram. These disciples were given regular methodical training, appropriate to each disciple. When after a period of tutelage, each of the disciples achieved the purpose for which he had come, the Guru, after initiating them on the path, sent them away.

This devoted disciple, who had come to the Ashram first and rendered exemplary and devoted service to his Guru, over such long years, when he saw what appeared to be favoured treatment of the Guru to the other disciples, who came after him, began to nurse, very imperceptibly, a feeling of grievance against the Guru. He felt he had been not only overlooked, but neglected and ignored.

This devoted disciple although burdened with this grievance against his Guru, never for a moment betrayed this fact in demeanour, speech or attitude. On the contrary, the disciple carried out all the work assigned to him by the Guru to his fullest satisfaction, day in and day out.

The Guru, ever observant and alert, was able through his Divinely Luminous Eye to see and understand all that was happening within the mind and heart of his devoted disciple.

One day, the Guru asked his disciple to fetch an object positioned at a place, access to which was only possible through a narrow passage way. At a particular point in this passage, there was a wooden projection overhanging from the ceiling of the narrow passage.

A person passing this point in this narrow passage would have to bend his head very low, in order to avoid hitting his head on the projection which was 6 feet in thickness.

At the behest of the Guru, the disciple approached the narrow passage to fetch the object. The speed with which the disciple negotiated the narrow passage was such that his head came into violent contact with the wooden projection.

The disciple, stunned and bewildered by the sudden and violent impact, placed both his hands on his forehead, over the point of impact and ran towards his Guru shouting that he had been severely hit on the forehead. Then the disciple encountered a bewildering spectacle. The Guru was himself groaning, with his hand firmly placed precisely, at the point on his forehead, similar to the point of impact on the forehead of his own disciple.

Blood was oozing at this point from the forehead of the Guru. The disciple, withdrawing his hands from the point of impact on his own forehead, discovered to his utter astonishment, that there was neither pain, swelling or oozing of blood on his own forehead in spite of the extreme violence of the impact.

Here at this point, it must be stated, that precisely at the moment the disciple struck the wooden projection, his Divine Luminous Eye was opened.

The Guru, addressing his devoted disciple said:

"My son, see! It is not your head that is wounded, but mine. You have merely experienced the superficial impact when you crashed into the wooden projection; but in reality it was I who received the wound at the time of the impact, resulting in pain, swelling and bleeding. You, on the contrary, my son, have escaped unscathed from this impact."

The Guru continued:

"My son! A truly devoted disciple of unswerving loyalty, superb integrity, sterling honesty and impeccable purity like you, is well and truly merged with his Guru, for all intents and purposes. Let it be clearly understood that no untoward incident would ever befall you, without first affecting me, for I am within you and you are within me."

The Guru continuing, said:

"The accident that you met with was apparent and not real, for the intrinsic suffering was borne by me.

"I deliberately contrived this accident, to uproot the silent grievance and resentment you had against me, that developed within the innermost recesses of your Heart (Qalb) for quite some time now.

"You were depressed, that I had ignored you and bestowed preferential treatment on the other disciples who came long after you. Here I want, pointedly, to draw your attention to the fact that all those disciples came from distant places to the Ashram and each of them had a specific purpose. The specific purpose each of those disciples had in mind was a final initiation by me in the path of Divine Wisdom.

"Each of these disciples, having reached that degree of Divine Enlightment by constant assiduity of effort and meticulous observance of my teachings in the Ashram, entitled himself for the final initiation by me, in the path of Divine Wisdom. Thereafter, each of them trudged back with my blessings to his native place, to be a source of Light and Understanding to the people seeking the path of Divine Rectitude.

"Further, I want to impress on you that each of those disciples came from a distant place and when his particular mission was over, returned to the same distant place."

The Guru continuing said:

"You my son, as my devoted disciple, are one of my household, and you are integrally a part of myself. I am within you and you are within me. Remember, you are not alone. No misfortune or calamity can overtake you, without first striking me."

Finally the Guru concluded by saying: "Your mind, hereafter should be at rest. Do your duty."

So saying the Guru went away, leaving the disciple all alone.

The devoted disciple all alone and undisturbed, deeply pondered over the exposition of his Guru for sometime.

During this reflection, the disciple realised that his inner eye was opened when his forehead struck the wooden projection in the narrow passage. He realised that the oozing of the blood from the forehead of his Guru signaled the moment of complete eradication of all worldly attachments to the world of Maya accumulated by the disciple during his long years of existence on this earth.

The disciple was also in a position to realise that the oozing of the blood from the forehead of the Guru also signaled the lifting of all the veils of darkness that had hidden the citadel of the Divine Noor (Divine Luminous Wisdom).

Still further, the disciple realised that the oozing of the blood from the forehead of the Guru signalised the transformation of himself into an authentic Gnana Guru.

Now, the entire being of this transformed disciple was suffused with the Lustrous Effulgence of Divine Wisdom.

The disciple, in spite of the above glorious achievements, maintained in his relationship with his Guru, the same unswerving loyalty and complete submission, typical and characteristic of his behaviour to his Guru in the past.

The Guru had a wife exceedingly devoted to him. She was the embodiment of virtue. The devoted disciple was accustomed to treat her with the reverence one bestows on his own mother. One day, the Guru before going to his daily devotions to the forest summoned his disciple and said:

"My wife has conceived a child and when the time comes for delivery, you should seek the necessary assistance and render all possible help to her."

The disciple agreed to implement the request of the Guru. Some months later, the Guru's wife, in the absence of the Guru, complained to the disciple of the onset of labour pains. The disciple ran as fast as he could to the nearest village and brought along a midwife.

Leaving the midwife in the room where the Guru's wife was labouring, the disciple closed the room and was waiting outside within hearing range, alert and attentive.

The disciple, now being endowed with Divine Illumination, saw with his eye of Divine Luminous Wisdom an old man approaching the entrance to the delivery room.

The disciple stopped the old man from going further into the room and blurted out.

"Who are you? What is the nature of your business that emboldens you, of all places, to enter the delivery room? What right have you to come here? Tell me, who are you anyway?"

The old man taken aback by this sudden remonstrance, replied: "You are indeed a man of Divine Illumination. Otherwise no ordinary mortal would be able to see me. Since you are determined to know my identity, I shall reveal it to you. I am Fate (Naseeb) charged with the mission of indicting on the head of the new-born babe, its Fate (Naseeb) and for this purpose I have a pen (Kalam) in my hand".

The disciple replied: "Before I grant you permission to enter the labour room, tell me precisely what it is, that you are going to write on the head of the new born babe.

The old man replied: "I do not write at all. I know absolutely nothing. It is the pen (Kalam) which I hold in my hand which writes on its own volition on the head of this new-born babe. I, personally, am able to read only after the pen (Kalam) has finished writing."

The disciple then told the old man that he would give him permission to enter the room provided he told him on his return what had been written on the head of the new-born babe.

The old man accepting the condition, went in. Simultaneously, there was heard the first cry of the new-born babe.

On this occasion, what was revealed was equally as startling. The old man said, "What has been written on the head of this new-born babe is unbelievable. However, what has been written is right. This child is a male child born to your most revered Guru, who has spent long years in his devotions to his Creator. He is indeed a person of surpassing moral excellence, revered and honoured by his fellow men. His devoted spouse is a woman of exemplary devotion and virtue.

"On the head of this male child born to such two good people is written in indelible characters and mathematical precision that the child, when it grows up to be an adult, would have to earn his sustenance by looking after a solitary lean cow."

So saying the old man disappeared.

The disciple heard the utterances of this old man in wrapt silence and was astonished at the fate earmarked for the male child of his revered Guru and his wife.

When the Guru came into the Ashram from his devotions in the forest later, the disciple appraised him of the birth of his male child and all that transpired in his absence.

A few years later, one day the Guru called his disciple and said: "Son! Your adopted mother is about to again deliver a child. I expect you to render all possible assistance as you previously did very successfully."

The devoted disciple most readily agreed to do his best.

After a few months when the Guru was away from the Ashram, the labour pains started and the disciple when informed rushed to the nearest village and fetched a midwife.

A few moments before the birth of the child, the old man who came, previously, again made his appearance at the entrance to the labour room.

The disciple standing outside the room, recalled his previous encounter with him. The disciple told the old man that he was at liberty to go into the labour room, provided he would tell him on his return what was written on the head of the new-born babe.

The old man agreed to the condition.

Encountering the disciple on his return from the room, the old man said: "See what has happened. This child is a female child. It is written on the head of this child that she would grow into maidenhood as a girl of surpassing loveliness and beauty. Her peerless beauty would be the envy of not only the men, but women as well. It is also written that blossoming into womanhood, she would earn her livelihood as an ordinary prostitute. She would be in great demand in her most infamous calling, on account of her extraordinary beauty."

The disciple was aghast. He asked the old man to be good enough to tell him how this Fate (Naseeb) came to be written in such a manner.

The old man replied: "An infinite number of factors operate in determining the Fate (Naseeb) of persons during their sojourn on Earth. I shall, however, give you an exposition of one important factor which will throw some light on your question.

"The Soul (Ruh) of a human being is of pristine purity, having radiated from the innermost recesses of the Divine Grace of Allah, Himself.

"At the moment of conception this Soul (Ruh) is symbolically covered by layers of genetic predispositions representing the quintessence of crystallised actions, stemming from particular attributes which in turn stem from the five elements in the physical composition of man. Some of these attributes and qualities are dominant in the minds of the parents at the moment of conception. This is one important factor in the life of a new-born babe when its Fate (Naseeb) comes to be written on its head."

The old man continuing said: "The Soul (Ruh) of the new-born babe accompanied by Wisdom comes from the innermost citadel, the Allah Himself. Wisdom is encased in the Soul (Ruh).

"It must be remembered that the new-born babe's physical composition is composed of the five elements with countless attributes and dispositions inherent in them.

"These predispositions become integrated with the attributes and qualities of the new-born babe and await the right moments for their particular and peculiar expressions in terms of human existence."

The old man continued: "The penetrating gaze of Divine Luminous Wisdom (Noor) sees the characteristics peculiar to each type of pre-disposition and records them with meticulous accuracy. This record is transposed in terms of human behaviour and written as Fate (Naseeb) in indelible characters on the head of the new-born babe. This record so written, unfolds with mathematical precision as to what is destined for this new-born babe, during its entire sojourn on Earth."

The old man in conclusion told the disciple: "My exposition is only one important factor as to how a particular aspect of Fate (Naseeb) comes to be written on the head of a new-born babe. There are of course an infinite number of other aspects of Fate (Naseeb) and their factors known only to those whose consciousness is integrated within the Divine Consciousness of Allah.

"The Fate (Naseeb) of a person cannot be altered even by an iota except through a Gnana Guru (Perfect Divine Guru).

"A person through absolute trust, determination and complete faith in Allah, can with the assistance of an authentic Kamil Sheik (Gnana Guru), who is integrated within the Divine Effulgence of Allah, have his Fate (Naseeb) altered."

Life thereafter returned to normal in the Ashram. The Guru as usual retired during the daytime to the forest for devotions and this Illumined Disciple was ever assiduous, regular and methodical in the discharge of all duties assigned to him by the Guru.

The children of the Guru were daily getting robust, healthy and strong.

One day when the male child was six years of age and the female child four years, the Guru calling his disciple said:

"My son! You are now in a highly illumined state. You are an authentic Gnana Guru in your own right. There are some 1008 seekers after truth, who are engaged in devotions in an Ashram adjacent to a mountain, some hundred miles from here.

"They are without a Guru and a guide to lead them in the path of Divine Luminous Wisdom.

"I desire that you should go over there and serve them as their Guru for twelve long years with a view to initiating each of them in the path of Divine Luminous Wisdom."

The disciple agreed to go and take charge of the Ashram as desired by his Guru.

The disciple, already an authentic Gnana Guru in his own right, was able through use of his extraordinary powers, to reach the Ashram adjacent to the mountains in record time.

There, the 1008 seekers after Truth were overjoyed at their singular fortune in meeting an authentic Gnana Guru competent and capable of directing each of them in the right path. All of them became his very devoted disciples.

After 12 long years the new Guru of the Ashram decided to extend his period by another 4 years as his work in the Ashram was one of continuous success and glory.

Then the new Guru of the Ashram in his meditation had occasion to remember his former Guru, his wife and the two children who would by now be 22 and 20 years respectively.

The Guru meditated for a while and then utilising his supernormal powers, saw that his Revered Guru and his spouse were buried in the premises of the Ashram.

The son 22 years old now, as written in his Fate (Naseeb), was tending a lean cow for his sustenance some miles away.

The daughter, a woman of 20 years of great loveliness and entrancing beauty, was engaged in the most infamous calling, as a common prostitute to earn her livelihood.

The new Gnana Guru (the former disciple) now invoked his Divine Powers to commune with the spirit of his former Guru, "Oh, my Guru, where are you now?"

The spirit of his Guru seeing that his former disciple was now an authentic Gnana Guru replied:

"I am here my son. God did not give me a good station. Although I prayed to God and practiced religious austerity in the jungle for all those years, I did not worship Him in the proper way. I did not attain the liberation that comes from true prayer.

"Nor did I leave that path behind and turn completely towards a householder's life, saying, 'This is happiness!' I had two children; I did not stop my worldly and sexual desire, nor did I give way to it and attain pleasure from it.

"Because of this, I did not get either heaven or hell, and I am suffering in the mid-station between the two. I did not go to heaven and attain bliss, neither did I obtain happiness from this worldly life. I did not achieve completion during my lifetime, nor have I found completion here.

26

"My son, I made a grave mistake. Of the two types of pleasures, I did not fully achieve either one. Please speak to God on my behalf. Since you are perfectly pure, your prayers will be fulfilled."

Then the new Gnana Guru thought of the son and daughter. Utilizing his supernatural powers, he found himself in the vicinity of the 22 year-old son tending a lean cow.

Calling him by name, the new Guru revealed his identity. The son, overjoyed on seeing the former disciple of his father, paid him obeisance and took him home.

Here the new Gnana Guru told him to sell his cow in the market place the next day and with the proceeds he was to give a small portion for safe keeping to a market vendor and with the balance buy food and clothes.

The son was bewildered at this strange order, for he did not know what he could do for a living when his solitary cow was sold. But his faith in the new Guru was such that the son carried out his orders to the letter.

The next day at 3:00 A.M. a cow appeared tied to the same tree where the previous cow was tied. The new Guru told him to do likewise with this cow and with the proceeds of the sale.

This process went on daily for six months and the market vendor had now quite a sum of money in the name of the son. The market vendor gave his only daughter in marriage to the son of the former Guru. Now he was blessed with a wife, a home, and money.

A cow continued to appear daily for another six months. The son, affluent and respectable, was now an honoured citizen of the village. Here is an instance of how the Fate (Naseeb) of a person was changed with the help and guidance of an authentic Gnana Guru.

Thereafter the new Guru, utilizing his supernormal powers, appeared in front of the house of the daughter of his former Guru, who was earning her livelihood as a prostitute.

The guards at the house at first refused permission of entry to the new Guru. After a great deal of persuasion, the guards allowed the new Guru inside the house.

When the daughter of his former Guru realised the identity of the new Guru, she paid obeisance to him.

The new Guru ordered her to give up her mode of living at once and put up a notice that she would sell herself permanently to only one person who would provide her with 500,000 rupees.

For weeks none came, as the cost of buying her was prohibitive. However, a very rich man, entranced and captivated by the beauty of the girl, sold everything he had and came with the 500,000 rupees to buy her.

The new Guru told her to accept the amount and be permanently attached to this person to the exclusion of all others. She had no need to worry about money as she had more than enough now.

Marriage however was out of the question in view of her antecedents. Nevertheless, she would be able to lead a conventional and respectable existence by being permanently attached to one person till death.

Here, too, is another instance of how the Fate (Naseeb) of a person can be materially altered by the intercession of an authentic Gnana Guru. The Fate (Naseeb) written on the head of a person is not permanent and absolutely irrevocable. If a person is possessed of Determination, Faith, and Trust in Allah, he or she can with the guidance of an authentic Gnana Guru materially alter his Fate (Naseeb) to a higher and nobler form of existence.

TRADITIONAL METHODS OF ALERTING MAN IN RELATION TO TIME OF PRAYER

The Kamil Sheik gave an exposition on the traditional methods of alerting man to the time of Prayer, which have been in vogue among the generality of mankind from the dim distant past down to the present day.

The Kamil Sheik (The Gnana Guru) in his exposition said that this world of ours is inhabited by immense varieties of human beings, belonging to different religions and creeds.

A considerable segment of people in this vast spectrum of humanity, belonging to these religions and creeds are engaged daily at prescribed times, in Reverential Prayer and Devotion to their Creator.

The time earmarked for the very first Prayer any day, is well before the streak of dawn. The religious leaders of the four religions adopt various methods to alert their followers (each method adopted being characteristic of their particular religion) to be present in time, for their first Prayer and Devotion to their Creator.

Each follower according to his religious persuasion repairs when alerted by his particular religious leader to the Temple, Mosque or Church, as the case may be.

In a certain religion, the followers are alerted through the pealing of the Temple Bells. The people of this particular religious persuasion, on hearing the pealing of the Temple Bells, repair themselves to the Temple premises well before the ritual and ceremonies in the Temple are scheduled to begin.

Similarly, the followers of the Christian Faith are sometimes alerted by the pealing of the Church Bells to be present well before the Church Services begin.

In the Mosque, the Mouzin (Priest) and Lebbe (Priest) alert their followers by time-honoured and traditional methods, the Call for Prayer (Azan), informing them in language unmistakable that it is time to come to the Mosque for Prayers.

The above exposition details the methods adopted by the leaders of the four religions to alert their followers to be present at their respective places of worship for offering Prayers to their Creator.

These religious leaders, in view of the functions they perform, are generally looked upon by their religious followers as men of singular nobility, unblemished reputation and distinction.

The Kamil Sheik (Gnana Guru) continuing his exposition said that these religious leaders ostensibly serving their Creator should appear to be very vigilant and alert in the performance of their inseparable functions.

But this is not so. These religious leaders being mortals, are subject to human frailties that assail mankind.

In consequence, at times they oversleep and the proper functions which devolve on them are done by their assistants.

The Kamil Sheik continuing his exposition said: Apart from these religious leaders, there are winged creatures, each of whom is possessed of two legs.

Though these winged creatures or birds are devoid of Divine Luminous Wisdom, they perform the functions of the religious leaders referred to earlier with meticulous precision and amazing regularity, each and every day, ever since man was first ushered into existence on Earth.

Each species of birds, through its peculiar and characteristic emission of sounds of sufficient volume and penetration, is able to alert people, within a particular range and radius, even before the first streak of dawn, that it is the time for the first prayer of the day.

The time of the emission of a particular sound by any specific bird occurs with mathematical precision exactly at the same time each day, regardless of the favourableness or unfavourableness of the weather conditions.

It must be understood that regardless of the weather condition, the sound emitted by a particular bird is of sufficient penetration, to alert people within a particular area to be in readiness for prayers.

When the sound emitted by a particular bird resounds in the ears of people within a particular range, the following truths emerge within the consciousness of these people.

First of all, they feel in the innermost recesses of their being their obligation to go to their place of worship and pray to their Creator.

Secondly, it dawns on them that they cannot tarry in their obligation, for if they tarry, the streak of dawn will soon appear and signal that the time for the First Prayer has passed.

Finally, these people realise that they should place themselves in absolute and unconditional surrender to their Creator at times of Prayer and He alone provides them with the sustenance for their existence on Earth.

In contrast, the birds of all species are indeed superb beings; in this sense, every second, they are constantly aware and ever conscious of the overwhelming Divine Presence of their Creator.

These birds indeed pass every single moment of their existence in continued and continuous awareness of their Creator. The Kamil Sheik (Gnana Guru) continuing his exposition said, that these birds are not afflicted by melancholy or grief and in consequence they do not oversleep at anytime and therefore there is no need at all for them to delegate their functions to someone else.

On the contrary, these birds are fully endowed with the Overpowering Divine Grace of their Creator, which enables them to be constantly aware of the precise manner in which they should perform their ordained duty.

The birds which perform the functions referred to above, apart from the cock, are the male birds of their respective species.

Each of these birds will emit their characteristic sounds precisely at 3:00 A.M. each and every day, singularly and cumulatively at different points on the Earth.

These peculiar and voluminous sounds penetrate the auditory nerves of all people deeply in slumber within a particular radius proclaiming the time for Prayers.

These sounds signal precisely that the streak of dawn is about to appear and it is time for man to fulfil his obligatory devotion and prayers to his Creator.

The sound emitted by each bird, well before the streak of dawn, is followed by similar sounds from other birds in the neighborhood. Consequently, this collective volume of sound from the diverse species of birds synchronizingly vibrates to all points within a particular area where a large number of birds have congregated.

Within this particular area, this massive sound from the birds causes a massive vibration within the auditory nerves of the people in deep slumber. These vibrations stir the consciousness of each person within the area and inform them that the streaks of dawn are about to appear, and that they should be up in time to fulfil their obligations of Prayers.

These birds are ever vigilant, ever active and ever watchful in the performance of their functions. Their vigilance is so sharp that even while apparently lapsing into sleep, they are not unmindful even for a moment of their obligations.

Further, during every moment of their existence, they are consciously aware as to when, how and the precise manner in which they have to perform their ordained functions.

The above is basic to their very existence, and each bird does not deviate even an iota from its ordained functions.

The Kamil Sheik (Gnana Guru) continuing his exposition said, these birds, although existing on Earth, are endowed with ears of such penetrating power and precision as to perceive the Divine Sounds radiating in Majestic Splendour from Heaven.

They are also able to perceive the vibrations emanating from the Devotions and Prayers of Angels and these birds are able to perceive the vibrations emanating from the Heavenly Cock as well as from the other varieties of male birds from the Heavenly Planes.

The moment the birds on Earth perceive the sounds and vibrations radiating from Heaven, they become aware of their ordained functions related to man and to the other created beings.

These birds, forewarned by these Heavenly Sounds, now move into action with superb precision and promptitude.

Immediately thereafter, which is precisely 3:00 A.M. each day, the birds on Earth emit a voluminous sound, both massive and penetrating, to people within a particular area, to awaken them and remind them that it is time for their very first Prayer for the day.

The Kamil Sheik, continuing his exposition, here interposed: It must be understood, that in God's Creation there are some birds which are extraordinarily receptive and superbly sensitive to Divine Vibrations and Sounds Radiating from Heaven itself.

The Kamil Sheik (Gnana Guru) continuing, said that Man (Insan), although endowed with Divine Luminous Wisdom, sometimes lapses in his regular and meticulous performance of his ordained daily functions.

However, the birds, although devoid of Divine Luminous Wisdom, have a penetrating awareness and instinctive knowledge of their ordained functions. In addition, these birds possess a very keen and sensitive pair of ears to pick up the Divine Vibrations which are outside the ken of ordinary functions.

Still further, they possess a consciousness so subtle as to detect even the slightest movement of both animate and inanimate objects moving about.

When birds are perched in the branches of trees and when thieves or beasts of prey prowl about the area trying to catch them for food, these birds possess a high degree of perception to detect, well in time, the thieves and beasts of prey and so make good their escape in double quick time.

This high degree of perception and awareness to danger possessed by these birds is present even when they are apparently asleep. Even at these moments of imminent danger, these birds are also tuned to the Divine Vibrations of their Creator, as well as the sounds of Devotions and Prayers of the Heavenly Angels. The awareness of these birds to Divine Sounds exists concurrently with their awareness of happenings on Earth.

The Kamil Sheik (Gnana Guru) here said that it must not be forgotten that whatever troubles, dangers or misfortunes afflict these birds, they are never remiss, even for a day, in the discharge of their ordained functions, namely, to alert the people in time for the first Prayer.

The above discourse details precisely the nature and the function carried out by the birds although they do not possess Divine Luminous Wisdom (Noor).

The Kamil Sheik here interposed and said that it is incumbent on men to pause and ponder as to whether it is man or the birds who have been faithfully adhering at all times in the observance of the Ordained Laws of God.

A knowledge of this makes us realise these intrinsic and rare qualities of birds, though unobtrusive in their existence, yet important enough in the over-all plan in Creation.

The Kamil Sheik, continuing his exposition, said that man, referred to above, generally performs his ordained functions for material gains only, while the birds carry out their ordained functions selflessly for the Glory of their Creator.

A true Man (Insan) should now realise, between man and the birds, which one really carries out the Divine Injunctions in methods not only noble, lofty and elevating but also acceptable to the Creator as well.

The Kamil Sheik here said that it should be the principal and primary endeavour of a Man (Insan) to ensure that he is possessed of a consciousness, ever-vigilant, ever-alert and ever-prepared, even in sleep like the birds, to detect and meet all manner of dangers.

Such a Man (Insan), the Kamil Sheik stressed, would be able to perceive the Divine Vibrations all the time like the birds.

The Kamil Sheik, in conclusion, said that a Man (Insan), endowed with this high degree of perception of the Divine Sounds, would possess a Resplendent Certitude (Iman) and his entire being will be lit with Divine Luminous Wisdom (Noor). In this state the Man (Insan) will know himself, as well as his Creator.

MYSTIC UNION

His Holiness Guru Bawa in his exposition of the Mystic Union said that realisation and integration with the Limitless Divine Effulgence of the Supreme Creator, God (Allah), should be the central aim, purpose and achievement of each and every human being travelling in the Divine Path.

His Holiness Guru Bawa continued that this glorious realisation is beset with formidable difficulties.

First of all, it is pre-requisite that Wisdom present in man should emerge.

It is only then that the man concerned can firmly discard all evil propensities within his Heart (Qalb) and be well and truly on the true path which would slowly, but surely, lead him towards realisation and integration with the Divine Effulgence of God (Allah).

In order to bring home the difficulties a person of rectitude has to face in achieving the above glorious objective, His Holiness Guru Bawa cited an illustration and stressed that a person should after reading this illustration reflect and ponder over the great truths in this exposition.

There existed, a gardener who specialised in the cultivation of sugar-cane.

The gardener devoted his entire time, labour and resources to make his sugar-cane farm not only productive but also the best in the neighborhood.

The farmer took great care, immense pains, and spent sleepless nights ensuring that evil people did not rob him of his sugar-cane when it reached maturity. In addition, he took all possible precautions to ensure that insects, pests and flies did not destroy the sugar-cane.

This never ceasing vigilance was amply rewarded, for he was able to harvest a very good crop of sugar-cane that particular season. After the sugar-cane had reached maturity, he cut the sugar-cane and sold it to the local market for a profitable price. Some bundles of sugar-cane, which he was unable to dispose of in the market, remained.

He placed these bundles of sugar-cane in a raised position in the midst of a room. Thereafter, the gardener poured water, about half a foot in depth and a couple of feet in width, around the area in which the sugar-cane was placed. The ants, in the area smelled the sweetness radiating from the sugar-cane. This smell was irresistible to the ants. The all-consuming love for the sugar-cane now became so pressing that the ants developed faith, trust and determination to somehow gain access to the cluster of sugar-cane.

The ants, so engrossed on their one-pointed determination to gain access to the cluster of sugar cane, hit upon a stratagem. They decided to scale the wall of the room, which they did without loss of time. Reaching the ceiling of the room, the ants moved onto the rafter directly above the cluster of sugar-cane. Coming to this position, the ants let loose their grip and fell in the middle of the cluster of sugar-cane.

Instantly, each ant started with alacrity to enjoy the delicious sweetness of the sugar-cane.

Engrossed in the all-consuming sweetness, the ants did not for a moment have any thoughts of any other matter. The ants were fearless, serene, contented and happy. Only one thought passed through the minds of the ants. They realised that when the owner came to remove the cluster of sugar-cane, they themselves would also be removed as they now formed an integral part of the sugar-cane.

His Holiness Guru Bawa continuing said: Man in his supreme efforts to realise and get integrated with the Divine Effulgence of the Creator God (Allah), has to conduct himself with the same skill, dexterity and concentration as did the ants in the illustration.

It is important, that within man there should first emerge Wisdom in such Resplendence as to bring to him with clarity and vision the Divine Truth.

This person should further possess unshakeable faith and determination to protect his Resplendent Wisdom and within his Resplendent Wisdom there should emerge Divine Forbearance.

From this Divine Forbearance there should radiate within his Heart (Qalb) the countless attributes of God (Allah).

It is this glorious state, comparable to the state of the ants enjoying the delicious sweetness of the sugar-cane, that man, overwhelmed by the Overpowering Compassionate Grace and Love of God (Allah), should forever relish and enjoy the Divine Nectar which is Everlasting and Imperishable.

In this Divine State man would be able to fully eradicate the 70,000 veils of hypnotic fascinations of Illusion (Maya) engulfing his Heart (Qalb).

Thereafter, this Divine Man is consumed within the Heart (Qalb) of his Authentic Gnana Guru. This interaction of the Gnana Guru and the disciple awakens the Divine Luminous Wisdom (Noor) in the disciple, for the Heart of the Gnana Guru is full of Divine Luminous Wisdom (Noor).

His Holiness Guru Bawa added that the ants underwent considerable difficulties, great perils and many obstructions to attain the supreme purpose of being integrated with the sugar-cane.

Man, who works to achieve the greatest purpose of his life on Earth which is the ultimate integration with the Creator, needs also to undergo immense difficulties and great travails. He should in a state of complete surrender fall into the innermost Heart (Qalb) of a True Gnana Guru whose Heart (Qalb) is filled with the Divine Resplendence of Noor.

The person, so integrated with the Divine Noor of his True Gnana Guru, will lose his identity. His soul (Ruh) will become merged with the Radiance of the Soul (Noor) of the True Gnana Guru.

The actions and qualities of this person become the actions and qualities of his True Gnana Guru in whose Radiance the disciple has integrated himself.

HOW TO REALISE HEAVEN BY
CONCENTRATED DEVOTION TO RIGHTEOUS LIVING

His Holiness Guru Bawa in his exposition about the realisation of Heaven by concentrated devotion to righteous living gave the following illustration about a dullard.

There lived long ago a young unmarried lady of surpassing beauty and sterling character, fully dedicated to the Divine Path of God (Allah). She was alone having lost both of her parents when she was young.

Every morning she used to awaken at 2:00 A.M. fully prepared to go to the proper place and to offer her prayers to God. In her daily endeavour she had no other single thought in the world for her entire Heart (Qalb) was permeated with love and affection for God (Allah). She had placed herself in a state of complete surrender to God (Allah) and became completely immune from the countless attractions radiating from the World of Illusion (Maya).

In close proximity to her residence was a Pillaiyar Temple. The Officiating Priest of the Temple was a young, virile, robust Brahmin. He had from time to time noted the movements of this young lady of great charm and beauty. Struck by the beauty of this young lady he started to scheme how he would be able to satisfy his lust and passion for her.

The Brahmin youth was up very early in the morning every day and waited by the path she travelled going to prayers. This convinced her that the Brahmin youth was up to some mischief.

He resolved that on a particular day he must seduce this young lady of incomparable virtue, charm and beauty.

The young lady, full of the Grace of God (Allah), became aware of the great danger threatening her chastity.

Being regular in her worship, she prayed five times daily and meticulously observed the Divine Commandments of God (Allah). Her face shone with Divine Radiance.

On the day preceding the one earmarked by the Brahmin youth to outrage her modesty, this lady made one reverential request to God (Allah). Since she had dedicated her body and soul to Him alone, she beseeched God (Allah) to take her life away from her in order to forestall the calamity that was about to befall her. God (Allah) acceded to her request and soon she was dead.

As she had no one to look after her, the Divine Angels took charge of her body. They took the dead body to her hut, placed it in a bed and properly dressed her in the traditional religious manner. Lamps were lit around the dead body. The neighbours, witnessing this strange phenomenon, were amazed how this lady, who lived all alone before she was dead, was given all the traditional paraphernalia associated with funerals.

Her neighbours concluded that it was Divine Help that had placed the dead body of this virtuous lady in this state of great dignity. The neighbours, struck by awe and reverence, pooled their resources and buried the virtuous dead lady with great dignity and scrupulous observance as laid down by the religious code of Islam.

His Holiness Guru Bawa continuing his illustration said that about this time there lived a very dull person, illiterate and bereft of Wisdom (Arivu). His only asset was that he was blessed with a body of immense muscular strength. Further, he was tall, robust and fearsome. His appearance caused terror in the hearts of people and enabled him to have his own way.

This dullard had an old mother to whom he was attached. He was her sole means of support. He did no regular work, but earned a livelihood for himself and his mother by murdering and robbing innocent people.

His method of attacking was to waylay travelling people carrying provisions or goods striking their heads with an iron rod. With one blow the skull of his victim was cracked and he fell dead. Then, the dullard took the provisions or goods of the dead person to his mother. This provided sustenance for both of them.

For years the dullard continued this ignoble means of livelihood. His old mother was a very noble and religious woman. She had an irreproachable character and she lived a life of exemplary rectitude.

One day the mother told her son that a person is accountable for his actions on Earth to God (Allah) on Judgement Day. Such being the case, the mother continued, it is incumbent on a person to always be engaged and involved in right action acceptable to God (Allah), for in this way he would be assured of a place in Heaven.

If a person was involved in actions that were wrong, unjust and improper, he would be consigned on Judgement Day to Hell. The dullard was aghast and stunned at what his mother told him. Since he had already committed 999 murders to rob people of their provisions and goods in order to provide sustenance for both of them, he asked his mother if such a person was guilty of wrong action and likely to be sent to Hell. The mother assured him that his actions in committing the murders were criminal in the extreme form and that he would be sent to the deepest recesses of Hell. The dullard replied that though he had committed these monstrous crimes he had done so only to provide sustenance for both of them. He continued that since his purpose in committing the murders had a good motive would he not be absolved from the consequences of his atrocious and heinous crimes.

The mother replied very emphatically that murder is murder, whatever the motive. In view of the exceedingly serious nature of the crimes he had committed she said that he would most assuredly be sent to Hell. The dullard, aghast at what lay in store for him resolved not to commit any more crimes of murder even to earn a livelihood.

Henceforth, he resolved to live a life of utmost rectitude, not only to atone for the crimes he had committed earlier, but also to assure his passage to the Heavenly Abode. The dullard immediately took up an honest livelihood to eke out a living to support his mother. He was exceedingly scrupulous to avoid doing any harm to his fellow men while engaged in earning his livelihood.

In the new sphere of existence the dullard's main pre-occupation was whether he might still go to Heaven. Obsessed with this thought, he accosted a Priest (Alim) in the market place and put to him the question which was uppermost in his mind. He asked him pointedly whether or not he would go to Heaven. The Priest (Alim), fully aware of the antecedents of the dullard whose thuggery and murders were common talk in the village, was afraid to offend the dullard lest he provoke his anger. The Priest (Alim) was fully convinced that if he roused the anger of the dullard, he ran the risk of being mercilessly chastised or murdered. In order to avoid this gruesome prospect, if he gave any other answer, he told the dullard that he would certainly go to Heaven.

The dullard, pleased with the assurance of the Priest (Alim) that he would go to Heaven, went about his work comforted for the time being. Some days later, doubts began to creep into the mind of the dullard and he went to the mosque to ascertain from a lower ranking Priest (Lebbe) whether or not the earlier assurance of the Priest (Alim) was true.

The dullard met the Lebbe within the mosque and asked him whether or not he would go to Heaven. When confronted with the question within the sacred surroundings of the mosque, the Lebbe was in a quandary about what to say, because he was aware of the antecedents of the dullard as a formidable thug and murderer.

The Lebbe thought deeply and furiously for if he gave a negative answer his life would be in peril.

If on the contrary he gave an affirmative answer, though it would satisfy the dullard, it would be a blatant falsehood uttered in the sacred premises of the mosque and, therefore, would be sacrilegious.

So, the Lebbe thought deeply to find a solution. He finally told the dullard that his place in Heaven was assured if he could grow flowering plants on a massive rock. He said that the day the flowers bloomed his place in Heaven was assured forever and ever.

The dullard was unable to understand the seeming impossibility of such an event coming to fruition. He took the utterance of the Lebbe as Divine Truth. Placing his complete Trust, Determination and Faith in the utterance of the Lebbe, the dullard went in search of a massive rock.

After an intensive search he found a secluded spot where there was a massive rock which was very flat and even. The surface of the rock was of reasonable dimensions. The dullard chose the rock and after cleaning it of all dirt he spread manure on the hard surface of the rock. He, in his stupidity, did not realise what he was doing.

The dullard, however, persisted in his stupidity. He spread the manure on the rocky surface and watered the rock regularly in the hope of seeing the emergence of flowering plants.

Adjacent to the rock was a burial ground. People from the vicinity brought the bodies of the dead to be buried in the place.

For six years the dullard continued his watch over the massive rock, day in and day out, waiting for the flowers to bloom. At the end of the sixth year the body of the virtuous lady, who was spoken of earlier, was brought by the neighbors to be buried. According to the traditional customs of Islam, this lady, who had died early that morning, was buried.

Barely three hours after the burial, the Brahmin youth, learning of the death of the lady of peerless beauty, was furious as he had been deprived of satisfying his criminal sexual lust. As a result, he decided to satisfy his monstrous craving using the dead corpse of the young lady.

The Brahmin youth opened the grave, took out the body of the lady and was about to commit the criminal act. The noise made by opening the grave reached the ears of the dullard who was keeping vigil over the adjacent rock. The strange noise moved him to check the source of the sound.

The dullard traced the noise to the grave of the lady. Approaching the grave, he witnessed the Brahmin youth about to fall on the corpse of the virtuous lady. The dullard was stunned with horror. He acted impulsively and within a split second dealt a deadly blow, striking the head of the Brahmin youth with his massive club. The youth fell dead.

Simultaneously, a wonderful phenomenon occurred for the massive rock began to bloom with a number of flowers. It presented a magnificent and gorgeous spectacle.

This singular act of Justice on the part of the dullard, as well as his very intense and concentrated devotion to realise Heaven, brought about this miraculous Divine Intervention.

The dullard saved the honour of a very virtuous and Divine lady.

The miraculous blooming of the flowers on the massive rock assured the dullard of a place in Heaven.

His Holiness concluded by saying that eternal vigilance, extreme devotion and one-pointed concentration on one's pursuit in the righteous path brings about the Divine Interaction which will, eventually, integrate this person with his Creator.

REALISATION OF THE CREATOR

Children! Let me give you an illustration:

There was a grove filled with tall trees, shrubs and wild plants of various kinds growing at random without any human supervision.

It is customary for people in the neighbourhood to dump all collected refuse, leaves and other discarded materials in this grove.

Further, quite a number of people in the vicinity utilise this grove as a place to ease themselves. The excrement discharged by these people formed a number of very small deposits at different points in the grove.

One day after it rained slightly, the beetles, which flourished in these small deposits of excrement, began moving all over the grove.

Thereafter, there was a meeting of the beetles and the strongest and fattest beetle took up the designation as King (Rajah) Beetle.

The beetles desired to have as their main food bits of delicacies from edible plants in the grove. This desire was translated into action when the beetles attacked the vital portions of the edible plants.

This destruction enraged the man in charge of the plants and he decided to set fire to certain places in order to annihilate the beetles which were causing such harm. The fire started blazing at certain points in the grove. This blaze attracted the community of the beetles. The King Beetle in order to investigate the phenomenon called a meeting of his four Ministers.

The King Beetle told his Ministers that they were seeing in the grove a new phenomenon and pointed to the blaze-like fire. The King Beetle thought that it was possible that the blaze which they saw was a different kind of food which they had never seen or tasted before.

They resolved that it was prudent and wise on their part to investigate and find out what, exactly, was the intrinsic nature of the blaze.

In pursuance of the above, the King Beetle sent one of his four Ministers to go to the blaze.

This Minister promptly complied with the order of the King Beetle and flew to the blaze. Circling round the blaze this Minister found the place increasingly hotter as he attempted to get closer. So, in sheer fright he gave up investigating further and returned to the King Beetle.

The King Beetle asked the Minister to report the results of his mission. The Minister reported that he felt heat. The heat was everywhere and approach to the blaze was impossible. The King Beetle was visibly annoyed at the inconclusive nature of the mission undertaken by the Minister, so he sent another Minister to find out exactly what the blaze represented.

This Minister, feeling honoured that he was charged with such an important mission, traveled to the place of the blaze. Thereafter, this Minister circled round the blaze, but found approach impossible. He returned to report to the King Beetle that what he saw was something similar to scorching heat of intense fury and that approach was impossible.

The King Beetle now showed visible signs of disgust at the failure of his two Ministers and now entrusted the important mission to the next Minister.

This Minister was more resolute and determined than the two previous Ministers and was determined to make an all-out effort to find out the nature, quality and attributes of the blaze.

This Minister, with considerable resolution and determination, flew with all speed to the blaze. When he approached the blaze the heat was overwhelming in its intensity and fury.

Undaunted, this Minister approached fairly close to the blaze and in consequence sustained visible and deep injuries all over his body.

Incapacitated by the blaze-inflicted injuries he thought that discretion is the better part of valour and retreated immediately. Coming back with considerable difficulty, the Minister reported to the King Beetle that the object he investigated had the qualities and attributes of fire. Therefore, closer approach to the blaze was out of the question.

Now, the King Beetle took stock of the situation and as a last resort decided to send his most capable and brilliant Minister, the Prime Minister.

The Prime Minister knowing all that had happened decided to stake everything in an all-out effort to know the intrinsic qualities and attributes of the blaze. With inexorable determination the Prime Minister departed on his mission. Approaching the fire more closely than the three preceding Ministers, he started circling the blaze.

He had hardly started when one of his wings got burnt. The Prime Minister discovered the nature of that destruction and was fortunate to save his life. He stumbled back to the King Beetle to report the findings of his mission.

The Prime Minister told the King Beetle that it was all fire and approach within its recesses meant certain death.

Now, the King Beetle decided to investigate the blaze himself and set out on the trip. Within himself he possessed such great determination that he never paused, even for a split second, to reflect on the difficulties he might encounter as he approached the blaze.

The King Beetle in keeping with his desire to know the nature of the blaze flew directly into the innermost recesses of the fire.

In consequence, the King Beetle was consumed and integrated with the fire and the fire was integrated with the King Beetle. The identity of the King Beetle was completely lost in the fire.

His Holiness Guru Bawa continuing his exposition said:

Similarly, Mankind is divided into 73 groups of humanity. Of these, 72 of the groups of humanity belong to one of the four religions. The four religions represent the four elements: Earth, Water, Fire and Air.

The 72 groups of humanity using their limited Wisdom and intellect project from each of the four elements a particular religion. The object of their worship is that particular element from which their religion originated.

Each of the elements, Earth, Fire, Water and Air, represents a particular religion and cumulatively they project 400 billion hypnotic fascinations from the world of Illusion (Maya).

In this illustration the four religions represent the four Ministers in the community of Beetles. The reactions of each Minister, when charged with the mission of finding out the identity of the blaze is indicative of the level of understanding of that particular Minister.

This is indeed the exact predicament of the followers of each of the four religions who employ material resources to find out the identity of the Supreme Creator.

It would appear that the followers of each of the four religions in their respective search for their Supreme Creator find themselves in the same predicament as each of the four Ministers referred to earlier.

The followers of the four religions represent the 72 groups of humanity.

The people belonging to a particular religion use the symbolic objects in a particular element as their concept of the Supreme Creator.

As stated earlier, the 72 groups of humanity draw their gods from the 400 billion hypnotic fascinations found in Illusion (Maya).

Only the 73rd group of Humanity belongs to the highest spiritual station represented by the King Beetle which realised the Supreme Truth by its total integration within the One Truth. To the 73rd Group of Humanity belongs the Perfect Man (Insam Kamil). He is a Divinely Resplendent Man who knows himself and who realises the crowning achievement of Man's sojourn on Earth is to know the Supreme Creator.

HOW TO ACQUIRE GNANAM (DIVINE KNOWLEDGE)

A fish swims in the sea. It is able to go everywhere in the wide expanse of the sea. It is able to move within the sea with ease and comfort. The sea is its natural habitat. In fact, the fish enjoys complete freedom in the sea and is able to get what it needs with ease and comfort. The fish is truly in a state of complete satisfaction and enjoyment.

Man, on the contrary, cannot swim like the fish in the sea. Owing to the very nature of his physical state, man is confronted with difficulties while swimming and he can only swim within certain limits. It is inevitable for man to give up swimming after a certain time for his strength can no longer cope with the strain.

His Holiness Guru Bawa continuing his exposition said:

Similarly, a true disciple should meticulously follow the Authentic Gnana Guru (Gnostic Guru) in the Ocean of Life. The Gnana Guru (Gnostic Guru) swims the Ocean of Life with the assurance and ease of the fish in the sea.

In the Ocean of Life the Authentic Gnana Guru (Gnostic Guru) is able to negotiate the 400 billion hypnotic fascinations of Illusion (Maya).

Unless the disciple meticulously follows the Guru, he will not be able to negotiate the Ocean of Life. The disciple who is ever vigilant, ever alert and ever watchful and who adheres very assiduously to the advice and guidance of his authentic and wise Gnana Guru will in time attain Divine Resplendence.

On attaining this glorious state the disciple will also be able to negotiate the world of Life with ease and comfort.

Such a disciple will eventually come to know himself and his Creator. This is the Summum Bonum of Man's life on earth.

ADVICE TO A DISCIPLE WHO WANTS TO
BE A GNANI (WISE SAGE)

His Holiness Guru Bawa gave an exposition of the various stages a disciple must pass through before he could become a Wise Sage (Gnani).

In the First Stage the disciple should place himself in complete surrender to the Guru without any reservation. In this act of surrender he dedicates himself to do any and every bidding of the Guru without any question.

Implicit and absolute obedience to the Guru is the First Stage of a disciple seeking Divine Wisdom (Gnanam). The person in this state renounces all material pursuits. He is non-attached to family and wealth. He is, in fact, completely free from all personal encumbrances.

In acquiring Divine Wisdom the Second Stage is for the disciple to be meticulously and scrupulously correct in his conduct and behaviour. This state of existence is comparable to a person walking on the edge of a sword which has been sharpened over and over 70,000 times. The person who walks on the edge of that sword has to be extraordinarily careful. The slightest deviation on the part of the walker means certain catastrophe.

In the Second Stage, the aspirant of Divine Wisdom (Gnanam) must show the same extraordinary care, vigilance and devotion in his day to day life as does the one who walks on the edge of the sword.

In the Third Stage, the aspirant of Divine Wisdom (Gnanam) should exhibit extreme vigilance, penetrating awareness and superb judgement in his conduct and behaviour. For no reason should he look backwards or sideways, but keep with unerring precision to the straight and narrow path of existence as laid down by his Guru.

The aspirant should exhibit a keen perception and avoid pitfalls and barriers that he is likely to encounter on his path and of which he has been forewarned by his Guru.

If the aspirant of Divine Wisdom (Gnanam) deviates from the path laid down by his Guru the aspirant will be confronted by degradation, demoralisation and destruction. A disciple, deeply saturated and immersed in Illusion (Maya), loses not only the continued guidance of his Guru, but will fail completely to attain Divine Wisdom (Gnanam).

The disciple who meticulously adheres to the path laid down by the Guru in the three stages detailed earlier and who scrupulously observes the advice tendered by his Guru will, in time, attain Divine Wisdom (Gnanam). In this glorious state he will come to know himself and his Creator.

SWORDFISH

The Kamil Sheik or Gnana Guru, in his exposition, said that in the ocean the swordfish is like the tiger. In the limitless ocean of Illusion (Maya) within the Heart (Qalb) of man the Divine Wisdom is like the Tiger.

The swordfish in its front part is endowed with a beak, like a sword, with a sharp cutting edge. The swordfish, in its passage through the ocean, is able to cut into pieces crores and crores of fish with its sword-like beak. In the limitless ocean of Illusion (Maya) within the Heart (Qalb) of man, there are lodged 70,000 evils of darkness and 4,000,000 crores of hypnotic fascinations of Illusion (Maya).

In order to negotiate successfully this limitless ocean of Illusion (Maya) the Resplendent Wisdom potentially present in man must emerge. Like the swordfish, in the vast ocean, utilises its sword-like beak to cut crores and crores of fish in the ocean, man, with his Resplendent Wisdom, should be able to root out the countless evils of darkness and the limitless hypnotic fascinations radiating from Maya.

Unless man uses his Resplendent Wisdom he will not be able to root out the limitless evil propensities within his Heart (Qalb).

A person, only when he roots out the entire hypnotic fascinations of this world and also of the 18,000 other worlds, which are present in his Heart (Qalb), will possess a Spotlessly Effulgent Heart (Qalb), in which state would emerge the Splendour of Divine Luminous Wisdom (Noor).

The Divine Effulgence of Noor engulfs his entire being and he comes to know himself.

When he comes to know himself he comes to know and realise his Creator.

FISH

The Fish swimming in the wide expanse of the Ocean has no eyelids. It sees straight and its vision is constant as the eyelids are never closed. After some time the vision of the fish gets blurred to a point when it is unable to see objects distinctly and clearly.

It is in this predicament that the fish gets entangled in the net spread by the fisherman to entrap the fish. In its blurred state of vision the fish goes on pushing forcefully into the net and in consequence is irrevocably caught.

The fisherman when he comes to remove the net takes with him entangled fish which will be eventually cooked for food.

The Kamil Sheik (Gnana Guru) here said that the fish was entrapped because of the absence of eyelids which blurred its vision. In consequence it was unable to see the net ahead of it. Further the inborn instinct in the fish, to escape from danger, was inoperable with the absence of eyelids.

The presence of the eyelids in the fish would have enabled it to size up and discriminate objects in its path. In so doing, it would have warded off danger through the active operation of its instinct.

Man is the noblest and rarest of God's creation. This man is potentially endowed with Divine Luminous Wisdom situated in the innermost recesses of his Heart (Qalb).

Within his Heart (Qalb) are also potentially present all beings in this world and the 18,000 other worlds as well.

There exist also within his Heart (Qalb) 400,000 lakhs of crores of hypnotic fascinations of Illusion (Maya), and the darkness of ignorance.

Further within the Heart (Qalb) of man there are six destructive Evils namely: Avarice, Anger, Stinginess, Lust, Sectional Religious Fanaticism and Envy.

Egoism, actions (good and bad) and the propensities of Illusion (Maya) are also present. These evils generate transitory pleasures and create a repository of erroneous knowledge, devoid of Wisdom.

All these aspects detailed above are crystallised within the Heart (Qalb) of Man.

In order to swim the limitless ocean of Illusion (Maya) Man should possess Resplendent Wisdom. It is only such a man who would be able to negotiate the limitless ocean of Illusion (Maya) with its countless hypnotic fascinations and 70,000 veils of darkness, each one saturated with the iniquity.

This man can, by his Resplendent Divine Wisdom (Pahuth-Arivu), eliminate all evil propensities, mind-monkey lust, passion, avarice, hatred, envy, caste-consciousness, religious fanaticism, linguistic pride, communal arrogance, iniquity and all the desires from within his Heart (Qalb).

A man with Resplendent Divine Wisdom is able to discriminate good from evil. He is able to root out all things that are perishable and evil.

Utilization of Wisdom is the birthright of Man who is the rarest of God's creation. Man using his Wisdom is well and truly on the way towards Divine Resplendent Wisdom.

On the other hand, the man who fails to develop his Wisdom is like the fish bereft of eyelids. Such a person leads a life of demoralisation, degradation, iniquity and meets with ignoble death.

This man is no better than the fish which finds its destination in the stomach of the fishermen for he meets with ignoble death and is consigned to Hell.

The Kamil Sheik (Gnana Guru) concluded that it is very important for man to be true to his Divine Heritage by working towards the emergence of his Divine Resplendent Wisdom.

Such a person will exhibit in his pattern of existence, behaviour and conduct the Glorious Attributes of the Creator.

He then becomes the Glorious Divine Image of God (Allah), honoured, revered, and ever respected by his fellowmen everywhere. It is this Man who would cut asunder the cycle of births and merge with the Effulgence of God (Allah).

ELEPHANT

An elephant in the search for its daily sustenance roams in search of food. In the process it pulls at anything and everything, in the wide expanse of the forest, which comes within the reach of its trunk. Further, the elephant strikes with its trunk indiscriminately anything and everything in its passage.

The elephant without exercising forethought strikes at all objects, in sheer perversity, and in this process one day it strikes at an armadillo (Alungu). The armadillo gets hold of its trunk. The grip of the armadillo is firm and unshakeable. The firm grip of the armadillo on the trunk of the elephant causes annoyance to the elephant. The elephant tries to get rid of the armadillo, but finds it difficult to get rid of. The grip of the armadillo becomes firmer and tighter.

The elephant gets increasingly enraged and in its fury strikes the trunk against the hardest tree in order to kill the armadillo, which has so firmly and so strongly gripped its trunk.

Every single stroke of the elephant's trunk at the tree is directed precisely to the point where the armadillo is positioned. The armadillo at the moment of impact gets a firmer grip on the trunk of the elephant and its body gets bloated up.

This process of hitting the trunk to eliminate the armadillo goes on for a considerable time. The result is that the ultimate position is worse than at the beginning. The elephant grows more and more desperate in its utterly futile attempt to get rid of the armadillo.

Physical exhaustion supervenes and the elephant eventually dies. Here the Kamil Sheik (The Perfect Guru) said: If only the elephant had exercised right knowledge it would have saved itself from its terrible end. The elephant need only to have moved to the nearest pond and there plunged its trunk deep into the pond.

The Kamil Sheik (the Perfect Guru) continued: In the same way man wedded to sectional religious fanaticism plunges deeper and deeper into the hypnotic fascinations generated by Illusion (Maya).

This man living and moving within the erroneous doctrines of his particular religious code is not only ignorant of the Divine Truth, but arrogant as well. This man is so unyielding and obstinate in his belief that he can best be compared to a wild elephant on rampage.

This man in his passage through the world gets immersed deeper and deeper in the hypnotic fascinations of Illusion (Maya). In consequence he becomes very vulnerable to poverty, disease and hunger. Once poverty, disease and hunger assail him, he tries to get rid of them with his worldly Wisdom, but fails in the end.

The Kamil Sheik (the Perfect Guru) continued: If the elephant utilised its instinctive knowledge rightly and plunged its trunk deep in the pond, it would have gotten rid of the armadillo and escaped alive in a matter of seconds.

Similarly, man when assailed by hunger, disease and poverty should go straight to an authentic Gnana Guru (Gnostic Guru) and submit himself fully to him for guidance. The Guru will guide him in such a way as to enable the Wisdom (Arivu) in the man to become emergent and resplendent and light his entire being with Divine Luminescence.

In consequence, the attributes of the Creator within man becomes active with Divine Splendour.

This person with his Divine Wisdom (Pahuth-Arivu) is able to negotiate the limitless ocean of Illusion (Maya) saturated with its darkness. Hunger, disease and age will not affect him.

He will be able to annihilate the limitless hypnotic fascinations of Illusion (Maya) which engulf his existence.

He will eventually reach a state when his Heart (Qalb) will become Spotlessly Effulgent.

In this glorious state there will emerge within his Heart (Qalb) the Divine Luminous Wisdom (Perr-Arivu). When his entire being is lit with Divine Effulgence, he will be able to eliminate poverty, disease and hunger.

Such a person is indeed free from death as he is integrated within the Divine Effulgence of Allah, or the Noor.

MARGOSA AND SANDALWOOD TREES

"There are present margosa and sandalwood trees. Even if these trees have been dead for a considerable length of time and their roots have completely deteriorated, they still retain one peculiar phenomenon.

The innate smell and other peculiar characteristics of these trees are present long after the trees are dead.

Even after decades, when these dead trees are burnt, the particular and peculiar smell of each tree radiates from them."

His Holiness Guru Bawa continued: "Similarly, man before he was ushered into existence in the world was in the form of a foetus in the womb of his mother. The foetus is impregnated with the dominant characteristics, not only of the parents of the unborn child, but also, carry the characteristics of its ancestors.

"The child is born and grows up into adolescence taking with it the above inheritance.

"This person, after he grows up, may develop his Wisdom and try to root out countless evil attributes inborn in him. Yet, however laborious his effort and however long the time he employs in this pursuit, he will not be able to root out the evil attributes from within himself.

"Like the margosa tree and the sandalwood tree which continue to radiate their peculiar smells many years after they are dead, these evil inherited characteristics operate in him, continually.

"Man in the course of his existence is off and on assailed by adversities. When these adversities are analysed in the searchlight of his Wisdom (Arivu), their origin can be traced to the time before his birth, when he was a foetus in his mother's womb.

"Many of his characteristics which bring about adversity were actually crystallised at the time of his conception which followed the cohabitation of his parents in their state of desire.

"The countless evil attributes, potentially present, within the Heart (Qalb) of Man can be traced back to a point of time before his birth, when he was a foetus within the womb of his mother.

"The heritage of man forms not only a repository of evil qualities acquired from his parents, but also from his direct line of ancestors.

"This heritage of evil can only be rooted out from his Heart (Qalb) by placing himself unreservedly and in complete surrender to a Gnana Guru (Gnostic Guru). Thereafter, the Gnana Guru through his penetrating Divine Glance and Utterances, directed at his disciple, will burn up the reservoir of evil qualities and develop the disciple's Wisdom.

"This Divine Fire of Wisdom, of the disciple, is powerful enough to effectively destroy the reservoir of evil qualities inherited by him, not only from his parents, but from his ancestry, as well. Therefore, a disciple who places himself in absolute and complete surrender to a Gnana Guru can effectively eliminate the heritage of evil within himself and will also become possessed of a spotlessly Effulgent Heart (Qalb).

"Such a person will reach and realise the Supreme State of Human Existence on Earth and will come to know himself.

"Further, such a person will have his Wisdom (Arivu) gloriously lit with the Divine Luminous Wisdom (Perr-Arivu) of Allah and this person will cut asunder the cycle of birth to which man is vulnerable.

QUESTIONS AND ANSWERS
UNDERSTANDING THE SECRET OF THE RUH (SOUL)

1. Question: What is Creation?

    Answer: The Wonderful miracle of Allah (God).

2. Q: Who is Allah (God)?

    A: The Immanent Divine Power which endows life and food to all created beings, light to the eyes, compassion, forbearance, calmness, righteousness, truthfulness, integrity and knowledge to the heart, smell to the nostrils, taste to the tongue, understanding, awareness, Wisdom and Serenity to the mind, Luminosity to the Soul, and finally Illuminates the Divinity in Man.

3. Q: What is the significance of Man?

    A: Man is the inner secret projection of the Divinity of Allah-u-thala (The Almighty God) and the Crown of His Creation.

4. Q: What is the purpose in creating Man?

    A: The main purpose is to proclaim the Glory of the Supreme Divinity which Allah manifested in Man and in the entire Creation.

5. Q: What duties devolve in Man?

    A: Principally to know himself, to assiduously strive towards the achievement of self-realisation, and to work indefatigably towards the elimination of suffering in service to all created beings.

6. Q: What is Islam?

    A: Complete, unconditional and absolute surrender to Allah (God).

7. Q: What is the Holy Quran?

    A: The Immutable Divine Truths of Allah (God) manifesting in words of Resplendent Glory through the Holy Prophet enshrined in the Holy Quran.

8. Q: Who is a Muslim?

    A: A Muslim is one who utterly gives his body, mind and Soul in

50

complete, absolute and unconditional surrender to Allah (God).

9. Q: Is such complete and absolute surrender possible?

    A: Yes. By scrupulous adherence to the Divine Commands enshrined in the Quran, practising assiduously, complete and utter selflessness in all actions and dedicating all one's work to Allah alone.

10. Q: How can this be practised amidst the demands of the material world?

    A: By being decisively wedded to virtuous actions and unswerving rectitude with constant and devoted worship of Allah (God) in the temple of one's heart.

11. Q: What is the Heart?

    A: The Judgment-Seat of Allah (God) and the Treasury of Divine Truths which radiate and illuminate the Wisdom of Man.

12. Q: What is Sufism?

    A: Sufism is the investigation of good and evil through the eyes of Wisdom. The annihilation of evil and the complete acceptance of good forms part of Sufism.

13. Q: Who is a Sufi?

    A: One who surrenders himself to the pursuit of Divine Truths.

14. Q: Who is a Moo-Min (True Believer)?

    A: One who has full awareness and knowledge of the 15 Authentic Secret Signs of the Holy Prophet is a Moo-min.

15. Q: What are the characteristics of a Moo-Min (True Believer)?

    A: The chief characteristics of a Moo-min are Faith, Selflessness, Love, Compassion, Tolerance, Integrity, Serenity, Mercy, Truthfulness, Forbearance, Purity and Justice.

16. Q: What is Faith or Iman?

    A: Iman is unshakable faith, tenacity and unflinching determination in the belief that Allah is Omnipotent, Omnipresent and Omniscient. Allah is the repository of all Divine Secrets including birth and death. The firm and absolute belief that Allah alone sits in Judgment on all our actions is Iman.

17. Q: What is Love and Selflessness?

    A: The spirit of Allah (God).

18. Q: What is Iklas (Purity)?

    A: Iklas means looking with absolute sincerity at every object. This is seen through the eyes of Wisdom.

19. Q: What is Compassion?

    A: Compassion means the Grace of Allah (Rahumath).

20. Q: What is Charity?

    A: Prompt help rendered to one's fellow beings with whole-hearted concurrence of one's conscience.

21. Q: What does Man normally observe?

    A: Man is first attracted to what grips his mind and fascinates his eyes. In this condition he is caught within the tentacles of Nafs Ammara (evil desires).

22. Q: What does Allah observe?

    A: The Divinely Luminous gaze of Allah is directed towards the spotless Purity in the Hearts of his Created Beings.

23. Q: What does a Moo-Min (True Believer) observe?

    A: The immutable Divine Truths first revealed by Allah manifested through the Holy Prophet and enshrined in the Holy Quran. The Moo-min finally looks at the Resplendent Effulgent Glory of Allah (God).

24. Q: What are the triple aspects revealed in the Glory of Allah?

    A: The Divine Luminous Gaze of Allah takes three Divine Attributes. In the *First* aspect it manifests the Holy Quran through the Holy Prophet. In the *Second* aspect the Luminous Gaze of Allah is focused in the heart of the Moo-min (True Believer) wherein are enshrined the Divine Utterances of the Holy Quran. In the *Third* aspect the Luminous Gaze of Allah is here directed at the Purity of the Hearts of all his Created Beings. Their speech, action and adherence to the Divine Commands come under the search-light of this Luminous Gaze of Allah. Each created being receives the Grace, Compassion and Blessing of Allah in proportion to his good actions. The Divine Truths of Allah emerge within the Divine Illumination of each created being in

Umul Quran (Mother of Holy Books).

25. Q: What is Forbearance?

    A: Forbearance is Limitless Grace from the Infinite Reservoir of Beauty, Truth and Goodness of Allah.

26. Q: What is Justice?

    A: Scrupulously adhering to the narrow path of Truth based on the Immutable Truths enshrined in the Holy Quran and Right Conscience fortified by the Grace of Allah.

27. Q: Who is Satan (Iblis)?

    A: One who is completely and absolutely divorced from the Divine Immutable Truths of Allah manifested through the Holy Quran and Right Conscience fortified by the Grace of Allah.

28. Q: How does Satan gain admission into the human body?

    A: Satan gains admission to the human body as a result of one completely losing Faith, Trust, Determination and Belief in Allah. In consequence the Iman (Faith, Certitude, Conviction) of this person is very shaky and vulnerable to the evil influence of Satan.

29. Q: What is the primary characteristic of Satan?

    A: The chief characteristic of Satan is to flout the Divine Commands of Allah.

30. Q: What is the cause of Suffering?

    A: Lack of tenacious Faith and Trust in the Divine Commands of Allah enshrined in the Holy Quran and non-awareness of the Divine Attributes of the Holy Prophet exposes one to intermittent suffering.

31. Q: What brings Everlasting Bliss?

    A: The chief ingredients which constitute Everlasting Bliss are awareness of the "Truth of Bismi", i.e. Creation, Preservation and Salvation, also full awareness of the Divine Injunctions or Commands of Allah and Realisation of the Divine Attributes of the Holy Prophet.

32. Q: What is the cause of Man's discontent?

    A: False words of Love on one's lips, nefarious and wicked

designs in the heart and stimulating friendship with evil thoughts in the mind, if continuously practised, bring acute misery and discontent in man.

33. Q: What is Wisdom?

    A: Moral Excellence, Unswerving Rectitude, Integrated Personality, Self-Restraint, Self-Knowledge, and Luminous Awareness of the Divine Injunctions or Commands.

34. Q: What is Life or Atma?

    A: Complete acceptance and realisation of the Divine Injunctions of Allah enshrined in the Holy Quran and assiduously putting these Divine Principles in daily actions. Awareness of the Divine Attributes of Forbearance, Compassion, and Justice exemplified in the life of the Holy Prophet.

35. Q: What is Knowledge?

    A: The imperishable Truths of the utterance of the Holy Prophet enshrined in the Holy Quran.

36. Q: What is Ignorance?

    A: When one does not know oneself.

37. Q: What is (1) Shariath,   (2) Tharikath,
             (3) Hakikath,   (4) Marifat?

    A: (1) Shariath—Complete awareness and full realisation of the Imperishable Truths enshrined in the Divine Injunctions of Allah.
       (2) Tharikath—In this state, Faith or Iman is placed in an unassailable and impregnable position based on immutability of Conduct, Trust and Faith.
       (3) Hakikath—The convergence of Allah and Moo-min (True Believer) in Divine Communion.
       (4) Marifat—Divine Truths crystallised in continuous Resplendent Glory in Luminous Space. Also Truth, Knowledge and Wisdom are enshrined in the Divine Illumination of Allah and merged in Infinite Bliss.

38. Q: What do the above distinctions connote in the life of Man?

    A: First of all, they connote scrupulous adherence to the Immutable Truths of Allah manifested through the Holy Prophet. Further, they connote Absolute Integrity, Forbearance, Serenity, Compassion, Love, Justice, Truthfulness, Righteous Conduct, Charity and all works done in complete dedication to Allah. Further they connote loving thy neighbour as thyself. Finally, in order to be fully immersed in the Divine Aura and Radiance of Allah one should be permeated and enveloped day and night with the imperishable Divine Truths embodied in the Holy Quran.

39. Q: What is Prayer?

  A: Man's prayer, is a Divine Instrument for shedding and eliminating the accretions of ignorance and evil attributes in Man.

40. Q: What are the wrong approaches to Prayer?

  A: Evil thoughts and harmful desires in the Heart (Qalb) of Man (Insan) militate against the right approach to prayer.

41. Q: What is the Authentic Prayer to Allah?

  A: In the Qalb (Heart) of Insan (Man) there should be impeccable Honesty, spotless Purity, unassailable Integrity, Tenacity of Purpose, and unshakable Faith in the Divinity of Allah. These are the chief ingredients which will enable Insan (Man) to achieve, successfully, the authentic Prayer to Allah.

42. Q: What is the body and soul of the above kind of Prayer?

  A: Unshakable Faith, complete Trust and absolute firmness of Belief in Allah are the main essences which cumulatively constitute the body. The soul of such a body is Kalima (Recitation of Faith). One should pray to Allah through the Luminescence of Kalima (There is no God but God).

43. Q: How can one achieve this Divine State of Existence?

  A: The impulse to Truth should take firm hold in the mind. Holding this impulse very tenaciously in one-pointed direction and by using the resources of one's intellect and knowledge one should achieve Wisdom and further make this Wisdom become Divine Wisdom. The Divine Wisdom is finally made Divinely Effulgent and Radiant in all directions. This Divine Luminous Wisdom transmutes into Rasool (Messenger of God) and is further transmuted into the Divine Illumination of Allah (God). This is the path towards the glorious consummation of the Divine State of Existence.

44. Q: What is Meditation?

  A: Absolute and complete non-violence in thought, word and deed in relation to all created beings is the main postulate of Meditation and super-imposed on this requirement is overflowing Love towards Allah.

45. Q: How can one put in practice this state of Meditation?

A: Knowing thyself and complete and scrupulous adherence to the Divine Truth and Spotless Purity of Heart are the chief ingredients that will enable one to put in practice this state of Meditation.

46. Q: What is Fasting?

A: Complete subjugation of the seven evil propensities inherent in the Nafs Ammara (evil desires), annihilation of all desires, compassion and pity for all created beings, amelioration of misery and disease in human kind and engendering happiness in mind and body to all one's fellow creatures. The above state is the essential pre-requisite to Fasting.

47. Q: When does this Fasting commence?

A: Fasting commences from the moment of attaining adolescence and Fasting is firmly established when he is in possesion of an Iman (Faith, Certitude, Conviction) which is complete.

48. Q: How do you observe Haj (Pilgrimage)?

A: Observance of Haj inexorably demands the complete annihilation of the seven evil desires inherent in Nafs Ammara and scrupulous adherence to the Divine Path of Allah. The Qalb (Heart) of Insan (Man) should be replete with the Divine Attributes of the Rasool (Messenger of God).
A person who complies fully with the above requirements will achieve the Glorious Consummation of realising the Divine Luminous Gaze of Allah.

49. Q: What is Mihraj (Ascension to Heaven)?

A: Mihraj is the triple glorious aspect of Allah divinely states as:
(1) Allah (God)
(2) Rasool (Messenger of God)
(3) Quran (The Holy Book)
Complete realisation of the triple Divine Truths in the innermost Qalb (Heart) of Insan (Man) will bring Divine Illumination and enable him to see the triple Divine Luminescence referred to above, gloriously embedded in the Divinely Effulgent Gaze of Allah. This Divine State is called Mihraj (Ascension to Heaven).

50. Q: What is the inner Kaa'ba (Mosque) or (Temple)?

A: The inner aspect of the Heart which is the place where Iman (Faith, Certitude, Conviction) resides and radiates His glory becomes the Kaa'ba.

51. Q: What is the outer Kaa'ba (Mosque or Temple)?

   A: Complete and scrupulous adherence without deviating an atom from the Divine Injunctions of Allah, realisation of the Divine Attributes of Rasool (Messenger of God) and righteous conduct is the outer Kaa'ba. This is part of the Divine Order immanent in Creation.

52. Q: What is the dominant quality of a Moo-min (True Believer)?

   A: Complete acceptance of the Divine Injunction of Allah manifested in the Holy Quran and the merging of the spotless purity of his Qalb (Heart) in the Triple Luminous Gaze of Allah.

53. Q: What are the authentic characteristics of an Insan (Man)?

   A: The inner Soul of Insan (Man) is gloriously replete with the Wisdom, Truth, Grace and Knowledge of Self in respect of birth and death. These constitute the authentic characteristics of an Insan (Man).

54. Q: How will the speech of Insan (Man) appear?

   A: The speech of Insan (Man) will be studded with the Divine Truths of Allah based on the immutable principles of Justice, Truth, Love, Charity and Goodness.

55. Q: What is the learning of Insan (Man)?

   A: The learning of Insan (Man) principally is scrupulous and unswerving adherence to the Divine Injunctions of Allah, absolute Integrity, true Justice, Forbearance, Compassion, Unity, Serenity of Mind and superimposed on these qualities are 70,000 additional Glorious Attributes of Allah.

56. Q: What is the mode of articulation of the Iman (Faith, Certitude, Conviction) in Insan (Man)?

   A: Complete adherence to the 6,666 Divine Injunctions of Allah manifested in the Holy Quran. These Divine Truths will permeate and condition the Iman (Faith, Certitude, Conviction) and mode of articulation of an Insan (Man).

57. Q: What is the demeanour of an Insan (Man)?

   A: The demeanour and appearance of Insan (Man) will reflect the Luminous Glory of Allah and His Holy Prophet enshrined in the Holy Quran.

58. Q: What do the eyes of Insan (Man) reflect?

A: The eyes of Insan (Man) reflect only the innermost Divine Essence and immutable Divine Truths of Allah enshrined in the Holy Quran.

59. Q: What causes the downfall of Insan (Man)?

A: Primarily the evil desires and in particular the seven evil desires (Nafs Ammara). These, then, will inexorably cause the downfall of Insan (Man).

60. Q: Whom does Insan (Man) deceive on Earth?

A: Insan (Man) on Earth deceives himself by making himself false witness to integrity and actively contravening the Divine Injunctions of Allah. Insan (Man) further deceives himself by denying the Divine Attributes of the Holy Prophet. Such an Insan (Man) is immersed in iniquity, gradually sinks into the mire of degradation and finally ends in destroying himself.

61. Q: What is the cause of the limitless and inordinate Love of Allah to His entire Creation in spite of patent evil in the world?

A: The reason for the limitless and inordinate Love of Allah to His entire Creation, in spite of patent evil, is that the Superabundant Grace of Allah is spontaneously available to each and every one within His Creation whether they seek His Divine Path or not.

62. Q: If Allah shows such inordinate Love and Compassion what happens?

A: By such Love and Compassion Allah progressively draws the evil out of man.

63. Q: What causes an Insan (Man) to deviate from the Path of Righteousness?

A: Insan (Man) deviates from the Path of Righteousness by his propensity for inordinate acquisition of land, gold and worldly goods. Further reasons are falling victim to the charms of women and giving way to his wayward impulses. By this he loses his moorings in Divine Truths, his Iman (Faith, Certitude, Conviction) becomes so infirm that his descent to self-destruction is accelerated.

64. Q: By what is Wisdom attracted and superseded?

A: Wisdom is attracted and superseded by the Divine Luminous Gaze of Allah, His Resplendent Effulgent Brilliance, His Overpowering Compassion and His Superabundant Grace. Further, it is the awareness that Allah and Allah alone is the

Supreme Arbitrator in respect to all our actions on Judgment Day.

65. Q: Who is authentically Great?

      A: The attributes of the authentic Great are; very highly developed Awareness, exceptionally profound Divine Knowledge and deeply penetrating Awareness of Right and Wrong. Although the dimensions of Insan's body when mathematically computed is infintesimal, the dimensions of his Divine Knowledge are beyond mathematical computation.

66. Q: Who are Sufis or Gnanis (Divine Wise Sages)?

      A: Sufis are those who are endowed with exceptionally deep understanding of the entire body of Divine Knowledge. Through penetrating awareness they are able to focus their intense Luminous Gaze on the innermost Divine Secrets within the Divine Truth of Allah. Then they are capable, with masterly ease, of propogating those Divine Truths to their fellowman with Grace and child-like simplicity.

Luminous Awareness of the imperishable innermost Divine Secrets of Allah and expounding them with the utmost lucidity to all created beings is the chief attribute, characteristic of a Gnani (Divinely Wise Sage).

The Sufi or Gnani realises fully the strength of the beliefs of his disciples to whom he has taught the Divine Truths of Allah and he hands over to each of them the Divine Sword of Allah with which the disciple can annihilate evil qualities and retain the good qualities.

The person who has the above capacity to know the attributes of his disciple truly possesses the Divine Illumination of Allah and is eminently fitted to be called a Gnani. The complete annihilation of the ego is another dominant characteristic of a Sufi or Gnani.

67. Q: Who is a Thirugnani (a highly developed Sufi or Gnani)?

      A: A Thirugnani is a person who possesses in full measure the Divine Illumination of Allah and through his Divine Luminescence has full awareness of the past, present and future.

68. Q: In the world who is wise and who is foolish?

      A: A wise man is one who has right knowledge, a true awareness of the transitoriness and impermanence of his body and who has annihilated evil through his Wisdom and who has effectively eradicated the seven evil desires inherent in Nafs Ammara.

Even after annihilating all the evil qualities referred to above the monkey in the mind will still bare its teeth and with tempting suggestions, tantalise one to embrace evil again. The only way to effectively eradicate the monkey from the mind is to have complete Trust and Faith in Allah, unshakable Belief in His Divine Injunctions and Iman (Faith, Certitude, Conviction), firm and resolute. The monkey in the mind finding it has no place at all disappears and with it goes all its inherent evil qualities.

A person who attains the above state becomes a fit reservoir to accept the entire Divine Truth of Allah and to protect His Divine Secrets with utmost care and vigilance. Such a person is a wise man.

A foolish man is one who is unaware and ignorant of the above Truths. The monkey within his mind runs riot and no attempt whatsoever is made to control the wayward impulses of this monkey mind. The wayward impulses are given concrete expression by the person concerned in a catalogue of evil deeds. Such a man is designated a fool.

69. Q: What does one find in a Moo-min Sheik (True Gnostic Guru)?

A: A Moo-min Sheik is one who has the Divine Luminous Faculty of expounding and propagating the HIKKMATH (Divine Secrets of Allah) with eyes of Wisdom. Allah has showered His Grace and inexhaustible Divine Knowledge on a Moo-min Sheik to be made known to His entire Creation. This inexhaustible Divine Knowledge is carefully protected and safeguarded by a Moo-min Sheik.

70. Q: What should be man's inborn nature?

A: Man's true inherent nature is a full awareness of the Divine Truths and adherence to the Divine Path of Allah in his daily actions. Through his eyes of Wisdom he should ascertain the innermost Divine Secrets in the body of Divine Truth and protect them with unflagging vigilance.

71: Q: Who is a dedicated Gnani (Divinely Wise Sage)?

A: A dedicated Gnani is one who has an awareness of the Divine Truth of Allah and with his eyes of Luminous Wisdom finds the innermost Divine Secrets of Allah.

He accepts all living beings as one and identical. He dedicates his entire life towards expounding and propagating the Divine Truth of Allah to all. He ameliorates misery, alleviates human disease and suffering and does everything to exalt and improve the condition of man.

72. Q: What is Siddhi?

A: Siddhi is the state in which a man possesses and uses self-acquired psychic powers for his own satisfaction and

60

advantage. Following is an explanation of how this power comes to a man and what it means.

An impulse to attain power from Maya (Illusion) comes to a man's mind as Maya-Mano-Sakti (Illusory Power of the Mind). The man ponders over this thought for a long time until it is magnified to a point where it occupies a position of importance.

He recites certain mantras suitable to the impulse and there emerges a Maya-Mano-Sakti (Illusory Power of the Mind) with potentiality of 10½ crores of forms. Looking pointedly at the Maya-Mano-Sakti with his original impulse there emerge 1008 forms. Out of these forms he sees beauteous form both inwardly and outwardly. This beauteous form in concrete shape appears in the Maya-Mano-Sakti inside him and as the Maya-Sakti (Illusory Power) outside him. From these two different positions this form speaks to the person concerned, were he to observe silence (Mounam).

The person now directs his gaze intensely at this form, he employs a certain technique and becomes aware of how best he can employ this form to carry out his purposes. Here he finally uses certain magic stratagems to actively vivify this form and reaches the stage when he is in a position to employ this now vivified form for his purposes. This state is called Siddhi. With the help of this Siddhi the person concerned will win over everything material but not his physical self. He can of course deceive the world, but he cannot cheat death.

This person cannot truly know himself by Siddhi nor can he subjugate the evil propensities inherent in Nafs Ammara (evil desires). Further he will suffer from an utterly false notion that he is great. Also, he will be utterly ignorant to questions such as: where he originated? from What he originated? where he is now? where will he go? who is he? and, finally, Who is his Creator?

In order to explain the concept of Siddhi more clearly I will give below the following illustration.

A man gets an impulse to control the sun and use it for his own purposes. With this idea in view, he starts to recite a particular mantra while sitting in an open area and looking pointedly at the sun for 40 consecutive days without batting an eyelid.

On completion of 40 days he is endowed with the entire powers of the Sun manifested in 1008 different forms. His eyes will now blaze in brilliance equal to the rays of the Sun. His gaze will be extremely dazzling and will make others close their eyes. In this state he sees himself enormously important. The possession of this enormous power which he utilises for his own purposes is called Siddhi. Just as the convex lens causes a wad of cotton placed underneath it to catch on fire by focusing on it the rays of the Sun, when man's impulse, mantra and Mano-Sakti (Mind Power) are integrated, it produces Maya-Sakti (Illusory

Power) from which emerges 10½ crores of powerful forms. When this man looks sharply at one of these powerful forms there emerges 1008 vivified forms in concrete shapes. The original impulse of the man, the mantras and Mano-Sakti (Mind Power) are integrated and a Maya-Sakti (Illusory Power) is created which draws out one powerful form and gives it life. This one powerful form made by the man is called Siddhi.

The man concerned uses the powers inherent in this Siddhi and thinks himself great. This assumption is false for this man can never know the Divine Truths of God, and will never know himself nor do any good to Allah's Creation. These are the qualities of true greatness.

I will give you an excellent illustration to bring home the truth that this man referred to above is even lower than a coconut tree.

A man plants a young coconut tree and waters it day in and day out for 6 years. The tree then starts bearing fruits from its crown. The owner receives fruit for years and years, amply repaying him for his services a thousandfold. Further, this coconut tree by its fruits and its constituent parts serve the needs of numerous of Allah's Creations.

On the other hand, the man who had acquired Siddhi by such prohibited techniques does not know himself, denies the Divine Truths of Allah, and is divorced from the Divine Path. In fact, he is a lost soul. His contribution to his fellow men is even less than the contribution of the coconut tree to God's creation.

73. Q: Who is an authentic Gnani (Divinely Wise Sage)?

A: A true Gnani is one who is fully aware of the secrets of his birth. He focuses the searchlight of his Intelligence on the repository of Divine Truths. These Divine Truths are tested and scrutinised very carefully with his eyes of Wisdom 70,000 times over till the immutable imperishable Divine Truths are subjected to the searchlight of his Divine Luminous Wisdom 70,000 times until only the Ultimate Innermost Divine Secrets of Allah remain.

The true Gnani further comes to the astonishing discovery that all these Divine Secrets of Allah are enshrined within him in a minutest particle within a minute particle.

Again with his Luminous Eyes of Wisdom the Gnani encounters 6 different coloured rays. On very close scrutiny he finds that these 6 coloured rays represent 6 aspects of Wisdom. His pointed Luminous Gaze is so intense and effective that all accretions are burnt out completely and the rays become utterly Pure and Divine. At this stage these 6 rays are almost invisible and crystallised into an infinitesimal and invisible particle. Within this particular particle are enshrined the ultimate Divine Secrets of the entire universe, the crores and crores of Allah's Creations, animate and inanimate objects, articulate and inarticulate beings and the 18,000 worlds.

Further the Gnani is in a position to control the 5 elements of his physical body through his Divine Luminous Breath and also purifies them.

He, with this Luminous Breath, transmutes these elements into heat which integrates one element with the other. The Gnani now integrates the Divine Breath with the Ruh (Soul). The Ruh is transmuted into Right Judgment, Right Judgment into Wisdom, Wisdom into Divine Luminosity, Divine Luminosity into Divine Illumination, Divine Illumination into the Divine Truth, and Divine Truth is transformed into a Divinely Brilliant Effulgence and this Effulgence merges with Allah himself.

The entire Universe and Creation is within the Divine Illumination of Allah. Within this Divine Illumination of Allah is the Gnani and within the Gnani is the Divine Luminosity of Allah.

A complete and full realisation of the above Divine Truths, and annihilation of all evil propensities and egoism and scrupulous adherence without deviating an atom from the above Divine Paths of Allah are the dominant ingredients of an authentic Gnani. In Maya (Illusion) there is no Gnani, in Gnani there is no Maya (Illusion).

May Allah Protect and Preserve His Divine Illumination in Insan (Man) and the Divine Luminous Wisdom endowed in Iman (Conviction).

AMEEN-YA-RABBIL-ALAMEEN
(So be it—Creator of Universe)

74. Q: Is it possible to attain Motcham (Salvation) through one's own endeavour, such as by learning or is it necessary to have a Guru to discover the Truth?

A: Son, your question is very subtle and abstruse. It needs very careful investigation. There are crores and crores of subjects on which learning is possible. Having mastered thoroughly one of these subjects a person finds some sort of livelihood. One's life in this world is in itself an important aspect of learning. In one's life one encounters numerous teachers at different points, but the learning so acquired cannot be, by any stretch of the imagination, satisfactory to meet the numerous problems caused by one's existence on this Earth.

First of all, a child when it begins to see acquires its knowledge through its parents. On this very susceptible and plastic mind of the child the parents effectively impart their inherent ideas and behaviour. This is the first quantum of knowledge that the child acquires in this world. The second stage of the child's knowledge begins as the child starts to go to school. Here the teacher of the school takes the child in his charge and imparts worldly knowledge to the child. The quantum of the knowledge imparted to the child increases with the passage of years. In his adolescence the teachers extend the range of knowledge to a wide field.

When the boy grows to a man he becomes academically well qualified to be called a person of great erudition. At this stage he may acquire the coveted title of Bachelor of Arts and Master of Arts. This vast knowledge acquired at a school, college or University, principally through books, fits him only for a particular vocation in life.

Then, there is knowledge acquired by one's experience. Here the person acquires knowledge through observation and whatever he experiences becomes part of his total quantum of knowledge. This knowledge is wide and includes the Sun, Moon, Stars, Light, Darkness and Knowledge of 84,100 thousand varieties of Allah's Creations on earth. This vast knowledge of the Seas, Oceans, Mountains, Species in the Vegetable Kingdom, etc., is infinite. This knowledge cannot be acquired even in a number of births. It is, therefore, evident that the knowledge one acquires from parents, books and from self study cannot, by any stretch of the imagination, be deemed even to a small extent sufficient to attain Motcham (Salvation).

At this point he encounters a Gnana Guru (Gnostic Guru). This Gnana Guru, through a proper initiation of this person actively kindles the Divine Spark in him. The Divine Spark now envelops this person. Under the Divine Luminous Gaze of the Gnana Guru all the accretions and dross in the repository of his knowledge are burnt out and only useful knowledge and the imperishable Divine Truths find permanent lodging in the heart of this person.

The Gnana Guru now actively imparts Divine Knowledge which is enthusiastically and eagerly grasped and assimilated by the person concerned. The person before the advent of the Gnana Guru saw a Guru (teacher) at every stage of his life.

This led him nowhere and he was very far away from Motcham (Salvation).

When this person finally met the Gnana Guru who not only kindled the Divine Spark in the repository of knowledge found within him, but also actively imparted further Divine Knowledge which Divinely Radiated in his Heart.

Through constant and continuous awakening of the Divine Truths enshrined in the Heart of the person concerned, the Gnana Guru enabled the person to come closer to Divinity and finally he achieved the glorious consummation of attaining Motcham (Salvation). This knowledge was present within him and not learned through contact with the outside world.

SECTION II

ILLUSTRATIONS

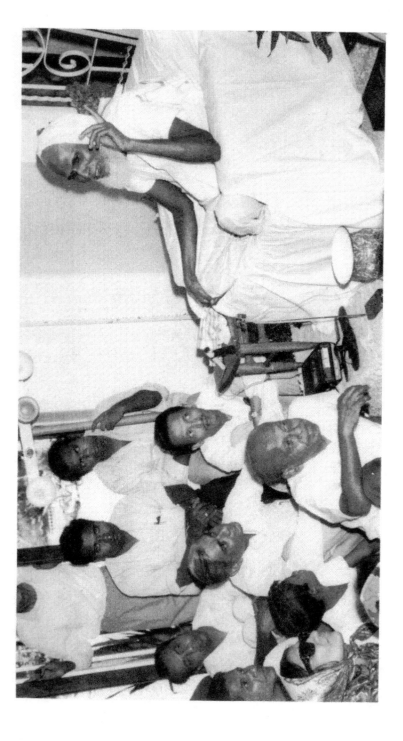

At 7:00 P.M. on 3/17/70

1. Book Learning

His Holiness Guru Bawa tells his disciples:

The more one reads books, the more one's intelligence gets warped. But if one has developed Divine Luminous Wisdom (Perr-Arivu) the Effulgence of God will appear within him.

Explanation: By reading books on theology and philosophy one cannot realise God within oneself, as most of these books are contradictory and confusing to the mind. One should develop the firm conviction that God is One, no matter what names may be given to Him in various languages and in various religions, and also, that all human beings are the children of God and are sisters and brothers of one family. With this Conviction one should develop one's Wisdom (Arivu) to a state of perfection and live according to the dictates of Divine Luminous Wisdom (Perr-Arivu). If one does this, he will then be able to see the Effulgence (Jothi) of the Ultimate One within his Heart (Qalb).

2. The Physical Body

His Holiness Guru Bawa says:

Wisdom (Arivu) tells the Soul (Ruh or Atma), "Look at how the physical body lays like a log, after you, the Soul, has departed. Look at this donkey, i.e., the physical body, which when it was alive leapt and gamboled. Now it lays like a block of wood."

Explanation: When the Soul (Ruh or Atma) is in a state of torpor caused by the hypnotic fascination of Illusion (Maya), Wisdom (Arivu) explains to the Soul, "O Soul, you are living in the house, i.e., the physical body. Along with you several others, namely, the five elements, dwell in this house. The five senses of sight, hearing, smell, taste and feeling are aroused and operate in this house when something comes into contact with the body. The darkness of Illusion (Maya), which attracts the senses, also dwells within this house. So do the seductive forms and the hypnotic projections of Illusion (Maya). Also found within this house is Ignorance (Agnana) of the Truth or Reality which is allied to the above forms and projections of Illusion (Maya). Science (Vingnana), which results from craving and which has developed into Ignorance (Agnana), is also in that house. A degraded state of Wisdom (Ariveenam), which considers destruction to be its prerogative, is another resident of the house. Another one found there is the hypnotic attraction of sexual joy which causes the degradation of Wisdom as its profit-making venture. All these claim ownership of this house. Can you see how they leap, dance, shout and wail, O Soul?"

3. The Intellect

His Holiness Guru Bawa says:

When the Intellect functions erratically, destruction follows.

Explanation: Man, the rarest and noblest of God's Creations, should hold on steadily to the Truth or Reality pointed out by Wisdom (Arivu). If he loses the Truth and enters the state of degradation of Wisdom (Ariveenam), his Intellect will function erratically. As a result, he will

65

harm the Created Beings of God. This, in turn, will result in his meeting with harm. This harm or fate is the result of God's Justice. Children, you should understand this well!

4. The Spiritual Master (Guru Shaik) says:

Son. Here is a word of advice for you. Only one who is free from these 'six' is the real wife. In this world only 'one' is the true friend.

Explanation: These 'six' are the six evil qualitites of Craving, Hatred, Miserliness, Lust, Arrogance and Envy. A human being should get rid of these evil qualities and develop God's characteristics of Love and Compassion. Love filled with Compassion can be considered to be the real wife of Wisdom (Arivu) in Man.

God, who pervades the entire Universe, is the only true friend of the Wisdom (Arivu) of Man.

5. His Holiness Guru Bawa says:

Even if one lives in a room carved within granite, he cannot escape death. Neither can he rid himself of his Debt of Birth (Piravi Kadan).

Explanation: You were created out of Earth. The Earth contains four hundred billion hypnotic projections. You should first repay this debt to the Earth. You should then free yourself from the divisive forces of 'I, mine' and 'you, yours'. You should completely eradicate your egoism. You should realise who your Creator is. You should merge with your Creator. Only then, can you escape death. Otherwise, you are sure to meet with death and you will not be able to repay your debt of birth.

6. The Guru (Spiritual Master) gives the disciple a Divine Message:

Child, listen to an illustration!

There is no flaw in God's Creation. Devotees, Friends, Those who have faith in God; you must all reflect on the following and understand it well. God, the Primal One, is Effulgence (Jothi). The Soul (Atma) is the form of that Effulgence. It is the flawless pure Light that emanated from God. It is the reflection of God. That reflection is Man. God's form is the Resplendence of Divine Luminous Wisdom (Perr-Arivu). It, too, has no flaw. It, too, is free from sin or guilt. It has no physical or astral form. It is merged with the Effulgence of the Primal One. If that Effulgence is seen shining brightly, the reflection will also be bright. If that Effulgence does not shine, the reflection will not shine. Everything will end. Man should rid himself of the degraded state of Wisdom (Ariveenam) for in that state he blames God for his misfortunes and illness. He should reflect and find out what the Truth is.

Here is a word of explanation to our friends. In our ignorance we blame God. One person is lame. Another is unable to use his hands. Another is dumb. Another is blind. Another is deaf. People meet with death in various ways. All over there is poverty, disease and hunger. There are one hundred and fifty million types of symptoms of diseases. In the state of our unintelligence we blame God for all of this. In this era of science we should reflect a little on our attitude.

I was speaking about the Soul (Ruh or Atma) earlier. There is nothing wrong with the Soul. It was in existence before the Creation of the World. It is the Effulgence of the Reflection of the Primal Effulgence. That Primal

Effulgence (God) gives everyone whatever he or she desires for the self. Then, He witnesses how this man uses the ability granted to him. Remember, the Soul is spotlessly pure. God keeps that spotlessly pure Soul as an atom within an atom within His Created Being.

Listen to the following illustration. You know, in this era of science, how the nature of a thing is artificially changed. Let us take the case of the grafted mango tree and the natural mango tree. A farmer plants a mango seed. It may be the seed of a sweet or sour mango. It germinates and grows. Within one year, the farmer cuts off the top part of the plant and he grafts onto the stump the shoot of an old mango tree which he has selected. He applies fertilizer and irrigates the plant. The plant grows. The farmer removes all the shoots that appear on the stump of the plant and allows only the grafted shoot to grow. The grafted shoot sends out branches. When this grafted tree grows into a large tree, it brings forth flowers at the same time as the mother tree from which the graft was taken. The fruit of the grafted tree have the same characteristics as those of the mother tree. In this modern age of science you will find that the nature of various trees are changed by grafting. Within two years the grafted tree bears fruit which have the characteristics of the mother tree from which the shoot was taken, not the characteristics and nature of the fruit of the stump of the tree on which the graft was artificially implanted.

Let us apply this illustration to life created by God. The Soul (Ruh), created originally by God, is of spotless pure Radiance. It has no veils covering and hiding it. It has no darkness. It has no defect. One Ray of Light of God divided into six sparks. Five of these became the five senses. the other one, the Spotless Pure Radiance, remained as the Soul, which remains as Grace within the Grace of God.

That Grace shines in the infant. If allowed to grow in its own way, the infant will grow up as a man shining with Grace. But within one year of its life, the infant's natural growth is changed by its environment. An artificial life is grafted on it by its parents. One hundred and fifty million thoughts and desires of the parents influence the mind of the infant. The parents cut off the spotless purity of the infant's Soul and graft on it the shoot of Illusion (Maya). The infant is made to develop ties of blood and earth. The various aspects of Illusion (Maya) listed as follows, are grafted on the life of the child by the parents: love of gold and of property, blood ties, friendship, birth, death, disease, joy, sorrow, disgust, fatigue, the diverse forces of 'mine' and 'yours' (my religion and your religion, my daughter and your daughter, my god and your god), creed and race, education, titles, status, jobs and billions of such desires and prejudices. These qualities developed as a result of succumbing to the hypnotic attractions of Illusion (Maya) and resulted in the degradation of Divine Wisdom (Ariveenam). Just as the farmer removes the natural shoots growing from the stem of the original mango plant and allows only the shoots growing from the grafted portion to grow, the parents remove the natural tendencies from the growing child and impose on it the artificial life of Illusion (Maya) with all its inhibitions, prejudices and wrong desires. They allow only these divisive tendencies of Illusion (Maya) to grow in the child. It is as a result of the implantation of these artificial tendencies of Illusion (Maya), referred to above, by the parents in the child, that the child falls a victim to hunger, disease, senility, and death. The child develops the prejudices and characteristics of its parents in this artificial life of Illusion (Maya) imposed on it by the parents.

But the natural tendencies and characteristics remain in the roots and the stem of the original mango tree on which a shoot from another mango tree was grafted. If the farmer has allowed the natural shoots coming out of the stem below the graft to grow, the fruit from those branches would bear the natural characteristics of the original plant. Because he did not do so and only allowed the shoots from the grafted part to grow, the fruit bear the artificial characteristics foreign to the natural characteristics of the original mango tree growing from the earth. In the same manner when the parents impose their desires and prejudices on the child, it develops this artificial life under the influence of Illusion (Maya). If the infant had been allowed to grow according to its original nature in a natural environment, the Truth in him would have grown naturally and he would become indestructible.

There is the natural and the artificial aspects in our lives. We have witnessed the effects of these two aspects of life. Therefore, instead of blaming God for our misfortunes and accusing God that He has no eyes and that He is wrong, it is better for us to realise and regret that though we are born as human beings our Gnostic Eye has become blind. Please reflect on this and develop your real Wisdom (Arivu). When the Wisdom (Arivu) is fully developed it will become Resplendence (Perr-Arivu). Then we will come to know the real nature of our birth. Then we will know who is at fault — we or God!

Because the natural shoots of the mango tree were removed and its real nature was suppressed, the artificial graft grows fast and bears fruit. In the same manner, because the parents suppress the natural growth of the infant, the grafted life of Illusion (Maya) grows fast and bears fruit prematurely. As a result, the child becomes liable to several births. If Nature had developed in the child, Nature will appear in it. That 'Nature' is Effulgence. It will have no births. It originated from God. It will disappear in God. This is His Truth. Children, understand this well!

7.   At 8:45 P.M. on 3/17/70

Child! Please listen to an illustration.

A person who was tired and thirsty went to a pond to drink water. The water level was very low in the pond. He said, "O water, why are you so low in the pond? Will you not come up to the place where I am standing? Do you expect me to come to the place where you are?" Thus he scolded the water. Then he sent down into the pond a vessel, the size of a peanut, and tried to draw water, but he could not draw sufficient water to quench his thirst. He made several such attempts to draw water with such a minute vessel. The result was the same. So, he became angry. He said to the water, "I came to you so many times and still my thirst has not been quenched. Till you come to me, I will not come to you", and he went away in anger.

There are many such beings with human faces. They develop the five senses. Their actions are guided by craving, hatred, miserliness, vanity, lust and envy. They hide behind Ignorance (Agnana) caused by Illusion (Maya). They live in sexual joy. Their life is guided by ties of blood, friendship, race, creed, etc. They get immense joy from their desires arising from their lower mind. They develop their body and strengthen it and proclaim, "Who is equal to me?" They get worldly glory and obtain titles of honour from the world. Later these people search for a Spiritual Master (Guru) and seek his services for their spiritual advancement. They go to him to get rid of the miseries of birth and death.

But when they go to a Guru they do not surrender their 'self' to him in humility. Instead, they tell him about their status and titles of honour and what they have learned about theology and philosophy and try to convert the Guru to their view instead of listening to him with an open heart. They boast to him, "Do you know who I am? Do you know my worth and status?" They get angry with the Guru for not giving them respect for their learning and worldly status. So, like the man who went away in anger from the water in the pond without quenching his thirst, these people get angry with the Guru and go away from him without quenching their spiritual thirst.

Children! It is best to avoid such people. We should not teach Divine Truths to such people who are full of vanity and egoism. If you try to teach such people the Divine Truth, there will be danger to God's Truth and your Divine Wisdom (Pahuth-Arivu).

That man brought only a vessel the size of a peanut to draw water from the pond and quench his thirst. These people bring the vessel of the darkness of Ignorance (Agnana) they obtained by studying theology and philosophy to quench their spiritual thirst and pay back their debt of birth and to obtain freedom for their Soul (Atma). That man could not quench his thirst with the minute vessel he brought. These people can not obtain freedom for their Soul (Atma) with the darkness of Ignorance (Agnana) which they obtained by book-learning, even if they take several births. That man's anger and the anger of these people is of the same category. Beware! Be careful! Avoid such people! They are a danger to us and to the Divine Truth. You should teach Divine Truths with love only to those who have the real Wisdom of Man.

At 9:15 A.M. on 3/18/70

8. His Holiness Guru Bawa said:

There are numberless 'holy men' who wander in the forests. There are an appreciable number of 'holy men' in the world who wander within the villages and towns. There are practically no 'holy men' in the world who wander within their own 'Self', remove the animals within the forests in their 'Self', clean their mind and find out the Truth that shines within.

9. His Holiness Guru Bawa explains the meaning of 'Samathi'.

'Samathi' is 'Sama-Athi'!

Child! The world has been speaking of 'Samathi'. Various meanings have been given to this word.

I will explain to you what 'Samathi' is. The Tamil word 'Samathi' is made up of two words, 'Samam' and 'Athi', The word 'Samam' ordinarily means equality or peace. In this special context it means: adoption of the Divine qualities of Compassion and Love for all beings. 'Athi' means God Who is the embodiment of Compassion and Love for all beings.

A person is said to have reached the state of 'Samathi' when he becomes the embodiment of God's qualities of Compassion and Love for all beings — when he Loves and shows Compassion to all created beings as if

69

they are himself. Sitting naked with legs crossed and wearing symbols of religion is not 'Samathi'. When a person sits naked, he loses his sense of modesty, fear, reserve and culture. Such a person, even if he sits cross-legged, cannot be said to be in a state of 'Samathi'.

There is a custom of burying the corpse of 'holy men' in a cross-legged sitting posture. This is wrongly called 'Samathi'. When he was living, he was unable to bear the weight of the world. When his Soul has fled, his corpse is made to sit cross-legged and his body is made to be rigid. It is put in a grave and covered with a load of earth which he has to bear in addition to the load he earned while living. This is called 'Samathi'. The religious rites are performed and offerings are made. He is asked to rise from the earth in order to grant benefits to one. This is utter foolishness. It is good to know what the real meaning of 'Samathi' is. It is not 'Samathi' to preserve the dead body by dehydrating it using lime and salt to cover it. When a man lives, he needs salt for his sustenance. If he needs salt even after his death, he cannot be considered to have reached a state of 'Samathi'. If salt, which is needed to develop the body during life, is needed to preserve the body by dehydration after death, then it cannot be called 'Samathi'.

At the time of Creation (Athi) when the Effulgence of the Soul (Atma or Ruh) spread its Rays, the flower of its Heart (Qalb) opened. When on earth He developed into a True Human Being (Insan Kamil). In that state his Heart (Qalb) opens within the Divine Luminous Wisdom (Perr-Arivu). Then, in his love for God the flower of God's Grace opens. When Man has realized his true self and the three Spiritual Flowers open and hover over God, God is attracted by the sweet scent of these three flowers and becomes merged in that fragrance. This merging is 'Samathi'. Covering the dead body with salt is not 'Samathi'.

10.   ## At 10:30 A.M. on 3/18/70

Child! Please listen to an illustration.

The cobra asked Garuda, the King of the Eagles, "Garuda, how are you?" The Garuda replied, "You are now in the wrong place. If you were in your proper place, I can inquire after your health. But now you are not in your proper place. Therefore, how can I inquire after your health?"

This is a story in Tamil mythology (Puranas). Lord Vishnu was flying in the sky on the back of Garuda. Lord Vishnu was sitting on the coils of a five-headed cobra which served as a cushion when he was flying on the back of Garuda. The five-headed cobra spread its hood over the head of Lord Vishnu to protect him from the heat of the sun. When Lord Vishnu was flying in the sky on the back of Garuda, the nose of the cobra was near the nose of Garuda. It is when they were in that position that the cobra inquired after the health of Garuda. Garuda replied as stated earlier.

Now, Garuda and the cobra are enemies. The cobra will die if only the shadow of Garuda falls on it. Cobras hide in holes when they see Garuda approaching. If by chance cobras are found outside, Garuda will tear them to pieces with its talons. Thus, the cobra was able to inquire after the health of Garuda from its position on the back of Garuda, as it had obtained the help of Vishnu (Krishna) and Vishnu (Krishna) had obtained the help of the cobra.

In the same manner, when the Resplendence of Truth (Oonmaiyin Jothi) flies riding on the five elements, Earth, Fire, Water, Air and Ether, with the hood of the five-headed cobra of the five senses above it. In fact, both the five elements and the five senses depend on the help of the Resplendence of Truth for their existence. When they are in this reversed state, the five-headed cobra, i.e., the five senses saturated with the dark blue poison of Illusion (Maya), inquires after the health of Garuda, i.e., the physical body of man which is made of earth, in the same way as the cobra inquired after the health of Garuda. It is then that the Radiance of Divine Wisdom (Pahuth-Arivu), which rose from the Unique Effulgence, tells the five senses, "If you talk to me from your proper station I could have given a fitting reply to you for inquiring after my health. But, now you are in a station which is really not yours. Therefore, how can I give you a proper reply?" It is the Resplendent Wisdom of the Soul (Atma-Oli-Arivu) which replied to the five senses.

A man should be in the proper station when he advises others about something. Otherwise his advice will not bear result. A man should try not to explain the nature of Reality and its Effulgence when he has not overcome the five senses. When he is living under the influence of the five senses and receives their help, a man, if he starts preaching about Reality, will receive grace and sorrow. We must understand this well. When we are living within the world of the senses, we cannot preach about Reality which is beyond the world of senses. Only when one has conquered the senses will he be able to know Reality. Only then can he preach about Reality. It will be like the five-headed cobra inquiring after the health of Garuda, if a man, while living under the influence of the five senses and obtain their help, tries to preach to others about Reality and its nature. It will only be a mockery.

11.   **At 6:40 P.M. on 3/18/70**

His Holiness Guru Bawa explains about 'Karu' (Seed) and 'Uru' (Form).

'Karu' in Tamil in this context means the seed which is of the size of an atom of an atom. 'Uru' means 'Mantra' (Vibrant Words of Power) which have been activated by incantation.

The Mantra that was incanted to turn the seed (Karu) into form (Uru) is called the Five Sacred Letters (Aintheluththu). In Arabic the five letters are 'Aliph', 'Lam', 'Meem', 'Hey' and 'Thal'. They are called 'Panchadcharam' (Five Sacred Letters). They indicate the five elements, Earth, Fire, Water, Air and Ether. The physical body of man is made of these five elements.

The incantation of the five letters, the 'Panchadchara mantra' is only one-fourth of the purpose of life, i.e., the development of the physical body is only one-fourth the purpose of life. Three-fourths of the purpose of life is the use of 'Madthi' (Fourth State of Conscience or Judgement); to find out the nature and real purpose of every part of the body for spiritual progress; to prepare an estimate of the profit and loss account of life; and to make a real evaluation of life and the body. Then, he should use Wisdom (Arivu) to escape from the clutches of the physical body and the world of senses which are merged in the physical body and the torpor caused by the hypnotic fascination of Illusion (Maya). This ability is the most important ability a man can have. Then, he should realize the Vast Space within himself. In that state he should realize Divine Wisdom (Pahuth-Arivu), develop it and realize the Light of Wisdom, i.e., Divine

Luminous Wisdom (Perr-Arivu). Then he should realize God, who is the Plenitude of the Light of Divine Luminous Wisdom, and merge in Him. We came out of Him in the beginningless beginning. We should merge in Him. This is the purpose of life on earth. The various stages in this progress are Seed, Form, Mantra, Judgement, Wisdom (Arivu), and Divine Wisdom (Pahuth-Arivu). In the course of these six stages in spiritual development, we must realise who we are. As a result of our Self Realization the Divine Luminous Wisdom (Perr-Arivu) resonates within us.

12.   At 7:15 P.M. on 3/18/70

Child! Please listen to an illustration.

Does the fowl know what a diamond is? No. It can only recognize refuse. Its joy in life is derived from the refuse. The insects and worms in the refuse dump are its food. If it sees a diamond, it will throw it away with its claws and search only for worms.

There are people like the fowl who enjoy only the dirt of the lower self. They are selfish people who are the embodiment of the darkness of Illusion (Maya). They are guided only by their five senses. They are motivated by craving and anger. They are always longing for gold, sex and property. Such people, who are like the fowl, will not listen if the Guru gives discourses on Divine Qualities that men should develop. A really good man should believe in the oneness of mankind, that there is only One God and that all human beings are equal to himself. He should develop the qualities of Peace, Patience, Compassion, Mercy, Liberality and other Divine Qualitites. The Guru will teach them these qualities. The Guru will further give them discourses on the nature of Reality, the fullness of God's Grace, the Resonance of Wisdom (Arivu) of Man when it is fully developed, etc.

But those who live in dirt, like the fowl, will not accept the Guru's teachings. Like the fowl that throws away the diamond and searches only for insects and worms, these people will discard the Divine Teachings of the Guru. They will only dig up the refuse heap of sinful acts in the material world and feed on the worms of the hypnotic torpor caused by the attractions of Illusion (Maya). They will even try to teach the Guru that only they know what is true. If the Guru does not accept what they tell, they will try to destroy the Guru and the Truth preached by him. The Spiritual Master (Gnana Guru) tells his disciples that one should not waste his time preaching the Truth to people who have been thriving on the dirt of Illusion (Maya). Instead, one should teach the Truth to those who have pure Wisdom (Arivu).

13.   At 7:35 P.M. on 3/18/70

Child! Please listen to an illustration.

A person finds that his body is covered with dirt. To remove it he jumps into a pond of water. If he just soaks his body in the pond and bathes or swims in it, will he be able to remove the dirt from his body? No. When he is in the pond of water, he must rub his wet body well and scrub the body. Only then, will he be able to remove the dirt from his body. The dirt will mix with the water of the pond. But does the water continue to hold the dirt in it? No. the dirt will settle out and join the dirt at the bottom of the pond. The water will become clear.

The dirt of Ignorance (Agnana), the dirt of dark Illusion (Maya) which causes hypnotic torpor in the spiritual state of man, enters the mind of a man endowed with Divine Wisdom (Pahuth-Arivu) through the five senses. As a result of the hypnotic torpor caused by this darkness of Illusion (Maya), he fails to discriminate between the good and the evil, and succumbs to the divisive forces of 'yours and mine' and 'you and I'. In this state of degradation one hundred and fifty million types of dirt of the darkness of Illusion (Maya) sticks to him.

When he is in that state, he searches for an authentic Spiritual Master (Meignana Guru), finds him, falls at his feet and requests him to remove the dirt of the darkness of Illusion (Maya) from him. In the same way as the person who got into the pond of water, soaked his body in the water, rubbed the body thoroughly, washed it well and thus removed the dirt from his body; this man, too, should use the 'water' of the resonant discourses of the Guru on the Truth and Grace of God and rub his five senses and his inner self thoroughly with it and remove the dirt from them. If he does so, the dirt of Illusion (Maya) which stuck to his self will be fully removed.

Just as the man, who gets into the pond of water and stays there without rubbing his body, will not be able to remove the dirt from his body, so the man who goes to the Guru will not be able to remove the dirt of Illusion (Maya) from himself unless he makes an effort to use the discourses of the Guru to clean his five senses and his inner self. He should put the teachings of the Guru into practice.

He should submit himself fully to the Truth within the Guru and rub off the dirt of Illusion (Maya) from his self.

Just as the water took the dirt from the man's body and without retaining it deposited it with the dirt in the bottom and edge of the pond, the Guru will remove the dirt which stuck to this man due to Ignorance (Agnana), the effect of Illusion (Maya) and the five senses. The Guru will throw it back to Illusion (Maya), the source of the dirt. The Guru will not keep the dirt arising from Illusion (Maya) within himself. He will not allow it to go back to his disciple. He will throw the dirt back to the source from which it came. Only after this happens, the path that will lead to Realization and Liberation will appear before the Divine Wisdom (Pahuth-Arivu) of the disciple. Thus, the Guru (Shaik) explained to his disciple how the disciple should make use of the Guru's discourses.

14.   At 8:00 P.M. on 3/18/70

Child, please listen to an illustration.

Special books meant for children whose ages range from one to seven years are being published in English. The words, sentences and stories with pictures are presented in such a way as to suit their various states of Intelligence and Wisdom. To arouse interest in the children's minds pictures of human beings, cats, rats, bears, rabbits, horses, asses, dogs, foxes, squirrels, cattle, deer, leopards, tigers, monkeys, crows, peacocks, ducks, bats, crocodiles, fish, beetles, bees, flies, mosquitoes, ants, insects found on grass, insects found on trees, snakes, carrots, beets, cabbage, leeks, brinjals, plantains, snake-gourds, the sea, ships, etc., are printed in the books in attractive colours. The stories, songs and morals are presented to suit the various states of their intelligence. The parents buy these children's books. The children read the books and the parents explain the stories to the children, pointing out the merits (right) and sins (wrong) of the stories. Thus, the parents increase the intelligence and knowledge of these young children and help them to understand the morals. Son, you have seen such books!

Among old and learned human beings there are many who have taken several births and who are still in the state of knowledge of small children as far as their spiritual progress is concerned. They also paint pictures similar to the pictures printed in the books meant for children. According to their intellect, they draw the pictures of various types of created beings with human faces and give them various names. They write stories, treatises, poems, songs, etc., in praise of the pictorial forms created by them. They devise dances in adoration of these pictures or forms. They sing songs of piety before these forms or pictures to the accompaniment of instrumental music such as Veena, Cymbals and Drums. They dance before these forms to the accompaniment of music. From generation to generation they show these pictures and forms to these grown-up people who are still in a state of childhood as far as spiritual progress is concerned and explain the implications of the pictures. These grown-up men in this state of spiritual childhood get into a state of ecstacy in their devotion to these pictures and forms. They worship these forms, do penance and ask them to grant benefits.

They explain to these adults in the state of spiritual childhood, "These teachings, mythologies and epics have been in existence for several aeons. They have been handed over from generation to generation. Therefore, they are natural. They are true. They alone are suitable to us." They state further, "These have been in existence from the ancient times. Do not forget them! Do not give them up! Stick to them!" Thus, they show the faces in these pictures and forms to these 'grown-up children' who have been taking births from aeon to aeon, teach them the meaning of the poems, and make them act their part on the stage of life in this world. In the same way as parents show the pictures in the children's books to the real children who are actually in a state of purity and teach them morals, these people show these pictures and forms to these adult 'children' who have taken several births to enable them to pay their debt of birth and obtain Liberation of the Soul (Atma).

Know well that there are two types of children in the world. There are the adult 'children' who have taken birth after birth. The other type of 'children' are those who have taken birth as Man, the rarest and noblest of God's creations, who will be able to see these pictures and the stories and sentences in the book, reflect on them and understand the Truth. You should know the nature and ability of these children. You should teach only the latter type of children who are able to grasp the Spiritual Truth fast, the path that will help them to pay back the debt of birth and obtain Liberation. If you teach these children, it will give Spiritual Greatness to them, make them know their birth-right as Man, see the beauties of God's qualities and realise the Glory of their Creator. So said the Spiritual Master (Gnana Guru) to his disciple.

The Guru states further to the disciple: But this teaching will not suit the adult 'children' who have taken several births. They will be happy only with the pictures, stories, songs, dances and dramas referred to earlier.

It is good for us to know the two types of children. Do not preach to the 'children' who have taken several births, who are happy only with pictures, forms and songs. If you do so, it will bring danger to you, to Truth and to God. If you preach to those rare children who are able to quickly grasp the Truth, they will be able to understand the nature of Divine Wisdom (Pahuth-Arivu) and Grace.

15.   At 9:15 A.M. on 3/19/70

Child! Please listen to an illustration.

Priests of the four religions in the world use various methods as indicated in their religions to call their followers at the pre-dawn period to come to the temple, church or mosque to offer prayers to God and worship Him. In certain religions they ring the large bell in the temple or church tower to call the devotees to the temple or church. In the mosques the Mouzins or Lebbes (Muslim Priests) shout in a loud voice calling the devotees to come to the mosque to offer prayers to God. These are the customary methods followed in this world. The people of the world give honour and respect to those who do this job.

Among these people who do service to God some, on occasion, oversleep and fail to do their duty to God on time. Sometimes if they have private domestic work, they get others to do this work.

But, child! In addition to these people, birds with two legs, which do not have Divine Wisdom (Pahuth-Arivu), awake these people and others and call the human beings at the pre-dawn period to prayer saying, "Come to offer prayers to God. Pray to God. It is dawn. With all your heart love God who gives you food. Come quickly." The mind of these birds is always attuned towards God; whether they are awake or asleep; whether it is day or night. When they are fatigued or in a bereaved condition or asleep, unlike human beings, they do not send others to do their duty. Because of their instinct they have an innate love for God. So, they do their duty to God by awakening all at dawn.

Birds like the peacock, cocks, etc., awaken people at 3 A.M. and tell them by shouting in a loud voice in their bird-language, "It is dawn. Come to offer prayers to God. Pray to God. Do your duty." The noise made by the birds enters the ears and minds of human beings and reminds them that it is already dawn. These birds do not at night fall into such a state of deep sleep as to forget their environment and their senses. When they are sleeping their sense of perception and awareness is always active. With their sensitive ears they listen to the Voice of God, the prayers of the angels and the songs of the birds in Heaven. When they hear these sounds, they invite the human beings to wake up and say their prayers as it is already dawn. Birds with such keen instinct exist in nature.

These birds are devoid of Divine Wisdom (Pahuth-Arivu). God has created them with such keen instinct and power of hearing for the purpose of awakening human beings in time so that they may offer their prayers in case they forget to rise early and obey His command.

If thieves or animals stealthily climb up the trees to catch these birds when they sleep at night, they fly away and save their lives. They are able to do so because, even when they sleep, their sense of awareness is always active. It helps them, not only to save their lives at night, but also to listen to the Voice of God and the prayers of angels, and to awaken Mankind during the pre-dawn period to offer prayers to God. Though these birds do not have the faculty of Divine Wisdom (Pahuth-Arivu) they do not fail in this duty of theirs to God to awaken Mankind to pray to God. We should reflect and find out who does their duty to God to His satisfaction, the Mouzins, Lebbes (Muslim Priests), priests of other religions who sometimes fail to do their duty or send others to do their duty to call others to prayer, or these birds which never fail to awaken mankind at the proper time by using their bird language.

The former, i.e., the priests, will not do their duty if they are not paid. The latter do their duty to God without any salary and without any selfishness. We are also God's creation. The birds are also God's creation. But we should reflect and find out who is doing the duty to God better.

Just as the birds, even in their sleep, do not lose their sense of awareness which, in addition to saving their lives, permits them to listen to God's Voice and the Prayers of the Heavenly Beings; man should also use his sense of perception, awareness, Divine Wisdom (Pahuth-Arivu), Iman (Faith, Certitude and Conviction) and the clarity of mind arising from these states of consciousness to hear God's Voice and the prayers without any desire of benefit for himself. He should know what is good and what is evil, and avoid the evil. He should adopt the characteristics of God and do his duty to God. Only such a service will enable man to attain the Divine Heritage that is his birthright. Whether he is in a state of joy or sorrow, or whether he is feeling fit or tired, he should always listen to the Voice of God and the Prayers of the Heavenly Beings and do his duty. Only such a person can really be called a Man.

I do not wish to elaborate on this. If one looks with Divine Luminous Wisdom (Perr-Arivu) that arises from the clarity of Wisdom obtained as a result of Faith, Certitude and Conviction (Iman), one will be able to attain this state of perception, awareness and Wisdom (Arivu) with which he was doing his duty to God. There is no need to speak again and again on this. So said the Spiritual Master (Gnana Guru) to this disciple.

16.   ## At 10:10 A.M. on 3/19/70

Child! Please listen to an illustration.

It is to preserve our modesty that we wear clothes. The cloth is woven with a very large number of threads of cotton. It is also worn to preserve one aspect of man's honour in society.

A man's life is subject to hunger, disease, aging, and death. It is also subject to contagious diseases spread by the four hundred billion hypnotic projections of Illusion (Maya). To remove these afflictions and preserve the honour of his existence and to avoid future births, man must use the threads of the teachings of the Guru and weave them into a cloth in the loom of Divine Wisdom (Pahuth-Arivu) and with the resulting cloth of Divine Luminous Wisdom (Perr-Arivu).

17.   ## At 6:40 P.M. on 3/20/70

Child! Please listen to an illustration.

'Buryani' is a preparation made of rice, meat and bones. If you place 'Buryani' before a dog, which part will it eat? It will eat only the bones. The dog enjoys eating the bones. It is its nature.

The body of man is made of five elements. It develops on the essences of the earth, the fire, the water, the air and the ether. If the Truth of God (Allah) is placed before it, it will discard the Truth of God (Allah). Like the dog which prefers the bones, it prefers the joys of the taste produced in the tongue, the visions seen by eyes, and other attractions of the material world.

Whatever effort is made to teach it the knowledge of the Truth of Wisdom (Gnana or Arivu), it will assimilate only the essence of the five elements. The more a dog bites the bone, the more blood will ooze from the gums of its teeth. The dog considers its own blood which oozes into its mouth, down its teeth, to be the essence coming out of the bone. So, it goes on biting the bone more and more.

In the same way, the earth, i.e., the body, enjoys biting what arises from earth, i.e., desire, passion and physical vision. Just as the avaricious dog enjoys biting the bone which is in the flesh, the body enjoys the physical pleasures of sex and the pleasures of the world. The earth enjoys eating things which arise from it. Children! You should understand the implication of this discourse.

18. Child! Please listen to an illustration.

Once upon a time there lived a King. He was interested in music, dancing and higher education. He told his minister, "I wish to hear good music, and see dances and dramas. How can we set about it?" The minister replied, "May it please your Majesty! All the people in our country are very good musicians, dancers and actors. If we invite some people, others will protest. By a beat of a drum let us make known that a competition will be held on a particular day six months from now. All experts in music, dance and drama can compete. The winners will be given prizes by the King." The King ordered the minister to take action accordingly. The minister did so. He also erected a stage in an open space of one thousand acres.

When the people heard about the competition, they desired to teach music and dancing to everyone, even to children six months old, hoping to obtain the prizes. The entire population stopped doing any other work. They were busy continuously training themselves in music and dancing. Since they did not work, they became afflicted with disease and poverty. They lost the radiance of beauty that shone in their faces when they were wealthy and ate well. Still their desire to obtain the prize from the King did not diminish. Their thirst for titles was not quenched.

On the day fixed for the competition the open space of one thousand acres was filled with musicians and dancers. There was a high stage from which the King would see all the dances and dramas and listen to music. There was a lower stage in front of the stage built for the King. Twenty-five people could stand on it. All the people who had gathered in that open space were actors, musicians and dancers. Even children, three years old, and old people on the verge of death were competing. There was no one there to witness the dances or enjoy the music, except the King and the minister.

The King requested the minister to blow the conch and announce that the competitors should stand on one side. The audience should stand on the other side. The minister did so. All who were present were competitors. None had come to see the dances. The King had a Guru who was seated beside him. The King asked the Guru, "Since all are dancers and musicians, to whom can I give the prizes?" The Guru replied, "Let all the actors act and sing. You can give the prizes to the best actors and singers." So the King requested them to act on the stages provided for them.

All danced and sang. Nothing could be understood. The noise was louder than the noise made by the braying of seventy thousand asses brought together in one place. It was not possible to decide who was singing. The King's ears could not distinguish the voices. Some voices were like a large number of foxes that were howling.

The minister asked the King, "To whom are we to give prizes?" The King replied, "I like music and dancing. But only today I came to know that 'this' is music and dancing!" The Guru asked him how he came to this conclusion. The King replied, "It was like the howling of forty thousand foxes and the braying of seventy thousand asses in the same place at the same time. My eardrums are about to burst as a result of this cacophony. I did not hear any music." The Guru requested him to give away the prizes. The King said, "This terrible noise has affected my ears, my heart and my Divine Wisdom (Pahuth-Arivu). I do not see any good result from this competition. To whom am I to give the prizes?"

The Guru told the King, "You are fond of music and dancing. Know well from today that this will cause suffering and pain to your Divine Wisdom (Pahuth-Arivu) in this birth. Even if you know it, the world will not leave you alone. The number of competitors is such that your kingdom itself is not enough to divide among them." The King inquired from the Guru, "Then what shall I do?" The Guru asked him, "You saw the dances and listened to the music. Whose performance was the best?" The King replied, "I do not know." The Guru said, "Let the competitors give their opinion as you do not know. After they give their opinion as to whose performance was best, God will give them the prize they deserve." "How can I do this?" asked the King. The Guru told the King, "Tell the people 'You were the competitors. You were the audience. Let the best actors and performers come forward to get the prizes' ". The King announced this to the people accordingly.

Then all the people rushed forward saying, "I am the best actor." They pushed each other and rushed forward. This resulted in fights. They quarrelled among themselves to determine who was the best actor. In the fights that ensued many lost their legs, many their arms. A large number were killed in the fights. The arena for music and dancing had become a battlefield. The relatives took away the corpses. Finally, none remained in the arena.

The King told the Guru, "There is none in the arena. To whom am I to give the prizes?" The Guru replied, "The music and dancing you were fond of has ended in death and destruction. The arena for music and dancing has become a battlefield. Know this well. Eagles have come in large numbers to the battlefield to eat the corpses of the people who had lost their Wisdom. The eagles have become the audience. You can only offer the corpses as prizes to the eagles. You cannot give them anything else. The 'corpses' who came to sing and dance and the eagles who came to appreciate have filled the stage you erected. Men of Divine Wisdom, the rarest and noblest of beings, did not come here to get your prize. Therefore, you should realise that what gives you joy actually causes pain and destruction. Therefore, you should discard things which give joy to the senses."

Comment: The above King was fond of fine arts and dancing. Similarly, among those who are anxious to see God, there are devotees, Siththars (those who have gained control over the forces of nature), Muktars (those who have realised God), priests of various religions, priests who extol caste and race, people devoted to service wearing symbols, and artists who decorate the four hundred billion hypnotic projections of Illusion (Maya). On the stage of the world there are 'learned' people who preach the word of God, extol His Glory, sing songs from mythological epics, Vedanta (Philosophy) and Siththantha (Religion), perform ceremonial rites and make offerings to God to merge with God. These are people who are similar to the actors and musicians who competed before the King. These people have studied theology and hymns and obtained titles. They sing these devotional songs with fervour.

Just as those people mentioned earlier went before the King to show their skill in music and dancing to obtain prizes, these people with titles in theology and Yoga, given by the world, who obtained fame as priests of the world, went before God Almighty, the Primal Effulgence, to act their part on the stage of Divine Wisdom (Pahuth-Arivu) and obtain their prizes from Him. These people obtained titles on the philosophy of religions just as they obtained titles in the world. They lived in the world of senses. They lived within the folds of religious fanaticism according to the open tenets of their individual religions. They obtained titles in the world for their excellence in a state of spiritual degradation (Ariveenam) and the blemish of foolishness. They took the form of the five elements. They wore robes to suit their mental visions. They obtained glory for showing miracles to the physical eyes. They lived as priests of the world, not as priests of God. It is with these attributes that they went before God Almighty to act their part and show their skill on God's stage of Divine Wisdom (Pahuth-Arivu) and Grace.

The King was fond of music and dancing. So, he got the experts in music and dancing to perform before him on the stage. God Almighty also wants to see human beings acting the part He likes. God likes persons who have discarded desire for land, gold and sex, who have forgotten their self, who have developed the Divine qualities of Love for all beings, Compassion, Patience, Forbearance and Tranquility, and who have taken the Truth into their Heart with their Divine Wisdom (Pahuth-Arivu). God wants to see such people act their part before Him on the stage of Wisdom (Arivu) and Grace.

So, God created the stage of the world with equal rights for all and promised to give His Kingdom to the best actor. Just as all the subjects in the kingdom appeared on the stage before the King to exhibit their skill in music and dancing and obtain the prizes from him, all human beings in the world; Yogis, Sannyasis (people who have renounced the world and who have locks of hair tied up on their head), devotees, Siththars, Scholars, Muktars, Gnanis (Gnostics), those who lead household life, and people in the eighteen thousand worlds full of the four hundred billion hypnotic projections of Illusion (Maya) — all of these appeared, in attire and symbols appropriate to each of them, on the stage of the world created by God to act before Him their part and obtain the Kingdom of God from Him.

God asked them to act their part showing their real character. In that stage of equality everyone acted his own peculiar part. None acted the part of God showing His Divine characteristics. They wore the enticing illusive dresses of the four hundred billion hypnotic projections of Illusion (Maya) and acted their part exhibiting their religion, creed, race, caste, titles of honour, social status, lust, their Yoga, Veda, Vedanta, Siththantha Philosophies and their connected steps of Sariyai, Kiriya, Yogam and Gnanam, which give rise to one hundred and fifty million births. None came there with God's Beauty and God's Characteristics to act His part and obtain His prize.

The stage prepared by the King who wanted to hear the best music and see the best dances turned into a battlefield flowing with blood. In the same manner, the stage of the world erected by God became the battlefield flowing with human blood and the flood of Ariveenam (state of spiritual degradation) leading to Hell. There was none who acted the part of God to obtain the Kingdom of God from God. Just as the King was unable to give the prize for music and dancing to anyone and had to keep it himself, God also took the prize for Himself and remained God. In God's stage of equality, it is very rarely that a man is able to act the part of God assuming God's characteristics and obtain the prize of the Kingdom of Heaven from Him.

Child! If you live within God and God lives within you, the Kingdom of God will be within you. All God's characteristics will be within it. If you understand this and understand the nature of the world and eradicate your Self, you will be called the Perfect Man or God-Man (Insan Kamil or Manu-Eesan). So said the Insan Kamil (Gnana Guru) to his disciple.

19.   **At 8:10 P.M. on 4/1/70**

Dr. Selvaratnam inquired from His Holiness Guru Bawa how a person can renounce the world, merge with the Guru and reach God. His Holiness replied thus:

Child! Please listen to this illustration and reflect on it. There is a type of hare called 'Vari Muyal'. They have both the male and the female genital organs in them. They live together in pairs and bring forth cubs. They have the power to change their sex. One year they live as male and female and bring forth young cubs. The next year the male will become the female and the female will become the male. The live together and bring forth cubs. The next year they will change their sex. Thus they live as males and as females in alternative years. One year the male genital organs are active. The next year these become inactive and the female genital organs become active. Thus they lead a life of balance in nature.

In the same manner, in the cage of the physical body of Man, the rarest and noblest of creations, craving generated by the senses (Pulanin Asai) and the hypnotic attraction of seductive Maya (Mayaiyin Mayakkam) live as male and female. For some time the craving generated by the senses becomes the motive force of the physical body and it acts like a male, whilst the hypnotic attraction of seductive Maya becomes the passive factor and it acts like a female. Then the hypnotic attraction of the seductive Maya becomes the active factor and it acts like a male, whilst craving generated by the senses becomes the passive factor and it acts like the female. In this way the craving generated by the senses and the hypnotic attraction of seductive Maya play alternative roles and guide the physical body through a life of sexual joy like the particular species of hare referred to earlier.

There are both these factors within the physical body of man. In two or three minutes sexual joy becomes predominant like the male and mates with craving. In two or three minutes sexual joy becomes passive like a female. Then craving becomes the active factor like the male. It mates with sexual joy which becomes the passive factor like a female. The hypnotic projections of Illusion (Maya), the five senses and the desires created by them, mate with one another; one factor being predominant at one time and the other factor being predominant at the other time. Then desires engendered by the five senses and the hypnotic attractions of seductive Illusion (Maya) increase the power of the five senses which create the ties of blood, resulting in the creation of four hundred billion hypnotic projections of Illusion (Maya) in the mind.

When the body is undergoing the ever-changing small joys caused by the senses and Illusion (Maya), there takes place a fundamental change. With the body is the natural product, the Bliss par excellence (Perinpam). This is the Bliss of God's (Allah's) Grace, which has been dormant. This, the Bliss par excellence (Perinpam) of God's (Allah's) Grace, arises from Divine Luminous Wisdom (Perr-Ariyu). When Divine Wisdom (Pahuth-Arivu) develops in Man, his body escapes from the clutches of the sensual pleasures. In that state the Divine Wisdom (Pahuth-Arivu) merges with the Bliss par excellence of Divine Luminous Wisdom (Perr-Arivu). This Bliss of Divine Luminous Wisdom (Perr-Arivu) emerges and surveys everything within that Timeless One in a state of Silence, Love, Compassion and Patience. When Divine Wisdom (Pahuth-Arivu) emerges in Man, he is freed from the influence of the sensual pleasures of the body and merges with the Guru, i.e., the Bliss par excellence (Perinpam) of the Grace of God (Allah).

In that state, the Guru becomes the disciple, and the disciple becomes the Guru. In that state the Light of Wisdom (Arivu) and the Light of the Soul (Atma) merge. Wisdom (Arivu) becomes Soul (Atma); Soul (Atma) becomes Wisdom (Arivu). In a second they reverse the position. Again the same change takes place, like the change of sex of the striped hare in alternate years. In an atomic second Wisdom (Arivu) becomes Soul (Atma) and Soul (Atma) becomes Wisdom (Arivu) and vice versa. Then they change in the unatomic state. Then the Soul (Atma) shines as the Embodiment of Wisdom (Arivu). The state of Guru and disciple disappears in the state of Wisdom (Arivu) and Soul (Atma). This state of Wisdom (Arivu) and Soul (Atma) also disappears. Then it becomes the Resplendence of Wisdom (Arivu) within Wisdom (Arivu). Within that Resplendence appears the Fullness of Divine Luminous Wisdom (Noor). Within that appears the Unique Effulgence which is brighter than the brightness of one billion suns. That Unique Effulgence without equal is God.

Just as the male and the female striped hares changed their sexes in alternate years and brought forth young ones and developed their species, the craving generated by the five senses and the hypnotic attraction of seductive Illusion (Maya) hold sway alternatively and make the body undergo sensual pleasures. Thus they developed the hold of the sinful five senses over the mind of man, developed the sway of Illusion (Maya), increased the hypnotic torpor caused by projections of Illusion (Maya) and speeded up the spiritual degradation (Ariveenam). When the Soul (Atma) of the disciple gets out of the clutches of the above and merges with Divine Luminous Wisdom (Perr-Arivu), which is replete with the Fullness of Bliss par excellence of the Grace of God (Allah), the Guru, when the Soul (Atma) merges in Wisdom (Arivu) and Wisdom (Arivu) merges in the Soul (Atma), that state which emerges is the state in which the disciple merges with the Guru. This state leads to the emergence of the state where the Soul (Atma) merges with the Guru and God. In that state the five senses which were dominant become powerless. When the mind becomes powerless and still, Soul (Atma) and Wisdom (Arivu) will merge and shine as Grace and God. That state is the state in which God, the Soul (Atma) of the disciple and the Wisdom (Arivu) of the Guru merge, when these three, the Triple Flame, merge in the place where they divided earlier in the Primal State, where only One exists. The person who has reached this state becomes He. Within Him exists you and I. The Spiritual Master (Authentic Meignana Guru) will shine in this state and merge with you and make you merge with God. This is the meaning of merging with the Infinite. Thus His Holiness Guru Bawa replied to the question raised by Dr. Selvaratnam.

20.   **At 9:00 P.M. on 4/1/70**

Sangeetha Pooshanam Ratnavel addresses His Holiness Guru Bawa and asks, "Your Holiness! Cannot a devotee make use of the scholarship and Wisdom gained by education to overcome the influence of the material world, worship and meditate and reach God without the aid of a Guru? Cannot one overcome Illusion (Maya) without the assistance of a Guru?"

His Holiness replied: Well, what you say is correct up to a point. You can overcome the world. You can make yourself invisible to others and move about in the world. You can fly in the sky. You can get the dwellers of heaven to do your bidding. You can walk over water. You can study and gain knowledge up to a point. You can study Yoga and Divine Wisdom (Gnana). You can do all these things. But it is very difficult to control the mind and meditate. If you want to control the mind you need a Guru. Please listen carefully and understand what I am going to say.

To remove the causes of birth, to get final salvation and reach God, the aid of a Guru is essential. There are certain eventualities which cannot be overcome with the aid of your Wisdom. In those circumstances your Wisdom becomes powerless.

I will give you an illustration: Take the case of the mongoose. It lives in holes and bushes. In some holes snakes also live. The mongoose and snakes are natural enemies. The mongoose can kill only certain types of cobras and snakes. The mongoose cannot kill the types of cobras called 'Athisedan' and 'King Cobra.' If the mongoose attacks them, they will kill the mongoose. The mongoose rolls on certain herbs if it is bitten by snakes in the course of a fight and gets rid of the poison. Then it will again attack and kill snakes and cobras. But it does not have the strength to kill the types of cobras mentioned above. Even if the these cobras hiss, the mongoose will die.

So, when the mongoose sees such powerful types of cobras, it will not attack them. It will go to its chief, the King Mongoose, and carry the latter on its back to the place where such a cobra is. It will be accompanied by the other followers of the King Mongoose. It will show the powerful type of cobra to the King Mongoose. The moment the King Cobra feels the smell of the King Mongoose, it will lie prostrate. It will not show its courage. When the King Mongoose leaps from the back of the mongoose across the body of the King Cobra to the back of the other mongoose on the other side, the King Cobra in the process, will get cut into two or three pieces and die.

The ordinary mongoose can kill only ordinary snakes and cobras, but not the King Cobra, etc., which are very powerful. In the same manner, a person who has learned on his own Yoga and Divine Wisdom (Gnana) and done penance, can control the senses connected with the world of Illusion (Maya) only to a certain degree with his intellect and Wisdom. But he cannot overcome hunger, disease, old age, death, attended evils (Karma), Illusion (Maya), craving, hypnotic torpor caused by the forces of Illusion (Maya), egoism, etc. Unless these are overcome, he cannot achieve Union (Yoga), Divine Wisdom (Gnana) and Salvation. He cannot merge with God. God cannot merge with him. He will not be able to free himself from the cycle of births.

To overcome Illusion (Maya), etc., the aid of the Spiritual Master (Authentic Meignana Guru) is essential, just as the services of the King Mongoose were necessary for the mongoose to get the King Cobra killed. Just as the King Cobra lay down powerless at the sight of the King Mongoose, all the poisonous characteristics in man will become inert and get burned up when confronted by the Resplendent Wisdom (Perr-Arivu) of the Guru. Know this well.

21. Child! Please listen to an illustration.

The lotus plant grows in water. Its leaves float on the surface of the water. The lotus flowers open above the water. Though the lotus leaves float on the surface of the water, water does not stay on them. The lotus cannot exist without water, yet its leaves will not retain water on them. The leaves suck the water through the stalks for their sustenance. However, neither do the stalks keep water within them. the leaves will not keep the water on them. The lotus flowers will not keep the water on them. In the same manner, man lives in the sea of Illusion (Maya), i.e., the physical body full of craving composed of Earth, Fire, Water, Air and Ether. This man of craving, after death will be born again and he will die again and go on and on. This sea of Illusion (Maya), i.e., the body, shows itself in innumerable forms of varying degrees of beauty, conduct and action. This sea of Illusion (Maya) smothers the growth of Divine Wisdom. It makes man boast that he will do the impossible, that he will make ropes out of sand, etc. The physical body is the sea of Illusion (Maya), the seat of sensual pleasures. This sea of Illusion (Maya) is full of water arising from the springs of egoism, attended evils (Karma) and Illusion (Maya). The dirty manure, i.e., the six sinful actions, is also mixed in this sea of Illusory (Mayic) water. In this sea the light of Soul (Atma or Ruh) grows like the lotus. Like the lotus leaves, Divine Wisdom (Pahuth-Arivu) lies spread on the surface of this sea of Illusion (Maya). Just as the lotus leaves reject the water of the pond that may fall on them, Divine Wisdom (Pahuth-Arivu) will, without getting soaked in the sea of the five senses of Illusion (Maya), stand out showing the Truth, rejecting the false and the evanescent which thrive on the power of Illusion (Maya). Like the lotus flower which raises its head out of the pond, opens and shows its beauty, the Flower of the

Resplendence of Divine Luminous Wisdom (Perr-Arivu) comes out of the Truth in the body or the sea of Illusion (Maya) and spreads its Rays. The Resplendence of Divine Luminous Wisdom arising from God's Grace, the Bliss par excellence, spreads its Rays and shows its real nature. If the Soul (Atma) rejects the attractions of the body of Illusion (Maya) and merges with Divine Wisdom (Pahuth-Arivu) and manifests its real form full of Resplendence, God will come to pluck that Lotus Flower of Divine Luminous Wisdom (Perr-Arivu) from within the Heart (Qalb). That flower is His property. It does not belong to anyone else. If you understand these two aspects properly, you will get True Divine Luminous Wisdom (Meignanam). So said His Holiness Guru Bawa to his disciple.

22. Child! Please listen to an illustration.

The camel can travel anywhere on the open sand dunes of the desert. The world calls it the ship of the desert. In its hump it has a water bag. When the camel drinks water, it drinks enough water to quench its thirst for several days. The water it drinks is stored in the body in the vessels below the hump. It uses this water stored within its body to quench its thirst when it cannot find water in the desert. When the quantity of the water stored in its body has been reduced considerably, it will not obey its master in continuing its journey in the desert to the place where its master wants it to go. Instead, it will use its sense of smell and go to the nearest oasis and drink enough water to fill all the water bags in its body. Only after doing so will it continue on the journey across the desert in accordance to its master's bidding.

In the desert whirlwinds sometimes create large sandstorms. During a sandstorm the camel will stand still protecting its nose and mouth from the sand with an overhanging muscular flap. Sometimes the camel will be covered fully with sand. When the sandstorm has ceased, the camel will throw off the sand covering its body and resume its journey. Such is the power of the camel, the ship of the desert.

In the same way as the camel that has to cross the desert, man has to cross the Illusory (Mayic) forest of sexual joy and sensual pleasures full of thorny bushes and wild animals, such as bears, tigers, lions, elephants and poisonous creatures. In that forest of Illusion (Maya) dwell numberless cruel animals and four hundred billion projections of Illusion (Maya).

Like the camel in the desert assailed by the sandstorms, man, travelling through this dark jungle of sexual joy and sensual pleasure, will be assailed by the winds of suffering, poverty and disease. When he is assailed by these evil winds, he must stand firm and still with Faith, Determination, and Certitude (Iman) in God, like the camel which stands still during the sandstorm. Just as the camel replenishes the water reservoir in its body, man should, even in the state of torpor caused by his sufferings, draw in the water of the Clarity of Truth called Divine Wisdom (Pahuth-Arivu), use the Resplendence of Divine Luminous Wisdom (Perr-Arivu) to remove the darkness in the forest of existence which is full of cruel animals, poisonous creatures and evil projections of Illusion (Maya), and cross that forest.

The waves of the sea are more boisterous near the shore than in the middle of the ocean, where one will not feel the force of the waves. The man who has successfully crossed the waves of the vicissitudes of life with equanimity and reached the ocean of Divine Luminous Wisdom (Perr-

Arivu) which has no waves, will live in peace and serenity.

In that place he will have achieved the stillness of the mind, the beauty of the peerless Unique One, the characteristics of Him who has no characteristics, the mind of Him who has no mind, the race and creed of Him who does not belong to any race or creed, and reach that Plentitude which has no curtain to hide it. Man who has reached that state will shine as That Fullness that has no blemish. Only the person who sought the refuge of the Spiritual Master (Guru), listened to his discourses with an open heart, reflected on his Guru's teachings, came to a clarity of conviction, followed the path shown by the Guru and reached the above State of Fullness, can be called the disciple of a Divinely Luminous Guru (Gnana Guru). So said His Holiness Guru Bawa.

23.   **At 7:15 P.M. on 4/2/70**

Child! Please listen to an illustration.

A horse neighs, runs fast exhibiting its speed and beauty, and wins the race. In the same manner, the senses, the projections of the five elements, craving, lust, Illusion (Maya), hypnotic attractions of Illusion (Maya), attended evils (Karma), etc., in the Heart (Qalb) of man take various shapes and traverse the eighteen thousand worlds with the speed of the mind. The horse after running the race, returns to the stable where it stands and falls asleep. In its sleep it falls down with a thud. Then it awakens, leaps up and neighs to show that it is a hero. In the same manner, the five senses after traversing all these worlds return to the Heart (Qalb) of man in a state of fatigue. Without resting, the faculty of the mind remains restless in the Heart (Qalb), thinking of the scenes it saw, and is unable to decide which desire it should achieve. Finally, being unable to achieve anything and being tired, it becomes inactive for a moment like the horse which fell in its sleep. But in a moment, it becomes active again boasting of its prowess like the horse.

Knowing the nature of the horse, the rider fits the saddle, bit, and reins on the horse, gets upon it and goes to his destination, controlling the speed of the horse and the direction in which it is travelling. In the same way, Man should control the mind with the reins of Divine Wisdom (Pahuth-Arivu) and ride on it with Faith and Certitude (Iman). He should then bring the mind to the stable of the Heart (Qalb) and tie it to the log of Faith, Determination and Certitude (Iman). He should feed it with the food of Patience and give it the water of Compassion to drink. He should cover the body of the horse with the cloth of Forbearance and Peace and guard it with the Splendour of Divine Luminous Wisdom (Noor or Perr-Arivu). A person who learns the method from the Spiritual Master (Guru) and controls the wayward mind is the best disciple of a Guru. So said his Holiness Guru Bawa to his disciple.

24.   **At 7:35 P.M. on 4/2/70**

Child! Please listen to an illustration.

Both the male and the female turtle live in the sea. When the female turtle wants to lay eggs, it goes to the sea-shore, digs a hole in the sand and lays its eggs in the hole. Then it covers the eggs with sand and retraces its steps to the sea, erasing all its footsteps. After some time, when the eggs are about to hatch, the turtle will think of the eggs and swim towards the shore. Before the turtle reaches the shore, the egg shells will break and the young turtles will come out of the eggs.

Some go towards the sea, get into the sea and grow up as sea turtles. Some go toward the sandy areas and live there. Some go towards jungles and live there. Some go towards ponds and wells and fall into them and live there. These young ones adopt the characteristics that are suitable to the environment in which they are living and eat the type of food that is available there. Only the young ones which got to the sea become sea turtles. These sea turtles become very large and have great strength.

In the same way, craving and desire for sexual joy in men live together in the sea of sensual pleasure of Illusion (Maya) wherein the six evil actions thrive. They create new lives. Countless beings have been born in this sea of sensual pleasure.

The innumerable beings created by God live in the fifteen worlds and are divided into one hundred and fifty million (ten and a half crores) types of beings and succumbed to the four hundred billion hypnotic projections of Illusion (Maya). They have developed various characteristics to suit the environment in which they were living like the young turtles. Like the young turtles, which went into the sea and lived as sea turtles, many live in the sea of sensual joy of Illusion (Maya). Their religion, the deities they worship and the nations to which they belong are determined by the environment in which they live.

Wherever man may be born, whoever his parents may be, if he erases the place of his birth (origin) and the path through which he appeared in this world with his Divine Wisdom (Pahuth-Arivu), like the turtle which erased its foorsteps as it retraced its steps to the sea from the shore, he will be able to attain Liberation for his Soul (Atma). He will be able to get out of the clutches of joy and sorrow and the cycle of births. He will be able to get the full benefits of the teachings of his Guru and the Resplendence of the Grace of God. If he does not erase from his mind the path through which he came into this world with the help of his Divine Wisdom (Pahuth-Arivu), he will not be able to destroy the sea of sensual pleasure of Illusion (Maya) full of the six types of evil actions within him. So said His Holiness Guru Bawa to his best disciple.

25.   **At 10:15 A.M. on 4/3/70**

His Holiness Guru Bawa said:

My dear disciple! Please listen, reflect with you Divine Wisdom (Pahuth-Arivu) and get clarity of conviction. Take the case of the buffalo. The owner of the buffalo should know its nature and characteristics. He should know how to control it and get it to work for him. He should know its natural characteristics and have it work in such a way as to suit its nature. The biological nature of its body is closely connected with its natural characteristics. He should understand the biological processes of its body and give it work only during particular periods of the day. There is a large fat deposit in its body just below the skin. Therefore, when the heat of the sun in intense during mid-day, the fat below the skin of its body melts and produces an intense and unbearable heat within the body. When the body is in this state the animal will not obey the ploughman or the owner. They will not be able to control it. The buffalo will run towards a nearby pond and roll in the mud instead of bathing in the clear water of the pond. Its 'wisdom' is such that it thinks that, only if the mud sticks to its body, it can reduce the unbearable heat within its body.

A buffalo never drinks clear water. It will first go into the water, move about in it and make it muddy. Then it will drink the muddy water. That is its nature. It does not know the difference between clear and muddy water. It does not have that amount of intelligence. But, it is a very strong and courageous animal with great powers of endurance. Its owner should know these characteristics. He should get work from it before the sun becomes hot and then allow it to rest or wander as it pleases. When the sun goes down, it can be brought back to do more work. If the owner tries to get it to do work in the hot sun against its nature, it will end in disaster for the owner as well as to the animal.

Comment: The body of man is made of the five elements. This body appears as the embodiment of Illusion (Maya) and is fully under the hypnotic influence of Illusion (Maya). Within it is the restless mind. The mind is full of impressions caused by the hypnotic projections of Illusion (Maya) and degraded Wisdom (Ariveenam). The mind retains all the scenes the physical eyes have seen and scenes which they did not see but its imagination has conjured up. The mind enjoys seeing the beautiful mental visions it has created. The mind, which creates these mental and physical visions, is within the physical body of man created out of the five elements.

Like the buffalo the mind carries tremendous loads it actually can not bear. But it thinks and moves about with the idea that it can carry any size load. The Divine Wisdom (Pahuth-Arivu) of man should first analyse and clearly understand the characteristics and nature of the mind, the five senses and the five elements, if it is to control them and get them to work properly, just as the owner of the buffalo should know the characteristics of the buffalo if he is to get the best work out of it. The Wisdom (Arivu) of man should know when to allow the mind to wander and when to control it and how to make it work under its direction. If the Wisdom (Arivu) of man is able to control the mind intelligently, man will be able to win the Love and Compassion of God and live without undergoing suffering during his existence on earth. If one tries to get the buffalo to plough in the hot sun, it will cause injury to the ploughman and to the buffalo. In the same manner, if one tries to achieve Liberation of the Soul (Atma) while his mind is in a state of wavering, it will bring suffering to him and to his Wisdom (Arivu). A man with his Wisdom (Arivu) controls the unwilling mind and ploughs the field of his existence to sow the seeds of Truth and reap the harvest of Liberation of the Soul (Atma). However, the moment Wisdom (Arivu) lets go its grip, the mind will run away to the pond of False Wisdom (Agnana), look at the path through which man was born and the place where he sucked milk, fall into the pond of Ignorance (Agnana), stir up the mud, drink the muddy water of Ignorance (Agnana) and bring upon himself a state of hypnotic torpor caused by Illusion (Maya). It is just as the buffalo which runs to the pond and wallows in the mud.

You should not control the mind-buffalo and then allow it to wallow in the mud of the pond of Ignorance (Agnana) like the buffalo which is allowed to wallow in the mud after the ploughing is over. The mind-buffalo should be tied up with the rope of Wisdom (Arivu) and fed with the food of Love, Patience, Compassion, Forbearance, Peace and Contentment, mixed with the food of God's Grace which is full of God's characteristics. If you feed the mind-buffalo with such food, you will be able to control it and its activities. You should understand this well and put this into practice and continue to guide the actions of the mind wisely.

So said His Holiness Guru Bawa to his disciple.

26. ## At 11:00 A.M. on 4/3/70

Child! Please listen to an illustration.

Among the animals generally called goats, there are several types. One type is the sheep. Sheep graze in flocks. They bring forth only one young at a time. Their body and bones are very strong. Their flesh is capable of producing diseases such as eczema in man.

The sheep always live together in flocks. If one sheep goes in a particular direction, all the other sheep will follow, however narrow the path may be, pushing each other in the process. Even if there is a wider path elsewhere, they will not think of going through the wider path and later joining the others. They will go along the narrow path following the leader. It is the nature of a sheep to move ahead with its head bent low down, nibbling the roots of the Arugu grass and through breathing blowing away the dust.

If there is a well in their path and if the leader falls into that well, all the sheep which follow it will try to fall into that well. If a thief gets hold of one sheep and takes it, all the other sheep will follow that sheep with their heads bent low. They do not possess any faculty of wisdom to make individual decisions.

Just as there are several types in the species of animals generally called goats, among human beings, too, there are many races, many religions, many creeds and tribes. Among them there are people who are like the sheep. Such people show pride in their race, religion and creed. Like the sheep following their leader blindly, they will only feed on the grass roots of religious fanaticism caused by False Wisdom (Agnana). These human sheep will not eat the luxuriant and beneficial grass found on the sides of their path. Even if there are wide plains where they can graze freely and eat the beautiful and tasty grass; they will not disperse and eat this grass. Guided only by religious fanaticism and racial pride, these human sheep will follow only the narrow and difficult path taken by the leader.

These human beings will never disperse and go individually along the wider paths and reach the Wide Open Space which is full of sweet Spiritual Food and the Grace of God, the Wide Open Space where they can enjoy the taste of Truth, the never-ending Fullness, the Indestructible One, the Taste that has no taste, the Everlasting Bliss. These human sheep with two legs will only follow the narrow and difficult path taken by the leader. Their heads are bent down full of degraded spiritual Wisdom (Ariveenam) which is motivatea by religious bigotry. They follow the path of egoism in the dark cave of their mind leading them to rebirth.

You should avoid such human sheep. You should stand erect and look with the Eye of Wisdom (Arivu), see the Limitless Wide Open Space within you, the Plenitude that fills that Space, and consume that never-ending Plenitude. Then, you will remove from yourself the shackles of birth and death, joy and sorrow, and merge with That which is Free, That which is an Ocean of Bliss.

So said His Holiness Guru Bawa to his best disciple.

27. At 5:30 P.M. on 4/3/70

His Holiness Guru Bawa tells his disciple:

Various types of deer live in the forest. Each type has its own characteristics and its way of life. Among the deer, the Spotted deer and the deer with antlers, called in Tamil 'Kalai Maan', are the most beautiful. They have long red fish-shaped eyes. Their necks, ears and face are like the necks, ears and face of the horses. One is fascinated by looking at these beautiful creations of God. Poets have compared men to the stags and women to the does in their poems. The deer is a beautiful animal. Its face and its look and its calm nature show tranquility that shines on the face of an infant. But, it is ever ready to leap and run. In spite of its beauty, the deer is a suspicious animal and is always in fear of losing its life. When it moves about in the forest, if it hears the sound of the fall of its dung on dry leaves or the sound of its footsteps on the dry leaves, it will become agitated and leap and run forward without thinking of the danger that may befall it. When it runs thus, it is obsessed with fear and runs over mountains and hills, and jumps over pits. In doing so it sometimes falls into deep pits or steep valleys and breaks its legs and bones and dies.

Just as there are deer of various colours, among men there are white, black, red, brown and yellow people. The men derive their physical beauty from these five colours. Man feels proud of the colour of his skin and considers races of other colours to be inferior to him. Whatever the colour of the skin of man may be, his body is composed of the five elements of Earth, Fire, Water, Air and Ether, and he is subject to the influence of the five senses. But man does not realise this Truth.

Man is subject to hunger, disease, old age and death. The moment he feels that these calamities are approaching, he loses his sense of perception and the faculty of Wisdom. He forgets the superiority complex in his mind created by the colour of his skin. He forgets his vanity about his beauty. His only thought will be, "How can I escape these maladies?" Like the deer in the forest, which leaps and runs on hearing the sound of its dung falling on dry leaves, his mind and senses will run at a terrible speed in fear in the Illusory (Mayic) forest of human existence. Like the deer which, when running in fear of its life, blindly falls into deep pits, breaks its legs and bones and suffers intense pain and dies, this man also runs blindly through the Illusory (Mayic) forest of life, spurred by the fear that the above four maladies will kill him, and falls into the deep pit of the divisive forces of race and religion, breaks his bones, undergoes intense suffering and dies. This man lived on the basis that the beauty of his physical body, the beauty of the senses and the beauty of the elements are his beauty. But he dies leaving all his beauty on the earth. The man who nurtured carefully his physical beauty is unable to take it with him when he dies. He leaves the body made of the five elements in this world. The five elements in the body go back to their source. Earth returns to the Earth, Fire to Fire, Water to Water, Air to Air, and Ether to Ether. The man, who considered the above to be his beauty, in the end loses what he thought to be his beauty, loses the beauty of God, loses the beauty of the five elements, loses the Eye of Wisdom (Arivu), the Resplendence of the Soul

(Atma) and wanders on earth and in the spiritual world as a ghost or demon immersed in the darkness of spiritual degradation in a state of torpor.

That four-legged one is the deer in the forest. This two-legged creature is the deer in the country with a human face. You should understand the nature and characteristics of this human deer in the country and discard his mode of life. You should understand clearly the purpose of human existence. You should seek the Divine Wisdom (Pahuth-Arivu) which will show you the nature of your Soul (Atma) and attain God's beauty by adopting His characteristics and hereby avoid destruction. This is the reward of proper human existence. Such a man who has achieved this sublime state is called Man-God (Manu-Eesan) or Perfect Man (Insan Kamil). You should discard the nature of your beauty and obtain the beauty of God.

So said His Holiness Guru Bawa to his disciple.

28.   **At 6:45 P.M. on 4/3/70**

"Gnana Guru! (Spiritual Master) How can one control his senses?" inquired one disciple. His Holiness Guru Bawa replied:

There are hares and rabbits. People rear rabbits as pets in their homes. The rabbit brings forth eight to eleven young ones at a time, three months after conception. When the female rabbit is about to give birth to the young one, people keep the male rabbit in a separate cage to prevent it from killing the newly-born rabbits.

The female rabbit makes the necessary preparations for the expected event. It selects a suitable place and digs a hole like a cave in the ground. It will remove all the hair from its skin by scratching the skin. Then it spreads the hair in the hole to serve like a cushion for the newly-born rabbits as soon as they are born. It will not go out for food till the event takes place. It is at this time that the owners take away the male rabbit and keep it in a cage. After bringing forth the young rabbits the female rabbit will start eating food and feed the young rabbits with its milk. When the young rabbits grow up and reach a state when they can find their own food and look after themselves, the owners will take the female rabbit and put it in the cage where the male rabbit is.

Again within three months the female rabbit will conceive and give birth to young rabbits. Thus this type of rabbit is able to increase its progeny at a fast rate.

Comment: Man is the rarest and noblest of God's creations. The five elements dwell in him. Within the five elements thrive the six sinful actions of Craving, Hatred, Miserliness, Lust, Vanity, and Envy and the five enemies of the mind, Intoxication, Adultery, Theft, Murder and Falsehood. They play the roles of husband and wife. Both these sets of actions interact on one another and develop the sixty four sensual arts like the rabbit that brings forth young rabbits within ninety days of conception. Just as the female rabbit sheds all its hair to serve as a cushion for its newly born rabbits, man dedicates his body, money and soul for the development of the sixty four arts which give sensual pleasure. Each of these sixty four arts gives rise to thirty five million (three and a half crores) evil actions. The four hundred billion (lakhs of crores) of hypnotic projections of Illusion (Maya) dwelling within the cave of man's body develop their species in the same manner. With your Divine Wisdom (Pahuth-Arivu) you must understand this state of affairs.

The mind and the five elements live like husband and wife and multiply these evils within man. These evils are capable of destroying Divine Wisdom, Truth and God which have the potential for existing within Man.

If you wish to cut yourself from these shackles, you must reflect on the meaning of the four aphorisms given below and act accordingly.

(1) "Pirappu Oru Mayakkam": Birth is a state of torpor, i.e., Parents in a state of hypnotic fascination caused by Illusion (Maya) mate. At that time they are in a state of spiritual torpor. The result is the birth of a child. The born child grows in a state of spiritual torpor as it is influenced by blood ties and the environment. The child does not know its real Divine Nature because it is in a state of spiritual torpor.

(2) "Man Oru Thayakkam": Earth causes spiritual inertia, i.e., The material attractions of the world produce a state of spiritual inertia in man. If a man succumbs to the attractions of the material world he cannot make spiritual progress.

(3) "Manam Oru Kalakkam": Mind is always in a state of fear, i.e., The mind is never steady. It wavers. It is never sure of itself. It is always worried whether its projects will come into fruition or not. Thus it causes fear and loss of self-confidence in man.

(4) "Guru Moli Iyakkam": The word of the Guru causes motion, i.e., The words of the real authentic Guru (Spiritual Master) are powerful. His words awaken man from his state of hypnotic torpor and spiritual inertia, steady his mind, instill confidence and cause spiritual progress.

You should understand the meaning of the four aphorisms and submit yourself to the dynamic force of the Guru.

There are human beings who multiply their karmic evil actions like the rabbit. You know that if the owner allowed the male rabbit to remain with the female rabbit when it gives birth to the young rabbits, the male rabbit will bite the young rabbits and kill them. Like this, you should switch on the Light of Radiance of Divine Wisdom (Pahuth-Arivu) resulting from the Spiritual Master's (Guru's) powerful discourses and turn it within you and kill the progeny of the elements and senses within you with your Divine Wisdom (Pahuth-Arivu). Like the male hare, when your Divine Wisdom bites the progeny of these elements and senses, the bad odour of blood, milk, lymph, corpses, spiritual torpor, and the repulsive odour of the cave of Hell within you, which is darker than the darkest night, will emerge. Then the motive force of the Guru's words which gives rise to the Radiance will fall among these evils within the dark cave of the mind and drive away these evils and burn them to ashes. When a snake falls in the midst of a crowd of people, they will run away in all directions from that place. In the same way, all these evils will run away from the Radiance arising from the motive force of the Guru's words. The evils will all be burnt to ashes.

When the cave of your mind is freed from these evil forces of darkness, the darkness in the mind will disappear. The Grace of God will shine within you. The Resplendence of Divine Luminous Wisdom (Noor) will manifest itself. Reality will manifest itself. The Ultimate Unique One will manifest itself. You will reach the state in which you become free from the effect of actions, called good and evil in the world, and reach That

Ultimate Unique One. You should reflect and understand this well.

29.   At 7:45 P.M. on 4/3/70

Child! Please listen to an illustration.

The hen lays eggs and hatches them. When the chickens come out, it protects them carefully. When the sound of the hawks, crows, mongooses, and foxes are heard, it rushes to the place where the chickens are, gets them to come under its spread-out wings and then covers them with its wings to hide them from the eyes of the above-mentioned enemies. It protects them like this till they grow up into adult birds.

In the same way, the mind, like the fowl, protects and rears blood ties and evil actions with its two protective wings of the five elements and the five senses. It feeds them with one hundred and fifty million (ten and a half crores) of evil actions (Karma). It does not feed them with good actions. If you want to destroy the mind (the fowl) along with the senses (its wings) and evil actions (the chickens hatched by it), you should move towards good actions and the Truth.

When a disciple surrenders himself to the Spiritual Master (Guru), who is one within the fold of Turth, the Spiritual Master will bestow the Grace within him to the disciple, feed him with Love, give him the wings of Divine Wisdom (Pahuth-Arivu) and the Soul (Atma), the powers which he was unable to use hitherto, and the Light of the Eye of Resplendence of Divine Luminous Wisdom (Perr-Arivu). He will give him the two legs of 'Kalai', the afferent and efferent spiritual power that moves simultaneously with the inward and outward breath, called in Tamil 'Suriya Kalai' (the Art of the Sun) and 'Chandra Kalai' (the Art of the Moon). The Guru will enable the disciple to walk with these spiritual legs of 'Kalai', fly in the sky with these spiritual wings and kill and burn the mind and its progeny symbolised as the fowl and the chicken, and throw away the ashes of the evil forces into the sea of Illusion (Maya), their original source. The disciple who has obtained this power from the Guru, will find the method of releasing himself from these forces of evil and reach the Guru within him, i.e., the Ultimate Guru (God). You should study and reflect on these things and obtain that power and reach God.

So said His Holiness Guru Bawa to a disciple of his.

30.   At 9:40 A.M. on 4/4/70

His Holiness Guru Bawa told one of his disciples:

Child! A man tried his luck at various jobs to earn his living. But he was unable to get enough wages to lead his life in peace. He was also unable to achieve the Truth in this world. When he tried to follow the path of Truth, these was none in the world to employ him and pay him wages or give him food. "What a strange world this is!" he thought. He looked intently at the world with his eye of Intellect (Puththi). He saw that the world was full of actions which appeared disgraceful to the eye of his Intellect. The man who really ploughed, the man who really worked sincerely, did not get his due wages. He saw people dressing idols, putting beautiful ornaments on them and offering limitless amounts of food to them, though these idols could not stand, walk, speak or work. Such people had been given titles and posts. They develop ceremonies and conduct festivals for the physical eyes to see and relish. They also develop methods of increasing mental visions. Their minds are full of desire for sex. But they parade as devotees, worship God and request Him to grant them boons. They cause sacrifices of lives of created beings to be made and cause intense suffering to them.

This man saw all these iniquities. He developed the faculty of Wisdom, which is on a higher level than Intelligence. He came to the conclusion that in this world devoid of Wisdom, if he deceived the gullible devotees who have no Wisdom, he could lead a comfortable life.

So, he wandered about in the country singing songs from mythology, which cause a state of trance. In due course he went to the gate in front of the palace of the King. He shouted in a loud voice, "I will show God before you. Those who want to see God may come before me", and started singing mythological songs. When the King heard this, he came before him and said, "If you will show God to me, I will give you whatever you want". The man replied, "So far you have seen only deities which can be seen by physical eyes. I will show you God Almighty, Who cannot be seen by your physical eyes, Who cannot be seen by your mind, Who is full of Compassion. If you want me to show Him to you, you should give me whatever I ask." The King, who was deceived by his robes, his actions, and words, agreed.

The man informed the King of his requirements, namely a large fortress four miles in circumference should be built. To pay the wages of the workers, the King should give him one hundred million rupees every month. No one should go to that place for one year. He needed also yarn, looms, silver, gold and nine types of gems. After the period of one year is over, he will himself call the King and show him God. The King agreed and provided him all these things. He gave him gold, silver and other things. He gave him one hundred million rupees every month.

When the man obtained the above, he built a large palace for himself. He also built five hundred mansions for the five hundred workers who were working under him, and gave them all the money, gems, gold and silver they wanted, and converted them into very wealthy persons. In the meantime he wove a silk cloth three feet square with golden and silver threads and silk yarn. It was studded with the nine types of gems. It had a many-coloured beautiful border.

The period of one year was coming to an end. The King was in a state of great piety to God. He was performing continuous ceremonies in a state of fervour due to extreme devotion to God. The appointed day at the end of one year arrived. The man who agreed to show God to the King had invited all Kings, Siththars (people who had overcome the forces of nature), devotees, priests, masters of ceremonies, poets, scholars, mendicants, etc., who wanted to see God, to assemble in front of the palace gate.

On the appointed day, he decorated the palace and all the roads leading to it. He decorated all the chariots and palanquins. He decorated the elephant. The mahout, who controls the elephant, was in ceremonial dress. The man, who promised to show God, dressed himself in silk, wore a golden crown on his head, and went in procession to the palace gate on the decorated elephant with that embroidered three foot square silk cloth on his lap.

All the Kings, Chiefs, Siththars and others who wanted to see God were assembled there. He got down from the elephant and sat on the throne, put the King's crown on his own head, took the folded silk cloth and held it above him towards the sky and said: "There! you see God. All heavenly beings, angels, heavenly commanders and soldiers, sun, moon and others are there. Now you may see them."

Then he gave the silk cloth to the King and said: "If you look through it, you will see everything. But a person who is born in adultery will not see God. An illegitimate son cannot see God. Only a person who was born to one father can see God through this silk cloth. A person who is born to several fathers cannot see God."

The King looked through the silk cloth. He did not see God or any heavenly beings. The King thought for a while. He was in an embarrassing position. He thought, "If I say I did not see God, people will think that I was born in adultery. I was born to one father. I should not say that I did not see God". In the meantime, the person who came to show God said, "O King! Do you not see God there?" The King replied, "I do." "Do you see the heavenly beings, angels and others?" The King replied, "I do." The King had no other alternative. He had to say "Yes" as he was afraid that all who were gathered there would think that he was born in adultery if he said "No."

The man gave the silk cloth to the other Kings, ministers, Siththars, scholars, masters of ceremonies, etc., who were there. All said that they saw God. None said "No", as they were afraid that people would consider them to be born in adultery.

They all knew in Truth according to their Conscience that they did not see God. The man who came to show God also knew this. The King accepted Falsehood as Truth to save the honour of his family. So, the world accepted Falsehood as Truth and gave that man gifts. They treated him as the god who showed God to the Kingdom. None saw God. But the man who showed Falsehood as Truth was treated like God.

Comment: Like this man, people belonging to the four different religions, the theologians who have mastered Veda and Vedanta, the Holy Scriptures and Philosophies of the four religions, devotees who think that they have mastered Yoga and Gnana, devotees who keep the idols of the four hundred billion (lakhs of crores) deities before their physical eyes and conjure up mental visions regarding them, Siththars who have mastered the forces of nature, poets, scholars, masters of ceremonies and the pseudo-gnostics, earn their living. These people develop within their bodies one hundred and fifty million (ten and a half crores) evil actions and are liable to take thirty five million (three and a half crores) births. They develop the sixty four sensual arts and obtain honour for serving as examples of the meaning of the ninety six human madnesses. They develop within their mind the shape and forms of the four hundred billion (lakhs of crores) hypnotic projections of Illusion (Maya). They also develop in their mind the four hundred billion (lakhs of crores) mundane deities. They develop within them satanic forces of Egoism, evil action (Karma) and Illusion (Maya), the triple dirt. They commit sins arising from Craving, Hatred, Miserliness, Vanity, Lust and Envy. They allow the five enemies of the mind, Intoxicants, Adultery, Theft, Murder and Falsehood, to hold sway in their life. These are the 'devotees' who have come forward to show God to the people in the world, like the man referred to in the illustration. These are the Siththars, people who have overcome the forces of nature, who have come forward to show God. What they succeed in doing is to cause degradation to the human birth of man, the rarest and noblest of all creations, and make him take several rebirths.

These are people, who were unable to earn their living on their own, like the man referred to in the illustration. To eke out their existence they have sacrificed Truth and praised the world. They have accepted the degradation of spiritual wisdom (Ariveenam) with glee. They wallow in Ignorance (Agnana), discarding True Divine Luminous Wisdom (Gnanam). They share in the joys of the five elements. They enjoy whatever scenes they see in the world. Having lost their ability to listen to the Inner Voice, the Divine Monitory Apparatus, they have driven away Divine Wisdom (Pahuth-Arivu). They have accepted Falsehood, Envy and Treachery as guides for earning their living. They have discarded the Ultimate Unique One. They show to the world that the six sinful actions are God and that self-glory, honour, wealth, titles, posts of honour, craving, desire for sex, symbols, forms, names, egoism, pride, illusion, the darkness of ignorance, hypnotic torpor caused by Illusion (Maya), intoxicants, adultery, theft, murder, and falsehood, are considered to be Divine Qualities and personifications of God. These are the people who have come forward to show us God for the sake of feeding their own stomachs. They rule the world with their stratagems. They give prominence to religious bigotry. They take refuge behind the facade of religion, remove God from the world, and rule the world themselves. But, when hunger and poverty betake them they will lose all their religious fervour. If they suffer disease they will lose in a moment all they have earned. When they grow old they will forget who they are. When they die, they will be born again and will continue to take birth after birth and finally become food for Hell. Their liberation and goal is the achievement of Hell.

You should know all these things. Do not forsake the Truth for the sake of feeding your stomach. Do not destroy Divine Wisdom (Pahuth-Arivu) for the sake of the joys of the five elements. For the sake of the Earth, Fire, Water, Air and Ether, do not forget the purpose for which you were born. For the sake of the beauty of the scenes you see with your physical eyes, do not lose sight of the beauty of God, Who is the embodiment of Compassion. Do not sell your conscience for the sake of your mental visions. Do not forget the state of Truth, which will prevent re-birth, owing to fear arising from the sufferings you are undergoing as a result of having been born in this world. Do not try to look here and there for God Who exists as Divine Luminous Wisdom (Perr-Arivu) within Divine Luminous Wisdom (Perr-Arivu). In the illustration I gave earlier the King said that he saw God through the silk cloth for the sake of his family honour, though he did not see anything, because the man who promised to show God said that a person who was born in adultery will not see anything. Do not follow his example. Do not accept as Truth Falsehood and what you have not seen for the sake of the honour of the conventional religions of the world. Do not lose the Ultimate Unique One Who is Truth and your Inner Voice. God is not within the folds of any conventional religion. He cannot be found within egoism and vanity. He is without birth or death. He is Plenitude itself. He is Divine Luminous Wisdom (Perr-Arivu) within Divine Luminous Wisdom (Perr-Arivu). He is That within you. In that state, That functions as the Divine Monitory Apparatus. That points out your errors. That warns you what is good and what is wrong. That is God within you. That is your Inner Voice. The

Kings, ministers, scholars, spiritual aspirants, etc., forsook That and accepted Falsehood as Truth in public. Do not follow their example. Do not accept Falsehood as Truth for the honour of your conventional religion. Only that which comes as the Voice from within you warning you, is the Reality. All other things cause suffering to your Truth, Divine Wisdom and the Divine Monitory Apparatus. They will cause suffering to your Soul (Atma). You should clearly understand this. You should realise who you are, develop your Divine Wisdom (Pahuth-Arivu) and make it Resplendent, and make the voice of God resonate within you and give you warnings to help you progress. The very day you hear and understand this Inner Voice of God, you will escape from the sufferings of existence. The illusive joys of the world will disappear. You will reach the state of Liberation from the cycle of births.

So said His Holiness Guru Bawa to one disciple of his.

31. At 6:50 P.M. on 4/4/70

Child! Please listen to an illustration.

Let us take the case of a woman whose infant has died. When she is fully under the influence of sorrow arising from the loss of her infant, she will not be in a position to wail. Neither will she wail using similies and metaphors to show how dear the child was to her.

Similarly, when the heart of a devotee has melted as a result of the maturity of his love and devotion to God, he will not be in a position to sing hymns in praise of God to the accompaniment of music produced by musical instruments. Nor will he dance in a state of frenzy or trance. His heart and body will melt when he is in that state of full absorption in the love for God, and tears will run down his eyes.

When the mother is in a state of bereavement at the death of her loving child, she will be in such an emotional state of sorrow that her body will be in a state of torpor. She will not know what to do. She will not be able to wail. In the same manner, when the real devotee of God is fully absorbed in his love for God, he will not be a position to sing hymns in praise of God. His heart will melt and tears will flow from his eyes. It is only a mother who does not fully love the child who will, for the sake of the world, wail, using similies and metaphors to show how dear the child was to her. In the same manner, only a person who is not fully absorbed in his love for God will be able to sing hymns in praise of God to the accompaniment of music. For, if his heart has really melted due to love for God, he will not be in a position to open his mouth and talk. He will find it difficult to breathe. He will be crying and shedding tears. He will not be able to sing. Only when his heart has not melted, a devotee sings songs in praise of God and dances in ecstacy. This state is due to unsteady and wavering devotion to God. There are one hundred and fifty million (ten and a half crores) forms of such wavering devotion to God. When a devotee has fully surrendered his Self to God with his Divine Wisdom (Pahuth-Arivu), his body and heart will melt and tears will flow down his eyes.

So said His Holiness Guru Bawa to his disciple.

32. At 7:20 P.M. on 4/4/70

Child! Please listen to an illustration.

Look at the peacock. It has five colours in its feathers. When the peacock spreads out its beautiful tail, exhibiting the beauty of its feathers, displaying the five colours and dances round and round in a state of ecstacy, a life fluid falls out of its body like pearls. The peahen eats up these pearl-like drops. These mature in the body of the peahen and later come out of its body as fertilized eggs.

In the same manner, man's body is composed of five elements. These five elements have produced five Illusory (Mayic) forces which have five colours. The mind, which has these five colours, dances in ecstacy when it sees the hypnotic attractions of the world. Adjoining the mind is the Evil Mind called in Arabic 'Nafs Ammara'. This has seven sections like the seven colours of the rainbow. Like the peahen, the Evil Mind (Nafs Ammara) consumes the drops of hypnotic stupor coming out of the mind as a result of its fascination for the four hundred billion (lakhs of crores) hypnotic attractions of the world, and lays one hundred and fifty million (ten and a half crores) eggs and hatches them. The mind sees these satanic qualities hatched by the Evil Mind (Nafs Ammara) and considers these forces of craving to be its children and relations. It is overjoyed at the sight of these and dances in ecstacy. If the mind and its five colours, the five senses and the forces of craving which arose as a result of the mind succumbing to the seductive attractions of the five senses, are burnt with Divine Wisdom (Pahuth-Arivu), the Soul (Atma) will become spotlessly pure. Otherwise man will suffer from spiritual loss.

If you understand this, find out the nature of your egoism and vanity and allied satanic qualities, and free yourself from their influence at every moment, then you will attain Liberation of your Soul (Atma) in this birth itself.

So said His Holiness Guru Bawa to his disciple.

33.   ## At 5:55 P.M. on 4/5/70

"When there are a large number of disciples with a Guru, how can the Guru find out whether a disciple is good or unworthy?" inquired a disciple. His Holiness Guru Bawa replied:

Child! There are cobras which have laid a thousand eggs. There are turtles which have laid a thousand eggs. When the eggs are hatched, the young snakes which have the characteristics of the cobra are called cobras. They will follow the mother cobra. The mother cobra classifies the other young snakes which have different characteristics as rat snakes, vipers, green snakes, etc. Similarly, the mother turtle considers only the young turtles which came into the sea as turtles. It classifies other young turtles which went towards the sand or pond or jungle as pond tortoises, sand tortoises, jungle tortoises, etc.

In the same manner, the Guru will be able to find out easily the good disciples and the unworthy disciples. He will consider the disciples who have developed his characteristics as his children and the others who have not done so as unworthy disciples. When a fowl scratches the earth in search of food, if it finds diamonds, gems or pearls, it will discard them and only eat worms and insects. Disciples with the characteristics of the fowl, will discard the good teachings of the Guru, and give ear only to the bad teachings of the world. The Guru will know that such a person is not a good disciple and that he will not accept his Divine teachings.

The fowl scratches the earth and picks up worms and insects and eats them from dawn to dusk. Only when it is dark will it go up the tree or go into the cage to rest for the night. But its stomach will not be full in spite of all its efforts during the day. In the same manner, a disciple who is with the Guru who listens to the evil teachings of the world without absorbing in his mind the Divine teachings of the Guru, is like the fowl. Even if he is living with the Guru, he will not attain Divine Luminous Wisdom (Perr-Arivu) and cut himself free from the cycle of death and birth. He will not be able to overcome the maladies of hunger, disease, old age and death. If the disciple does not listen carefully to the teachings of the Guru, reflect on them and retain them in his Divine Wisdom (Pahuth-Arivu), the Guru will consider him to be unfit for Higher Divine Teaching. He will consider him to be like the fowl and not fit for knowledge of Divinity.

34.   ## At 6:05 P.M. on 4/5/70

"How can the disciples find out whether the Guru is authentic or an imposter?" asked one of the disciples. His Holiness Guru Bawa replied:

There are four hundred billion (lakhs of crores) Spiritual Masters (Gurus). They will live in hiding in seventy thousand tents constructed of veils. They will have thirty five million (three and a half crores) forms. If you wish to know, then you need a real Spiritual Master (authentic Guru) who can remove the disease in your mind, death, and the dirt of your birth.

When you are thirsty, only water can quench your thirst. Nothing else can. So, only the Guru who can remove the dirt of birth from you and quench your spiritual thirst can be called the Spiritual Master (authentic Guru). You will know when your thirst is quenched and when you find that your thirst is quenched, you will realise that your Guru is an authentic Guru!

35.   ## At 6:10 P.M. on 4/5/70

"People say that Destiny can be overcome with intellect. Can one overcome Destiny?" asked one disciple. His Holiness Guru Bawa replied:

You have asked a very intelligent question. Knowledge (Madthi) prepares an estimate of one's life and decides 'this is the limit'. But Destiny (Vithi) is beyond the limit. It is limitless. It is connected with God. If one is to explain Destiny (Vithi) it will not be possible for him to completely explain all aspects of Destiny even if he continued to explain till the end of the world. The limit you spoke of is called the limit of Intellect (Puththi). You think that you can overcome Destiny with Intellect. Destiny is the Flame of God. Knowledge (Madthi) is the subtle end of Intellect (Puththi). If you have surpassed Intellect (Puththi), then you have really achieved your objective. That achievement is Liberation from Destiny. It means you have reached God. Take the two letters 'Vi' and 'Thee' in the Tamil word, 'Vithee'. 'Vi' means Wisdom (Arivu). 'Thee' means Fire which is to say that your cycle of births been burnt by the Resplendence of Divine Luminous Wisdom (Perr-Arivu) which is represented by the letter 'Vi'. When the cycle of births has been burnt, what else do you want? What then, is 'Vithee', Destiny?

Once you have surpassed Knowledge which developed from your Intellect, then Divine Wisdom (Pahuth-Arivu) which originated from God will manifest itself in Man in all its glory and overcome Destiny which also originated from God. Therefore, overcome Knowledge which developed from Intellect. The Effulgence of Grace (Arul Jothi) appeared from God. Divine Luminous Wisdom (Perr-Arivu) originated from the Grace of God. Destiny originated from God's hand. It is that Divine Luminous Wisdom (Perr-Arivu), alone, which can destroy Destiny.

36. ## At 6:45 P.M. on 4/5/70

"People are searching for a Guru. They are moving about with the Guru. What is the meaning of the Guru?" inquired Mr. Ramachandran. His Holiness Guru Bawa replied:

Child! It is easy to explain the word "Guru". It is easy to seek a Guru. It is easy to meet a Guru. It is easy to be a Guru. But to a real disciple, the Spiritual Master (Guru) should be the Light which removes the darkness in the mind of the disciple. The disciple should hold that Light within himself and remove the darkness within him. Darkness is within the disciple. The Light of the Guru is also within him. With the help of the Guru who dwells within his heart, the disciple should gradually remove the darkness within himself. A dsiciple should take the Truth, the Guru, and keep it within his Heart. Then, only, the Guru can remove the veils of darkness surrounding the Soul which resides within the Spiritual Heart. If you keep the Light of the Guru outside, you cannot remove the darkness within.

37. ## At 7:00 P.M. on 4/5/70

"Is it essential to realise God before one reaches the age of forty? Cannot one realise God after that age?" inquired Mr. Ratnavethan. His Holiness Guru Bawa replied:

Child! To find and open the spring of Divine Luminous Wisdom (Perr-Arivu) in the well of life, one must dig out the dry earth and reach the layer of wet earth before he reaches the age of forty. When a person digs a well to find clear water for drinking, he must dig hard with Faith, Determination and Certitude without wavering and without feeling discouraged. He must continue to dig till he reaches the layer of wet earth. It is only then that he can discover the spring and dig it open. In the same manner, one should strive hard with a steadfast mind till he reaches the wet layer where the spring of Divine Luminous Wisdom (Perr-Arivu) can be discovered. This should be done before the age of forty. If he has achieved that much by the age of forty, the Guru will be able to open the spring of Wisdom (Arivu) in him. If one does not reach the wet layer where the spring of Wisdom (Arivu) can be discovered, before the age of forty, the influence of the senses will have become too powerful. The nerves will have become less sensitive. Forgetfulness will have increased. The unsteadiness of senility will have appeared. Signs of impending death will have appeared. Therefore, it is very difficult to attain Divine Luminous Wisdom (Gnanam) after that age.

Termites build up the colony where they live only in wet ground. They roll up the wet earth softened with the secretions from their mouths and build up their colony and live there. They cannot build colonies where there is no water and when the earth is completely dry. In the same manner, only if the wetness of Wisdom (Arivu) is manifest in you, will the Guru be able to use the wetness of Wisdom (Arivu) in you and with His Grace build up the walls of the well and open the spring of Divine Luminous Wisdom (Perr-Arivu). He will open your Gnostic Eye (Gnana Kan) and show within you everything in the universes and God Who is Omnipresent. If the wetness of Wisdom (Arivu) is not found within you, the Spiritual Master (Guru) will not be able to do anything. It is like a tree grown large and old which has fruit that is small and changed in taste.

During the period when one is young, his heart is open. It is receptive. You can put anything in it. The stock provided to you by the Guru can be kept inside and sealed by the Guru. The Guru's seal can be impressed clearly. The seal will stick clearly and will not break. When you have filled the house fully with hay, you cannot keep anything else inside it. You cannot even open the door. You cannot even open the ridge of the roof. In the same manner, when your heart is full of the hypnotic attractions of the world which cause spiritual torpor, it is not possible to keep in it the stock the Guru gives you. You cannot open the door of the heart. You cannot remove the ridge of the roof of the heart. Therefore, when your heart is empty, when there is room in the heart in your youth, you should obtain and keep the good stock of the Divine teachings of the Guru in it. That is the proper time. If you miss the opportunity presented in youth, it will be very difficult later. When your heart is full of trash, it is not possible to keep valuable goods inside, even if you wish to do so, as there will be no room. Therefore, it is essential for you to strive hard to realise God before you reach the age of forty.

38.   At 9:15 A.M. on 4/6/70

Child! Please listen to an illustration.

Take the case of the scorpion. It has a sting in its tail. It crawls on all its legs. If any insect, animal or man crosses its path, it will get hold of it with its claws and sting it with the poisonous sting in its tail.

We are all trying to learn Divine Luminous Wisdom (Gnanam) like the scorpion, without removing the sting in us. We have as our tail the five elements. At the end of this tail is the sting called egoism. Inside that sting is the poison of Illusion (Maya) caused by the degradation of spiritual Wisdom (Ariveenam). Just as the scorpion, when going in search of food, stings anything it meets on its way, these human scorpions sting those in their way when they are motivated by egoism. The men who are stung by these human scorpions are liable to lose their Divine Wisdom and Truth and die as a result of the poison. If we remove the sting of egoism from us, Divine Wisdom will develop in us. It does not matter even if the Earth, Fire, Water, Air and Ether hold sway over us. But egoism which exists beyond these five elements should be removed as it contains the poison of Illusion (Maya).

So said His Holiness Guru Bawa.

39.   At 9:20 A.M. on 4/6/70

"What is 'Gnana Kan', or the Eye of Divine Luminous Wisdom? Who possesses it?" inquired a disciple. His Holiness Guru Bawa replied:

Infants as well as adults have this Eye of Divine Luminous Wisdom (Gnana Kan). The infant sees God when it is born. If you do not recognise or see your individuality, you will see the Truth. If you see the Truth you will see the Ultimate Unique One. If your see Him, you will see all the Grace within Him. In that state, only He exists. Everything else will disappear. To know and attain that sublime state is the highest achievement of existence on earth.

40. <center>**At 5:10 P.M. on 4/6/70**</center>

Child! Please listen to an illustration.

A hare went early in the morning to graze on dewy grass. The top of the blades of the 'Arugu' grass were very sharp. As a result of the dew, the hare bit the grass in a hurry. The pointed blades of the 'Arugu' grass injured its nose. So the hare became angry. It said to the grass, "Are you so brave? You have stung my nose. I will not eat you." So saying, it went away. The hare in its anger did not eat the grass. The grass laughed at the hare's foolishness.

There are human beings like the hare. Owing to their degraded state of Wisdom (Ariveenam) they commit mistakes, fall into pits, and break the bones of their legs and hands. Being unable to climb out of the pit, they blame Omnipotent God, Who creates all beings, feeds them and protects them both in their joys and sorrows. They become angry with God and say, "You are blind! Are you God? What is the use of worshipping You? Are You the person who created all beings? You are not God. If You are God, why do You cause suffering?"

Some human beings blame the doctor when they go to him to get treatment for their diseases. If the doctor says, "Please wait a little. I will prepare some medicine and administer it to you", they retort, "Are you a doctor? How long have I been waiting? Do you think that there are no other doctors in this world?" and go away in anger.

Some people go in search of a Spiritual Master (Guru) to satisfy their spiritual hunger and to cure themselves of their diseases of birth and death. They go to him in a state of extreme devotion. They expect the Guru to welcome them with all ceremony, honour them and give them a seat of honour by his side. If the Guru does not do this, some people who go to the Guru to study Divine Luminous Wisdom (Gnanam) get angry because they have not been given special treatment by the Guru, and say, "He is not an authentic Spiritual Master. He is an impostor who is cheating the world. What does he know?", and go away.

There are many people who have been going about in search of God, singing hymns in praise of God. When they are tired of this method of trying to reach God, they go in search of a Guru. When they go to a Guru, instead of following his teachings, they try to find out the following particulars about the Guru. "Has he obtained Divine Luminous Wisdom (Gnanam)? Is he wearing ochre robes or not? Is he wearing holy ash on his forehead? Is he wearing only spun cloth or is he naked? What is his race and caste? Is he a Tamil or a Muslim or a Buddhist or a Christian?" If they find that he does not wear robes or symbols of religion, they jest about him and go away, because these people pay more respect to the external trappings, the robes, the religious symbols, etc., of the Guru than to his Divine Teachings.

Some people suffer from disease, poverty, loss in business, litigation regarding property, domestic trouble caused by their spouse and children,

101

unemployment, etc. They think that if they go to the Guru they will be able to find a way of improving their living and that God or the Guru will grant all their requests. They go to the Guru, tell him about their sufferings, and request the Guru to grant them wealth. If the Guru does not grant them wealth, they scold the Guru, emphasising their point with gesture of their eyes, mouth, neck, and head, and go away in anger.

All these people are like the hare which got angry with the 'Arugu' grass and went away without grazing it. They are the people who are guided by selfishness and who are bound to take several births. They will never study Wisdom (Gnana). Even if you lecture to them continuously for a month giving billions (crores and crores) of illustrations, they will never give up their wicked deeds. You must understand the nature of such people and give discourses. Most of the people in the Serendib Circle in Ceylon who come to study Wisdom (Gnana) are this type of person. But among them there are one or two who are really born as Man and are striving to be Man-God (Manu-Easan). They are in search of the Guru. They want to reach God. If such people come to you, you should teach them Wisdom (Gnana) and explain to them the Truth about God, whom it is very difficult to know. But such people will be very few.

If the hare does not eat the grass, what does it matter to the grass? It does not matter to the Guru or to God if people who wanted to study Wisdom (Gnana) to reach God, get angry with God and the Guru and go away. This is the nature of the world and the nature of its devotees.

So said His Holiness Guru Bawa to his disciple.

41.   **At 6:40 P.M. on 4/6/70**

Child! Please listen to an illustration.

Only the Spiritual Master (Guru) has the life-giving herb that can cure one's spiritual disease of birth and death, i.e., the disease of the effect of past evil actions. That herb is always fresh. It will never dry up or decay. It is indestructible. It is a life-giving herb which only the Guru knows. He will show this herb to his best disciple, i.e., the disciple who satisfies the exacting requirements of the Guru. He will uproot that herb and show him how to prepare the docoction from it, administer it to him, free him from the spiritual disease and bestow on him a life of bliss free from that spiritual disease. Because this disciple has surrendered himself completely to the Guru and is near him, the Guru will show him personally how to diagnose his disease, how and where to find that herb, how to extract its juice, how to prepare the docoction in the proper manner, how to administer it and cure himself of the disease. By unrelenting practice under the immediate supervision of the Guru, this disciple learns this, the nature and characteristics of the Truth and about Man's existence of earth.

If you try to find the immortal herb without a Guru, i.e., with your book knowledge, you may buy the herb from the shop-keeper, prepare it as directed in the book and administer it to yourself. But, without finding out from an experienced herbalist how to identify the herb and to prepare the decoction, then you cannot cure yourself of your disease. When you cannot identify the herb, if you buy what the shop-keeper gives you and treat yourself with it, you cannot get rid of your disease. You will be simply wasting your time taking that medicine. You will not gain anything. In fact, the medicine will give rise to other diseases. When you take more medicine to cure those diseases, you may get mental disorders. Thus, when you go on treating yourself for one disease after another, you will get all the four thousand four hundred and forty-eight diseases and there will be no cure for your endless disease.

In the same manner, if you try to cure yourself of your spiritual disease without the aid of a Spiritual Master (Guru), relying only on what you learned in books, your book learning will only help to develop your malady. It will prevent you from getting Liberation in this birth. It will only increase your disease resulting in thirty-five million (three and a half crores) births. You should understand this clearly. You should find the Guru who knows the precious herb and cure yourself of your spiritual disease of birth and death with his aid.

So said His Holiness Guru Bawa to a disciple of his.

42.   At 6:45 P.M. on 4/6/70

A bird which soars into the sky needs a support like a branch of a tree to rest on when tired. Otherwise it has to come down to the earth.

In the same manner, even if a spiritual aspirant flies in all the eighteen thousand worlds, unless he takes refuge under a Spiritual Master (Guru) he will not have any support to rest on when he is tired during the journey. If he does not have a Guru, then he will not have any place at all to rest. Therefore, he will never be able to proceed further to see God. If he does not have a Guru to rest on, he will have to come back to the world of Illusion (Maya) and become subject to several births.

43.   At 6:50 P.M. on 4/6/70

His Holiness Guru Bawa said:

In the modern world, people are learning various arts and crafts or other branches of learning without the personal guidance of a Spiritual Master (Guru). These are the students who wail and wander after assaulting and driving away the Spiritual Master (Guru) and losing their spiritual arm as a result. Such people assaulted and chased away Jesus, Muhamud (Sal), Gnostics and Nabis (Messengers of God). After driving these Spiritual Masters from their heart, they have only taken their words and discourses and study them like students who do not have the personal guidance of teachers (Gurus). There is, in the world at present, no Spiritual student who has learned things of the Spirit with the Guru and merged with the Guru.

44.   At 7:00 P.M. on 4/6/70

Child! Please listen to an illustration.

If the bowels are distended by gas, if there is rumbling in the bowels, or if there is a feeling of uneasiness as a result, a man will be suffering much. If there is a motion of the bowels, if the bowels are emptied, the man will become normal and happy.

We came into this world to realise God. In the same manner as the man who got rid of his discomfort by emptying his bowels, if man gets rid of the dirt of Illusion (Maya), he will realise God. Once he has realised God, there is no work for him in this world.

Child! All the men of learning cannot attain Divine Luminous Wisdom (Gnanam). If a piece of fibre falls on the sea it will not reach the shore. It will not sink. It will continue to float moving here and there till it decays.

In the same manner, if we become scholars, learned in theology and philosophy, we cannot reach the shore and leave the ocean of Illusion (Maya). We cannot attain Divine Luminous Wisdom (Gnanam). Where did Jesus study? Where did Muhamud (Sal) study? Divine Luminous Wisdom (Gnanam) can be easily taught to people who are not scholars. If the Spiritual Master (Guru) tries to teach Wisdom (Gnana) to scholars, they will try to argue with the Guru and teach him what they have learned in theology and philosophy. When that occasion arises, you will not know who the Spiritual Master (Guru) is. It will not be possible to know who the disciple is. If a rat snake catches a mouse, it will not be able to eat it as it is poisonous to the snake. Neither can it let go the mouse as the mouse will injure its eyes. It will be in a fix, not knowing what to do. Such will be the fate of the Spiritual Master (Guru) if he selects a scholar as his disciple. There is danger to the Guru if he teaches Wisdom (Gnana) to him. There is also danger to the Guru if he rejects him and sends him away. As a result there will be danger to the Truth, his life and to his Divine Luminous Wisdom (Perr-Arivu). As a result of this choice the Guru may meet with spiritual loss. You should understand the nature of the two types of people. One type is a person who is potentially capable of developing a very high standard of conduct, character, Divine Wisdom (Pahuth-Arivu), and finding out the Truth. He will not be a person who has become a scholar or a book worm. He will learn a lot from the experience he undergoes in the world.

If you discover such a person and teach the Truth to him, you can escape. He can also escape from the clutches of Illusion (Maya) and the cycle of births. But, you cannot bring to the shore the second type of person whose mind floats like a fibre in the sea of Maya. You cannot give Liberation to him. You should understand this well.

So said His Holiness Guru Bawa to a disciple of his.

45.   **At 7:15 P.M. on 4/6/70**

Child! Please listen to an illustration.

To train a dog, you should throw a single ball in a particular direction. The dog will pick up that ball and bring it to you. You should get that ball and throw it in different directions. The dog will go in search of the ball and bring it back to you. But, if you throw several balls in many directions, the dog will be confused. It will not be sure which ball it should pick up. Its mind will be wavering. So it will not learn anything and it cannot be trained.

In the same manner, only if a man comes with an open mind, without fixed book learning, is it possible to teach Divine Wisdom (Gnanam) to him. If he comes after learning eruditely all sorts of things about religion, it is not possible to teach him Wisdom (Gnana). He will try to find fault with the Spiritual Master (Guru). He will have doubts. His mind will not be steady. It will be wavering. His degraded state of Wisdom (Ariveenam) will manifest itself. He will not have Faith. Where there is no Faith the Divine Wisdom of the Guru will not develop. If Divine Wisdom does not develop, it will not be possible to understand Truth which is Fullness itself. Only if he throws away from his mind all that he has learned and comes to the Spiritual Master (Guru) with an open receptive mind free from any prejudice, can he attain Divine Luminous Wisdom (Gnanam). If he does not do so, he will never attain Liberation of his Soul (Atma), even if he takes one hundred thousand births. He will not be able to know That which is Divine Luminous Wisdom (Perr-Arivu) within Divine Luminous Wisdom (Perr-Arivu).

So said His Holiness Guru Bawa to a disciple of his.

46.   **At 7:35 P.M. on 4/6/70**

Child! Please listen to an illustration.

A hunter went out to hunt hares. He sent his hunting dog to chase the hares out of their hiding places in the bushes. The hare, on getting the smell of the dog, will jump out of the bush in fear, run and leap in all directions deceiving the dog. The hunter who wants to kill the hare for his food will chase the hare. His dog also will run after the hare. But the hare will run in circles and deceive them and finally come back to a bush which adjoins the bush it was in originally, and hide in it. Since the hare had run in all directions several times and the dog also had run all over following the scent of the hare, the dog will get confused and will not come back to the original place from which it chased the hare. The hunter who went after the hare following his dog will also get confused. He will continue to examine the confusing footsteps of the hare. The hare will hide in the bush, feeling that it has escaped.

Like the hare, man also should escape from Illusion (Maya). During the Pre-creation period, Man originated from God. Then he was born on earth. After his birth in the world, the dog and the hunter of worldly desires, and Egoism, bad actions and Illusion, chase him to bring him under their full control and consume him. Like the hare, man should evade them and hide within the Resplendence of Divine Luminous Wisdom which is by the side of God. Only then can he escape from Illusion (Maya).

So says the Spiritual Master (Gnana Guru), who imparts Divine Wisdom to his disciple.

47.   **At 9:35 P.M. on 4/6/70**

Child! Please listen to an illustration.

If a mosquito bites a person, he slaps himself with his hand and kills the mosquito.

Like the mosquito, the five elements out of which man's body is made, and the five senses, suck the blood of Truth from man's life. They are in his physical body. If he wants to eradicate completely the influence of those five elements, he should slap the pleasures of the body arising from desires caused by his degraded state of Wisdom (Ariveenam), with the hand of Wisdom (Arivu) and kill the physical pleasures of the body, just as the mosquito is killed by slapping one's own body. If he kills the physical pleasures of his body, the senses which suck the blood of the Truth in man's life, like the mosquito, will die.

When the man in the process of killing the mosquito sucking his blood slaps his own body, he causes pain to his body. In the same manner, when he assaults the senses with his hand of Wisdom (Arivu) he will in this world undergo sufferings caused by his mind, attachments of friendship and blood ties and the world. He should not pay attention to these sufferings and pains. He should kill the elements and the senses which suck his blood of Truth. If he does so, those sections of his make-up, physical and mental, which smother the emergence of Truth will become powerless. The man who slaps his body to kill the mosquito does not pay attention to the pain caused in the body by the slap.

The senses, the mosquito, sit on the body of craving and try to suck the Soul (Atma) and the Truth. When you slap the body of craving to kill the senses, i.e., the mosquito, it will naturally cause pain to the mind, the source of craving. Just as the attention of the man was on the mosquito, your full attention should be on your senses and craving so that you may completely remove craving due to the influence of the senses from your mind. Your Awareness and Divine Wisdom should always be on the alert to remove craving and the influence of the senses from your mind. If you are in that alert state, you will be free from physical pleasure or pain, mental pleasure or pain.

So said his Holiness Guru Bawa to his disciple.

48.   **At 7:35 P.M. on 4/7/70**

Child! Please listen to an illustration.

There lived a barber who used to go to the palace and shave the face of the King and dress his hair. He was also serving all important people. It was the custom to serve the people according to a programme. Whenever he had to go to the palace to serve the King, he had to obtain permission from the Commander of the troops and the Minister. Because he had to obtain permission from the officials, he got annoyed. As a result of disputes the relation between both parties became more and more strained.

One day the barber was dressing the head of an important official. Then he suddenly remembered that it was the appointed day for him to shave the face of the King. So, he served the official in a hurry and ran to the palace. In the meantime the King was anxiously waiting for the barber as it was already late and he had to go to the Audience Hall. While waiting for the barber, the King fell asleep again. When the barber came to the palace, he found the King sleeping. While the King was sleeping, the barber did his job without waking him up. Then the King woke up and found the barber standing before him. He scolded the barber and said, "Why are you so late? It is time for me to go to the Audience Hall." The barber replied, "May it please your Majesty! I had come earlier, finished my job and was waiting to see you and get your permission to go away." He held the mirror in front of the King. The King found that the barber had dressed his hair beautifully.

The King was highly pleased. He told the barber, "You are clever. You have done your job fast. What shall I do for you?" The barber replied "I require only your love, your Majesty! I should be able to have free access to come to your Majesty in the palace. I beg you to instruct the Minister, the Commander of the troops, and the Chief Executive Officer to allow me to come into the palace freely without any obstruction on their part."

The King gave a gold coin to the barber. He called the Minister and commanded him in the presence of the barber that he should instruct all to allow the barber free access to the palace. As a result of this order, the ego of the barber increased. Whenever he came to the palace, he started jesting to the Minister and others, "You used to stop me and ask me to stay here; stay there. What is your power now?" He would wink at the Minister, Commander of the troops and the Chief Executive Officer of the King, and shake his head at them in defiance of them. He thought to himself that, if he wanted, he could have the ministers dismissed, using his influence with the King. The Minister, the Commander and the Chief Executive Officer became angry because of the King's order and the impudent behaviour of the barber.

One day, the Minister asked the barber, "Why do you jest at us and show disrespect to us whenever you go to the palace?" The barber replied, "You must know what I can do. If I so desire I can get you dismissed in a minute." This reply led to a quarrel between them. The barber told the Minister "Beware! I will take action against you". The King and the barber had become very friendly. One day when the barber was cutting the King's hair, the King asked him, "How are the people? What are they saying?" The barber replied, "People state that the King is good and the Country is good. But they do not pay enough respect to the King because they have plenty of gold and silver in their houses. If all the gold and silver in the country is brought to the King's Bank, it will reduce their pride which is due to their wealth. Then they will respect the King." The barber told this to the King with a motive. He had an axe to grind. He wanted to humble the Minister, Commander and other officials, as their pride was due to their wealth. The King called the Minister and ordered him to search the houses of all the people in the country and confiscate all gold, silver, diamonds and other gems and bring them to the Royal Treasury and keep them there. So, the Minister and the officials searched every house and took charge of all the gold, silver, diamonds and other gems and brought them to the Royal Treasury. In the course of their duty they searched the house of the barber. The barber asked them, "Do you know who I am?" They replied, "We do not care who you are. We are carrying out the King's command." They searched his house and took away gold and silver including the gold coin the King had given him as a present.

Because of this the barber became very angry with the Minister and the officials. So, he planned to have them banished from the Kingdom. One day the King asked the barber when he was dressing his hair, "What is happening in the country? What is the general talk of the people?" The barber replied, "The people pay due respect to your Majesty. They talk well of you. By the way, I humbly bring to your notice that the Minister and the officials had taken from my house even the gold coin you gave me as a present. I told them that it was a royal present and that due respect should be given to it. They replied that they were carrying out the King's command and that I can report to the King. I am only sorry that these Ministers did not respect the King. All others honour and respect your Majesty." The King replied, "King's laws are applicable to all his subjects impartially. You cannot be treated in one way and others in another way."

The barber felt disappointed at the King's reply. He was determined to see that the Ministers and other officials were dismissed by the King. Next time, when he came to cut the King's hair, the King asked him about the opinion of the people regarding affairs of the State. The barber replied that the people were talking thus; "The King is impartial and just. But the Minister, Commanders and the Chief Executive Officers in the King's establishment are drawing money from the Treasury and are enjoying more comforts than the King himself. We are here to help the King. Why is the King keeping all these ministers and other officials paying them high salaries? If their salary is reduced, their ego will disappear. They will administer the King's laws impartially. There will be more money in the Treasury. If the King does not reduce their salary, they will ruin the country." He added that they are praising the King and that they do not have a good opinion about the Ministers and the officials.

The King said, "Is that so? What shall we do about it?" The barber replied, "May it please your Majesty! I have an idea. If we are to get the good opinion of the people, we should discontinue all these people. This will result in saving as their salary bill will disappear. The Treasury will be full of money. The people will talk well of the wise action of the King." The King said, "What you say is correct. But, to defend the country and the King, the services of the Ministers and the Commander and his troops are essential. Is that not so?" The barber replied, "Your Majesty! The citizens are capable of defending the country and the King. They can drive away any enemies. But, to protect the palace five hundred sturdy dogs are necessary. They will not allow even a crow to come into the palace. A cook will be needed to prepare food for the dogs. The only expenditure will be for rice and half a hundredweight of dried fish per meneem. The salary paid to the Minister for a month will be enough to feed the five hundred dogs for a year. The people of the country are patriotic. They will protect the King. What is the necessity for the Minister and other officials?" The King asked, "How can we defend the country if it is invaded by enemies?" The barber replied, "The people will defend the King and the country with patriotism. The five hundred dogs will not allow any enemy to come into the fort. Therefore, there is no need for them."

The King dismissed the Ministers, the Officials, the Commander of the troops and others. He ordered the barber to bring five hundred sturdy dogs. The barber brought to the palace five hundred sturdy dogs and a cook to feed them. Only the King and the dogs were in the palace. The barber served as itinerant Minister to the King. No one else was in the palace. At night the cook would unchain the dogs and allow them to move freely. Night and day the King could hear only the barking of the dogs. He could not have peace of mind. Day and night the dogs were fighting with one another. This ceaseless noise affected the King's ears and mind. He was annoyed that he had to suffer from this nuisance as a result of listening to the words of the barber.

In the meantime the Ministers, General and the Commander-in-Chief of the troops, who had been dismissed by the King, went over to the enemy King and sought office under him. They related to him all that happened. They told him, "Only the barber is serving as the King's minister. There are five hundred dogs in the palace. The people of the country have met with loss. They are undergoing suffering and are worried in their minds. We have come to you to request you to remove our grievance and the grievance of the people of our country."

The enemy King replied, "Is that so? For a long time I had an intention of seizing your country. I will mobilise my troops and invade your country now to help your people." The Minister who went to him for help said, "There is no need for an army. Two gunny-bags of dried fish are enough. Your Majesty can go with me and the Commander of the troops. You can go in a palanquin at night and capture the country." The enemy King asked why dried fish was necessary. The Minister replied, "In the palace there are only dogs. If we roast the dried fish and throw them before the dogs, they will take them in their mouths and run away. You can easily enter the palace, capture the King and seize the Kingdom."

According to the advice, the enemy King went to that country with the Commander of his troops, the Minister who had been dismissed and the Commander who had been dismissed. When they reached the gate of the palace, the dogs barked at them. They threw roasted dried fish in all directions. The dogs picked them up and went away from the gate. The enemy King and others broke open the door of the fort and the palace, entered the palace and captured the King. The two commanders told the King. "O King! What are you going to do now? Come to the prison." They took him before the victorious King. On the mast they sent up the flag of the victorious King and blew the conch to announce the victory. The King asked the captive King what he wanted to do. The captive King replied, "I am prepared to do what you wish. I have been brought to this disgraceful state because I listened to the advice of the barber whom I employed as a minister. I request your permission to talk for a few minutes with my barber-minister." The enemy King said, "I grant you permission." He ordered the commanders to take him to the barber-minister and said, "After he talks with the barber, he should be brought back and locked up in the prison." Saying this, the victorious King remained in the palace. The commanders led away the captive King.

In the meantime, the barber was dressing the hair of several people gathered in a place. Some of them asked the barber, "We heard some big noise from the palace. We understand that the enemy King has seized this Kingdom. You are the King's minister. What happened?" The barber replied, "What does it matter to us whether Ravana is the King or Rama is the King? If a man's wife leaves her husband and marries another, the Lebbe (priest) gets five Fanams of money as his fee. As long as I have the shaving knife with me, I earn twenty-five cents for every head I shave. Whatever happens, what do we care? What does it matter to us if the enemy King has seized this Kingdom?"

The commanders came there leading the captive King. They heard the words of the barber. The captured King told the barber, "By listening to your advice I have lost my country and come to this state. You remained as my only minister. Please advise me how I can get out of this situation." The barber replied, "Maharajah! I knew then that this would happen. As long as a person remains as a King, he undergoes sufferings. It is a fact that one King captures another King. If a person lives like me, he will not meet with any sorrow. If I shave a head, I get twenty-five cents. I do not fight or quarrel with anyone. I serve one thousand families. I will give you five hundred of them to serve. I will serve the other five hundred.

The captive King replied, "You have reduced me to the state of a barber. Today I have learned both aspects of the question of life." The minister who was there told the King, "O King who listened to the advice of the barber! Prison is the most suitable place for you for listening to the words of the barber." They took the captive King back to the victorious King and related everything to him. The victorious King told the captive

King. "O King! Who chased away the friends who protected your life and the country and instead kept dogs to guard the palace after listening to the advice of the barber, you cannot administer this country, as you did not know the nature of the barber, as you have no Wisdom and sense of royal justice and as you cannot understand what is good and what is evil. You are in the darkness of a state of degraded Wisdom (Ariveenam). The best place for you to live and die is the semi-dark prison." Then he sent the captive King to the prison.

Comment: Man is the rarest and noblest of God's creations. He has the highest degree of Wisdom (Arivu) among all created beings. He was born in this world to know who he is, lose his sense of individuality and see the greatness of his Lord, God. But there are many types of men. Many are like the King who listened to the advice of the barber. They are guided by the degraded state of their spiritual Wisdom. They wear the symbols of title, status, religion, tribe, etc., like ornaments. Their mind is also warped by these symbols. Their intelligence in its degraded state is blurred by the baneful influence of these symbols. The senses, in their state of torpor or in their active state when they frolic like the monkey, are influenced by these symbols. The hypnotic projections of Illusion (Maya) in their play show that they are influenced by these symbols. Like the barber who gave wrong advice to the King, these people advise men to follow the narrow path of their religions and creeds to reach the Unique One. They make men lose their Divine Characteristics and drive away Divine Wisdom (Pahuth-Arivu) from their Heart. They get them to drive away the Divine Qualities of Patience, Compassion, Liberality, Mercy, Merit, Justice, Truth, Peace, the Conviction that all mankind belong to the same family and that there is only one God for all. They also make them drive away the seven faculties of Divine Wisdom, viz.,

1. Unarvu — Perception
2. Unarchi — Awareness
3. Puththi — Intellect
4. Madthi — Practical Understanding; Knowledge
5. Arivu — Wisdom
6. Pahuth-Arivu — Divine Wisdom
7. Perr-Arivu — Divine Luminous Wisdom

All these Divine Qualities guard the Soul (Atma), within the cage of the physical body. Like the King who listened to the advice of the barber and chased away the minister, the commander of the troops, etc., from the palace and kept dogs to guard the palace, these people drive away all these Divine Qualities from within their 'Self' and keep the evil qualities of religious fanaticism, egoism, love for titles and status, and the divisive forces of race, religion and creed to protect the Soul (Atma), within the cage of the physical body. As a result of listening to such evil people, we lose the priceless heritage of human existence and the state of Liberation which we should achieve, like the King who lost his Kingdom and spent his days in prison till death, as a result of listening to the words of the barber. As a result, we succumb to hunger, disease, senility and death and become subject to several births. By listening to these people, who are full of religious fanaticism, egoism and vanity, and who have obtained titles and status, we come to this state of degradation like the King who listened to the words of the barber and lost his Kingdom and was finally offered by the barber himself the right to shave the heads of five hundred families. By listening to these people, Man, who is the rarest and noblest of God's creation, who was born in this world to reach God whom it is very difficult to know, becomes subject to thirty-five million (three and a half crores) births. One should know this. He should realise who he is and lose his 'Self' and know his Lord and merge within Him. That is the summum bonum of human existence.

You should understand this well. You should know the greatness of Wisdom (Arivu), and with Wisdom examine the nature of That Plenitude and understand the Truth in That Plenitude. You should discover Him who shines in the Truth and listen to the Resonant Voice coming from Him. You should understand the Effulgence radiating in that Voice. You should shine and activate your voice within that understanding of that Effulgence. If you reach that state, you will have achieved the highest state in your life.

So said His Holiness Guru Bawa to a disciple of his.

49. At 5:30 P.M. on 4/8/70

Child! Please listen to an illustration.

The Cobra has poison in its mouth. It hisses with anger. If it was not for these qualities, men would like to wear the Cobra round their necks, like garlands, because of its beauty and scent. Because of its poison, people are afraid to wear it round their necks.

Gypsies play on the pipe tunes called in Tamil, 'Naga Virari', to calm the hissing Cobra, bring it under the hypnotic influence of the music played by them on the pipe, make it dance and then lie down in submission in a state of hypnotic torpor. When it is in that state, he seizes it, removes its poisonous fangs and puts it in his basket. Later he trains that Cobra to dance to the music he produces on the pipe.

Comment: This physical body of ours is like an ant-hill full of holes where poisonous snakes live. The poisonous snakes of Earth, Fire, Water, Air, and Ether, the five elements, live in this body. They lay eggs and hatch innumerable young poisonous snakes. A large number of human beings in this world are in a state of torpor caused by the poisons of these snakes living within their physical body. These poisonous snakes feed on Egoism (Anawam), Evil Actions (Karma), and Illusion (Maya).

When the potential Man-God (Manu-Eesan) or Perfect Man (Insan Kamil) sees the poisonous characteristics of the five senses and their poisonous progeny within the physical body, he exclaims in fear, "O God! Wherever I look, I see snakes. Everywhere I see poison. Wherever I stay, I see evil. Wherever I lie down, I see demons. Wherever the mind wanders, I see deities who demand sacrifice of living beings. These snakes, the senses and their progeny, suck the blood from the body, melt the marrow in the bones, and make the nerves tired. They destroy good character. They destroy the faculties of Perception, Awareness and Intellect, and hide Wisdom (Arivu). They drive away Patience, Compassion and God from the mind. They torture Truth. They remove the good qualities of Modesty, Reservedness, Fear (to do wrong) and Culture from man. They spread their poison all over the body of man and the seed of life. They remove everything Divine from the mind of man. My God! My Lord! My Father!

111

What mystery is this? Save me! Save me!" These rare men run away from the influence of the senses, seeking refuge in God. The Perfect Man (Insan Kamil) or God-Man (Manu-Eesan) among them will adopt Divine Characteristics, play the pipe of Divine Grace and bring under the hypnotic influence of the Divine Music these evil characteristics of the senses, the poisonous snakes, catch them with the hand of Wisdom (Arivu) remove their poisonous fangs, put them in the basket of Divine Wisdom (Pahuth-Arivu), control them and with the power of Divine Luminous Wisdom (Perr-Arivu) make them dance according to the tune played by Divine Luminous Wisdom and again keep them under control within the basket of Divine Wisdom, and live in glory without fear in the three worlds.

In the same manner, if you seize the numberless poisonous snakes which live within the physical body, which is like the ant-hill with holes where snakes live, and remove the poisonous fangs of these snakes, the senses and their progeny, you can live with these snakes as their bite will not do any harm to you as they have been deprived of their poison. If you have done this, it does not matter where you live, whether as a recluse or whether you move freely in the world. You should reflect on this.

But, people whose Gnostic Eye is blind do not know the holes in which these poisonous snakes live. So they sit on the top of these holes, get bitten by these poisonous snakes, the senses and their progeny. The poison affects their body and rises up to the head. They wail, "It is Fate! It is Fate!" and run about in search of a snake-bite specialist, i.e., one who can cure them from the disease they call Fate. It is not possible to cure the mental aberration of these people. If you see such people, please avoid their company. Otherwise, these lunatics will also make you a lunatic. You should understand this well.

So said the Spiritual Master (Guru).

50.   **At 6:40 P.M. on 4/8/70**

Child! Please listen to an illustration.

There lived a mother and her son who was dull-witted. She brought him up and taught him Wisdom. But he was unable to understand anything. Up to the age of eighteen he was taught by various methods by the mother. But he did not gain any Wisdom. The mother tried her best to make him a man. But his faculty of sense-perception, awareness and intellect did not develop.

So, the mother thought that he may improve his Wisdom and intellect if he was sent out into the country to do business. So, she gave him some articles and sent him to the market to sell them. On the way some one asked him what he was carrying and requested him to give them to him. He gave them to him and returned home without getting money. Every day he did the same thing. He gave the articles to whomsoever asked for them and returned home without getting money. As a result they lost all their wealth. Only their bull remained.

The mother told him one day "We have now only the bull. Take it and sell it for one hundred rupees and bring the money." He wanted her to pre-pare and give him a parcel of boiled rice to eat on the way. She gave him the food parcel and sent him out with the bull. He went into the forest to sell the bull. It was twelve o'clock. Since it was noon, he became hungry. He saw a stream. He tied the bull to a tree. He sat down under the tree and ate the boiled rice in the parcel.

Then, when he looked up, he saw a Chameleon on the branch of the tree which was in front of the bull. It was moving its head. He asked the Chameleon, "O Brother Chameleon! Do you want the bull?" The Chameleon moved its head once. He said, "I have brought the bull to sell it." The Chameleon moved its head. He said, "Will you buy it?" The Chameleon moved its head again. He continued, "Are you asking for the price?" The Chameleon moved its head. He said, "The price is one hundred rupees." The Chameleon moved its head again. He asked, "Do you want me to leave the bull here?" The Chameleon moved its head. He asked, "Will you pay the amount?" The Chameleon moved its head. He asked, "Are you saying that you will give me the money tomorrow?" The Chameleon nodded its head. He asked, "Will you definitely give me the money tomorrow?" The Chameleon nodded. He said, "Well, brother! Shall I take your leave now? I will return tomorrow for the money." The Chameleon nodded its head. He left the bull tied up there and returned home.

When he came home, the mother asked him whether he brought the money after selling the bull. He replied, "I have sold the bull to Brother Chameleon. He promised to give the money tomorrow. I have come back home. Tomorrow give me a parcel of food. I will go and get the money and return." The mother asked, "How can the Chameleon give you money?" He replied, "He is a very good person. He asked me to come tomorrow for the money. He will give it." She said, "Anyhow, definitely bring the money tomorrow!" He agreed.

Next day, she sent him with a parcel of food. He went to the spot. The bull was not to be found. He saw the Chameleon basking in the sun. He asked it, "Brother Chameleon! Will you give me the money?" The Chameleon nodded its head. He asked, "Will you give me the money now?" It nodded. He asked, "Will you not give the money now?" It nodded. He asked, "You have taken the bull. But you are refusing to pay me the money. Is that so?" The Chameleon nodded. He said, "Let me see whether you will give me the one hundred rupees or not!" He took a stick and chased the Chameleon saying "See what I will do to you!" The Chameleon moved here and there and finally entered a hole. He said, "You have taken the bull. But you are refusing to pay the money. I will teach you a lesson". He started digging and enlarging the hole. Inside the large hole he saw seven cauldrons full of gold coins. The Chameleon also was there blinking. He told the Chameleon, "Brother Chameleon! You have so much money. Still you refused to give me the one hundred rupees due to me. Please give me the money now." The Chameleon nodded its head. He asked, "Do you want me to take the money?" The Chameleon nodded again. He took out one hundred rupees in gold coins and said "Shall I take them away?" The Chameleon nodded. So he went home with the money.

His mother asked him whether or not he brought the money. He replied that Brother Chameleon had given the money to him and related to her what happened. His mother thought there was a treasure-trove there. So, that night she went with him to that place and brought home all seven cauldrons full of gold coins. She knew his nature. She knew that the next morning he would tell everyone about the treasure they brought home.

113

This will reach the ears of the King. She knew the King would investigate and take away the treasure. So, she wanted to play a trick on him to deceive him and thereby deceive the people and the King. When he was sleeping that night, she prepared short-eats and threw them all over the courtyard. They she woke him up and said "It is raining short-eats. Come! See! He saw the short-eats everywhere on the courtyard, and was busy picking them up and eating them. When he was doing so, she threw further short-eats on him without his knowledge. He believed that it was actually raining short-eats. He ate up all the short-eats and slept again.

Next morning he woke up. He told everyone that they had brought seven cauldrons of gold coins. They asked him "When?" He replied, "Don't you know? It was on the night it was raining short-eats." People informed the King. The King went there with the captains of his army to investigate. They asked him when they brought the treasure. He replied that it was on the night when it was raining short-eats. When his mother heard this, she told the King, "He is a dull-witted fool. Did you ever see it rain short-eats?" The King and his people believed her and went away.

Comment: Men are the rarest and noblest among God's creations. But many among them study the mythology and epics and the works of Gnostics and devotees, and sing them with devotion thinking that they can merge with God by doing these things. The state of their Wisdom (Arivu) is like that of the dull-witted person who sold his bull to the Chameleon. They think that since the authors of these works have merged with God, they can also do so by singing these hymns and songs and shedding tears. These people have sold their treasure, Wisdom (Arivu) to Illusion (Maya), the Chameleon, and bought the article, False Wisdom (Agnana), to their home, their heart, and filled up the heart with it. They have got into a state of exhilaration by their devotion to the senses, the elements and the joys of the body. By attaining a state of exhilaration in the body, by singing these songs and hymns with melody that pleases the ears, they feel they have merged with the Ultimate Unique One. So, they wear ochre clothes, apply holy ash in triple lines on the forehead, put a chain of 'Uruthirakka' beads round their necks and hold in their hands a stick, a water vessel and prayer beads. They grow long nails. They grow long beards and hair which they tie up in locks on the head. They conjure up forms in their mind, adopt the characteristics of these mental forms they like, and proclaim to the world that they have merged with the Ultimate Unique One. But God has no form. If you ask them when they merged with God, they will reply that they merged with God at midnight when the five elements merged and took a form. Their answer is like the reply given by the dull-witted fellow that the treasure-trove was brought on the night it rained short-eats.

He showed the bull to the Chameleon, asked for money, and gave date for payment of the price of the bull. The next day he sat in judgment over the Chameleon and took the amount due to him himself from the treasure-trove in the hole where it was hiding when he chased the Chameleon. In the same manner, these people talk on their own, assess their worth themselves, declare themselves to be 'swamis' or 'holy men' and that they have gotten 'true divine wisdom' themselves. They take a particular form conjured up by themselves in their mind; they make the 'god', keep it, perform ceremonies before it, talk to it and deliver their judgment on themselves, as if it was given by 'god'. We can only pity them for their so-called honour, achievements and liberation.

If a Man-God (Manu-Eesan), whom it is very difficult to find, analyses their antics with Divine Wisdom (Pahuth-Arivu), he will find that all their so-called piety and wisdom are of no use. Child! If these people surrender their knowledge of their senses, elements, and the hypnotic attraction of Illusion (Maya) to an authentic Master of Real Divine Luminous Wisdom (Meignana Guru) he will tie them in a parcel and throw them into the sea of Illusion (Maya), and give them the never-ending wealth of Wisdom (Arivu). They can receive that wealth that never diminishes, wealth that is useful in both the worlds. They can obtain Liberation of the Soul (Atma) and live in both worlds.

So said the Guru to a disciple of his.

51.   **At 7:15 P.M. on 4/8/70**

The Spiritual Master of Divine Luminous Wisdom (Authentic Meignana Guru) gives an illustration to a disciple.

There lived a widow with her only son whose intelligence was sub-standard. The mother wanted in some way to teach him Wisdom. Her son was a fool of the first degree. She had plenty of money. She asked her son to go out and learn. He wanted her to give him a small bag full of money to enable him to go out and learn. She gave him a small bag of money as she wanted him to learn. He took away the money with him.

On the way an owl which was hiding in a hole in a tree peeped out and blinked when it saw him. When he saw this, he placed the bag of money at the foot of the tree and started singing;

> "O Brother! He is blinking
> Like an owl in the hole;
> O my girl! The king is able
> To sing a song."

Having sung the song, he addressed the owl and said, "Oh Brother! I am offering you this gift." He left the bag of money at the foot of the tree and returned home. The mother asked him whether he studied. He replied, "Yes. Tomorrow also give me a small bag of money."

Next day, the mother sent him with a bag of gold. On his way, he saw a mouse digging a hole in the pond of a paddy field. When he saw this, he started singing:

> "O my girl! He is digging a hole
> Like the mouse in the field;
> O my girl! The King is able
> To compose two songs."

He sang thus and left the bag of money in the field and returned home.

Next day he also asked his mother to give money to him. She gave him a bag of money. He went out with the money. He saw a palmyrah tree standing erect in the middle of the path. Immediately he started singing:

> "O my girl! He is standing erect
> Like a tall tree
> O my girl! The King is able
> To compose three songs."

He sang thus and left the bag of money at the palmyrah tree and returned home. The mother asked him whether he studied. He said, "Yes.

You should also give me a bag of money tomorrow."

Next day, the mother sent him with a bag of money. There was a channel with flowing water running across his path. A man came there and leaped across the channel. Immediately he started singing:

"He is leaping like a fawn:
The King has composed four songs."

He called him back and said, "My master! Take this money." He gave the money to him and returned home.

Next day also he went out with a bag of money. On the way he saw a woman running with a pot of boiled rice water for her husband as it was already late. He ran and stopped in front of her and started singing:

"O Girl! He is running
With a pot of rice;
O Girl! The King has
Composed five songs."

Then he told her, "My teacher! Please accept my offering", and gave her the bag of money and returned home.

In the meantime, a gang of thieves came to know that there was plenty of money in his house. So they came to his house late in the night. The mother saw them. She thought that if she raised cries, they would kill them. So, she quietly awakened her son and said, "Son! You went out to study all these days. What did you learn? Please tell me." One of the thieves heard this and looked at them blinking. At that time the son started singing pointing out his hand towards the direction where the thief was staying:

"O Brother! He is blinking
Like an owl in the hole;
O my girl! The King is able
To sing a song."

That thief scratched the back of the other thief who was quietly making an opening in the wall and whispered to him that he had seen them. At that moment the son started singing:

"O my girl! He is digging a hole
Like the mouse in the field;
O my girl! The king is able
To compose two songs."

The two thieves were surprised. They thought he had seen them both. So, they quietly got up and stood like tall trees. At that moment, the son started singing:

"O my girl! He is standing erect
Like a tall tree
O my girl! The King is able
To compose three songs."

When the thieves heard this, one said to the other, "They have seen us. Let us go. We should not stay here," and leaped out. As they leaped out, he started singing:

"He is leaping like a fawn;
The King has composed four songs."

When the thieves heard this they started running. As they did so he started singing:

"O Girl! He is running

With a pot of rice
O Girl! The King has
Composed five songs."

The thieves ran away in fear.

Comment: The education people receive in this world, the hymns they sing in a state of fervour, the special characteristics of their devotion to God, the methods they adopt to achieve Liberation of their Soul, the state they consider to be the actual state of merging with God, are analogous to the story given above. They learn the verse in the scriptures on Veda, Vedanta and Siththantha philosophies and the various methods of worship of the diverse religions from Masters (Gurus) who are devoted to the world. They don various types of robes and symbols and shine in this world merged in the six types of evil actions: Craving, Hatred, Miserliness, Vanity, Lust and Envy.

Like that man of sub-intelligence, who sang cute songs and saved his wealth, these people also, in their state of hypnotic torpor caused by the darkness of Ignorance (Agnana), sing cute songs to save their stomach from hunger. These people run and search, sing and dance or cringe for feeding their stomach. If their stomach withers with the hunger, all their peity and devotion to God will wither away. The spiritual state of these people who claim that they have achieved Liberation of their Soul is such that they will forget everything, even God, if they feel the pangs of hunger. The son referred to in the story gave his wealth and learned to sing songs and with these songs saved his wealth. In the same manner, these people save their stomach from hunger by dispensing craving and desire and earning material rewards. This is their aim. This is their achievement. This is their Liberation. You should know this well. Remember these aphorisms:

(1) For penance only one
   i.e., A person who does penance to merge with God should give up dualism and go as one — that he is one with God.
(2) For joy two
   i.e., For getting sexual joy which is considered to be the highest joy by the secular world, two are needed.
(3) For the corpse four
   i.e., Four people are needed to carry the corpse for burial.

You should understand the implications of these sayings. You should not remain as many. You should remain as one — that you are inseparable from God. If you attain that sublime state, it will become the effective remedy for the maladies of Hunger, Disease, Senility and Death. If you have reached that supreme sublime state, you would have achieved in this birth wealth that will never diminish.

So said the Master to a disciple of his.

52.   **At 8:10 P.M. on 4/9/70**

The Master (Guru) gives an illustration to his disciple:

There lived a wild cat. It used to leap up the trees and catch birds and eat them. One day a hunter saw that a large number of pigeons lived in a tree. So, he spread nets over the branches of the tree to catch them. When the pigeons came back to the tree as usual, many got caught in the nets.

The next morning when the wild cat went out in search of food, it saw the pigeons caught in the net. It climbed up the tree, ate as many birds as possible and took away the balance of the birds caught in the net to its lair. When the hunter came, he saw some feathers in the net. He thought that the pigeons must have gotten caught in the net, but some animal must have carried them away. So, he adjusted the nets and went away. Some pigeons got caught in the net that evening. The next morning the wild cat came there and ate all the pigeons caught in the net. For three days consecutively this happened. The hunter wondered, "How strange this is! Every day something is eating the pigeons. It must be the wild cat." So, he adjusted the nets in such a way that the cat would get caught in the nets when it moved on the nets to eat the pigeons.

The next day when the cat saw the pigeons caught in the net, it wagged its tail and leaped on the nets and got caught in the net. The net rolled up when he struggled to get out. A mouse, which was living in a hole in that tree, watched all this. When the cat saw the mouse, it prayed to it and implored it saying, "You are my god! You are my father! You are the saviour of my life! You are my friend! Save my life! I will always treat you as my god and pray to you." The mouse replied, "You are god to our god. You are our enemy. You are the god who kills us and sends us to the land of the god of death. Wait for some time. Let us watch the developments!" The cat replied, "We will not kill you. Our tribe will worship you in future. We will love you. Save me." The mouse replied, "O our master! It is our duty to run away whenever we see you. Be patient for a while. We are small people. You are great people. We should be very careful and wait for the opportune moment to help the great people. If we help them at the wrong moment, we are liable to lose our lives." The cat again implored, "The hunter will be coming soon. He will kill me! So, save me!"

The mouse thought, "Even if he is my enemy, it is my duty to save him. Even if he is in danger and I save him when his attention is on me, he will kill me and eat me the moment I save him. When he is actually in danger of his life and when his attention is drawn to someone else, then if I save him, he will run away to save his life. Then I can also escape from him." The cat vowed several times that he would do no harm to the mouse and begged it to save him. But the mouse kept quiet without moving to help the cat.

Then the hunter appeared with bow, arrows, trident and sword. He saw the pigeons and the wild cat caught in the net. He exclaimed, "O cat! You have got caught. See! I will kill you!" He started climbing up the tree. The cat became agitated with fear. He found it difficult even to breathe owing to extreme fear. He looked intently at the hunter who was climbing up the tree. The mouse thought this was the most opportune moment. It quietly went up the net and quickly cut up the folds of the net within which the cat was caught, and ran away and hid in its hole. The cat made use of the opportunity to leap out of the net. It ran for its life. The hunter was sad because the wild cat had escaped. He took the pigeons caught in the net, adjusted the nets again and went away. The mouse remained in the hole in the tree.

The wild cat was hungry for two days, as it was caught in the net on the previous day. That day also it was unable to catch any food. So it thought, "The mouse which saved my life is living in that hole in the tree. If I catch him and eat him, it will be enough for this day." So, it went up that tree up to the hole. From there it called the mouse, "My god who saved my life! Where can I see a god like you in this birth? I have come to worship you and keep you in my heart. Please come out a little." The mouse replied from within the safety of the hole, "I am thankful to you for your love and adoration. You are our eternal enemies. There has never been any connection between you and us. We never transacted any business with you. You live on branches. We live in holes. We are not of equal status to stay in the same place and express love to each other." The cat replied, "God who saved my life! Is it not my duty to kiss you at least once and go away? Please come out so that I may worship you and express my gratitude." The mouse replied, "It is our duty to help one when he is in danger of losing his life. You are great people. I am small. It is not proper for me to come and sit near you and talk to you. If you keep your love for me in your heart, it is enough." The cat became angry and said, "You, little mouse! I was starving yesterday. Today also I could not catch any animal or bird for my food. So, I came to catch you and eat you. But, you are wise. Wait and see what I will do in the future!" The cat went away from that hole.

Comment: There are people who are in a degraded state of Wisdom (Ariveenam). They are religious fanatics. They are enemies of Truth and Divine Wisdom. If you wish to be of any help to them, you should do it at the proper time in an indirect way and escape from them like the mouse in the illustration above. If you help him at the wrong moment, he will try to do harm to you, like the cat which later attempted to kill and eat the mouse that saved its life. Therefore, you should render assistance at the opportune moment and escape from them. You should understand this clearly.

You should know the mental force generated by the senses arising from the Earth, Fire, Water, and Air. You should understand the characteristics of the body which is the enemy of the Soul (Atma), and the actions of the senses. Fire burns everything. Wind will break and overturn anything. Water will erode everything and will carry away everything on its way. Earth will receive all forces and power and keep them within it. It absorbs the pure as well as the impure, and grows. It is the essence of the earth that develops your physical body. It becomes blood, skin, tissues, fat, etc. Finally the earth consumes the same body. You should know this. You should know from where you came. You should know to which place you will finally return. You should look after the body and help the body in the same way as the mouse helped the cat. You should not come under the influence of the body. Though you are living within the body, you should live as if you were out of it. You should help your friends and those who love you at the opportune moment. You should not think of getting any reward, help or gratitude from them. Like the mouse, you should render help to others at the correct moment and escape. Otherwise, the ties of the world (Agnana) will consume you in the same way as the cat which tried to entice the mouse out of the hole and consume it. You should know this well.

So said the Master (Guru) to the disciple.

53. **At 6:50 P.M. on 4/13/70**

The authentic Spiritual Master tells his disciple:

Please listen to this illustration. There lived a beautiful young virgin. She was a queen of chastity. She used to walk with her eyes looking intently on the large toes of her feet. Several people who saw her beauty and her gait used to remark, "Look at her style. Look at the way she walks. Look at her dress," and poke fun at her. Some would follow her and try to get hold of her hand and remove her chastity. When a man tried to deprive her of her chastity, the whole world will aid and abet him. None came to her help. There are only a few in this world who would go to her help to save her chastity and character.

When men or women of excellent character, chaste wives and Gnostics go in search of the Truth of God and try to reach It, the whole world will join together to destroy their Truth, their Conscience, Compassion, Forbearance, Peace and Love of God in their minds like the persons who tried to destroy the chastity of the virgin. They will come in waves to destroy these noble persons. None will come forward to save the Truth and the Seeker after Truth. These people are in a state of torpor caused by the degraded state of Wisdom (Ariveenam) by the darkness of Illusion (Maya). They are under the influence of Craving, Hatred, Miserliness, Vanity, Lust and Envy. You should get above this state, develop your Wisdom (Arivu), make it shine, and with that Light cross the dark forest of existence which is full of animals, guided by the five senses, and go beyond. This will be good for you.

54. **At 7:20 P.M. on 4/13/70**

The authentic Spiritual Master tells his disciple:

Please listen to an illustration. The goat searches for its food very actively in the day time. Whatever grass, herbs or leaves it sees, it gobbles them up quickly without chewing or masticating. Then the goats lie down together in a suitable place and leisurely chew their cud. While chewing their cud, they enjoy the tastes of the different types of grass, leaves and herbs they had earlier swallowed; they throw out what is bad and send back to the stomach only what is good for them. While they chew their cud, their mind is drawn towards God. They close and open their eyes now and then, or lie down with closed eyes as if sleeping, or stand when they chew their cud. When they chew their cud, they do not forget to enjoy the taste; at the same time they do not cease to think of God. Their intelligence, which enables them to throw out what is bad for their stomach when they chew their cud, is also active.

Comment: There are also flocks of goats with human faces. Night and day they run about seizing from others food, flesh, property, gold and riches. They gather in a hurry for themselves joy and sorrow, freedom and slavery, heaven and hell, anger and sin. They run about here and there in a hurry and gather all things, like the goats and bring them home. The goats, after swallowing all types of food in a hurry, rest in a place and leisurely chew their cud and throw out what is bad for them and send back to the stomach only what is good for them. But these human beings do not, when they rest at night, ruminate over what they did during the day. They do not analyse with their Wisdom (Arivu) the good and the bad, merit and

120

sin. They do not reject from their mind what is bad and enjoy the taste of the good. They do not throw out of their minds those things which are harmful to their existence, like the goats which throw out what is bad for their stomach when they chew their cud. What type of creations are they? Are they men? Or are they animals? They do not try to find the answers to these questions. They do not try to find out whether they are the highest among animals or whether they are the rarest and noblest among human beings. The animals, the goats, sleep without sleeping when they chew their cud and enjoy the taste of the food and at the same time develop their intelligence by drawing their mind towards God. In the same manner, man should also sleep without sleeping and reflect and find out who he is and the purpose of his existence on earth. But, he does not do so. Like the goats, these animals with human faces bite something here, and bite something there without knowing what is good and what is bad.

If among these people anyone was really born as Man, he should give up the company of these flocks and try to enjoy the real taste of his existence on earth. In joy and sorrow, in good health and in ill health, in walk and in rest, in his work and in his duty, he should enjoy the real taste of his existence with his Wisdom (Arivu), like the goat which enjoy the taste of the food while it chews its cud. He should reflect on God, and night and day he should keep his attention fixed on God. With his Divine Wisdom, he should understand the nature of his existence on earth, the nature of the body in which he is housed, the nature of the senses within the body, the nature of the darkness within the senses, the nature of the hypnotic torpor caused by the darkness of Illusion (Maya), the nature of the state of sleep caused by the torpor, the nature of actions without clear perception performed in that state of sleep, the numberless births caused by these actions, the nature of sin connected with these births, and the Hell which exists within these sins. He should, like the goat, throw out all these which are harmful to his Soul. He should understand that God (Allah), the all Powerful Lord of all the worlds, is the only food for his Wisdom (Arivu), the sweet taste for the body and the Light for removing the Darkness of Illusion. Man should throw out everything else from this birth. Then he will have the privilege of knowing the real qualities of Man, the rare nature of human birth and the sweet taste of The Unique One. He will be the disciple who has achieved Liberation in this birth itself. You should understand this well. You should give up all which cannot be digested by the Soul. You should persevere day and night with firmness of Conviction and Certitude and live within your Wisdom (Arivu). Keep this firmly in your mind.

So said the Authenitc Spiritual Master (Meignana Guru) to his best disciple.

55.   At 7:45 P.M. on 4/13/70

Child! Please listen to an illustration.

A cobra has poison in its four fangs. It has the characteristics of the eight mythological cobras which guarded Heaven on eight sides. Instead of the thousand legs of the mythological cobra, it has a thousand scales on its body. There are a thousand types of snakes. The cobra has the characteristics of all these. It mates with the rat snake. Then it goes to the bush full of 'Erukala' plants, lays eggs and watches the eggs till they are hatched. At that time if anybody goes near that bush, it will become angry and hiss and spread its hood and try to bite that person, thinking that he is an enemy who will harm it and the eggs. If the man goes away from the bush out of fear, the cobra will become normal and watch its eggs. When the eggs open up, the young cobras leap out of the eggs. The mother cobra will eat up the young cobras which fall near it. A few young cobras leap far away from the mother and escape death. They develop as real cobras of the highest order. It should be noted that the cobra which watched over the eggs carefully eats up the young cobras as they come out of the eggs. It eats its own progeny.

Comment: When man comes into existence in this world, the five senses in the mind, the five-headed cobra, take crores and crores of shapes of the hypnotic projections of Illusion. This five-headed cobra mates with the rat snake, the hypnotic torpor of Illusion, and lays four hundred billion (lakhs of crores) eggs in the bushes of the dark forest of Illusion, in the thorny bushes of poisonous characteristics of Illusion, in the holes of Envy and in the caves of Illusion which give rise to the divisive forces of 'mine' and 'yours', and watches over them carefully.

Like the cobra which eats the young cobras coming out of the eggs, the senses, the earth, consume human existence. If man, though born as a result of the mating of Desire with the Senses, leaps out of the reach of desire and the senses, like the young cobras which leaped out of the reach of the mother cobra, he will not be swallowed by death caused by the senses and the earth.

In that state he can survey with Divine Luminous Wisdom (Perr-Arivu) the senses, the torpor caused by the hypnotic attraction of the world, the origin and the end of poisonous characteristics. He can burn up all the poisons and go beyond. He can go beyond and see Him, the Embodiment of Divine Beauty, mate with Him and give birth to the Effulgence of Grace, the Resplendence of Divine Luminous Wisdom; and nurse it, develop it and make it spread its Radiance all over the Universe. Only a person who has reached That State and obtained That Result has obtained Liberation in this birth.

Just as the cobra mated with the rat snake and developed its progeny, man should develop the Effulgence of Grace and make it shine. If he does so, the whole world will become Effulgent. In that state there will be no darkness. Where there is no darkness there will be no blemish. Where there is no blemish, where everything is spotlessly pure, there will be Fullness. That Fullness is Eternal Purity. A person who reaches That State becomes He. Man and Man-God become He. That is the State where One is merged within the Other. You should understand this well.

So said His Holiness Guru Bawa to his disciple.

56.   **At 9:10 P.M. on 4/14/70**

A disciple asks the Guru, "How can a disciple obtain from the Guru the priceless wealth the Guru has?"

The Guru replies: My friend! My disciple, who has come with body and Wisdom (Arivu) to merge with me! Yours is a very intelligent question. Please listen to an illustration and reflect on it carefully.

You know that there are seven oceans, which can never go dry, in which crores and crores of beings created by the Grace of God live. There are more beings in the oceans than on the land, which serves as a stage for Mankind. Only if you develop a strong desire for those things in the ocean and exhibit love for them, can you get hold of them. They will not come out of the ocean to the shore. The Thing you desire to get hold of lives in the large and limitless ocean of Wisdom (Arivu). If you wish to get That you should turn into water similar to the water in the ocean of Divine Wisdom. Even that is not enough. Just as the water in the ocean goes up the canal and the water in the canal goes down to the ocean and merge, your Wisdom (Arivu) should merge with It. That should merge with Wisdom (Arivu). In that state, the Rain of Grace, Unarvu (Perception), Unarchi (Awareness), Puththi (Intellect), Madthi (Practical Understanding; Knowledge), Arivu (Wisdom), Pathuth-Arivu (Divine Wisdom), and Perr-Arivu (Divine Luminous Wisdom), should fall on the canal of your Wisdom (Arivu) and flow down it and merge in the Ocean of Effulgence of Divine Grace, the Reflection of the Ultimate Unique One. The rain water should flow down the canal of Wisdom (Arivu) as the water of Divine Love and Compassion and merge in the Ocean of Divine Grace. Then the beings and things in the Ocean of Divine Grace will come up to meet this Water of Divine Love and Compassion. Then you can get hold of them. Reflect on this a little.

In the same manner, in the ocean of the Divine Luminous Wisdom (Perr-Arivu) of the Spiritual Master (Guru), God's Wealth, the whole Universe, Divine Grace, the secrets of heaven, the secrets of the earth, the secrets of the three worlds, all Truth, swim and play about. Wherever it rains, the water flows down the canal (rivers) to the ocean. In the same manner, if Faith in the Spiritual Master (Guru) rises in your heart, and if the water of Love of God and Compassion flows down the canal of your Wisdom (Arivu) from your heart, and falls into the Ocean of Divine Luminous Wisdom full of Divine Grace, the Divine Grace and the Divine Wealth in that Ocean will swim up your canal of Wisdom (Arivu) and Love and fill your heart, like the ocean fish which will swim up the canal to the pond of rain water. All the wealth, all the things living in your Guru will swim up the canal of the Water of Love and Compassion and live in your sea of Wisdom (Arivu). In that spiritual state you have obtained what is in the Guru. That is the state in which you and the Guru establish contact, through the canal of Love, in the Ocean of Divine Grace and merge and obtain That Divine Thing. This is the path of contact between the Guru and the disciple. This is the path through which you can obtain That Divine Thing.

Child! You have to flow with the water of the seven essences: Unarvu, Unarchi, Puththi, Madthi, Arivu, Pahuth-Arivu and Perr-Arivu. The water of these seven essences should go and merge in the Ocean of Grace of the Guru, then the mirage of the seven 'Nafs Ammara', Lower Mind, will disappear.

So said the real authentic Spiritual Master to the disciple.

57.   **At 6:40 P.M. on 4/14/70**

Child! Please listen to an illustration.

I will tell you something about the small ant, the intelligent and the most active being among God's creations. It moves about actively and gathers all necessary food in the ant-hill to enable it to carry on its existence in all types of weather. It makes use of the experience of the past dangers and erects a house which is capable of meeting all future dangers. So, it is able to live in safety during floods, drought, heat and cold, and wind and cyclone.

When it is actively engaged in searching for food, if it sees that any other small ant is dead, it does not wait for kith and kin to carry it home. It carries it home where its kind live. It does this service with determination and faith. We call that being which works with determination and faith an ant. It has no Divine Wisdom (Pahuth-Arivu). It is guided by its intelligence.

Comment: Man, the noblest and rarest of creations, is born with Analytical Divine Wisdom (Pahuth-Arivu). But, he considers the four hundred billion (lakhs of crores) hypnotic projections to be useful to him. He spends four hundred billion (lakhs of crores) aeons in physical and mental visions of these forms. He tries to bring under his control their powers. He tries to see the fifteen worlds. He does penance through Yoga to turn his mental visions into physical visions and make use of them. He intends to do innumerable acts like these. He thinks about them. He searches for them. He rules the world. He lives. Finally he dies. He takes birth again. But this man, who has such prowess, cannot do what a small ant is able to do. He is afraid to use his Analytical Divine Wisdom (Pahuth-Arivu) and face the Truth. He is so heavy that the world cannot bear his weight. When an ant dies, another ant is able to carry it to its house, whatever the weight of the ant may be. But the earth itself cannot carry the weight of this man with Pahuth-Arivu who does not use it. If he dies, four people are needed to carry him. If he lives, he needs the help of a thousand people. What a large number of relations he has! Still, his body is so heavy that, when he is dead, one man cannot carry him.

But the ant has given up the world and keeps only its intelligence for its use. But man has given up the great faculties of Divine Wisdom, i.e., Unarvu (Perception), Unarchi (Awareness), Puththi (Intellect), Madthi (Practical Understanding; Knowledge), Arivu (Wisdom), Pahuth-Arivu (Analytical Divine Wisdom), and Perr-Arivu (Divine Luminous Wisdom). He keeps with him only the Lower Mind (Nafs Ammara), the mirage. He carries in his mind the mental visions and the physical visions. Therefore, his weight is such that four people are needed to carry him to the cemetery for interment. Even when he is alive, he needs the assistance of a thousand people to wake him up. There are two types of ants, man, the ant which cannot carry itself, and the small ant which can carry itself. We should understand the nature of these two types of ants.

Child! The ant is able to build a home to protect itself from ill winds, heat of the sun, fire and water. Man should know that his home, the body, is built of the five elements of Earth, Fire, Water, Air and Ether. He should analyse the nature of his home. He should find out the good and the evil effects of air in it. He should understand the nature of the five elements and their good and evil effects; He should understand the nature of earth, its joys and its hypnotic effects. He should analyse the nature of water, the joys and sorrows it generates. He should analyse ether, the seven colours of the seven Nafs (Lower mind), the thunder and lightening in it, its disturbances, its beauty and its limitless mysteries. He should understand the esoteric meanings of these five elements. He should understand the nature of the four hundred billion (lakhs of crores) hypnotic projections living within these five elements. He should understand the nature of the fifteen worlds which adjoin the world of five elements. He should understand the forces of darkness, and the light in them. He should know the limitless void, the sun, the moon, and the stars. Like the ant which used its intelligence to avoid the load of the world, man should use his Wisdom (Arivu) to avoid the loads of joy, sorrow, hypnotic attractions, mental visions and physical visions. Just as the ant carried the body of another ant of the same species to its home, man should carry his Soul (Ruh or Atma) full of God's Grace to God's (Allah's) home full of His Grace, which is the home of the Perfect Man (Insan Kamil). If he does so, there will be no need for four people to carry him to the burial ground. There will be no need for a thousand people to look after him in the world. The above is the knowledge and understanding that it is the birthright of man, the noblest of creations, to have. We were born in the world to know this mystery. Find out a method to carry you, yourself.

So said His Holiness Guru Bawa to his disciple.

58.   **At 7:20 P.M. on 4/14/70**

Child! Please listen to an illustration.

There are a large number of beings created by God in the seven oceans which are very difficult to fathom. Those beings cannot live without water. Yet the beings in the seven oceans thought that they could measure the length, breadth and depth of the seven oceans if they all drank the water of the ocean.

Comment: Man is the rarest and noblest of all creations of God Almighty, the Lord of the Universe. He thinks he can measure God by studying the religions, philosophies such as Vedanta and Siththantha, mythology, epics, and the divisive force of race and creed, like the fish which thought of measuring the ocean by drinking the water in the ocean. They enter the divisive forces of 'I am great; you are not'. They climb up the Triple Dirt of Egoism, Evil Action and Illusion. They survey the six sinful actions of Craving, Hatred, Miserliness, Vanity, Lust and Envy. Within them they build the beautiful fortress of Illusion and employ the elements and the senses to watch that fortress. He appears like the chameleon to the senses. Then he states, "God is like me. This is his colour. Just as I change, he also changes. Who is greater than I? There is no power greater than I." Thus, in his state of degradation man tries to fathom God.

These men judge God, who is All-Pervading, with their degraded state of Wisdom (Ariveenam), think that man and God is one and are trying to swallow God like the fish which tried to swallow the water in the ocean. The fish cannot swallow the ocean. They cannot measure the ocean. They cannot exist without the water in the ocean. In the same manner, man and his Soul (Atma) cannot exist without God, the Ultimate Unique One. This world also cannot exist without God. The fish which tried to swallow the ocean die when the ocean gets agitated and hot. In the same manner, when man tries to measure God with the yard-stick of his degraded wisdom, he gets burnt and dies when God spreads the Rays of His Effulgence. Man does not think of these things. Man is trying to measure God. He boasts "What can God do?" and gets caught in the shackles of his evil actions, which cause suffering, and dies. Therefore, embrace God with Love and Compassion in the stillness of mind, God who is limitless and who is full of limitless Love and Compassion. The day you do so you will obtain Liberation for the Soul (Atma). You will realise His joy.

So said the Guru to the disciple.

59.   At 7:55 P.M. on 4/14/70

Child! Please listen to an illustration.

If you want to sew up a big hole in the cloth, you have to first get the thread to go through the small hole in the needle. In the same way, to sew up the great hole of existence, you must make the thread of God's Love and Compassion go through the hole in the needle of Wisdom (Arivu). If you do so, the path through which you go out of the world and then come back into the world will be sewn up and blocked. If the path is blocked, there is no more birth for you, no more death for you; no joy; no sorrow; no senility; no death; no fatigue; no want; no end; no Hell; no Heaven; no day; no night; no state of sleep; no state of wakefulness; no torpor; no illusion; no forgetfulness; and no memory. You will shine as Effulgence. If you know that state, you will know the real state of existence.

So said the Spiritual Master (Authentic Meignana Guru) to his disciple.

60.   At 8:25 P.M. on 4/14/70

Child! Please listen to an illustration.

A person wanted to know the secrets of the seven oceans; the Black Ocean, the Red Ocean, the Blue Ocean, the Silver Ocean, the Gold Ocean, the Milk Ocean and the Ocean of Illusory (Mayic) Mysteries. These seven oceans surround the raised land of the earth. There are innummerable raised land-islands in the ocean. He went round the shores to find out the mysteries of these oceans. He did not get into the oceans. As a result of going round and round along the shore, he lost his Wisdom, his Intellect, his Intelligence and his Awareness. He fell down senseless. He revived. Again his desire to look at the ocean became active. He began to go round and round the shore. Though he took one hundred and fifty million (ten and a half crores) births, he was not able to discover even an atom of the mysteries of the ocean.

He was unable to know the mysteries of the Ocean of Blood. He was unable to know the mysteries of the Ocean of Illusion (Maya). He died. He was born again. He died. He repeated this process till he sank in the Hell of Illusion (Maya). He was unable to develop the faculties of Awareness, Intelligence, Intellect and Divine Wisdom. He did not search for a Spiritual Master (Guru) who could change his memory and develop his Wisdom (Arivu). He did not discover any method to prevent rebirth.

Child! Great men have exclaimed, "If we lose the opportunity presented by the present human existence to realise God, we do not know whether we will be born again as a man or an animal in the future." Man, the rarest and noblest among God's creations, wanted to see the ocean of God's mysteries, the ocean of Illusion (Maya), mental visions and physical visions, and go round these to see God, Who is without a veil covering Him, and His Grace. Child! When you stand on a raised ground covered with veils, you cannot see God Who is All Pervading.

But, if you wish to understand the ocean of Illusion (Maya), and the seven oceans, you should merge within the clarity of the Divine Luminous Wisdom of an Authentic Spiritual Master (Meignana Guru). He will live in the wide open Resplendent Shore beyond the Ocean of Illusion (Maya). He will know within himself all the oceans and keep them under control. He will have seven ships to sail across the seven oceans. The seven ships are; Unarvu (Perception), Unarchi (Awareness), Puththi (Intellect), Madthi (Knowledge), Arivu (Wisdom), Pahuth-Arivu (Analytical Divine Wisdom), and Perr-Arivu (Divine Luminous Wisdom). He will serve as the captain of these ships when they sail across these oceans. He will take in these ships those who desire to go to that wide open Resplendent Shore. With the help of that Authentic Spiritual Master (Meignana Guru), you can find out the nature of the seven oceans, and the mystery of the islands in the seven oceans. You can find out the mystery of your birth and your death. You can find out who you are. You will know how to become deathless. You will know where the Eternal One is. You will merge with Him.

But if you go round and round the island of egoism and religious fanaticism which are surrounded by the ocean of Illusion (Maya), you will never know the mystery about your birth and death. You will only become liable to several crores of births. You should understand this well.

Know this well and get into the boat of Divine Luminous Wisdom of your Spiritual Master (Guru). Remember this clearly. If you get into the boat of Divine Luminous Wisdom of your Spiritual Master (Gnana Guru) and go with him in it, you will be free from Birth, Hunger, Disease, Senility and Death. As a result you will receive the Light and Clarity, and reach the Ultimate Unique One, get His characteristics and merge with Him.

So said His Holiness Guru Bawa to his disciple.

61.   **At 8:55 A.M. on 4/17/70**

Dr. Selvaratnam tells His Holiness Guru Bawa, "Swami! I have read many books on religion. While I was reflecting on every one of your ideas and illustrations, I was reminded of the various interpretations given in the books. In the books I read I was able to understand various ideas." His Holiness asked: "What idea in the books did you understand?" Dr. Selvaratnam did not give a direct reply. He explained certain ideas according to what he learned in books. His Holiness replied:

There is a great deal of difference between what you learned in books and the meaning of the illustration I will now give. What you studied is a book (Puththakam). This Tamil word can be divided into two words, 'Puththu' and 'Aham'. 'Puththu' means the forms of deities worshipped in the world, deities which are really the four hundered billion (lakhs of crores) hypnotic projections of Maya (Illusion). 'Aham' means the world. You are reading the 'Puththakam', i.e. the world in which deities which are the hypnotic projections of Illusion (Maya) are worshipped in the form of idols.

If you want to develop their power, you have to first erect a beautiful house or temple for them. You have to create a form to represent its qualities out of earth or the five elements. You have to paint colours on the idol. You have to engrave the eyes so that they may appear to look at you. You have to dress the idols with silk clothes with golden borders. You have to deck the nose with nose-gays made of diamonds and other gems. You have to place a crown made of the nine types of gems on its heads. You turn it into an object of the world. You consider it to be the inner home of the world. You make it artistically beautiful to attract and hypnotize the people. You create rules for performing ceremonies before it. You create rules for worshipping it. You compose hymns to be sung before it. The people of the world follow these methods and conduct festivals in its honour, dance and sing its glory in a state of false devotion and fervour and enjoy themselves. You need the materials of the world to decorate the idol and make it more beautiful.

So, what you sang is about the world of the hypnotic projections of Illusion (Maya). This is the world which makes itself the happy dwelling place of the hypnotic projections of Illusion. What you have learned is like a craft learned without the guidance of an instructor. You decorate the idol with clothes and beautiful jewels and enjoy the sight. In the same way, you decorate it by singing songs and enjoy hearing your own music. This is the inner and outer meaning of the story you have learned in the books. Reflect on this a little. If you do not have these materials of the world, you cannot decorate the deities of the world. This is the lesson you have learned. You are in the form of these deities, hypnotic projections of Illusion (Maya). Your inner self is in the shape of the world. Reflect on this. Unless you have Wisdom (Arivu) you will not be able to meet the Spiritual Master (Guru). If you do not surrender fully to the Guru, you will not be able to know the Limitless Ominipresent Beautiful One, the Ultimate Unique One, whom you cannot decorate with the beautiful things of the world.

Dr. Selvaratnam asked, "Can one show disrespect to others?". His Holiness who was able to know the state in which he was, and his mind, replied: What you say is correct in a way. Your mind has been absorbed in the intelligent method of seeing God given in my illustration earlier. In that state you have asked this question. Please listen.

A man of excellence, one who knew the Truth, a person with Divine Luminous Wisdom (Gnani), was doing penance in the forest. He was singing about God. He was writing songs and singing about his experiences about what he saw, about Grace, about Reality, about God's actions, about His beauty and about the world. He was not singing those songs for the benefit of the animals in the forest. The animals cannot understand them. Because they are unable to understand his songs, the animals think that he is insulting them by shouting. He sang in the forest not for the benefit of the animals which are without Analytical Divine Wisdom (Pahuth-Arivu). He was doing his duty. A man will one day come to him to get that Wealth of Divine Grace. That wealth is for him. That holy man was telling that, singing that. Are we, You and I, men? No. We are the animals referred to. What he sings will appear to be an insult to us. But what he sings is not an insult to Man. Man needs his songs. Other animals do not possess Analytical Divine Wisdom (Pahuth-Arivu). So, they may say anything. Truth will appear to be an insult to them. Only mental visions will appear to be Truth to them.

In the same manner, your mental visions appear to be true to you. When your mental visions are destroyed, when Egoism, Causative Action (Karma), and Illusion disappear, Wisdom (Arivu) will appear in you. When Divine Wisdom appears in you, you will understand the Truth I was speaking of to you. From what you say it appears to me that the Truth I tell will appear to be an insult till you get rid of Egoism, Causative Action (Karma) and Illusion.

Dear Doctor! I will add a few words. Please reflect on them a little. God is the Ultimate Unique One. What is God? What type of Thing is It? What is Its Origin? What is Its shape? What is Its beauty? Who created It? When did It come into being? Is It a single element? Is It composed of several things? Can It be commonly seen by man? Is It beyond the physical sight of man? Can It be seen only after undergoing great difficulty? Can you see It by offering fruits, coconuts, arecanuts, camphor, and incense? Can you see It by offering boiled milk rice? Is it a Thing which does not require these things? Is It a Thing which you see in your mental visions? Is It a Thing which can be embraced only by the Soul (Atma) and Wisdom (Arivu)? Is It a Thing which is very difficult to know? Or is It a Thing which can be seen in hills and forests in physical form? Is It a Thing which can be made by the hands of man, and painted and decorated? Can It be made by mental visions? Or is It a Thing which is beyond the beyond which can be known only by Real Wisdom (Arivu)? Is It a Thing which is Wisdom (Arivu) within Wisdom (Arivu)? Does It have a wife and children? Or is It without a family? Is It beyond the pale of race, caste, religion, creed, scriptures, Vedas, Vedanta philosophies? Or is It to be found only within the folds of a particular religion in the world?

Is It a Thing which will open Its mouth and eat the food It is fed with? Or is It a Thing which will consume only the Resplendence of Divine Luminous Wisdom, given It with Divine Wisdom full of Love and Compassion? Is It a Thing which you make and worship? Or Is It a Thing which you cannot worship with your mental visions? Is It made of the five elements? Or is It something beyond the elements? Is It a Thing which demands the sacrifice of the mind, the body, goats, bulls, and fowls and cranes? Or is It a Thing full of Compassion with Compassion and Love? Is there a different God for people of my race and people of your race? Or is It something which transcends you and me and is immanent in all created beings? Is It something that can be reached by your mental visions? Or is It something beyond the reach of your mental visions? Is It a Thing which can be created by the Coppersmith or by the mind? Or is It something that cannot be made by the Coppersmith or the mind? Is It something That can be visualized only by Wisdom (Arivu)? Or is It something that can be made and decorated by the five senses and the five elements? Is It something which depends for livelihood on what you earn and save? Or is It something that does not need even an atom of your material savings? Can It be seen by all? Or is It something That can be discovered only after a great deal of effort by the Divine Luminous Wisdom (Perr-Arivu) of a Man-God (Manu-Eesan) who it is rare to find among men?

Which of these things is God? From your book-learning, what did your Wisdom see as God? What did your mind see as God? Think well and answer. You all have a large number of deities made of the five metals. You make your god, paint it, apply 'tilak' on its forehead, open its eyes, clean the dross from the copper figure, keep it in one place, give food to it to prevent hunger, disease, senility and death to it, and then request it to grant boons.

You make the deity; you open its eyes; you protect it; you dress it and decorate it; you offer it food, flesh, ghee, milk, peeled fruits; you offer incense and request it to eat these things. You lock it up in rooms. Then you scold it saying "God! Have you no eyes? Have you no mouth? Have you no tongue? Do you not know the sufferings I am undergoing? God who is blind!" Thus you scold the god whom you make, saying "You have no mouth! You have no eyes! You have no tongue! You have no nose! Are you lame?".

God has no eyes. You give him eyes. He has no nose. You give him a nose. He has no ears. You give him ears. You keep a god like this all over the world. Then you scold him, "God! You have no eyes!" Is it proper to speak of God like this? Is it proper to insult God like this? Dr. Selvaratnam! Is it not an insult for you to make a god yourself and scold it? Is what I speak more insulting than this? Child! Think well and find out whether I am in Ignorance or you are in Ignorance. The world talks of God like this. You know that these deities you make cannot speak or laugh or walk. Is it in keeping with Wisdom to say that is has no eyes; it has no mouth; it has not granted me any boons? Reflect a little. All of you have a large number of deities. Finally you are asking God this question. You are telling a blind person, "You are blind". You are telling a dumb person, "You are dumb". You are telling a thing that does not walk, "You have no legs". You make offerings of food to something that does not eat and you eat the offerings. You sing devotional songs to deceive it. It is you who enjoys singing the devotional songs.

Please reflect on this. God transcends race, caste, religion, creed, scriptures, Veda and Vedanta philosophies. He cannot be made by man. He is Limitless, beyond the pale of everything. He cannot be found within the limits of the elements. He has bo birth or end. He is One who cannot be seen by anyone who has not developed the seven faculties, viz., Unarvu (Perception), Unarchi (Awareness), Puththi (Intellect), Madthi (Knowledge), Arivu (Wisdom), Pahuth-Arivu (Analytical Divine Wisdom) and Perr-Arivu (Divine Luminous Wisdom). One who does not love other beings as he loves his own 'self', one who does not have Patience, Compassion, Liberality, Mercy, Truth, Justice, Love for all beings, Friendship, Modesty, Reservedness, Fear to do evil, Culture and other such Divine Qualities, will not be able to see God. God is Immanent in all created beings. He is Divine Wisdom. He can be seen only by Wisdom (Arivu). He is the Primal Unique One. He is the Inner Essence of everything. He has no astral or physical form. He is the Primal Effulgence. He has no shadow. He is beyond the pale of everything. He is One who can be seen by the Divine Luminous Wisdom of Man-God (Manu-Eesan). Only the very great people with that rare high state of Divine Luminous Wisdom can see him. Let us, you and I, try to see Him who dwells as Divine Wisdom within the Divine Wisdom of Man-God (Manu-Eesan). Try to find out the true path.

Child! If you lock yourself up inside a dark windowless room, you will be aware only of the bad odour emanating from your perspiration and the bad odour of your breath. If you come out into the open plain, the bad odour of your perspiration will be removed by the natural breeze. When that bad odour has been removed, you will enjoy the blowing of the natural breeze in the wide expanse. Doctor! Please reflect a little on this. You and I have to get rid of the bad odour of our senses. If we get the natural scent of Wisdom (Arivu), the bad odour of the senses in our existence will be blown away.

Child! The face is the most important part of the human body. If the head is not available it is not possible to say whose body it is. In the same manner, the seven faculties of Unarvu, Unarchi, Puththi, Madthi, Arivu, Pahuth-Arivu, and Perr-Arivu consitute the face a man must have to see God. This is the face of Divine Wisdom of a Man-God. God will not know that he is His child, His devotee, unless the man has this seven-fold face of Divine Wisdom. If this face is not there in the presence of God, the man may become liable to several births. The head is the most important part of the body among the created beings of God. In the same manner, it is these seven faculties of Perception, Awareness, Intellect, Knowledge, Wisdom, Analytical Divine Wisdom and Divine Luminous Wisdom that I mentioned, which are essential for a Man-God (Manu-Eesan). Please understand this clearly.

So said His Holiness Guru Bawa to Dr. Selvaratnam.

62.   **At 9:50 A.M. on 4/18/70**

Mr. Thambaiah was explaining Divine Luminous Wisdom (Perr-Arivu) clearly to his wife, daughter and others. His Holiness Guru Bawa who was listening to this, was reflecting on what he was telling. Mr. Thambaiah was telling them, "You must know the real nature of the world. You must adjust yourself and do everything in an intelligent way. You people have a pure trusting heart free from treachery and stratagems. The world will note this and take advantage of this. So, if you are not careful, it will bring disgrace to you. It will bring disgrace to the Master who is full of Divine Luminous Wisdom (Gnani). You must examine everything intelligently and do it." He referred to his wife as Fool number One and his daughter as Fool number Two.

His young daughter replied, "Whatever you preach to others, your heart will be full of those words when they come out of you. You should find out what those words are. After that only you should observe others and advise them." Mr. Thambaiah said, "This is the world of Illusion. People of the world are of various types. As far as I know, I have not seen a straight man. Therefore you should understand how you should act towards others."

His Holiness, understanding his motive and the state of his mind, said: Mr. Thembaiah! Look at the sea. The wave has to form itself from the water in the sea. It goes and dashes against the shore and returns to the sea. Only then can it be sea water. But if it goes beyond the shore and falls into some low ground or hollow, it will dry up in a day. It cannot remain as sea water. It has dried up. Please reflect a little on this.

Comment: The disciple should intelligently pick up the words that come from the Guru, the sea of Grace full of Divine Wisdom. These words are the waves of the Sea of Grace full of Divine Wisdom. If the words go beyond the limits set by the Guru, the words will disappear and lose their effect, like the waves which go beyond the shore and fall into a low ground. The words of Divine Wisdom arising from the Guru should go and dash against the shore of Illusion (Maya) and remove the dirt of Illusion (Maya) and come back to the Guru. But if the disciple goes beyond the discipline of the Guru, his Divine Wisdom will disappear.

131

A real disciple of a Guru should be like the pearl oyster, which lives on the bed of the sea. When the cold wind indicating the imminence of rain begins to blow and the sky is full of dark clouds and there is thunder, the pearl oyster leaves the bed of the sea. It comes up to the surface of the sea and keeps its mouth wide open high above the surface to receive the drops of rain water. As soon as two drops of rain water have entered its mouth, it will close its mouth, go back to its home in the sea bed and hold itself firmly to a rock, in a state of exhilaration, forgetting itself, till the pearls mature in it.

If the disciple wants to pay back the debt of birth, if he wants to obtain Liberation of His Soul (Atma), if he wants the Wisdom (Arivu) and Soul (Atma) to merge to prevent rebirth, if his Divine Wisdom is to merge with God, he should adopt the form of Divine Wisdom, Faith, Determination and Patience, open the mouth of Wisdom (Arivu) and push out the tongue of Forbearance and Peace, prevent the inflow of sea water of hypnotic torpor comprising the water of Illusion (Maya), thoughts of Illusion (Maya), desire for objects of Illusion (Maya), mental visions and physical visions, and receive the rain drops of Grace like the pearl oyster.

The excellent disciple who lives with the Guru should withdraw within his body after getting the rain drops of Grace and keep himself attached to the Guru's heart like the oyster which will go down to the bed of the sea and attach itself to a rock till the pearls mature. The pearl of Grace will mature in him in the same way as the pearls will mature in the oyster. If he does not do so, if he develops in the world as one who is subject to the influence of the senses, the senses will consume him in the same way as the mother cobra eats up the young cobras when they hatch from the eggs she laid. You should reflect on this and understand it well.

So said His Holiness Guru Bawa to his disciple Thambaiah.

63.   **At 7:15 P.M. on 4/21/70**

Child! Please listen to an illustration.

A type of deer called, in Tamil, 'Ukkulan' lives in the forest. If you chase it, it will run faster than an ordinary deer. If you chase it continuously and come near it, it will hide its head inside heaps of dry leaves or in holes. When it hides its head, it thinks that it has completely hidden its body. If any dog catches it, it will kick it with its hind legs. If man tries to catch it, he will be kicked by its hind legs. Therefore, men club it to death, and take the carcass to cook for food.

Comment: There are human beings with the characteristics of the 'Ukkulan' deer referred to. When they are chased by Poverty, Disease and Senility, they also hide their head in the Darkness of Illusion of False Wisdom (Agnana); they bury their heads below the heaps of dry leaves of crores of deities and crores of thoughts. Then they think that they have disappeared or merged in God; that they have become 'Swamis' or Holy Men; that they have become men of Divine Luminous Wisdom (Gnanis); that they have become dwellers of Heaven (Devas); that they have obtained powers of healing; and that they have reached Heaven. They place their head within the hole of their book learning and senses, and show their body, the elements, outside to the world. When they are in that state, Poverty, Disease, Suffering, Fate, etc., which were chasing them, will club them to death and consume them. In their degraded state of Wisdom, they are full of vanity, thinking that they have become real devotees of God and men of Divine Luminous Wisdom (Gnanis). They become victims of Death and become subject to several births.

You should know their external trappings, their appearance and their actions. It is good for you to avoid their company. If you join them and hide your head within crores of deities, you will not see the Truth. You will see only the world of Illusion. You should remove your vanity and ego and develop humility. You should lose your 'Self'. You should forget your body-consciousness. The Resplendence of your Soul (Atma) should disappear in the Effulgence of the Ultimate Unique One. Then only can you escape Death. If you only hide your head like that deer and keep your senses out, you will never reach God.

So said His Holiness Guru Bawa to his disciple.

64.   **At 7:40 P.M. on 4/21/70**

Child! Please listen to an illustration.

A Guru tells his best disciple: If you catch a monkey living in the forest and bring it to the village and keep it before a mirror, it will see its own reflection in the mirror. It is not intelligent enough to think that it is its reflection in the mirror. It will think that it is another monkey. It will like to see it, embrace it and kiss it. Being unable to succeed in its attempts, it will cry and wail. Again it will attempt to hug and embrace the reflection in the mirror without knowing that it is its (shadow) reflection. When the monkey is in that state, it will not eat any food or fruit or any tasty dish placed before it. It will continue its attempt to hug and embrace the reflection in the mirror. It is guided by its blood ties. It wants to get hold of the reflection which it considers to be a monkey like itself. In that state, it will not pay attention to the tasty food.

In the same manner, if you keep the mind-monkey in front of the mirror of the darkness of False Wisdom (Agnana), the reflection shining in the mirror will be that of the senses and the elements which lead to False Wisdom (Agnana). Like the monkey which tried to catch and embrace its own reflection in the mirror, this mind-monkey considers the four hundred billion (lakhs of crores) hypnotic projections of Illusion (Maya), seen in the mirror of False Wisdom (Agnana), as his religion, his race, and his relations and tries to get hold of them, embrace them and play with them. Like the monkey which refused to eat the sweet food placed before it, the mind-monkey also will not desire, touch or eat or drink God's fruit of Divine Luminous Wisdom (Perr-Arivu), the milk of God's Grace and the honey of Divine Grace, even if you offer them to it with love, when the mind-monkey is in that state of craving. It will only desire the hypnotic projections in the mirror of the darkness of Illusion. It will not drink this Divine honey, or eat the fruit of Divine Luminous Wisdom (Perr-Arivu), and the food of the Light of Wisdom (Arivu). The mind-monkey will always be dwelling with those who possess the dark mirror of hypnotic Illusion (Maya) which develops the strength of the mind-monkey. You should consider all these aspects of people and teach Wisdom only to the deserving.

Let us now consider the monkey which was brought to the village from the forest. Take away the mirror in front of the monkey. Take a stick and place its end on the droppings of the fowl. Then smear the droppings of the fowl, sticking to the end of the stick, on one hand of that monkey. The monkey will smell again and again the droppings of the fowl smeared on its hand. Then it will rub the place in the hand again and again till sores appear on the hand. It will continue to smell the place again and again, take that stick and dig up the sore and make the wound deeper and deeper. The wound will putrify as a result. Finally the monkey will die of tetanus.

Similarly, a person with the mind-monkey, once he smells the excreta of egoism and sexual joy in his hand of Wisdom (Arivu) and Awareness (Unarchi), will smell it again and again and rub the place in the hand very hard repeatedly till it becomes sore and the wound festers. Finally he dies as a result of the effect of sexual joy which sucks the life out of him. Till he dies he continues to indulge in sexual joy, under the hypnotic influence of dark Illusion (Maya), again and again till he dies as a result of tetanus in the infected wound of Existence. Such monkeys exist with human faces and appear like men. You should study their character and conduct carefully. There are these human monkeys as well as the monkeys in the forest. You must note them carefully. You must not teach Divine Luminous Wisdom (Perr-Arivu) to such people. You should teach Wisdom only to people who are potential Man-God (Manu-Eesan).

So said the Guru to his disciple.

65.   **At 8:05 P.M. on 4/21/70**

Child! Please listen to an illustration.

Look at the streaked lizard called, in Tamil, 'Aranai'. Its body is full of poison. It asked God to give it a boon so that when it bit a human being he would die immediately. God replied, "You have forgotten me. You are asking me for a boon with egoism. I grant you the boon. But I am also imposing a condition. You will go near a man with the intention of biting him. The moment you come near him you shall forget your intention." The streaked lizard is poisonous. If it bites, the man will die. But, whenever it sees a man it will approach him with the intention of biting him. When it comes near him, it will forget and go away.

Comment: Among human beings also there are people like the streaked lizard. They search for God. They desire to reach Him and merge in Him. So, they search for a Spiritual Master (Guru) to help them to attain Divine Luminous Wisdom (Perr-Arivu), fly in the heavens, and see God. When they find such a Guru and go to him, they forget all the above noble desires, like the streaked lizard which forgets to bite human beings when it comes near them. Instead, they request the Guru to give worldly boons. They request him to grant them his blessings to have wives, children, cattle, house, property, gold, titles, jobs, etc. They request him to give them power to rule the world or to destroy the world, like the ten-headed demon, King Ravana. There are people who continue to request the Guru to grant them similar boons. Such is the state of their senses and their Wisdom (Arivu).

People commonly ask "Did these people renounce the world because of famine? Or did they renounce the world because their inborn nature was religious?" The man of the first category will give up the robes once the famine is over, forgetting his original purpose like the streaked lizard. Unlike the streaked lizard, the man who took to the robes because of his inborn religious nature, will not forget his purpose. He will go to the Guru with one purpose. He will come with the strong faith that only God Is and that all other things are ephemeral. His one-pointed attention will be drawn towards God. He will succeed in reaching God.

Therefore, do not preach Wisdom (Arivu) to people who are forgetful like the streaked lizard, or people who are like those who renounced the world because of famine. If you preach Wisdom (Arivu) to such people, Truth will be destroyed. If Truth is destroyed, the world will get destroyed. As a result, people will suffer from poverty and disease. They will undergo pain and suffering. You must study the nature of these people and preach to them.

So said His Holiness Guru Bawa to his disciple.

66.   **At 7:40 P.M. on 5/2/70**

Child! Please listen to an illustration.

A drunkard had drunk five to ten bottles of toddy (liquor) and was coming along the road. He was under the impression that he was going home from the liquor booth. When he takes one or two steps he thinks he is going home. When he staggers this way and that way on the road, he still thinks that he is going straight home along the road. If he knocks against another man, thinking that he was going straight along the road, he will quarrel with the other man thinking that it is the other man who purposely knocked against him. If he falls down on the road, owing to his drunken condition, he will lie on the road in a semi-conscious state. When he lies like that, he will be under the impression that he is lying at home. At that time even if the King or God went along that road, he will not have the sense of modesty, reservedness, fear (to do harm) and cultures. Even if his clothes are in a state of disarray, he will not feel ashamed. He will be under the impression that he is with his family at home.

Comment: The senses and the elements in the body of man are normally attracted by the world. A real Man of Divine Luminous Wisdom (Meignani) will have brought the senses and the elements under control. He will have burnt up all ties such as blood ties which bind him. He will have removed from his 'Self' the divisive forces of race, caste, religion and creed, and the sense of possessiveness 'mine' and 'yours'. He will have gotten rid of egoism, that 'I am greater than you'. He will have removed from himself with his Divine Wisdom the Ignorance, which gives rise to the six sinful actions motivated by Craving, Hatred, Miserliness, Vanity, Lust, and Envy, and thrown it into the sea of Illusion (Maya) in Hell, in which he was born. He will have removed the mental veil of sexual joy before him. He will be drunk with That which gives Bliss par excellence. He will have no consciousness of his 'Self'. He will gaze at the Effulgence of the Ultimate Unique One That pervades the whole Universe. He will be absorbed fully in the beauty of Divinity. Within that Effulgence he will see the mystery of various creations, the good and the evil, the mysteries of Hunger, Disease, Senility and Death, the mysteries of birth and death. He will see numberless scenes, their implications and their end. He will see the Indestructible One. He will know the destructible. He will enjoy seeing all these things within That Unique One.

After being in that state of Unconsciousness of Self, if he opens his physical eyes and looks, he will see that several aeons have passed. Numberless kings have ruled and died one after the other. Kingdoms would have changed. The sea would have become land. Land would have become sea.

Now, the man who was lying unconscious, after taking too much liquor, thinks when he regains consciousness, "What! Was I lying on the road! I was actually lying at home. Who brought me here?"

Both the drunkard and the Man of Divine Luminous Wisdom (Gnani) have given up the comforts of beds and mattresses, the comforts of home, the comforts of clothes, the comforts of food and the comforts of the physical body. The drunkard has no sense of personal honour or shame. The 'Gnani' also has no sense of personal honour or shame. The drunkard was lying on the road without the cloth covering his body. The 'Gnani' also was lying like that. When the drunkard regains consciousness, he sees the joys and sorrows of the world; he realises the ties of the world. He sees that his senses and elements are active. But the Man of Divine Luminous Wisdom (Gnani) sees the Plentitude, the Perfection that has no beginning or end, That Fullness of Bliss par excellence.

Both the drunkard and the 'Gnani' were lying in the same manner. The drunkard was unconscious as a result of the influence of alcohol, and was lying in the darkness of Ignorance (Agnana). The 'Gnani' was lying in a state of spiritual wakefulness seeing the Resplendence of Divine Luminous Wisdom (Perr-Arivu). Though both the drunkard and the 'Gnani' did not have any sense of personal honour, the drunkard was lying in darkness, but the 'Gnani' was lying in the Light of Wisdom (Arivu). The drunkard was in a state of joy with Illusion which causes torpor. The 'Gnani' was in a state of Bliss par excellence with the Ultimate Unique One. The drunkard is liable to several births. But the 'Gnani' has become deathless. Both were in different levels and in different states. They obtained results suitable to the state in which they were.

The state of character, the state of worship, the state of the mind, the state of mental control, the state of meditation, the state of Yoga, the state of craving, the state of sexual desire, the state of intoxication caused by liquor, and the state of torpor in men, differ. It is the state in which he loses consciousness of his 'Self' that determines the reward he will get. The drunkard obtained the reward of rebirth. The 'Gnani' obtained the reward of the state of Fullness and Perfection. In both these states, they have lost consciousness of personal honour. The state of the 'Gnani' is different from the state of the drunkard. The drunkard lost his consciousness of personal honour as a result of degradation caused by forsaking Wisdom. But the 'Gnani' lost his consciousness of personal honour in a state of Divine Luminous Wisdom. You should understand these two states.

So said His Holiness Guru Bawa to his disciple.

67.   **At 4:40 P.M. On 5/8/70**

A Guru tells his disciple:

Child! You have come here with your mind loaded with sorrows and pains and many desires. Listen carefully to the following illustration.

There lived a beggar, who used to beg everywhere. If work was available, he would work. He eked out his living by begging and by doing odd jobs, whenever they were available.

One day he came along the Palace Road. The Princess and her maids were playing ball upstairs in the Palace. The ball bounced over the wall and fell on the road in front of the beggar. The beggar took the ball and looked up. The Princess and her maids looked down the road and over the wall. When they were looking out, the beggar saw the beautiful Princess and fell in love with her. So, he went to the gate of the Palace to give the ball, personally, to her and to enjoy her beauty close at hand. The Princess and her maids came down to the Palace gate.

The commander of the soldiers who guarded the Palace gate, had been thinking for a long time of killing the King and marrying the Princess. When the beggar came to the Palace gate with the ball, the Commander assaulted him, kicked him and snatched the ball from him. The Princess who saw this, told the Commander, "Are you a Commander? Are you a man? You are showing your prowess on a poor man and torturing him!" The Commander replied, "Does this beggar know your greatness, Princess? He may form a low opinion about you. So, I assaulted him and snatched the ball from him. Here is the ball." The Princess sent a maid to get the ball from him. She obtained the ball through the maid and told the Commander, "Only God knows what is in one's mind. One who does not use His Wisdom is a fool. It is his nature to call all wise men he meets fools. In your mind you are forming plots. So you think that others are also doing the same thing. This is the attitude of a fool. Such a person will not understand compassion, truth, patience, their nature and the Grace they emmanate." Then she bade good-bye to the beggar and went away.

The beggar prostrated himself on the ground and rose. He had been listening to the conversation between the Commander and the Princess. The sweet words of the Princess increased his love for her. He went away in a reflective mood. He thought, "I am a beggar, she is a Princess. How can we ever marry? It is impossible." But he could not get rid of his love for her.

He continued to lead his life of begging. In the meantime, the Princess reached marriageable age. The king thought, "I have become old. It will be better if I get my daughter married to a Prince and hand over the Kingdom to her while I am alive." He discussed this with his daughter. The Princess told her father, "I will marry only a person with proper beauty and fullness of character who has reached that which is Omnipresent." Her Guru had taught her to reach that stage.

The portraits of a large number of handsome Princes were received by the King. The Princess rejected all these portraits and refused to marry any one of them. The King felt sad and consulted his Minister. The Minister consoled the King and said, "Do not feel sad, Your Majesty! We may publish the requirements of the Princess by the beat of a tom-tom. A man who has all these qualities will come." The King ordered him to do so. The requirements were published by way of a tom-tom. The conditions published were as follows: Those who have true beauty, fullness of character, and who have obtained the beauty of that which is Omnipresent, and who have come to know it and understand the meaning and nature of it, can meet the Princess and explain it to her. Such a person can marry her and rule this Kingdom. If anybody fails to give the proper meaning to these questions, they will be placed on the leg of an elephant and trampled to death.

There were a large number of people who considered themselves very handsome. But since they were unable to explain the meaning of her words, they were afraid they would lose their lives. So, none went to the Palace. Two or three months passed. Since none turned up, the King consulted his Minister. The Minister suggested that they ask the Princess where such a person could be found. The King agreed.

When they asked the Princess, she replied, "People who have this beauty may be found everywhere. They may live beyond the towns and villages. They may live in the forests. They may live in the Himalayan mountain range." When the King and the Minister asked her to confirm whether they could be found in the Himalayan Mountains, she replied that they could be found there as holy men or wanderers.

So the King and the Minister sent their troops to the Himalayan Mountains in search of them. The beggar, referred to earlier, thought that he could marry the Princess if he went to the Himalayas and learned to answer the questions. Because of his obsession for her, he grew a beard. He thought that if he went to the Himalayas, they would also take him to the Princess. So he went there. He did not know any Mantras (holy words meant for incantation). So, he just kept on saying "Narayana, Narayana" (Narayana is one of the thousands of names for God). The King's soldiers ignored him. They went up the mountains and searched. They saw a man standing on one leg. Another man was sitting. Another man kept his mouth wide open. Another was reclining. They all remained in the postures they had assumed like statues without moving. The soldiers shook these people and asked whether any one of them wished to marry the Princess and rule the Kingdom. None replied. But the holy man who was in a reclining posture told them, "There may be a person who would like to marry the Princess. Go and search for him." The soldiers came down the mountain, searching.

The beggar, who saw them coming down, ran away, begged and had his meal. Then he came to his place by the side of the road and kept on incanting the words, "Narayana, Narayana". The soldiers came to him and asked him to marry the Princess and rule the Kingdom. He recognized the Commander of the soldiers who had kicked him earlier and who was begging him now to come with him to the Princess. He did not want to go with him. He wanted the Minister to come and invite him. So, he told them, "Oh people! who are the King's men. Oh Commander! Let the people concerned come. You may go away." They told the King and the Minister what had happened. In the meantime the beggar regretted his action and wondered whether they would return.

The King sent his Minister. The beggar told him, "You are only the Minister. Let the King and the person concerned come. You may go." After sending away the Minister, the beggar wondered whether the King would come.

The Minister told the King what had happened. The King said, "I will go and invite him. Get the Palanquin (passenger carriage) ready. Get all the gifts ready. The Princess told the King that she also wanted to accompany the King and see this man. They all set out on the journey and reached the foot of the Himalayas.

The beggar begged and took his meals. Then he sat by the side of the road waiting for the King. The King and the Princess bowed and paid obeisance to him. Then the beggar felt happy that the beautiful Princess whom he loved had come. The King requested him to take charge of the

Princess and the Kingdom. At that time, the beggar thought, "When I repeated the word 'Narayana' without any purpose or piety, the man who assaulted me and the King and the Princess, all have fallen at my feet. I begged and ate. I repeated the word 'Narayana' without any aim. But, if I repeat the word 'Narayana' with real piety and fervour, the eighteen thousand worlds will fall at my feet."

So, he related to the King what had actually happened. He told him, "I repeated the word 'Narayana' without any piety. I took up the role of a holy man because of my love for a woman. I want to lose this body, know God and reach Him. You may get your daughter married to someone else." Then the Princess said, "I will marry this man who has this Divine Beauty, who has obtained the characteristics of God and who has known God." The beggar said, "Go away; I want to reach God." The Princess replied, "I also want to reach God." She sat by his side. Both of them said in union, " 'Ohm! Namo Narayana!' " Both spirits merged together and wandered around the world.

There are people like this beggar in this world, who are subject to craving, sexual desire, attachment, joy and sorrows. Like him, they succumb to the hypnotic fascination of sex and go about in search of some place where they can get satisfaction. They reach the Guru. The Guru comes to know the loads of attachment, friendship, desire, lust and the world which they carry in their minds. He will know the obsession each is having. The Guru will administer the spiritual medicine to remove the obsession. He will then feed them with the honey of Grace available to him and feed them with Wisdom (Arivu) and try to remove their loads. This beggar stood firm, even after seeing the Princess whom he loved, but he still wanted to know God. He knew that if he developed Faith in God, he would be able to rule the Universe. In the same manner, if man also develops Faith in his Guru, Faith and Determination in the Truth and stands firm with Patience; whether he is faced with bewitching beauty or agonizing pain, the Guru will remove him from his spiritual disease and from his cycle of birth and take him to God. If the man does not have the characteristics of Faith, Determination and Wisdom (Arivu), teaching Divine Truths to him will be like teaching to an ass. To succeed in anything, a man must have Faith, Determination, Certitude and Patience. If he has these qualities, only the Guru will be able to remove the world of Maya from him. So said His Holiness Guru Bawa to his exemplary disciple.

68.   **At 9:15 A.M. on 5/10/70**

His Holiness Guru Bawa addresses his disciples thus:
Children! The lowest of God's created beings is the worm. It lives in dirty places and where there is human excreta. It lives in water. It lives in putrefied wounds and tissues. It enjoys living in places full of foul smells. It also lives in the last Hell. Therefore, in both worlds it lives in the same type of place. It enjoys the taste of foods fit for Hell. All other beings try to get rid of the worm. These worms cause trouble to whatever being in which they live.

In the same way there are worms of Action (Karma) in the form of human beings who enjoy living in the deep pit of the Hell of sexual pleasure. Their number is countless. These human worms live in places which emanate bad and repelling smells like the dwelling places of natural worms and germs. Only a few with human form are born as Men, grow up as Men, live as Men and disappear as Men. Just like the germs and worms which hide in dirt and who enter wounds and the body, these good men pierce the body which is full of craving caused by the darkness of Ignorance (Agnana) with their sharp, deep Penetrating Light of Wisdom (Arivu) and burn out the pus and bad odour of all impermanent things and go beyond in search of, and meet, the One Permanent Being which is beyond the beyond. In the place where this Man's Wisdom (Arivu) sees That Permanent Being, he will have developed to the stage where God will attract his Wisdom (Arivu) towards Him just as a magnet attracts a piece of iron towards it.

In that stage God is called the Ultimate Unique One, that is, Wisdom (Arivu) within Wisdom (Arivu). When this Man reaches that stage, people will chase him away from this world in the same way as worms and germs are killed with insecticides. You should, therefore, regardless of what happens, never lose heart. If you go on analysing your inner self, you will reach God.

69. ## At 12:30 P.M. on 5/10/70

His Holiness Guru Bawa tells his disciples:

Children! Please listen to a small explanation. You can study Divine Wisdom (Gnana). You can study the world. You can study books. You can study religions. You can study anything. But to put into practice what you have learned you need the services of a Guru. It is not enough, even if the Guru shows you how they can be put into practice. The misguided wrong wisdom of the disciple should first be removed. His Ignorance (Agnana) should disappear. His Egoism (Anawam) should be annihilated. His sense of duality, 'mine and yours', should disappear. Envy and Treachery should be weeded out of his mind. In the mirror of his heart the mercury of Wisdom (Arivu) should be applied to make it clearly reflect the image falling upon it.

When Wisdom (Arivu) is applied to the heart of the disciple, then the Light of the Wisdom of Divine Grace from the Guru falls on it and the power of the disciple's heart can be brought out clearly. If the mercury of Wisdom (Arivu) had not been applied to the mirror of his heart, there would be no reflection forthcoming from the heart. It will be dark. When the heart is in this state, it does not matter what is the power and intensity of the Light which the Guru may focus on it, for the Light will not be reflected with brilliance. The effect will be like that of candle light in a dark place.

But if the disciple applies the mercury of Wisdom (Arivu) to the mirror of his heart and keeps it spotlessly clean, then, when the Light of Divine Wisdon full of the Guru's Grace falls upon it, it will reflect the Light with dazzling brilliance. All the scenes within the citadel of the Heart will be seen. You should understand this well and take necessary action to purify your heart.

At 12:50 P.M. on 5/11/70

Dr. Selvaratnam asked His Holiness Guru Bawa: "Swami. Some people say that every happening in their lives is due to their fate. Is that correct?"

His Holiness Guru Bawa replied, "A man loses his Wisdom first. Then he meets with sorrows and pains. In the Pre-Creation period God, the Primal Unique One, was meditating within Himself. At that time His Resplendence of Grace (Arul Jothi) shone within Him. God placed it before Himself and looked at it with His Eye of Grace. When He looked at it He saw 124,000 'Rays of Light' coming out of it. God thought, 'What a mystery this is.' Then He considered Himself to be a mystery; the Resplendence that rose within Him as His Respository of Grace and the Rays of Light that came out of that as the Secret of Grace. The Original Manifestations (Athi Porul) He could not keep within Himself. He could not keep it within the 124,000 Rays of Light. He proclaimed, 'There is nothing equal to This. This is Trust (Amanitham). All have equal right to It. This is My property. Who is prepared to receive This?' Then, He asked the Rays of Light to look at It. The 124,000 Rays of Light looked at It. Their sight got blurred. They said, 'God! This has swallowed within It all our brilliance. We cannot bear the power of its Resplendence.'

"On hearing this, God kept It in His Hand and asked the mountains, earth, sea, trees, etc., 'Who is prepared to receive this Trust (Amanitha Porul)? Come forward.' While others did not come forward, Earth did and told God, 'I will receive It. I will take charge of It.'

"When God heard this, He said, 'O Earth! I am going to create you in My Image with My Beauty. I will keep within you, My Grace, My Trust (Amanitha Porul) and the whole Universe. I will keep within you Myself, this Trust (Amanitha Porul) and all the Rays of Light that came out of the Trust.

" 'Whatever you may dispose of, you should return My Trust (Amanitha Porul) to Me. It will be found within everything. I will be creating from you. Everyone will have a right to It. This is My Trust and at the end This should be returned to Me.

" 'I give This to you, O Earth! It is your duty to return It to me. You have done a great injustice to yourself, because you have come forward to take charge of This Precious Article which all others have refused. This has only One Colour. It is one with Me. It came out of Me. It saw only Me. But you have within you numberless objects, numberless colours, numberless luminosities, darkness with an intensity that none can measure, numberless characteristics and states of torpor. Because you contain all these things, you may forget the fact. That is, you must return the Trust to Me from whom It came. You may not have the determination and steadfastness, so you may drop It or you may sell It for the love of alluring colours and forms.

" 'Amanitha means another person's property which has been given to you to keep in trust. If you fail to return it to the person who gave it to you, you will meet with losses. Since you came forward to take care of Something which none can, you must look after it very carefully and return It to Me.

'If you return It, you will be able to rule the whole Universe which I have kept within you and live, forever. You will have no birth, old age or death. You will have infancy or youth. You will assume My characteristics.'

"We are the creation referred to. We are called Man (Adam). Our Human Life is called Soul (Jeevan) or (Atma). Soul (Jeevan) is Life (Sivam). Life (Sivam) is Man (Adam). We are Man (Adam). If we realise who we are, then, where is Fate? It would be foolish not to return that which God gave us. We have failed to estimate our birth and our life, because we have lost our intellect and we have had to suffer. As a result we are subject to several births. Know this well. This is what is wrongly attributed to Fate.

"God has kept the whole Universe within Himself, and kept that Trust (Amanitha) within you and kept Himself and all the Rays of Light (Olis) within the Trust (Amanitha) and given It to us long ago and asked us to return It.

"You should find It and give It to the One from whom you originally got It. This is your obligation and duty. That is not Fate. You borrowed That (Amanitha Porul). You are a debtor. You must return that debt.

"When due to your foolishness you fail to return that debt, you write your own destiny. God is not to be blamed. You are determining your fate by what you earned. This is what Dr. Selvaratnam, other doctors and my children in the Serendib Sufi Study Circle and all other devotees should know."

71.   **At 10:40 A.M. on 5/12/70**

Children! Please listen to an illustration.

A fisherman tried his hand at various jobs. But he did not succeed in any of these jobs. A thought arose in his mind. "I have tried all jobs. But I did not succeed in any job. What job will help me to lead my life and also help me to get Spiritual Freedom. Whom shall I consult?" He walked along in this reflective mood.

In the meantime four brothers who had received four types of education and who needed four types of jobs, obtained the permission of their parents to go out into the world and seek jobs. They went to an elevated area of ground under a banyan tree and sat there. They asked each other what they had studied and what job they wanted. The eldest brother said that he had studied Sariyai (he knows the way people live in the world without knowing right or wrong). The second said that he studied Kiriyai (he knows the theory of realising the Truth, but his actions are material). The third said that he studied Yoga (he knows the theory of finding the Truth, but is attracted by the world). The youngest said that he studied Gnanam (he knows the theory of Knowledge of Truth but he has no True Wisdom). Then they began to discuss the merits of what they studied and argued with each other. This led to quarrelling. They quarrelled with each other and went along four roads which branched from there.

Later they again met at another junction and sat there under a tree facing four different directions. Some villagers accepted the person who had studied Sariyai as their Guru. Some accepted the person who studied Kiriyai as their Guru. Some accepted the person who studied Yoga as their Guru. Some accepted the person who studied Gnanam as their Guru.

At that time the fisherman, who was trying to find a job which would help him to lead his life and at the same time help him to get Spiritual Liberation, came that way. He was attracted by the crowd and wanted to seek advice there.

He met the Guru who had studied Sarayai and said, "I have tried my hand at all jobs. What is the job that will help me to lead my life and help me to attain Spiritual Liberation?" The Guru asked him what job he did last. He replied that he had been selling dried fish. The Guru told him, "Now, if you sell fish, you will be able to get Liberation of your Soul (Atma)." He asked the Guru, "Where can I get the fish?" The Guru replied that it is found in the sea.

After listening to him he went to the Guru who had studied Kiriyai and told him, "To carry on my life and to get Liberation for my Soul (Atma) I propose to catch and sell fish. Where is the sea from which I can obtain fish?" This Guru replied, "The Sea? Do you want to obtain Liberation of your Soul (Atma)? Go to the open space and search. You will find the sea."

The man could not understand him. So, he went to the third Guru who had studied Yoga and asked him, "I want to catch and sell fish. Where can I find the sea?" "Do you want to know where the sea is? Go to the wide space and look. You will see waves. If you go to that place, you will see the sea", that Guru replied.

Then the man went to the fourth Guru and asked him where the sea could be found. He replied that it is blue in colour. Fish live in it. You may catch them.

After listening to him, the man went in search of the sea. He went to an open wide space and looked. It was a wide expanse. He did not find the sea or the fish. Then, he went to the place in the wide plain where he saw waves moving. He found that the sea was not there, that his feet did not get wet and that there were no fish. When he was returning, it became night. He sat under a tree and looked up. Since it was night, the stars were twinkling in the sky. A traveller passed by. He asked the traveller what was seen in the sky. He replied that it was a fish and went away. Then he thought, "What the fourth Guru said is correct, but I can not catch the fish. How can I go there, catch and sell the fish and lead my life and obtain the liberation of my Soul (Atma)?"

He went to another Guru. That Guru asked him, "Son! What is the matter? How many Gurus did you have?" He replied, "I had four Gurus. But I was unable to earn my living and obtain freedom for my Soul (Atma)." He related everything to him in detail.

The Guru replied, "What the Gurus said is correct. You have undergone suffering in your attempt to get freedom for your Soul (Atma). They told you what they learned from books. These four Gurus are Earth, Water, Fire and Air. They were born from the world. They are the four religions of this world. They are the four elements. They are the four faces. The four faces are the four steps. The four steps are four types of worship. They are not the types of worship for Spiritual Liberation which you wanted.

First, the dried fish is your dried up body. You have been selling your body which had dried up as if the embryo in it had been roasted. You did not get the desired result. Give up selling this dried fish and sell fresh fish. Fresh fish is the ray of Divine Luminous Wisdom (Noor). It is the Perfect Man (Meem), the Resplendence of Grace that originated from the Primal Unique One. Your embryo was in the shape before it developed and you were born. It was a ray in the form of a fish. It is smaller than an atom. There is the Soul (Atma) which developed within the embryo. Seize that ray and sell it. Then you will be freed from re-birth. It is good to know this.

143

Second is the open space. The sea of Illusion (Maya) spreads everywhere where Mayakkam, a state of spiritual torpor caused by the influence of Illusion (Maya), exists. In that sea of sexual pleasure is found that fish. Catch it and sell it.

Third, when you go to the open space and observe, you will find moving waves. It is a mirage. You know the waves of your mind. The mind retains everything it sees in the form of visual impressions. A state of spiritual inertia caused by the hypnotic fascinations of Illusion (Maya), the world, the sky, water, air, fire, darkness, Illusion are all kept within this mind. Your mind tries to embrace all four hundred lakhs (one lakh is 100,000) of crores (one crore is ten million) of enticing and alluring projections of Illusion (Maya). But your mind was unable to succeed. Yearning for them, you went in search of the sea to gain Spiritual Freedom and travelled in spite of hunger and disease in the wide expanse and reached the waves of sorrow in your mind. Within that wide expanse of your mind you should search for the Effulgence of Divinity found within the Resplendence of Divine Luminous Wisdom lodged in the innermost recesses of your heart. That which is Soul (Atma) is in a free state.

Fourth, about the fish in the sky. The Throne of God on the Top of the Head (Arsh), the Triple Flame of God (Aliph), Light (Lam) and Perfect Man (Meem), the Triple Rays, the Divine Luminous Wisdom (Perr-Arivu) and God are there. The Atma Guru (the True Guru who has discovered God and Self by his Wisdom) shines from the forehead in a state of Formlessness and spreads its Resplendence and Resonance everywhere. Get hold of it. The Effulgence of the Soul (Atma) is there. Receive it.

This Guru explained to him all the implications of what he said. He prepared him for his spiritual ascent, and when he had progressed fully, he enabled him to reach God. The Guru who had reached That Object which is Wisdom (Arivu) within Wisdom (Arivu) is the Atma Guru, who was in the form of Divine Luminous Wisdom and Divine Grace, who was able to do this.

This Atma Guru further tells him, "Son! There are the four Religions (Vedas). There are the teachings of these four Gurus which cause a lot of mental and spiritual suffering and a chain of rebirths. Their teachings are the four Vedas—the four religions—the four steps—the four elements. These Gurus consider themselves to be great but have hidden their Lord. They have encouraged caste divisions, destroyed righteousness, developed unrighteousness, destroyed Divine Wisdom and spread Ignorance (Agnana) and chased away real Divine Wisdom (Gnana). They have developed the sixty-four alluring arts which serve their self-interest. They are in league with the three moods, the six sins, and the five grave crimes. They are devotees who develop egoism. They are fond of sex. They attempt to rule the three worlds. They are devotees who show the visions of the mind and physical visions as worlds of exquisite art (and cause the embryo of desires to be fertilized and grow in the womb). They finally consign your corpse to the Fire and then to Hell. They are experts in the sixty-four arts. They are the people who have obtained the freedom of this world. You should understand the nature of their teachings. You should know the Primal Unique One, Who has no shape or form, Who is the light of your heart, Who is in the form of Grace, Who is the Effulgence of Divine Luminous

Wisdom within your heart. That is Spiritual Freedom. So the fifth Guru, full of Grace, explained this to that devotee.

So said his Holiness Guru Bawa to his disciples.

72.   **At 7:20 P.M. on 5/18/70**

Man is the highest and noblest of God's creations. His body is made of the five elements. When he is born, his body contains all necessary faculties. But he has no moustache or teeth. A few days after his birth, the infant begins to laugh. It is a beautiful sight to see the infant laugh, though he has no teeth. Later, teeth appear in the mouth of the infant. He makes the world happy by laughing, showing his sparkling clean teeth. He shows his joy and sorrow with his teeth. He uses the teeth to bite the things of the world and enjoy the tastes.

Later hair grows on his upper lip. He calls it his moustache and twists and twirls the ends to show his egoism, vanity and courage. But the teeth which appeared after he was born fall out before his death: the teeth with which he laughed and attracted the world. Before the hair on the head, which appeared earlier, becomes grey, the moustache which appeared later, which he twirled to show his courage, becomes grey. This is the Fate of the teeth and the moustache which appeared later.

Man builds up the physical body and the attributes of the body with blood and attachments due to blood relationships. He kills other beings and uses them as food for his body. He exhibits his strength, courage, physical brawn and attractive body, and feels happy as a result. He has forgotten the Soul (Atma) which appeared in the Pre-Creation period and the beauty of the Divine Wisdom of Grace of the Ultimate Unique Effulgence, and is intent on developing the physical body which came later and is attracting the attention of the world, just as did the teeth and the moustache, which appeared after the body came into the world. But when he is past forty, his nerves become less sensitive and fail to work properly. He loses his attractive beauty. His hair becomes grey. His skin gets wrinkled. His blood supply is reduced. His stamina disappears. He develops intolerance and shouts at everyone in the same way as a dog barks at everyone. His egoism and overhastiness disappears. Since he has failed to realise who he is, he drops from That One from which he originated in the beginning, just as the teeth drop before the man dies. He paid attention to the development of something which appeared later. He exhibits his body and enjoys the world, forgetting what is in store for him. He wanders like a ghost, gets obsessed and dies.

But if he had obtained the beauty of That One from which he originated in the beginning, the whole universe would look at him and feel happy at his sight, in the same way as the world felt happy when he, as a toothless infant, smiled and laughed. Everything in the Universe would be attracted towards him. Everything would merge within his beauty. Since he failed to get that Divine Beauty in his body, but only paid attention to the beauty of the physical body and lost the earlier Divine Heritage, he becomes subject to several rebirths. If you understand this, and develop the inner Divine Beauty, with that Beauty, you can keep the physical body, which came later, attractive and protect it. Otherwise, just as the teeth which dropped, this body will also be destroyed. You should understand this well and act accordingly.

So said His Holiness Guru Bawa to his disciples.

73.   **At 7:50 P.M. on 5/18/70**

An exposition on the brain:

Child! The brain has four hundred lakhs (one lakh is 100,000) of crores (one crore is 10 million) of petals similar to the petals of the lotus flower. Each petal has ten and a half crores of births. In each birth one can see four hundred lakhs of crores of shapes and colours. These colours and shapes are seen in mental visions and in physical visions. In addition, in dreams and in wakeful states, at night and in day time, during sleep and when one is wide awake, in states of hypnotic torpor and fatigue, and in states of degradation of the intellect, projections of the mind appear. Through these projections the darkness of hypnotic fascination of Illusion (Maya) appears. In this darkness one sees scenes enacted. These scenes will show the sun, the moon, the stars, the planets, the clouds, fire, water, air, the earth, the sky, the sea, the rising land, ships, emeralds, gold, gems and other scenes of darkness of the demons living in the four hundred lakhs of crores of types of worlds.

Human intelligence submits all these scenes which appear in the panorama of the human mind in its dream state, i.e., the good and bad actions, joys and sorrows, success and failure, the armed forces, the wars, and other actions caused by the ten and a half crores of powers in each petal of the brain. Human intellect, which is in a state of spiritual degradation, analyses these scenes, and prepares an assessment of one's worldly life. It assesses what it saw in the dream as victory, as joy, and what it saw as defeat, as sorrow. This analysis reacts on his senses and on his physical body and causes a shock. The nerves and bones lose their stamina. Because of the state of fear induced by the shock, all the diseases which were latent in the body come out in the open and chase away his Divine Wisdom (Pahuth-Arivu), hide his Divine Luminous Wisdom (Perr-Arivu), make him lose the Divine Effulgence within him, churn the physical body and make it a wreck, and torture his soul. As a result, he gets fatigued, loses his senses and dies.

The powers in the petals of his brain work only to satisfy the desires of the senses and the elements. As a result, his aims and desires lead to ninety-six types of obsessions, eighty-four types of diseases caused by the wind, 4,448 types of tissue disorders, four hundred lakhs of crores of mental diseases caused by the hypnotic fascinations of Illusion (Maya), diseases of Action (Karma) caused by the ten and a half crores of births, and the end of three and a half crores of births. They also lead to the understanding of the sixty-four Arts and Crafts (Kalas), the satanic state of the thirty-two attributes of the human body. They also lead to a spiritual sleep caused by inertia induced by ninety-five out of the ninety-six powers of the human mind. They also lead to the commission of the six sins: craving (Kama), hatred (Krotha), miserliness (Loba), lust (Moham), vanity (Matham) and envy (Macharyam). These are caused by the state of Spiritual Ignorance induced by Egoism (Anawam). They also lead to the darkness of Hell caused by Egoism (Anawam), Action (Karma) and Illusion (Maya). They also lead to the moods or the 'three strong evil qualities' (Rachitham, Thamaltram and Sathvicam) which torture the faculty of Wisdom (Arivu), and the five dreadful sins of intoxication, lust, theft, murder and falsehood, which are enemies of Spiritual Progress. The diseases caused by all these states impinge and influence the mind, which in turn influences the senses. Again, the senses influence the mind. The mind influences Illusion (Maya), Illusion (Maya) causes spiritual inertia and hypnotic torpor which influences the alluring projections of Illusion (Maya). These influence human existence, which result in Actions (Karma). These actions influence the subconscious mind. The impressions in the subconscious mind influence the petals of the brain which elucidates the meaning. This in turn influences the power which makes use of the intentions of the mind. This results in the destruction of the glorious heritage of human existence. As a result, man loses his Spiritual Wisdom and slips down the path of degradation and destruction.

But, if this Spiritual Wisdom of man shines in Resplendence, removes the darkness of Illusion (Maya), chases the mind away, controls the influences of the five elements in the physical body, burns the five senses, repulses the attractions of the earth, opens the Gnostic Eye and cuts off the influences of the physical eyes, enables man to know his Self and know beforehand what is in store, sees what is in front and merges in That One which has neither end nor destruction. It will be the summum bonum of Human Existence and the Glory of The Ultimate Unique One (Paraparam). That Glory is Fullness. That Fullness is God. God is Man-God (Manu Eesan). That 'Manu Eesan' is God. You should understand this well. You should know the nature of the Petals of the Lotus of the Human Brain. So said the True Gnostic Guru (Meignana Guru) to his disciples.

74.   At 8:10 P.M. on 5/18/70

Children! How can one obtain Divine Wisdom (Pahuth-Arivu)? What is its nature? In what shape and in what manner should the iron safe of the heart be kept? I will give you an illustration.

Elephants like to eat wood-apples. It does not break the fruit and eat it. It plucks the wood-apple from the tree and swallows it. The hard shell of the wood-apple as a whole is thrown out of its body with its dung. All the essence in the fruit has been absorbed. Only the shell has been thrown out.

In the same manner, when the Wisdom (Arivu) of man picks up Good, Truth, Learning, Gnana, Patience, Compassion and such teachings and puts them inside the heart, Divine Wisdom (Pahuth-Arivu) should absorb the essence and throw out the rest from the heart just as the elephant throws out the shell of the wood-apple from its body after absorbing the essence. Only the essence should remain in the heart. Then the heart will become Light. The heart will become pure, sanctified and develop in the atmosphere of Divine Grace. It will not be heavy. The Gleam and Radiance will be there. But the refuse will not be there.

Only if a man's heart is in that glistening state, will he become a True Man (Insan) and get the Beauty of God. If he keeps the refuse of the world in his heart, on the other hand, the heart will be heavy.

Gnanis (Gnostics) say "Clean your heart with Wisdom (Arivu). Rub it and clean it. Keep it as clear as crystal. If one wants the heart to shine like crystal, he must seek the essence of Truth with Wisdom (Arivu). Otherwise the heart will not shine like crystal."

So said the Guru to his disciples.

75.   **At 12:10 P.M. on 5/19/70**

Children! Please listen to an illustration.

Look at the elephant. It has the strength of sixty to one hundred men. It is able to do in a day, work that one hundred men cannot succeed in doing. It is able to raise very heavy loads according to its strength. The essence of Water, Air, Fire, and Earth are in its body to a great extent. This gives it great strength. The elephant is able to carry on its back eight to ten people. It eats branches of trees, leaves, plantain trees, kitul trees, coconut plants and coconut leaves—things which other animals cannot eat. The elephant, which is not afraid of wind or rain, is afraid of a bird called "Anairanch-pul", whose feet have talons which can tear away the skin and flesh of the elephant. Man uses the elephant-goad, which has the shape of the talons of the bird, to frighten the elephant and control it.

Just as the elephant carries heavy loads, man also carries in his mind very heavy loads, heavier than the loads carried by the elephant. Just as the elephant carries on his back eight to ten people, man gets his elephant of egoism to carry the heavy load of the ten sins: intoxication, robbery, murder, falsehood, craving, hatred, miserliness, lust, vanity and envy, which are activated by the five elements and the five senses. He takes the form of craving and looks at everything with the eye of egoism and rules the world. Man develops the arrogance of egoism, rides on the elephant of vanity and attempts to carry the world and rule it.

But there is the disease called Death awaiting the elephant of egoism. Just as the elephant is afraid of the talons of the "Anairanch-pul" bird, man is afraid of Death. He is only afraid of Death. But he is not afraid of God, Truth, Conscience, the Divine Monitory Apparatus, Justice, Reality, Patience, Compassion, Love, Mercy, Charity, Pity. He will not even be afraid of the Effulgent Form of Truth.

So said His Holiness Guru Bawa to his disciples.

76.   **At 7:45 P.M. on 6/10/70**

A Yogi called Swami Puri from Assam in North India, during the course of his tour in Ceylon, came to Jaffna. During his stay in Jaffna, he paid a visit to His Holiness Guru Bawa on the 10th of June, 1970, at 7:45 p.m. accompanied by some of his followers who are natives of Jaffna. He was welcomed and given a chair on which to sit. Others who were present there sat on the floor. Swami Puri thanked His Holiness Guru Bawa for treating him with honour and said, "I have heard about you. So I came to meet you and find out your ideas about certain matters. I shall be glad if you will explain the methods of worship and meditation (Thiyanam) followed by Islamic Mystics (Sufis). I came late. I apologize for it. We were in meditation (Thiyanam) at our temporary residence. As a result we are late."

His Holiness Guru Bawa replied, "It does not matter. Do not be worried about being late; a little before you came, I was speaking to those present here about the type of meditation you people were practicing and the methods of worship and meditation adopted by Islamic Mystics (Sufis). I was explaining these things to Peter, the Divisional Revenue Officer, Nadarajah, Sangeetha Vidwan Ratnavel, Father Tampoe, Sabaratnam and others. I will repeat now what I told them earlier."

His Holiness Guru Bawa spoke in detail about meditation as follows:

"Brother! What you are practising is not Meditation (Thiyanam). To understand what is meditation and to practice it one must first be aware of its meaning and its implications. To sacrifice one's evil characteristics and evil propensies at the alter of the fire of one's Radiant Wisdom (Oli Arivu) is Meditation. To burn to ashes one's evil qualities in the fire of one's Radiant Wisdom is Meditation. To sit still closing one's eyes is not Meditation. To throw one's evil qualities into the fire of one's Wisdom (Arivu) and to burn it to ashes is Meditation. Meditation is a continuous process. When one is walking, sitting, sleeping, or is in a state of wakefulness, or when one is engaged in his profession or doing his duty, in fact, every moment of one's life, one should sacrifice one's evil thoughts to the fire of Radiant Wisdom. This is real Meditation. To sit still with closed eyes and neglecting one's duty is not real Meditation."

Mr. Somasekaram, former Director of Education, who came with Swami Puri said, "When we close our eyes and meditate, we can make our minds become still. When the mind is still we can merge with God. We were doing this type of Meditation".

His Holiness Guru Bawa replied, "Is that what you think? Can you still the mind by that process? The waves in the sea are never still. That is natural. As long as the sea exists, the waves and tides will be there.

"One's mind is like these waves; it is never still. Like these waves, one's mind moves hither and thither over the four elements of one's physical body, namely, Earth, Water, Fire and Air. Innumerable waves arise from one's mind. There are seven layers of waves in the sea, one arising on top of the other. When you look at the surface, it may appear as if there are no waves. But at the bottom, you will find waves moving. A little later, when you look at the bottom of the sea, the waves will appear to be still. But at the middle the waves will be moving. If you look later, at the middle, the waves there will appear to be still. Then at the top, you may see the waves moving.

"So it is with the mind. You sit still with your eyes closed and think, 'I am seated, my eyes are closed, I have controlled my mind. My mind is still.' But actually the mind is never still. The waves of the mind move every second endlessly without rest. Every wave of the mind creates seventy thousand (70,000) minor waves out of itself and seventy thousand mental vision or pictures. You are deceiving yourself when you think that your mind is still when sitting immobile with closed eyes. Actually, you were sitting idle without doing your duty. You did not succeed in stilling the waves of your mind. Thus you are committing a very great mistake. You are neither meditating, nor are you doing your duty."

Mr. Sabaratnam translated into English what His Holiness Guru Bawa had said in Tamil. Swami Puri said that he accepted fully what His Holiness Guru Bawa had said.

His Holiness Guru Bawa continued:

"Brother! God has three duties to perform. Man, the most wonderful creation of God, has only one duty to perform. This we were discussing before you arrived. Do you know what his duty is?" Swami Puri said that he did not know. His Holiness Guru Bawa said, "It is God's duty to Create, to Protect and to Succour. He is doing his duties without fail. But man has only one task to perform, that is, to give up the visions of the mind and the visions of the physical eyes. He has to forget the visions that his mind

149

creates. He should not keep them in his memory and as a result of this develop a desire in his subconscious mind, that one day he can physically achieve what he has seen in his mental vision. If man concentrates on his daily duties alone and neglects the one most important duty, he will simply be wasting his precious time."

Swami Puri said that he agreed fully. His Holiness Guru Bawa further said, "Brother, you said that you were practicing Meditation in accordance with the Saiva (religion) and Vedanta (philosophy). Then, you should be aware that Reality, the Ultimate Truth, is beyond the limitations of caste, colour, creed and religion. Do you agree that Reality is beyond the limitations of caste and creed?" Swami Puri replied that he agreed. His Holiness Guru Bawa said that the state of Perfection (Pooranam) is beyond the ultimate limits of the Veda (religion) and Vedanta (philosophy). It is not within the reach of a particular religion of creed, such as Vedas, Vedanta or Saivism. It is not within the reach of any particular caste. It is Universal. It is common to all mankind. Do you agree?" Swami Puri agreed.

His Holiness Guru Bawa added, "I was told earlier that you were teaching your followers to practice Meditation within the restrictions imposed by Vedanta. God is not within the limits of Vedanta. He is beyond. If you teach your followers to meditate in an area where God is not, you are not preaching His Truth.

"Let us consider for a while the nature and habits of crows. When they see a crumpled piece of black cloth of an umbrella, they mistake it for a dead crow. They will then gather around the black cloth and cry 'Ka, Ka' while sitting on fences, trees and shrubs. They think that one of their kind has died; they cry as if conducting its funeral and then depart. But the piece of black cloth remains where it is.

"In the same way, human beings are enticed by the symbols and rituals of the four religions. They run after the people who wear these symbols, shout their praises, give them fame, name and honour in this world. They mistake everyone who wears these symbols of religion for the real man of God in the same way as the crows mistake the black cloth for the real crow. You were speaking of Saiva Siththantham (religion) and Vedanta (philosophy). You are wearing the ochre robe (Kaavi). On seeing the ochre robe, these people are singing your praises like the crows. You also appreciate their praise. You are in a station where God is not; but still you are wearing the ochre robe. You should leave this station and go higher and beyond to where God is. That will be necessary for your self-realisation.

"Assam is far away. You have come from there to Lanka (Ceylon), an island beyond the southern tip of India. Ceylon is very far from Assam. There is a lot for you to learn in Assam. Your visit here will serve no purpose. People here have been attracted by your symbol. If you teach them Meditation without reaching the highest spiritual station where God is, they will desert you in the same way as the crows, which mistook the piece of black cloth for a crow and deserted the black cloth. You should know this well. You should go higher and higher, beyond the beyond and know Him. Do you understand what I have said?" Swami Puri replied in the affirmative and agreed with what His Holiness had said.

His Holiness Guru Bawa continued, "One should know that Meditation roots out all the evil qualities in a person. Only a diamond can cut a diamond. One should adopt the Divine Qualities of God and with the Divine Compassion that results from this, one should cut oneself away from the vicious hold of the senses and these foolish symbols and thus cut the cycle of birth. The darkness of Illusion (Maya) should be cut with the diamond of Divine Grace which is activated within one by adopting the Divine Qualities of God. Illusion (Maya) defies destruction. God is the true diamond which can cut all these things including Illusion (Maya). With this true diamond, one should cut oneself free from the hypnotic fascinations of Maya and from the egoism and fanaticism which grows out of strong adherence to the rituals of conventional religions. If you do not possess this true diamond, you will not be able to cut yourself free from the clutches of Illusion (Maya), even if you take ten and a half crores (105,000,000) of births. If you are in a state where you cannot cut yourself free from Maya and the cycle of births, you will not be able to know God. You should know this well. You were speaking of Sufi Meditation and Vedantic Meditation and wanted to know about the differences. This is like a person attempting to cut one diamond without having another diamond to cut with. To cut the diamond of Illusion (Maya) you should go beyond the beyond and reach the station where God is and meet Him, and obtain the true diamond of His Grace. Do you agree with what I have said?"

Swami Puri replied that he fully agreed.

His Holiness Guru Bawa continued, "Look at the Earth! It contains myriads and myriads of hypnotic fascinations of Illusion (Maya) to which men succumb and bring about their own degradation. God, in His Glory and Perfection, examined the nature of the Earth very carefully, sifted it and selected the constitutents that He needed, melted them and filtered the molten liquid and took the essence from which He created Man, the noblest of His Creations. Further, God has reduced the eighteen thousand worlds and all the created beings within the eighteen thousand worlds, both visible objects and invisible objects, articulate and inarticulate beings, things that can move and things that cannot move, into a particle within a particle. The size of this particle is almost beyond description. Take an atom of an atom. Divide that into seventy thousand particles. Take a particle of one of those particles. You can imagine the diminutive dimension of that infinitesimal particle. God, having reduced the eighteen thousand worlds with all the beings and things in them to the size of this minutest particle, enclosed it within a Ray of His Divine Effulgence, and kept it inside Man whom He created as His noblest creation. If man can know himself, his innermost state, the state and nature of God's Creation, the Glory of his Creator, and the Divine Treasure mentioned earlier, he will then realise how infinitesimally small are the eighteen thousand worlds and all the beings and things within it. If one were to divide an atom into forty million particles and take one particle out of those particles and look at its size, he will find that all the eighteen thousand worlds are smaller than that infinitesimal particle. It will be so small that if man can realise this, he will be able to rule the eighteen thousand worlds; the world of gods (Devas) and this Earth. He will then realise that he is the King of all these worlds. He will come to realise that none else can equal him as the repository of Divine Grace, Power and Status. You should understand this."

Swami Puri replied that he understood what His Holiness had said. His Holiness Guru Bawa continued further: "The Tamil traditional Myths (Puranas) speak of Maha Vishnu (a Hindu High God). Maha Vishnu would fly all over the world and enter and leave the hearts of devotees. He had a vehicle. It was a mythological bird called Garuda of the eagle family. Maha Vishnu used to fly seated on the back of the Garuda. On the back of the Garuda was a mythological five-headed cobra which formed a coil of its long body to provide a seat for Krishna (Maha Vishnu) while its five-headed hood served like an umbrella to protect Krishna from the heat of the sun. When the Garuda was flying, the nose of the cobra came near the nose of the Garuda. It should be noted here that the Garuda is a bird which kills snakes whenever it sees them. But in this safe position, the cobra without any fear for the Garuda, its natural enemy, sarcastically inquired after Garuda's health. Garuda replied, 'How can I under the present circumstances speak about our mutual health? If you ask this same question from your normal position, I could give you a proper reply. Now, you are in a place which is not your normal station. Therefore, how can I give you a fitting answer?' This discussion occurred in a situation where the Garuda was below and the cobra was above."

His Holiness Guru Bawa explained the meaning of this Traditional Myth. He said, "The two wings of the Garuda signify Craving and Infatuation. Its body indicates Illusion (Maya). Its two legs indicate good and evil actions. Krishna indicates the Radiance of the Soul (Atma) or Divine Wisdom (Pahuth-Arivu). The five heads of the cobra signify the physical body made of the five elements, Earth, Fire, Water, Air and Ether. Illusion (Maya) and the five senses which are indicated by the Garuda and the five elements indicated by the five-headed cobra thrive because of the assistance rendered to them by the Soul (Atma). In the illustration given by me, the Garuda is able to carry Krishna and the five-headed Cobra is able to protect Krishna from the heat of the sun, because of the help rendered to them by Krishna. In the seat of our heart is the Radiance (Jothi) of the Divine Wisdom. It is this Divine Wisdom which is carried by the five elements, which constitute the physical body which in reality is an illusion.

"As told in the Myth, Krishna or the Divine Wisdom (Pahuth-Arivu) sought and obtained the help of enemies referred to as the Garuda and the Cobra who are inimical to one another and who attempt to kill one another in their desire for dominance. The Soul (Atma) is now on friendly terms with its natural enemies and has extended its help to them and even sought their help. Thus, when Atma had not seated itself in its proper station, how could it overcome its enemies? How could it kill them? In fact, this Soul (Atma) has put itself in a state of endless misery by extending its help to its own enemies and obtaining their help in turn, due to its wrong judgement."

His Holiness continued; "In the same way you have also lost your proper station. You have imprisoned yourself within the symbols of conventional religion, within the confines of Veda, Vedanta, caste and creed. You have conditioned yourself within these restrictions. Within the ambit of these restrictions, you are preaching and you are practicing Meditation according to your preaching. This will result in misery for the Soul (Atma) and the suffering of several births. Therefore, for the sake of your spiritual liberation go beyond Veda and Vedanta, beyond the beyond. Did you understand what I have said?"

Swami Puri said, "What you say is true. I have to search for The Reality beyond Veda and Vedanta."

His Holiness Guru Bawa replied, "If that is so, do not look this way. Look beyond. Do not preach to the world. Learn for your own spiritual advancement."

His Holiness added, "In the Tamil traditional mythologies we learn of the form of Nadesan (Hindu Deity). We have observed the people worship the statue of Nadesan. In the statue, we see the figure of Nadesan standing on one leg trampling firmly on Muyalakan (a triple-headed giant of Hindu mythology) with his other foot raised in a dancing pose. He is carrying the four elements, Earth, Fire Water, and Air in his four hands. Sages, in ancient times who had the clairy of Divine Wisdom, who were supremely wise and who had achieved perfection drew a sketch of the Vision of Nadesan as it appeared within their Divine Luminous Wisdom (Gnanam). Only the Divinely Wise Men can understand the inner meaning of the sketch of Nadesan that the Sages drew. The common people in the world cannot understand this inner meaning. They have given various interpretations to the figure of Nadesan according to the state of their intellect and Wisdom and given it a name and use it as an object for Divine worship. They worship the statue with the same reverence as some worship God Almighty.

"When that true Sage concentrated his true gaze with his eye of Grace at the Radiance of Divine Luminous Wisdom (Perr-Arivu), His Perr-Arivu began to shine in Splendrous Lustre. The Resplendence of his Perr-Arivu extended from Awwal (first) to Akhir (last) and its rays enveloped all the worlds. The Resplendence of Perr-Arivu did not see any other form. It absorbed everything within itself and it shone by itself as a Unique Entity. In that state, His Perr-Arivu did not see any other form. It absorbed everything within itself and it shone by itself as a Unique Entity. In that state, His Perr-Arivu trampled on Muyalakan, the triple-headed Giant of Egoism (Anawam), Action (Karma), and Illusion (Maya) with the foot of his Radiant Wisdom, and grasped the physical body of Illusion (Maya) composed of the four elements. In one hand he held the Earth, in another hand, the Fire, in the third hand, Water, and in the fourth hand, Air symbolized by the Primeval Drum (Udukku). Displaying these four elements in its hands on all four sides, it danced with the leg of Perr-Arivu raised, which extended all over the world and the universe. Everything became it and danced within it.

"In this state, the Perr-Arivu split Maya into its four constituents of Earth, Fire, Water, and Air and reduced each of the elements to the infinitesimal particle of a particle of an atom of an atom and holding these four in its four hands proclaimed to all, 'Look at what is in my hands! Do you think that men cannot carry their weight?' And it continued to dance. It is this vision that the Sage, who realised his true self and knew who he was, saw and sketched. This has now been turned into a beautiful article of sculpture. Today the people of the world, who are unable to carry the weight of the earth, worship idols and statues and in the degraded state of their misguided knowledge have given various names and interpretations to this piece of sculpture and worship it.

"One must understand this and become the embodiment of Radiant Supreme Wisdom, i.e., Perr-Arivu. That which in its Resplendence would hold while dancing the crescent on its forehead, the sun in the vertex of its head, the world in its waist, the sea of Maya in its stomach, the fire in its rectum (Moolam), the messengers of God in its Heart (Qalb), the attachments of blood and sex in its chest, Illusion (Maya) between its legs and Hell underneath its leg of Wisdom. It is the Perr-Arivu which dances as the Resplendence of the Atmic Brilliance of Supreme Wisdom.

"That Resplendent Supreme Wisdom of Perr-Arivu envelops the whole universe and dances, observes all things, absorbs all within it and reigns over them, shows compassion on men and saves them. The all encompassing Ultimate Reality (Paramporul) shines in all its Divine Effulgence, as Divine Effulgent Wisdom within that Resplendent Supreme Wisdom of Perr-Arivu. Understand this well. You will be able to see the Resplendence of your Supreme Wisdom only when you get out of the shackles of race, religion, and caste. Come away from the four elements of your body i.e. Earth, Fire, Water, and Air and carry them in your hands and say, 'Oh! These four elements are but the four religions of the world', and throw them away. You should understand this well.

"You have been stating that you were practising and preaching Vedanta and Meditating without first throwing away the elements of your body and without allowing your Resplendent Supreme Wisdom (Perr—Arivu) to shine in its Glory. You have a long way to go to Reality."

Swami Puri asked His Holiness whether there is rebirth and whether he believed in rebirth. His Holiness Guru Bawa replied that he will not be born again. But people who are like the piece of black cloth and the crows, have to be born again. "I believe that I will have no rebirth. The ultimate end of Intellect (Puththi) is Vedanta (Intellectualism). Those who are in that state of consciousness and below are liable to be born again. They stay within the ultimate end of Puththi and strive to achieve their aim with its help. But with its help they will not be able to get liberation for their Soul (Atma). As a result they have to take several births. If one goes beyond the boundaries of Vedanta and Puththi, and goes beyond the beyond where the Ultimate Divine Effulgence is, he will have no more births. I have explained this to you earlier. If you had reflected carefully on what I said earlier, you would have realised this.

"Man is the rarest and the noblest of God's creations. He is surrounded by the hypnotic fascinations of Maya, the senses, the five elements, cravings, attachments, lust, vanity, worldly titles of honour, worldly jobs, the Vedas, the Vedanta, the divisive forces of colour, race, religion, caste, and creed, ignorance, egoism, and myriads of thoughts and desires. It appears to me that in your mind you think that these are of use to you. If you seek the aid of these things, if you stay within the fold of conventional religion like Vedas and Vedanta for the sake of getting glorious titles and praise of the world, you will meet with spiritual death. You should remember this.

"I will give you another illustration. A fox used to steal from the villages the food it liked, bring it to a hiding place behind a banyan tree near a pond, and eat it. A crocodile lived in that pond. It desired to catch the fox and eat it. One day the fox brought a fowl it had stolen to its normal hiding place near that tree by the pond and started eating it with

154

relish. Accidentally, the bowels of the fowl fell into the pond. The crocodile in the pond got hold of the bowels in its jaws. The fox told him, 'Brother, the bowels belong to me. Please give it to me!' The crocodile thought that it could get friendly with the fox by giving it the bowels and later eat the fox itself. The fox had become strong by eating a large number of things. Let him become strong by eating these bowels, also. So it gave the bowels to the fox. The fox ate it and became friendly with the crocodile. The crocodile also became friendly with the fox with the idea of seizing it by deceit one day and eating it. The fox also continued the habit of bringing daily various stolen food and eating it under the tree near the pond.

"In the course of time, the crocodile and the fox became very intimate. Taking advantage of this situation, the crocodile told the fox, 'Brother! my wife and children desire to see you. Our palace and our property are on the other side of the pond. We will be happy if you will come there and see them!' The fox replied, 'There is water in the pond; how can I come through the water?' The crocodile replied, 'You can get upon my back, I will carry you there.' So, the fox got on the back of the crocodile. When the crocodile was in the middle of the pond, it could not help asking the fox, in his joy at the prospect of dining on the fox, 'Brother! You were eating large quantities of various types of food. How tasty your liver and your fat will be!' The fox asked him, 'Do you want to eat my liver, Brother?' The crocodile replied, 'It is for that purpose that I brought you here.' The fox knew that he was in danger. So, he said, 'Brother! I have left my liver behind in my house. If you had told me earlier, I would have given it to you.' The crocodile asked him, 'Is that so?' The fox replied, 'If you take me back, I will take it and give it to you and then you can eat it.' So, the crocodile brought the fox back to the bank of the pond.

"The fox jumped onto the land and told the crocodile jeeringly, 'You stupid crocodile! Did you want to eat my liver? You will not be able to catch me any more. Ooh! Ooh!' The fox howled and ran for its life. The crocodile felt very sad at the thought that there is many a slip between the cup and the mouth.

"In the same way, if you lean on your brethren in this world, who are like the crows that cried over the piece of black umbrella cloth, and wear ochre robes and carry a copper vessel, and attach yourself to the ways of Meditation restricted by Vedas and Vedantas, race, religion, caste and creed, and place your faith in the sun and the moon and the hypnotic attractions of the world and its colours, and seek their help, praise and titles, this attitude will certainly kill and consume you.

"Attached to one's physical body are the entities projected by the five elements; namely, the senses, the conventional religions and religious fanaticism, the castes, Vedas, foolishness, anger, sin, darkness, egoism, vanity, jealousy, deceit, backbiting, falsehood, theft, liquor, murder, lust, tyranny, ill treatment, haste, impetuousness, visions of the physical eyes, visions conjured by the mind, the desire for woman, gold and property, the divisive forces of I and you, mine and yours, the feeling of I am great, and you are not great. All these and, similarly, four hundred lakhs (100,000) of crores (10 million) of hypnotic fascinations of the darkness of Maya will attach themselves to your Puththi and remove piety from your mind and will show you the nature of the five elements of your birth, i.e., Earth, Fire, Water, Air and Ether. They will feed you with earth, water, fire, air, and enlarge your physical body under the pretext of rendering help to your Soul (Atma) and will consume your Divine Wisdom and your birthright as Man, in the same way as the crocodile intended to eat the fox. If you get the help of these things to act as food to you they will certainly consume your birthright. You should know this well, and if you run for your life, from these crows who are following you and run away like the fox which escaped from the crocodile, and go beyond the boundary of conventional religion and worship, to beyond the beyond, you will escape.

"And in that open space that Resplendence (Perr-Arivu) will shine. In that Resplendence, (Perr-Arivu) will be the Primal Plenitude. You will be merged in that Plenitude and Perfection. That Effulgence will be merged in you. Within that Effulgence will be found everything. If you remain merged in that Effulgence, and then take an atom and divide it into seventy thousand pieces, and take a particle, of a particle, of a particle, of a particle, of that piece and look at it, you will see in it all the visions you saw with your mind and your physical eyes. Then you will come to know everything. If you reach that state, you will not be born again. If you do not reach that state, you will be born again. Do you understand what I have said? Do you agree?" Swami Puri said, "I endorse with all my heart all that you have stated."

His Holiness Guru Bawa said, "At least hereafter, remember this well. God has three duties to perform. The Perfect Man (Manu Easen) has only one duty to perform. God Creates, Protects and Succours. Your duty is to give up the visions created by the mind and the visions of the physical eyes and proceed further in your Spiritual Journey. This is Meditation (Thiyanam). Do you understand?"

Swami Puri said, "I accept all you said. Because I came to you I was able to learn what I should learn. I will put into practice your teachings. Please accept my thanks", and he went away.

77.   At 6:10 P.M. on 6/13/70

His Holiness Guru Bawa gives an illustration to his disciples:

A man may build a very beautiful palace with a large number of rooms for various purposes and decorate them with emeralds, diamonds, and other gems. But if he fails to brighten the palace with lighted lamps, the place will remain dark and become the dwelling place of satan and demons.

The physical body is the house of man, the noblest and most beautiful of God's creations. Man (Insan) was born to rule the universe. If he fails to get the Radiance of the Wisdom of God's Grace to shine in his heart, his physical body will become the home of satan and demons, just as the palace which is not brightened with lighted lamps will become the home of satan and demons. Man should ponder over this and understand this well, and shine as Radiance in the Resplendence of God's Grace. Then, only, will his physical body in which he is housed become the House overflowing with God's Grace. Children! You should understand this well.

78.   At 6:40 P.M. on 6/16/70

His Holiness addresses his disciples and tells them: "Children! I will give you an illustration."

The cobra, a poisonous snake, lives in the forest. To entice it and catch it, the Snake Charmer plays a tune called 'Nagavarali' on his pipe. The cobras, which enjoy this particular type of music, come out of their hiding places and hasten towards the place where this man is playing the tune 'Nagavarali'; and spread their hoods and dance to the tune. They become hypnotically fascinated by the music coming from the pipe. As the cobras forget themselves and are absorbed fully in the music and dance, this man takes the root of the cactus tree and holds it near the noses of the cobras. At the smell of the cactus root, the cobras fall down senseless. This man then immediately gets hold of the cobras by their necks and pulls out their poisonous fangs and puts the snakes in his basket. He trains these cobras and exhibits them in various places and ekes out his living.

In the same way, man gets hold of the poisonous hypnotic fascination of the darkness of Maya called Ignorance (Agnana) and makes it dance to his tune, himself dancing in front of it. He takes to all these antics to feed and look after his wife and children, his cattle and property. Like the cobra, this foolish snake in human form dances, enjoys his own dance and praises himself in the world of Maya. He controls the forces of Maya and gets the plaudits of the world. Just as the cobra moves its head this way and that and dances, this foolish man also moves his head and pokes it into many things in various places and tries to control Maya. This man has not gotten rid of the evil qualities and tendencies of Maya in his mind. In whatever manner he may disguise himself, these evil qualities and tendencies in his mind always wait for an opportunity to attack him and kill him in the same way as the cobra, which dances to the music produced by the man from his pipe, waits for an opportunity to attack and kill him. If the man is careless, the cobra will bite him. In the same way, if man is careless, the evil qualities and tendencies of Illusion (Maya) in his mind will attack and kill him. Therefore, man should be ever vigilant to prevent the poisons of Illusion (Maya) from attacking him and causing him spiritual and physical death. Children! Remember this well.

79. At 8:05 P.M. on 6/16/70

His Holiness Guru Bawa addresses one of his disciples and says:

Brother! Look at this bug. It sucks human blood. That blood turns into bug's eggs. The bug's eggs hatch and become young bugs. If you crush the bug that has sucked human blood, in that place, hundreds of young bugs will come out in due course. They themselves will bite you and suck your blood. If you crush them and kill them after they have sucked your blood, thousands of bugs will hatch from them. They will bite you all over the body and suck your blood in plenty.

Guided by Ignorance (Agnana), man feeds on the five elements of Illusion (Maya) i.e., Earth, Fire, Water, Air and Ether and grows. This Ignorance (Agnana) itself causes suffering and misery to man. When man attempts to remove the cause of his suffering by Ignorance, in the same way as he crushes the bug, the result is more suffering because Ignorance (Agnana) multiples like the bug. When he tries to remove his suffering, new sufferings appear in various guises, as he does not know the correct method of removing Ignorance (Agnana) itself. There is no end to this chain reaction. The more he attempts to remove the darkness of Ignorance

(Agnana), the darker it becomes.

But, if he is able to get the services of a real authentic Perfect Guru (Kamil Sheik), The Perfect Guru will apply the proper repellent and prevent the bug of Ignorance (Agnana) from coming near the man, and apply the ointment of Wisdom (Arivu) to soothe pain caused to the man by the bite of the bug of Ignorance (Agnana). In this way, the bug is spared its life, but prevented from approaching the man and causing any pain to him in the future. The man is cured of the pain caused by the bug earlier, and saved from attack by the bug in the future. The man is able to get peace of mind and sound sleep.

The Perfect Guru will apply necessary remedies to prevent the bug of Ignorance (Agnana) from coming near the man. The Perfect Guru also will indicate to the man his relationship with God. As a result, this man's Radiant Wisdom will become brighter day by day and his mind will become more and more serene.

If man tries to remove his suffering with his own effort without seeking the help of a Perfect Guru, his misery will increase day by day. If he wants to escape from this world of Illusion (Maya), he should seek the help of a Perfect Guru (Kamil Sheik).

80.   At 9:30 A.M. on 6/17/70

There are a large number of fish in the sea. As long as they move about as they please in the sea, they cannot be cooked in the cooking vessel. Only the fish that are caught on the fishing line can be cooked in the cooking vessel.

A large number of people visit the Guru. But they do not take his teachings into their heart and practice what they hear from him. They do not follow his instructions. They do as they please. Such people are of no use to the Guru in the same way as the uncaught fish which moves freely in the sea are of no use to the cooking vessel. Only those who listen carefully to the Guru and accept his teachings fully and put them into practice in their daily life can be of any use to the Guru. In the same way as only the fish that has been caught can be turned into a tasty curry by the cooking vessel, only the people who accept the Guru's teachings with their whole heart and put them into practice in their daily life can be made by the Guru to realise their Divine Heritage so that they may be of use to humanity.

81.   At 10:15 A.M. on 6/17/70

A stork stands still in the pond, patiently without moving, though it sees schools of fish moving about in the distance. It waits patiently until one fish leaves the school and comes toward it alone. When the fish gets within its reach, the stork will seize it.

When man allows his mind to wander in the sea of Illusion (Maya), indulging in the hypnotic joys of the senses, then Wisdom (Arivu), the flame of Gnosis, will not come near him in the same way as the stork will not move toward a school of fish swimming freely in the distance. Only when man gives up his kith and kin and comes alone, losing his ego and self-identity, in a state of innocence, with his mind and senses in a state of inaction as a result of fatigue caused by swimming hither and thither in the sea of Maya, Arivu, the flame of Gnosis, will take possession of him and prevent him from escaping again into the sea of Maya.

82. **At 10:20 A.M. on 6/17/70**

Children! I will give you an illustration:

Take the case of a large sailing ship which sails on the high seas. When it sails on the sea, it has to avoid sandbanks, rocks, reefs, sharks, large fishes, whales, etc. The Captain of the ship scans the sea with his telescope and steers his ship along a course avoiding all these obstacles. In case he accidently comes across these dangerous fish and whales, he cuts them to pieces with the long swords in the ship and guides the ship on its course. When he steers the ship on its course, sometimes very small prawns, which are the size of rice bran, will come in millions and stick to the propeller of the ship in such a mass that it will not be possible for the ship to move. To chase these minute sized prawns from the propeller and hull of the ship, the Captain will throw bags of bran into the sea. The prawns will leave the ship and rush towards the place where the bags of bran were thrown into the sea and eat the bran. In the meantime, while the prawns are busy eating the bran, the Captain will steer the ship away from them and make it sail on its proper course.

In the same way, when man sails on the sea of life which is actually the large ocean of Illusion (Maya), in the ship of Divine Wisdom (Pahuth-Arivu), he has to avoid many obstacles in this ocean of Illusion (Maya) such as Earth, Fire, Water, Air, Ether, etc. He will have to cut them to pieces with his sword of Wisdom (Arivu) and sail further in that ocean along the proper course. When he sails along carefully, his worldly desires, attachment to wife, children, friends, joys, sorrows, etc., stick to the keel of his ship of Divine Wisdom (Pahuth-Arivu) like the prawns of the minutest size referred to in the above illustration, and prevent the ship of Divine Wisdom (Pahuth-Arivu) from moving. As a result, man will not be able to advance spiritually. If even the slightest trace of desire, attachment, joy, sorrow, doubt, etc., remain in the mind, little by little these will accumulate and become such a big mass that man will not be able to progress spiritually in the ocean of Illusion (Maya). To get rid of these, he should throw overboard from his ship of Divine Wisdom (Pahuth-Arivu) the things that belong to Illusion (Maya), things such as gold, property, etc. He should rid himself of his material possessions which attract him and give up whatever he desires. Then Illusion (Maya) will leave him like the minute sized prawns, which leave the keel and hull of the ship to eat the bran thrown overboard. Only by throwing these things away can we escape. Then only, can we cross the sea of Illusion (Maya), the sea of blood, the black sea, the sea of currents, the sea of magnetic force, the sea of air and crores of such seas. If we cross all these with the help of Wisdom (Arivu), only, then, can we become Man.

83. **At 7:40 P.M. on 6/18/70**

Children! Listen to an illustration:

A tiger in the jungle is caught alive and trained to do many tricks in the circus shows. It is kept in a cage. While inside the cage, it goes round and round withouth resting, waiting eagerly for its food. Its full concentration is on food. When it is inside the cage, if it sees any animal which can serve as its food, it will straighten its tail, bend its back and jump at the animal.

But it will only knock itself against the iron bars of the cage and fall down. It thinks it is still in the forest and not inside the iron cage. So, it jumps at the animal forgetting that it is inside the cage.

In the same way, there are roaring human tigers confined within the cage of Egoism and Religious Fanaticism. They know not what is good or what is evil. They do not know where they are, where they come from and where they have to go. Like the tiger which goes round and round the cage with its whole concentration fixed on obtaining its food, these human tigers move about with their mind concentrated on achieving their selfish aims even at the risk of killing others. In that attempt, he knocks against the bars of the cage of Egoism and Religious Fanaticism and dies. He is obsessed with an extreme sense of Egoism arising from the Religious Fanaticism of Ignorance (Agnana). Even if the sun and the moon change their course, these people will never swerve from their path of Egoism and Fanaticism.

There are four-legged tigers living in the jungle. They do not know what is good and what is bad. But there are two-legged tigers living in the country. The tigers in the forest will die one day at the hands of the lion. But these two-legged tigers will one day become the victim of Yemen, the Angel of Death.

Therefore, we should know well where we are living and where we are bound to go after death. So said His Holiness Guru Bawa to his disciples.

84.   At 7:55 P.M. on 6/18/70

If a dog gets a sore in the body it will be able to lick it with its tongue and cure it. But if he gets a sore on the top of its head, it will die, because the wound is in a place where it cannot lick with its tongue.

If the faculty of Wisdom (Arivu) which will enable him to discern the Truth, does not develop in man, the sore of Ignorance will develop in his brain and kill him in the same way as the sore on the head will kill the dog.

85.   At 8:05 P.M. on 6/18/70

God rules man within and without. He pervades the whole universe. He pervades beings who can move about, immovable things, beings which can speak, beings which cannot speak. He is found within everything like magnetic power.

If you commit a crime or do something which is against your conscience, after some period of time you will get suitable punishment or meet with sorrow. At that time, when you reflect on the cause with your faculty of Intelligence (Puththi), your Divine Monitory Apparatus, The Divine Conscience will explain to you clearly the reason. "What you did is wrong. You assaulted him. He never committed a crime. You are sure to die sooner or later. You will be subject to God's Judgment. Go to the person whom you assaulted. Seek his forgiveness." Thus, something tells your Intelligence (Puththi). It brings fear to you and warns you. That which tells you this is God. Only one who listens to that inner voice or Divine Conscience and follows the path of Truth is Man. None else is Man. Know this well!

86.   At 8:15 P.M. on 6/18/70

Wind in the body goes out of the body, through the mouth as well as the

160

anus. The mouth emanates a bad smell. The wind goes out of the mouth with the sound 'Eh!' Through the anus it goes out with the sound 'Ah!' Both these openings emanate a bad smell. If the mouth is not cleaned regularly and washed, it emanates a bad smell. So too the anus. Both these openings are unclean. So we should ponder a little as to where cleanliness is. Even the orifice of creation emanates a bad smell. The opening that goes in search of the basic organs needed for creation, urged by passion, also emanates a bad smell. If one keeps the mouth clean, controls his passions and his tongue, he can remove the stench of this birth. If the sexual urge in the other orifice, desire and egoism, are controlled, the stench of the orifice of creation can be removed.

87.   **At 9:00 P.M. on 6/19/70**

Brother! Listen to an illustration.

In this world dogs grow up very fast. What is the reason? Man must reflect on this and find out the reason.

Man eats all types of delicious and nutritious foods. The consumed food leaves the body as feces in ten to fifteen hours. Dogs eat this excreta with great desire. It will take man twenty four hours to absorb all the nutrients in the food he eats. But he throws it out of his body in ten to fifteen hours in a state of half digestion. So seven-eighths of the essences of the food is absorbed by the dog when it consumes the human excreta. This helps the dog to grow fast. That food gives the dog 96 elements. This is the reason why it grows so fast.

Six thousand drops of blood become one thousand drops of fat. This again is converted into one drop of marrow in the bone. When the dog eats a bone four inches long, it absorbs twenty-one grams of calcium. The dog eats the brain, marrow, and bones which contain calium and fatty acids. It gets the necessary salts from the calcium. As a result, the dog grows fast into a very active and courageous animal.

In the same way, if man also eats sinful food and food which encourages sinful actions, he will also grow up fast. He will hide the Truth, and do sinful actions against his conscience and dictates of Wisdom. Such a man will make a name in this world very quickly, attain power and glory and rule the world. He will gather great wealth, but lose his character. He will destroy the true and the good. He will obtain great glory in the world. Then, he will lose all this fame, become the meanest of the mean, die and become subject to several births and hell. In the same way as the dog fattened on base food, this man grew up fast, feeding on evil actions.

But if you are to be born as a Man and grow up as a Man, it will take a long time. You will have to undergo a lot of suffering. If you consider those sufferings to be joys and proceed on your Spiritual Pilgrimage, and escape from these two types of beings, you will have earned the real bliss which is True Man's heritage. So said His Holiness Guru Bawa to his disciples. Real devotees free themselves from all attachment. But goldsmiths steal gold surreptitiously.

88.   **At 9:40 P.M. on 6/19/70**

'Thaala', the sweet scented screw pine, grows luxuriantly on saline land. It is its nature. But can it remove one's hunger or quench one's thirst? No! If you get hold of it and pull it, its serrated leaves will cut and injure you.

In the same way plants which are not really useful will grow up fast, without dying off. But they will be of no use. But good plants, plants that are really useful take a long time to grow; and they grow with great difficulty. Evil grows fast. What is acceptable to Truth takes a long time to develop. Man should make use of his Divine Wisdom and understand this well.

One who strives to develop the good, that which serves the cause of Truth, even in the face of suffering and loss, and develops it, is called God-Man (Manu Insan). One who develops that which helps the Truth, that which our Lord appreciates, that which bestows Grace and Compassion on devotees, that which is liked by the Primal Reality (Athi Param), that which he consumes in the face of odds and difficulties, without caring for loss or suffering, is really God-Man (Manu Insan). He who develops the Truth without any selfish motive by using his Resplendant Wisdom is the noblest of human beings.

89.   At 9:55 A.M. on 6/19/70

'Eddi', the nux vomica tree, will be very healthy and have luxuriant leaves wherever it grows, whether in the forest or in the hot climate or in the cold climate. It will not die or decay easily. It will not allow other trees near to thrive.

In the same way, a man who does harm to others and leads a selfish life will materially be healthy and beautiful and clever. He will not allow others to thrive. He will not help them. Such a man and the 'Eddi' tree are antagonistic to Truth and real Wisdom. Danger lurks near the person who seeks and relies on the help of a selfish heartless man like the 'Eddi' tree. He is sure to suffer at the hands of God. You should understand this well. So said the Guru to the disciple.

90.   At 4:20 P.M. on 6/19/70

A doctor covers his nose, mouth and head, excepting the eyes, with cloth, and wears gloves on his hands when he performs an operation on a patient. He does this to protect himself from the disease of the patients and the bacteria and dirty smell that emanate from the patient. By doing this, he saves himself and tries to save the life of the patient.

In the same way, man suffers from ten billion types of 'contagious' diseases arising from the hypnotic fascination of the darkness of Illusion (Maya) which causes sin and Ignorance (Agnana). The following are some of these 'contagious' diseases: the disease of Action (Karma); the disease of egoism; the disease of caste; the disease of selfishness; the disease of religious fanaticism, which says 'My God is Great; Your God is not powerful'; the disease which proclaims, 'I am different from you; you are different from me'; the disease of lust; the disease of theft; the disease of falsehood; the disease of intoxication; the disease of vanity which proclaims, 'It is mine'; the disease of the feeling of mine and yours; the disease of killing other beings and eating their 'flesh' to protect one's own life; the disease of disunity; the disease of pride, which proclaims 'there is none greater than I!'; the disease of jealousy; the disease of back-biting and wounding the feelings of others; the disease of the triple sins of egoism, bad action and illusion. The above diseases hold man in a vicious grip. There are more than ten billion types of these diseases. All these diseases

162

can be grouped under the four great maladies of hunger, disease, old age and death. As a result of these maladies, man becomes the victim of death.

Like the doctor, the person who is really born a Man; the person in whom Radiant Wisdom sheds its rays; the person who grow up with Divine Compassion, adopting God's characteristics; and the person who lives with Divine Forbearance; should wear the cloth of Truth to protect the Compassion and Forbearance and Peace of God in his self, and help to cure people suffering from the above diseases.

But if these diseases are contracted by you, they will kill you. To safeguard yourself from these contagious diseases, like the doctor, you should protect your body. Within your body is a child called the Unique Ultimate One, i.e., God. It is sleeping in the form of Divine Love. You should protect that Divine Child within you from the Disease of Ignorance which will chase away the child from you, by covering it with your Resplendent Wisdom. If you do so you will not have any sorrow. So said the Gnostic Guru to his disciple.

91.   **At 5:40 P.M. on 6/19/70**

Child! Listen to an illustration.

There are two types of fish; fish made of celluloid and fish found in the sea. You have to pay cash to buy either of them. You buy the celluloid fish to satisfy your children. It is a thing of beauty. The sea fish satisfies your desire and removes your hunger. Both are called fish.

The demon fish when it is in its home, the sea, eats other fish and gambols and swims about as it pleases. The celluloid fish remains still in the place where it is kept. Both the celluloid fish and the real fish look alike. But they are different in their nature and origin. One was created by man to deceive the eyes of the children. The other was created by God to show the intricate nature of His created beings.

In the same way, there are two types of men, among the human beings created by God. One type of man considers the worldly life, the sea of Maya which causes Ignorance (Agnana), hunger, disease, senility, and death, to be real and considers this sea of Illusion (Maya) to be his real home and swims about, joyfully, in it. He does not know what is good and what is evil. He does not consider other lives to be as valuable as his own life is to him. In the sea of Illusion (Maya) where he lives, he seizes whatever he sees and gathers whatever his mind desires, and eats them with glee. He develops egoism and religious fanaticism.

These people are really demon fish with human faces. Without knowing what is good food and what is bad food, without knowing that other lives are as valuable as their own lives are to them, they seize and kill and eat whatever living beings they see. They know not what is good and what is bad. These people enjoy whatever they see. They eat whatever their mind desires. These people are the demon fish of the sea of Illusion (Maya). They are similar to the type of fish found in the sea which consumes whatever it sees. These demon fish of the world of Maya with human faces deceive their body and the world and satisfy their hunger.

There is another type of fish which satisfies the eyes and the mind of children. The students of Gnana (Gnosis) who are learning the injunctions of God have the same characteristics as small children. They like to see and enjoy the bliss of God's Grace which is Eternal, Faultless, and Ever-Full.

To these devotees, who have realised Divine Wisdom (Pahuth-Arivu), Divine Luminous Wisdom (Perr-Arivu), and the Truth, God shows the beauty of His Grace to satisfy their minds in the same way as the father shows the beautiful celluloid fish to the crying child to satisfy its mind.

The children take the celluloid fish in their hands and stop crying. In the same way these seekers of the Truth take God and place Him in their Heart (Qalb) and remove all their worries and sufferings. Such people are the real Men. They love others' lives as they love their own. They are always fascinated by the good. They lose themselves completely in the Goodness that is God and remove their worries and sufferings.

Thus, you see, there are two types of men, similar to the two types of fish referred to. One type of man realises who he is, comes to know his Creator, and understands His nature and mysteries. The other type of man seeks joy in the place of his origin and swims, joyfully, in the sea of sex and causes the degradation of his Wisdom. One should reflect on all these aspects, live as a man and merge in God as God-Man (Manu-Insan). That is the mission of human existence. But many who are born as man, grow up as wicked men and end their lives in degradation.

It is a man who consumed the world. It is a man who consumed himself. Out of these two, who is the real man? You should find out. The world will respect the first one. But God will not respect that man. Know this well! So said the Gnana Guru (Gnostic Guru) to his disciple.

92.   At 6:15 P.M. on 6/19/70

Children! You have been born in this world to go round the world and observe what is happening. You should understand the real nature of the world by observing everything in the world carefully. If you wish to be a real man in this world, you should know that two things are essential.

There is a saying: If an elephant has become over energetic, feed it with plantain (banana) trees to bring it back to its normal state. If a man, too, has become over energetic, feed him with the leafy vegetable called 'Keerai' to make him normal.

In the same way, feed a man who is misguided by Ignorance with Wisdom (Arivu). Feed the demonaic who is full of egoism and religious fanaticism with things of Illusion (Maya) which have a hypnotic fascination for him and generate Ignorance (Agnana) in him. Only then can you escape from the demonaic man and join the company of real man. You should do this with great circumspection. Remember this well when you wander in this wide world. So said the Guru to his disciples.

93.   At 7:40 P.M. on 6/19/70

If a crystal mirror is cleaned and polished with a polish of very high grade and extreme purity, dust will not easily settle on it. It will slip off. Whatever little dust that may settle on it can be easily wiped off with a cloth. But if smoke, oil, fats, and similar oily things settle on the mirror, it is very difficult to remove these things from the mirror. So, care has to be taken to see that the mirror is not exposed to these things. The mirror should be protected from smoke, oil and fatty acids. In a mirror which is kept in a place with a pure atmosphere, you will be able to see your reflection very clearly. If it is covered with smoke, oil, and fat you will not be able to see your figure in it.

The mind of man is like a mirror. Sixty-four kinds of arts settle on this 'mind-mirror' like smoke, oil, and fat. Visions of the mind settle on the mirror of the mind like smoke. Attractive figures with hypnotic fascination projected by Illusion (Maya) appear in the garb of pseudo-divine forms, which can bestow on you what you desire, settle on the mind as though they were Divine Light, confuse and misguide man. You should analyze these things with your Wisdom (Arivu), find out their real nature and prevent them from settling on the 'mind-mirror'.

You are the noblest of God's creations. You are endowed with rare and noble qualities. You have the faculty of Divine Wisdom (Pahuth-Arivu) for you are God's representative on earth. Within your Heart (Qalb) is placed all the eighteen thousand worlds, the secret of God, the secret of your birth, the secret about death, the secret of all God's creation, the secret of the sky, the earth, the sun, the moon, and the stars. God has placed all these within your Heart, the seat of His Pure Grace. Do not allow the attachments of the five elements and the five senses and religious fanaticism to settle like smoke on your Heart (mind-mirror) which is full of His sacred Grace. Always wipe these things from your Heart (mind-mirror), so that His Grace is not hidden.

Unless you keep your 'mind-mirror' clean and pure, you will never be able to see your own self. You will not be able to realise who you are. You will not be able to discover the Mysteries of God. If you want to see your self and God, you should keep the 'mind-mirror' spotlessly clean and protect it from being covered with the smoke and oil and fat of attachments arising from the five elements and the five senses and from religious fanaticism. If you succeed in that, that very day you will become Man-God (Manu-Eesan). If you become Man-God (Manu-Eesan), that Ultimate One will become your Friend. If He becomes your Friend, all His creations will render homage to you and become your followers and as a result become His devotees. You should reflect on what I have said and understand it well. So said His Holiness Guru Bawa to his disciples.

94.   At 11:00 A.M. on 6/20/70

You have to dive to the bottom of the sea and take the pearl oyster and cut it in two to obtain the pearl inside it. If you do not do so, thinking that to do this is a sin or because its odor is repulsive, you will not be able to get the pearl. Therefore, you will not be able to assess its value, nor will you be able to inform the person who desires to buy it of its value.

In the same manner, if one beats up, breaks, and kills with his Wisdom (Arivu) the attachments which encase the Heart (Qalb), he will be able to get the pearl that is hidden within the ocean of Illusion (Maya). If he wastes his time in thinking of the attractions of the senses, the love of those dear to him and to whom he is attracted, the fascination of the images projected by Illusion (Maya) and the pros and cons of sin according to his limited intellect, he will never be able to obtain that Effulgence of Grace (Arul Jothi).

Just as the pearl diver dives into the sea and gets the pearl, one should dive into his own physical body, which is a limitless sea of Illusion (Maya) with unending waves, and annihilate the manifestations projected by the five elements. In other words, annihilate Ignorance (Agnana) which is like the oyster, and look within. There he will find the pearl of the Effulgence of Grace (Arul Jothi). He will assess its value and find out that it is a precious pearl, the value of which is not possible to assess, because it is a pearl of such perfection. He can take this rare and unique pearl without fear and keep it securely in the safe of his Radiant Soul (Atma Jothi).

Just as the pearl is found within the foul-smelling oyster, within this physical body of man, which emanates foul smells owing to Darkness (Agnana), is found that rare pearl of Effulgence of Grace (Arul Jothi). As the pearl can be taken only after the oyster is cut up; the pearl of Effulgence of Grace (Arul Jothi) can be obtained only if one cuts asunder Darkness (Agnana), the manifestations projected by the five elements, the five senses and Illusion (Maya). If he does not do so, he will never obtain it. He will never be able to put an end to his cycle of births. So said the Gnana Guru to his disciple.

95.   At 5:30 P.M. on 6/20/70

His Holiness Guru Bawa tells his disciple:

My son! The mind travels faster than the wind. The light of Divine Luminous Wisdom (Perr-Arivu) travels at a speed several times faster than the speed of the mind. Within the split second taken by the eyelid to close and open, the Light of Divine Luminous Wisdom (Perr-Arivu) would have visited all the places it wanted to survey, rested in all the places where it wanted to rest, taken away all it wanted to take away and come back to its abode. It travels very much faster than the mind.

But mind cannot traverse in the worlds where Wisdom (Arivu) can travel. Wisdom (Arivu) can travel both in the worlds of the mind and in the worlds where the Limitless Transcendent All Pervading One is found. The senses, the elements, and the manifestations of Illusion (Maya) projected by the elements cannot traverse in the worlds of Wisdom (Arivu) and the World of God. Wisdom (Arivu) can observe what is within and what is without, the Inner Reality, the Good and the world of the Grace of God which is beyond the limit of the worlds of sound and vibration. But the senses and the elements can see only the world of mental visions and the worlds of physical vision. You should reflect and perceive as to which faculty will enable you to see the world of God and the other worlds. After realising that it is only the faculty of Wisdom (Arivu) that can help you to see these worlds, you should traverse the world of Wisdom (Arivu) and observe the world of Grace within it, and within the world of Grace, see God, and within God see your own self, and see His Divine Ray which pervades every nook and corner of the Universe, and see God who shines as Effulgence in that Ray. Make up your mind to search for Him and see Him with your Wisdom (Arivu).

96.   At 5:40 P.M. on 6/20/70

Brother! Listen to an illustration.

In day time one hears many sounds. The sounds arising in the neighbourhood are heard clearly. But the sounds arising in the distance are not heard clearly and distinctly. Why? In the day time there are a lot of extraneous sounds caused by the sun, the wind, the vibrations arising from the earth, etc. Therefore, sounds cannot be heard clearly in the day time, but in the night sounds can be heard more clearly and distinctly.

In the same manner when the five senses of man are active, he will not be able to hear the voice of True Wisdom (Unmai Arivu).

But in the night when he sits on the mat or bed, he loses contact with the earth. So he is able to hear sounds more clearly at night.

In the same way, only when he cuts himself off completely from the influence of the earth, i.e., the material world, he will be able to clearly hear the resonant voice of God's Grace through his faculty of Wisdom (Arivu). Therefore, my children! You should control your mind which is the workshop of your five senses, cut yourself off from the influence of the material world and listen to the voice of God's Grace.

97.   At 6:35 P.M. on 6/20/70

Brother! Listen to this illustration.

The precious green gem, the Emerald, is found within the earth. Whatever method you may adopt to dig it out, you have to look at and observe its characteristics by holding it against a light. Then, only, will you be able to see its true characteristics and assess its intrinsic value. Otherwise, you will not be able to assess its real nature.

Just as you have to hold the Emerald against the light to see its real characteristics and assess its worth, you will have to examine every religion against the light of Wisdom (Arivu). Then, only, will you understand the real worth of every religion. Otherwise, you will not be able to distinguish between the good and the evil in the practices and observances of any religion. You should understand this clearly. So said His Holiness Guru Bawa to a disciple.

98.   At 11:40 A.M. on 6/21/70

There is a legend in Hinduism that the sage 'Agasthiyar' converted the waters of the seven oceans into an atom and swallowed it. It does not mean that he drank all the water of the seven oceans in a literal sense.

The correct concept is as follows: The seven seas indicate the seven evil souls (nafs). He had converted the seven evil souls (nafs) into an atom and thrown it into the fire of Wisdom (Arivu) and burnt it. As a result, the natural Truths in the whole universe conversed with him.

99.   At 5:10 P.M. on 6/21/70

A Point of View:

The world is vast. To the man, bereft of Wisdom (Arivu), the world is large. But to a man endowed with Wisdom (Arivu) the world is like an atom. The man bereft of Wisdom (Arivu) will not be able to travel round the world and observe all its mysteries even if he takes several births. To a man of Wisdom (Arivu) the world is too small to travel as it is smaller than an atom to him.

Man should burn to ashes with his Wisdom (Arivu) the ninety-six attributes of the mind, wrong knowledge, the three and a half crores of hypnotic fascinations of Illusion (Maya) and the ten and a half crores of hypnotic forms projected by Illusion (Maya). The world will then disappear within Wisdom (Arivu). And only Wisdom (Arivu) will remain. All else will have disappeared. So said His Holiness Guru Bawa to his disciples.

100.   **At 5:50 P.M. on 6/21/70**

Brother! Listen to an illustration.

A blind man and a deaf man, who were friends, went to the theatre to see a dramatic performance. After the performance was over, the blind man told his friend, the deaf man, "How sweet and exhilarating the songs and the music were. It pleased the ears and enchanted the mind." The deaf man replied, "Fool! There was no music. Nobody sang. There was only acting and dancing. How beautiful the dances were!" The blind man said there was no dancing or acting. There was only music and songs. Both hotly argued their points of view and parted as enemies. The blind man lost the help of the deaf man, and the deaf man lost the help of the blind man.

In the same manner, those of us who are deaf to the inner voice of God and those of us who are unable to see God with eyes of Wisdom (Arivu) fight among ourselves saying, "That is false, this is false. My religion is true; your religion is not true. I belong to a high caste; you belong to a low caste. What I tell is the truth; what you tell is false. I am great; you are not great." Not knowing the Truth, we fight among ourselves and suffer and finally die. We should reflect on these senseless quarrels. So said His Holiness Guru Bawa.

101.   **At 6:15 P.M. on 6/21/70**

There is a saying:
> "Man created wealth,
> Earth (i.e. attraction of the
> material world) caused death,
> God created Character."

If you gather wealth to protect your body, you will lose your character. Only the person who has adopted the characteristics and qualities of God can be called Man.

102.   **At 7:05 P.M. on 6/21/70**

Children! Listen to an illustration.

A man catches a parrot and keeps it in a cage and teaches it to speak like a human being. It learns to repeat what he has taught.

In the same manner, Illusion (Maya) gets hold of this beautiful man and imprisons him in a cage, rears him, and teaches him words of Ignorance (Agnana).

The parrot repeats the words it has learned without knowing the meaning of those words. When a thief comes, it says, "A thief is coming". When the thief hears it, he will throttle the neck of the parrot and kill it.

In the same way, when this man makes use of the words taught him by Illusion (Maya) for his personal benefit, death will put an end to him in the same way as the thief killed the parrot. Such a man will reach Hell from which he will not return. So said His Holiness Guru Bawa to his disciples.

An Aphorism:
> Whatever you look at laughs at you. You laugh at them. Wisdom (Arivu) laughs at your ignorance. Therefore, look at your own foolish self and laugh at its antics. This will be good to you like a tonic.

103. ## At 9:15 A.M. on 6/22/70

Brother! Listen to an illustration.

A cock calls the hens when it finds a beetle and feeds them with it. In the same way, though you are made of earth, you feed the desires in your mind by offering them gold, property, attachment to wife, children, relations, etc. Likewise, in the same way as that vain cock will one day become the food of man, the man who has demonic qualities will also one day become the food of the earth. Like the cock which reared the hens, you are developing the bonds of attachment. You should shed tears over the insensitive state of your Ignorance (Agnana).

104. ## At 9:50 A.M. on 6/22/70

Brother! Listen to an illustration.

Parrots are kept at the entrance to the Meenachchi Temple at Madura. Whenever anybody enters the temple to worship they cry, "Pallan (high caste) is coming! Paraiyan (low caste) is coming!" If the worshipers are really Palla (high caste) or Paraiya (low caste) people, they will be taken aback, stop there, and blink. The attendant of the Temple will chase them away. So they will not be able to worship in the Temple. If he is really a Paraiya (low caste) man, and through courage if he gets into the Temple, he will be able to worship and come out.

In the same way, the world has created many castes, conventional religions, and creeds. Like the parrots which cry in the above temple "Pallan (high caste) is coming! Paraiyan (low caste) is coming!". In this world the foolish human parrots shout, "My religion is great! My religion is true! I belong to high society! You belong to a low social order!" If you, without listening to their preachings, proceed with courage towards the Truth, you will reach God.

But if you tarry in doubt, like the real Paraiyas (low caste) and Pallas (high caste), who were confused when the parrots started crying, "Pallan (high caste) is coming! Paraiyan (low caste) is coming!", you will be killed by the world. You will not be able to reach God. You should reflect on this and understand well and avoid these ignorant human parrots, who act as preachers of religions. So said His Holiness Guru Bawa to his disciple.

105. ## At 10:50 A.M. on 7/1/70

Brother! Listen to this illustration.

In the ocean there are rocks, sand banks, ships and boats which sank thousands of years ago. You cannot drain the ocean dry. When we sail across the ocean in a ship we have to take drinking water from the land, as the water in the sea cannot be used for drinking. It cannot quench our thirst.

In the same way, in the mind which is the ocean of Illusion (Maya) are found attachments and actions which follow us from birth to birth. We do actions out of our free-will in this birth, actions due to our fate of bondage, actions due to our attachments due to blood affinity and crores and crores and actions caused by our desires. These actions exist in our minds in a latent form. There is none who has drained away this mind, which is the ocean of Illusion (Maya). There is none who has destroyed mind. There is none who has fathomed the mind fully. There is none who has purified the mind fully. In our young days we tried to drain the mind, but it never went dry, and at the end of each attempt it became full. Thus we gained experience of the truth of the mind. Therefore, when you cross the mind, which is the ocean of Illusion (Maya), you should exercise Patience and Forbearance and quench your thirst with Truth, and cross it. This is how you may succeed.

Your must know full well that the mind cannot be drained away just as the ocean cannot be drained away.

106.   At 5:10 P.M. on 7/1/70

Brother! Listen to this illustration.

A tank is full of water. If you want to irrigate your crops, you must open the necessary number of taps in the regulator and allow only a limited quantity of water to flow out. Then, only, will the crops thrive. If you open all the taps in the regulator and allow all the water in the tank to flow out, your crops will be washed away.

In the same way, you should control the waves of the mind. In the 'tank' of your mind you must fix the taps of Wisdom (Arivu) and regulate and control the desires. If you allow the waters of Illusion (Maya) in your mind to flow out without restrictions, the crop called Truth will be washed away. If you want to protect the crop of Truth, you should control the water of Illusion (Maya) in your mind with the taps or the regulator called Wisdom (Arivu). Then, only, can you protect the crop of Truth.

107.   At 6:00 P.M. on 7/1/70

An Illustration:

Children! We sow paddy in the field. Before the paddy germinates, the weeds germinate. Weed seeds are found in nature. For every paddy plant that germinates, five weeds germinate. You must root out completely all the weeds to allow the paddy to thrive.

Your body has been created out of five senses and the five elements called Earth, Fire, Water, Air and Ether. Within these are found the seeds that cause Man to succumb to the hypnotic fascinations of Illusion (Maya). When the Soul (Atma) is sown in this field, your physical body, the seeds of the five elements of Illusion (Maya) germinate stronger and earlier like the weeds, and smother the crop of the Soul (Atma).

If you remove these weeds which smother the growth of the Soul (Atma) with your Wisdom (Arivu), your Wisdom (Arivu) will attain fullness. You should understand this well. So said His Holiness Guru Bawa to his disciples.

108.   At 6:40 P.M. on 7/1/70

Look at the clock. There are twelve numbers on the face of the clock. The minute hand goes round passing the twelve numbers and coming back to the original number from which it started.

In the beginningless beginning the Soul (Atma) appeared. The body in which the Soul (Atma) lives has twelve openings. The Soul (Atma) will make a full round, complete the twelve openings and come back to its original place like the minute hand of the clock.

At 7:10 P.M. on 7/1/70

Children! Listen to an illustration.

If a tree grows luxuriantly in an open plain, men will go and stand under its shade to avoid the hot sun and the rain. They will say, "Here is a good tree which has spread out its branches on all sides giving full protection."

Later on when the tree grows up into a tall straight large tree, they will forget what they said earlier and say, "The timber of this tree will be very good for furniture, beams, rafters, reepers and doors for houses." They will cut the tree down with an axe, saw it, smooth it with a chisel, smooth it with sand paper, apply suitable paints, and polish the articles of furniture, etc., and show them with pride to the world.

God has created Man, as the rarest and noblest of His creations, as His representative on earth. Man should use the powers of his Wisdom (Arivu), the Grace of God and his physical power to help human beings who are suffering from the delusions of Illusion (Maya). He should love other beings as he loves his own self. He should be Just to them. He should show Compassion to them. He should adopt the Divine Qualities such as Compassion, Liberality, Pity, Virtue, Justice, Truth, Patience, Forbearance, and with Tranquility of Mind and a sense of Duty protect the suffering human beings under the shade of his Love and Compassion. But, after some time the world will forget all these good and noble actions. The people of the world will persecute and try to kill his good qualities and use him for their selfish ends. Finally, in the same way as men cut the tree that gave shade to them and converted its timber into household articles for their selfish use, they will also destroy the man in whom these Divine Qualities flourished who had helped them.

Children! In the same way as the tree stood in the open place and protected the men with its shade from the sun and the rain, you should also stand in the open unlimited space of Knowledge beyond the limits and restrictions of conventional religion, and with the knowledge of limitless Wisdom (Arivu) bestow on those people, who are bereft of Wisdom, the Wealth of God's Grace without expecting any reward or gratitude from them. Then you should merge yourself in the fullness of Wisdom (Arivu) that fills the limitless space of knowledge and hide in it. Otherwise, they will destroy you and the Truth in the same way as they destroyed the tree.

Children! you should do everything you want to do without expecting reward or help from others. Then, keep aloof from their persecution. If you seek the help of others, they will praise you for sometime. Then they will speak ill of you. Remember this clearly. There is no glory or fanfare for you. There is no subtraction or multiplication for you. There is no promotion or demotion for you. There is no rise or fall for you. You should meet with equanimity whatever happens to you.

You should be humbler than your followers. You should show yourself to be more insignificant than the most insignificant person. You should appear like the dust. If you show yourself to be the most insignificant and smallest of God's creations, you will be able to understand the intelligence and predilections of the beings in this world with your Wisdom (Arivu). When there is danger to the Truth, you can escape easily as you are an insignificant person. If you stick to the Truth, just as a magnet sticks to a piece of iron, you will be able to hide in it. This is the main aim and end of life. So said the Gnana Guru (Gnostic Guru) to his disciples.

He added further: If you expect your relations, whom you helped when you were prosperous, to help you in your adversity, they will never help you. They will destroy you as the people destroyed that tree.

As the people come to the shade of the tree for protection from sunshine as well as from rain, these human beings will come to you for succour when their physical bodies, which are composed of the five senses and the five elements, become tired and run down. They will also come to you when they are under the hypnotic influence of seductive Illusion (Maya) to seek your help to achieve their ends. They will consider both of these to be temporary sufferings. If you seek help from such people, you will meet the fate of the tree. To them an attempt to reach God is also suffering. To them an attempt to live prosperously in the world with a selfish motive is also suffering. So, they have no peace of mind. Therefore, do not seek their company to save your peace of mind. It will only cause you danger. So said the Meignana Guru (True Gnostic Guru) to his disciples.

110.   **At 7:45 P.M. on 7/1/70**

Children! Listen to this illustration.

The snake is beautiful to look at, is it not? But it has a deadly poison in its mouth. Whichever animal or living being is bitten by it will be affected by its poison and its life will be in danger. The snake does not have the faculty of Divine Wisdom (Pahuth-Arivu) to distinguish between good people and bad people. The ears of the snake are the same as its eyes. Its eyes have no eye-lids. It has very sharp eyesight. It lives in holes gazing intently outside with its eyes. When there is thunder and lightning, the cartilage inside its poisonous fangs will burst, ejecting the poison into its own mouth. As a result it dies.

In the same manner, there are men with beautiful physical bodies of Illusion (Maya). They have the evil qualities of wrong knowledge, the poisons emanating from the six types of evil actions (Aruvinai), the darkness of Ignorance, and the heartless qualities of the demonaic blood in their Heart (Qalb). With these, they live in the physical body with its nine openings and like the holes in the ant hill, live in it thinking that the physical body, which is the seat of darkness of Illusion (Maya), Ignorance (Agnana) and rebirth, is their permanent home.

They do not have the eyes of Wisdom (Arivu). They do not have the eye-lids of Wisdom (Arivu) to enable them to think and reflect and understand the real nature of things. Just as the snake keeps the poison of its fangs in its mouth, these people keep their evil propensities and qualities in their Heart (Qalb), look at the world with their eye bereft of Wisdom (Arivu), hear the drama acted in the world with the ear of the physical vision of Illusion (Maya) and enjoy the acts. They get confused when they hear the voice of God calling them to account for their actions because of their selfishness, avarice and evil nature, and they die from the poison of their own evil actions. Therefore, do not keep evil qualities in your Heart (Qalb), because you will die of them. So said the Gnana Guru.

172

111

At 8:40 P.M. on 7/3/70

The fish in the ocean has no eyelids though it has eyes. It swims on the top as well as on the bottom of the ocean and lives on the food it catches. But many fishermen draw their nets in the ocean to catch fish. Because it has no eyelids, the fish is unable to distinguish between the water in the ocean and the net. So it goes headlong into the net and gets caught. If it had eyelids, it could see better by closing its eyelids now and then, and could distinguish between the water and the net.

In the same way, people of the world, in order to procure their food and joy, swim above and below in the ocean of Illusion (Maya) that causes Ignorance and Darkness (Agnana). They do not possess the eye-lids of Truth and Radiant Wisdom. Their misguided joys and piety and the hypnotic joys of the ocean of Illusion (Maya) appear to them to be real devotion to God Almighty. They are sure to get caught in the net of desire which is spread in the ocean of Illusion (Maya) and they will die like the fish. You should understand this well.

In the same ocean where the fish live, the foul smelling pearl oyster keeps the maturing pearl in its mouth and dives to the bottom of the ocean and secures itself to a rock, until the pearl within it matures. It will not allow itself to be moved away from the rock by the waves. Pearl divers catch the pearl oyster and bring it out of the ocean. Till then, the pearl oyster remains at the bottom of the ocean, firmly holding to the rock.

So, in this world of Illusion (Maya), many people swim about on the top and in the bottom of the murky ocean of Illusion (Maya), like the fish, and lead a selfish life seeking only the necessities for their physical body. They finally die.

But, a few take within their Heart (Qalb) the Truth, and attach themselves firmly to the Grace of God and hide in the bottom of the ocean of Illusion (Maya), like the pearl oyster, until their Pearl of Radiant Wisdom (Gnana) matures. Then, a Gnana Guru (Gnostic Guru), who possesses the Pearl of Radiant Wisdom (Gnana) takes it and assesses its value. These few find that its value cannot estimated by anyone but a Gnana Guru. In the same way as the divers who swim below to the bottom of the ocean and take hold of the pearl oyster, a man, if he loses himself, discovers the Gnana Guru, who has matured the Pearl of Gnana, embraces him and secures himself firmly to the Gnana Guru. The man will realise the beauty of Man-God (Manu Eesan), and realise God and obtain His Grace.

If he swims across the ocean of Illusion (Maya) and enters the place where the darkness of Illusion (Maya) cannot penetrate and looks carefully, he will see, beyond the darkness, the Gnana Guru who possess the Pearl of Divine Grace. If he does not do this, the ocean of Illusion (Maya), which causes spiritual degradation, and the net of desires will appear to him to be the same as the sea and the net appeared to be to the fish. He will mistake the net to be Divine Grace and as a result of his ignorance get caught in its meshes and perish. Know this well and save yourselves with the help of Wisdom (Arivu). So said His Holiness Guru Bawa to his disciples.

112

At 9:50 A.M. on 7/3/70

Man treats everything he sees as a symbolic illustration of God. Then he treats the symbol as God. Then he makes it the Ultimate Reality and worships the symbol as Reality. He honours the symbol and makes use of it for his material life. This makes him ultimately guilty of sacrilege to God. It makes him an enemy of Truth. He becomes an evil force which restricts the development of Truth. He creates an atmosphere hostile to the emergence of True Awareness. His action sets in motion a cycle of births which carries with it the effects of his previous actions. He becomes the embodiment of sin. He becomes the victim of Hell and is subject to continuous births. Know this well.

It is very difficult to be born as Man. It is very difficult to obtain self-realisation and freedom from future birth. It is difficult to be a real devotee of God. It is very difficult to know and understand all this. It is very difficult to reach God. To reach That Unique One, you should develop Faith, Certitude and Determination. Children! Come forward to pay back the debts of birth. So said His Holiness Guru Bawa to his disciples.

113.   At 6:10 P.M. on 7/3/70

Listen to an illustration:

A man plants and regularly waters a coconut seedling. The seedling sends out its roots to all sides in search of water and grows. The man pours water on the young coconut tree for only three years. But the coconut tree, returning its gratitude, lives for 120 years and gives him coconuts and other produce.

In the same way, God, at the time of Creation, in the present time and in the future time, pervades man within and without, feeds him, shows compassion to him and protects him. But man does not praise God (Allah). The coconut tree itself shows its gratitude to man by giving its produce to him for 120 years. Then to what extent should man show his gratitude to God and praise Him? What can we say of the man who does not show at least the same amount of gratitude to God which the tree shows to man. After three years, the coconut tree sends out its roots in search of water and grows, though the man has ceased to pour water on it, and in due course gives its produce to him. In the same manner, man also should enter the Truth and draw out God's Grace with his Wisdom (Arivu), and come to know the Saviour who Feeds him, Protects him and Saves him. He should Praise Him, Worship Him, Show Compassion and Love to all His creation and bestow on them the benefit of the Fullness of Wisdom (Arivu) and the Divine Grace of the Truth. Such a Man is the Noblest of Men, and a Man with Divine Characteristics.

114.   At 6:35 P.M. on 7/3/70

Son! The eye is large. But if a small particle of dirt falls in the eye, it cannot see. It is the same way with the Gnostic Eye of Divine Luminous Wisdom (Perr-Arivu), for if even an atom of worldly desire falls in it, the Gnostic Eye will disappear. You should understand this clearly. So said His Holiness Guru Bawa.

115.   At 6:55 P.M. on 7/10/70

There was a difference of opinion between the "Mother" of the Ashram and Gejavalli. His Holiness Guru Bawa addresses them and tells them:

Children! Do not argue as to who is right and who is wrong. Justice will remain as Justice. Mistakes may be made. When a child makes a mistake, do we chase the child away from home? The child has made a mistake. When he gets Wisdom, he will reform. God has created numberless beings, He gives food to them and succours them. He shows compassion even on a murderer. He shows love even to sinners. He grants them whatever they want as a boon from Him. That is God's Duty.

But later there is a Day when He will investigate their intentions, requests, and their actions. On that day they will be judged one way or the other according to what they earned during their life on earth. Therefore, there is no need for you to argue or fight over such small matters. You have no right to pass judgement on the actions of others. That is God's Duty.

The world will not leave alone the Man who searched for Him with Wisdom (Arivu), developed a state of love towards Him, treated all beings with compassion, and finally came to know Him. The whole world will oppose such a Man and chase him away. When that situation arises, God will accept that Man who was attached to Him, and take him within Him.

There is no place in this world for such a Man. He has a place only in God's Bosom. The Man (Insan) whose Wisdom (Arivu) has become Resplendent meets with all types of troubles and tribulations in this world. This happens for the purpose of taking him to God. God will grant whatever his devotees wish for. God has got the power to give or take whatever we wish. Both of you should understand this.

God has Compassion over all Created Beings. He causes hardships in the material world to those who are devoted to Him. As Truth develops in such Men, the world will progressively discard Them. God bestows Compassion, Love and Justice on all, tests them and their Faith in Him and draws them towards Him. God does not have Ignorance (Agnana) i.e., the state of degradation caused by the hypnotic fascination of Illusion (Maya). He has full Effulgence. He does not exist in two worlds. There is only one world for Him. Therefore, He bestows Compassion on all beings without showing anger or hatred against any being. You should understand this well. You should adopt His Divine Characteristics.

116.   **At 10:20 A.M. on 9/17/70**

One Mr. Subramaniam complained to His Holiness Guru Bawa that his life was full of sorrow, trials and tribulations. His Holiness replied:

The world is like firewood. It has two types of firewood; joy and sorrow. Wisdom (Arivu) is the fire. The world is firewood for the fire of Wisdom (Arivu). What is recognized by the five senses is also firewood. There is only one thing that connot be burnt up by the fire of Wisdom (Arivu). That is God. Wisdom (Arivu) can burn everything else, but not God. When Wisdom (Arivu) merges in God, Man becomes God-Man.

To travel along the path of Wisdom (Arivu) and to burn out the material world from man's life is to travel along God's path. What you consider to be trials, tribulations and sorrow is firewood which is to be burnt by the fire of Wisdom (Arivu). The mind brings trash home from all the 18,000 worlds. This should be burnt up by the fire of Wisdom (Arivu). This is like refuse fit to be burnt up by the Radiance of Wisdom (Arivu). We have come to this world to know and understand this. There is nothing that cannot be burnt up by the fire of Wisdom (Arivu), except God (Allah).

It is easy to preach. It is difficult to put it into practice. If you look intently with your Wisdom (Arivu) at joys and sorrow, you will know how they are caused. If you are guided by your senses, you will meet with sorrows; but if you are guided by Wisdom (Arivu), you will get perpetual joy.

Do not be affected by the sorrows in the world caused by the five senses. The world is a stage. We are actors. The people in the world will say, "This act is bad, that act is good!" Do not be happy when they praise you. Do not feel sad when they find fault. If you understand this well, you can lead your life in tranquility.

117.   At 6:30 P.M. on 9/17/70

His Holiness Guru Bawa told Mr. Nadarajah, D.R.O., Child! Listen to an illustration:

Ancient Hindu Myths (Puranas) speak of Karu Mal and Thiru Mal. Karumal indicates desire. Thirumal indicates the mind. The mind and desire were discussing about God in the following manner: "People speak about God, Where is He? What is His nature? We must search for Him and find out."

Thirumal (Mind) told Karumal (Desire), "I will search in the Upper World. You search in the Lower World. Let us find out where He is."

Thirumal (Mind) searched for God in the Upper Eight Worlds. Karumal (Desire) dug into the earth and searched for Him in the Lower Seven Worlds. Karumal (Desire) did not see Him there. Thirumal (Mind) also did not see Him in the Upper Eight Worlds. So each of them came to the conclusion that there is no God.

Even if Karumal and Thirumal, Desire and Mind, search for God in all the 18,000 worlds, they will not be able to find Him. Only when Mind and Desire disappear, will Wisdom (Arivu) appear. If Wisdom (Arivu) matures and shines brilliantly, shedding its Radiance everywhere, one will be able to understand the nature and characteristic of Param Porul (The Ultimate One).

118.   At 7:05 P.M. on 9/17/70

Mr. Moyse requested His Holiness Guru Bawa to explain the meaning of the word 'Thiruthoothar'. His Holiness replied as follows:

'Thiruthoothar' (Messenger of God) is Divine Luminous Wisdom (Perr-Arivu), which originated from God in the beginningless beginning, i.e., the period before Creation. It is the representative of God and pervades everywhere for all time, i.e., the period antecedent to Creation, the period of Creation, the present and the future.

One in whom the Effulgence of Divine Luminous Wisdom (Perr-Arivu) shines in full measure is the 'Thiruthoothar' of God. He is the Messenger (Thoothar) of Divine Luminous Wisdom (Perr-Arivu) at the time of Creation of the Soul (Atma), in the present, that is in this world, and in the future, that is in the next world. He is the 'Thoothar' of the Triple Flame (Muchchudar) of the three worlds: the Past, the Present and the Future.

At 10:15 A.M. on 9/22/70

His Holiness Guru Bawa tells Usman:

Child! In the early days of Islam there lived a Guru (Sheik) with some disciples. He was teaching them how to worship God and how to fast. He explained to them in detail about Prayer and Worship and asked his disciples to do as he did.

To perform the cleaning of the body before prayer (Wolu) he requested that each of them bring a pot of water. They did so. When the Guru (Sheik) was pouring out water from the pot to wash his hands, the pot, accidentally, fell down and broke to pieces. When the disciples saw this they foolishly thought that this was also part of the ceremony to be observed. They threw down the pots of water and broke them to pieces. When the Guru asked them why they did this and told them that his pot of water had accidentally fallen down and broken to pieces, they replied, "You asked us to do exactly what you did. So, when your pot broke to pieces, we followed your example and broke our pots."

The Guru told them, "Let us forget what happened. Bring more fresh pots of water and perform 'Wolu'." After they did so, he took them to the Mosque. The Guru was taller than the disciples. When he went into the Mosque, his head knocked against the top door frame as he was a little too tall. He did not mind it. He went into the Mosque. The disciples who were following him observed this and thought that they should also do the same. So, everyone of them knocked his head against the top door frame and went inside the Mosque. The disciple who came last was not tall. He was the shortest among them. He jumped up to knock his head against the door frame. He did not succeed. So, he jumped again. He could not succeed. So, he kept on jumping.

The Guru (Sheik), who was inside the Mosque, wanted to start the prayers. So, he asked, "Have we all come in?" Then he turned his face towards the entrance to the Mosque. There he saw the short disciple continuing to jump towards the top of the door frame.

He asked the others why he was doing this. They replied, "You told us to do as you did. We saw your head strike against the top door frame, at the entrance to the Mosque, when you entered the Mosque. So, we also jumped towards the top door frame and struck our head against it and entered the Mosque. But he is not tall. So he is unable to strike his head against the top door frame in spite of all his efforts. That is why he is continuing to jump." The Guru (Sheik) addressed that disciple and told him, "My head struck against the top door frame because of my carelessness. But everyone of you has been imitating me! There is no need for you to strike your head against the top door frame. Come into the Mosque!" Then he conducted the prayers.

Some months passed by. On the day before the Ramazan fast started, the Guru (Sheik) called his disciples to the Mosque. He told the disciples, "Nalaikku Nonpu. Aanapadujal Nonpu pidiththukkondu Nalaikku vara Muthalil pallikku Varukinranaro Avarthan en pillaikalil Sirappanavar." What the Guru (Sheik) told them was that the disciple who comes first to the Mosque on the next day after observing the fast will be considered to be the best disciple. Now, in Tamil, the words 'Nonpu pidiththukkondu' can mean 'After catching Nonpu.' The disciples did not know that the meaning of 'Nonpu' was fasting. They thought Nonpu was an animal or some person whom they must overpower and tie up and bring to the Mosque.

So, they divided themselves into groups and went in different directions with hoes, hatches, ropes and clubs to catch 'Nonpu'. One of these groups, on their way, saw a man about fifty years old coming that way. They ran towards him and asked him who he was. He replied, "Nan Nonpu; ennai onrum seiyatheerkal", meaning that he was fasting and they should not do any harm to him. The word 'Nan Nonpu' can literally mean 'I am Nonpu'. It can also mean 'I am fasting'. The disciples decided that he was Nonpu. So, they told him, "We have been searching for you without taking food or drink." The man replied, "Nan Nonpu! Nan Nonpu!" The disciples told one another, "Catch him! Tie him up! We came in search of him. Beat him up!" They assaulted him with their hoes and hatches and felled him to the earth and tied him up to a long pole and carried him to the Mosque and placed him before the Guru (Sheik).

The Guru (Sheik), who was surprised, asked them, "I did not see any of you in the Mosque in the morning. Why did you assault this old man and bring him?" They replied, "You told us to catch Nonpu and come. (Nonpu pidiththukkondu vara). Nonpu tried to run away. We seized him, tied him up and brought him to you. This is Nonpu." The Guru (Sheik) replied, "You have only beaten up a man, seized him and brought him. I told you to set your mind towards God (Allah), fast and come to the Mosque (Allahvuday a Niyyaththu Vaiththu Nonpu Vaikkumpadiyallo nan sonnen).

Then the Guru (Sheik) untied the ropes with which the old man was tied up, sprinkled water on him, freed him and saved his life. The Guru (Sheik) explained to them in detail what Nonpu (Fasting) is. The disciples said, "Is that so? We did not know. You should have explained every thing in detail then. If you had done so, we would have followed your instructions correctly."

All the actions in our society are also like this. I act like this; my disciples act like that. This is how we study and teach about God. Our aim in life appears to be to laugh at others and hurt their feelings, to speak ill of them when they are not present, to feel jealous of others, to cause pain to the Created Beings of God (Allah) and to destroy them by deceit. Only if you give up these evil qualities will you be able to get the Grace of God.

In the various religions there are Gurus similar to the one referred to in the illustration given earlier. They do not know the inner meaning of the books of God which they have studied. They do not know what the real interpretation is. Their main aim is the well-being of their physical body. They develop the vision of their physical eyes and the visions of their mind. Their actions and teachings are guided by selfishness. So, they teach their disciples in the wrong way telling them, "Do as I do." They do not teach the truth about Reality to their disciples in their youth. In the illustration it was shown that the disciples, instead of fasting, assaulted and tied up a man who told them 'Nan Nonpu', meaning 'I am fasting', misunderstanding the instructions of the Guru (Sheik). In the same way, the world is being led astray by the wrong instructions of these Gurus. Just as the disciples broke the earthen pots when they want to pray, these people destroy the Truth about God. Because of these Gurus, the disciples lose their valuable Spiritual Heritage on earth.

120. **At 4:25 P.M. on 9/22/70**

Brother, Listen to an illustration:

When the rat snake and the cobra are in a state of embrace, if man goes near, they will chase him and bite him. Although the rat snake has no hood like the cobra, at that time it will appear like a cobra, and chase man.

Because the rat snake was, at the time, in a state of embrace with the cobra, it assumes the shape and characteristics of the cobra, spreading its head like the hood of the cobra, and chases. The cobra will also follow it.

People who have succumbed to religious fanaticism also act in like manner. In them the rat snake of ignorance and the cobra of religious fanaticism lie embracing each other. Since they are guided by ignorance and religious fanaticism, they know not the difference between the great and the small, the man who knows and the pretender.

During the period the snake stays in a place protecting its eggs in the period of incubation, it will chase and bite anyone who disturbs it. In the same manner, ignorant people, full of Ignorance (Agnana), spend their time protecting their earthly possessions, e.g., house, property and gold. Those who preach the Truth cannot approach them. Those who try to preach the Truth to such worldly people will meet the fate of the man who approaches the place where the snake lies protecting its eggs.

You should preach the Truth only to a person who comes in search of the Truth like the bat which uses its sense of smell to reach the place where fruits are found in abundance.

If you try to explain Reality to the people who have fully succumbed to the material world, they will chase you and kill you like the snake. That snake breathes on air and moves on its belly. This human snake moves on two legs. These people feed on the senses and walk with the two legs of ignorance and religious fanaticism. To these human snakes the man with knowledge of the Truth and Divine Wisdom and Impartial Justice is an enemy. Men of Truth and Divine Wisdom should avoid these people.

121. **At 6:30 P.M. on 9/22/70**

Children! Listen to an illustration:

When a calf is born to a cow, the cow licks up all the dirt and slime on the calf and saves the calf because of its attachment to the calf.

Man does not realize that before he was born his conception took place in dirt, that he was nourished in dirt and that he came out of a dirty orifice. Urged by the sin of his birth and sexual desire, he again seeks the place of his birth and derives pleasure in wallowing in that dirt, forgetting the fact that he was born as Man to obtain a Glorious Spiritual Heritage. He is unable to use his emergent Divine Luminous Wisdom (Perr-Arivu) and differentiate between the pure and the impure.

Born as a result of impure carnal desire, he thrives on the food of impure carnal desire, under the influence of the triple dirt of Egoism (Anawam), Action (Karma), and Illusion(Maya) and the attachment of blood. The only difference between the cow and the man is this: The cow has four legs, the man has two legs. You should understand the implications of what I said and adjust your life. So said His Holiness Guru Bawa.

179

122. **At 7:10 P.M. on 9/22/70**

Children! Listen to an illustration:

When a bull starts on a spree of butting, it turns its face towards the earth, turns the horns aside and butts those in front of it. Till its frenzy is over, it goes on butting whatever it meets on its way, whether it be man, animal, tree or heap of earth.

A religious fanatic is similar to this bull in his actions. He will not look up and see reason. He will always look down and the area of his vision will be restricted. He will charge on like the bull, irrespective of the consequences. He is guided by wrong knowledge (Ariveenam). He is urged on by the divisive forces of race, religion, egoism and bigotry.

It is not possible to teach the Truth about Reality to such people. If you attempt to do so, they will charge against you and kill you like the frenzied bull on its spree of butting.

123. **At 9:10 A.M. on 9/24/70**

His Holiness Guru Bawa addresses his disciples in the Ashram and tells them:

You all appear as loyal, loving disciples. I will describe to you the common features and differences that exist between the Guru and the disciples.

Some who go to the sea to fish use a line and catch fish. Some use swords and cut up the fish that come to the shore in search of food. Others use nets and catch fish. Some go to the deep ocean in ships and use metal nets to catch big fish. Some go into the sea in large boats with thousands of lines and catch big fish. The man who goes in a ship to the deep ocean, catches a large quantity of fish, preserves them in ice, or cures them into dried fish and makes his catch available to a large number of people in the world. The man who fishes in the boat is able to supply fish to a limited number of people. The man who catches fish with nets divides his catch among his relatives. The man who stands on the shore and catches fish with the line or with the sword supplies his catch only to his family.

In the same way, people assimilate the teachings of the Guru according to the degree of their intelligence and their intellectual capacity and attitude. If a disciple of a Guru is like the man on the shore catching fish with the line, he will not be able to make much use of the Guru's teachings. Though he is with the Guru, he will be guided by the affinities of blood and attractions of the material world. His intelligence is such that he cannot mend his ways. The man who caught fish with the sword, will always devote his intelligence to the furtherance of his selfish material ends, though he is with the Guru. The person, who is like the person who catches fish with nets, will bring his whole attention under the sway or worldly Intelligence (Puththi) and bring the Intelligence (Puththi) under the sway of the hypnotic attraction of Illusion (Maya). He will devote his full attention to the management of his material wealth, always expecting profit from his actions, though he is with the Guru. The man, who is like the person who fishes in the boat with thousands of lines, will always be under the influence of his status and family connections, though he has an inner faith in his Guru, and he will always be doubting the veracity of the teachings of his Guru. He will not accept the teaching of the Guru in full.

The disciple, who is like the person who sails in the ship in the deep ocean and catches large quantities of fish with iron nets and serves a large number of people in the world, is the true disciple. He will give up all selfishness and attachment to the world and live for the benefit of Mankind. He will develop the spirit of Compassion and devote his body, spirit and wealth to the service of his Guru. He will listen to every one of his Guru's teachings and with full attention imprint it in his mind and heart. The teachings of the Guru will influence his Emotions, Awareness, Spirit of Compassion and Love and his emergent Divine Wisdom. He will mould his inner and outer life according to the teachings of his Guru and reach the feet of God.

The disciples of a Guru will be able to absorb the teachings of the Guru according to the state of their intelligence and intellectual capacity and mental attitude. Like the various types of people who catch fish in the sea, the disciples will be able to get the Divine Wisdom (Arivu) according to their worth, ability and mental attitude.

Although you are with the Guru, unless you are like the person who sails in the ship and catches fish in large numbers, you will not be able to get the Light of Grace in the ocean of Wisdom (Arivu) and become fully aware of the inner meaning of the Guru's teachings.

124.   **At 7:20 P.M. on 10/8/70**

Seyed Ahamed told His Holiness Guru Bawa, "There is a saying, 'One who realises his self will realise His Creator.' Please explain the meaning of this." His Holiness explains the meaning of the saying as follows:

The Soul (Ruh or Atma) is God's (Allah's) Grace (Dhat or Arul). It depends on Him. This Surat (body) is made of five elements: Earth, Fire, Water, Air and Ether. These five elements are inimical to one another. But they all have Faith in God (Allah). From the day they developed Faith in God (Allah), their enmity disappeared and they started dwelling together. Since they have Faith (Iman) in God, they are indestructible. Their power is never destroyed. They exist for ever.

In the same way as a house is built of five elements, God has built a house for the Soul (Ruh) out of the five elements on an agreement. When the period of agreement is over, the Soul (Ruh) must get out of the house.

In the sea over the earth is the water; above the water is the air; above the air is fire; above the fire is ether (colour - blue). In the same way, all these five elements are found in this body. At the end of one's life, when the body is interred in the earth, the five elements in the body return to the respective five elements in the earth. When that happens, what remains? Who are you? What can you call your own? In the physical body of yours there is nothing that you can call yours. This is only a rented house where the Soul (Ruh or Atma) lives. When the period of agreement is over, you have to get out of this rented house. When that happens, the Soul (Atma) has to return to the Creator as it is His property. If you understand this, you can understand your self.

If one knows that this is a rented house, he will know himself. You will know that this body is not your house; this is not your property! In that state you will know Soul (Atma). The Creator (God) has explained this clearly to Noor Muhamed, the Effulgent Divine Luminous Wisdom (Perr-Arivu).

God (Allah) has told Muhamed, "Oh, Muhamed! I have not created anything without you." Muhamed is God's (Allah's) Effulgence, His Beauty (Zeeneth). Muhamed is in the Divine Luminous Wisdom (Perr-Arivu) of Soul (Ruh). It is merged in God. God's beauty is not the body. It is not the "I". It is the Truth. That Truth is God.

The Soul (Ruh) is God's property. It is sacred and pure; it is Effulgence. It is that light that has come from Him that is living in this rented house. After it has studied the world and come to understand what it is, it sees its Lord, and reaches God. In that state one who has known his self knows his Creator. Understand this clearly.

Without understanding this, as long as you identify your self with the physical body, there is death. If you realise that this body is a rented house, and know your self, you will know that this is not your house or your property. In that state, you will come to know the Soul (Atma), the Creator.

So said His Holiness Guru Bawa to Seyed Ahamed.

125.   At 11:00 A.M. on 10/10/70

Susan Matthews, an American lady, who paid a visit to His Holiness Guru Bawa, described to His Holiness the present trends of the American people. His Holiness asked her "In your country you have advanced a great deal in the field of Scientific Research. But how far has your country progressed in spiritual things, in Ture Gnosis (Meignana)?" She replied, "There has been a little more change in American Society now than before. Many people are interested in Eastern Philosophy, Religions, Mythology, and Meditation. But there are no Ashrams (Holy places) like this in the West where one can learn about spiritual advancement. Also, there are no competent Gurus."

His Holiness Guru Bawa replied, There is no need for you to consider Ashrams to be necessary. It is not necessary to learn spiritual advancement from Ashrams. Ashrams are very difficult to run.

The attitudes of the people of the world are different. Only a few people will have the Emergent Divine Wisdom to understand the real nature of the world. You have to perform a duty in this world. God is not far from the person who performs this duty. The person who performs his duty will become Manu Eesan (Man-God) so long as he develops the Divine Luminous Wisdom (Perr-Arivu) of God. If he leads his life truthfully according to the dictate of this Divine duty, within his Emergent Divine Luminous Wisdom (Perr-Arivu) he will hear the resonance of the voice of God and the nature of Wisdom (Arivu), and see the Effulgence of the Soul (Atma).

The lady asked His Holiness, "The present trends of life in the West are not conducive to spiritual development. Therefore, how can we go along the path of spiritual advancement? In America this question is being raised everywhere."

His Holiness replied, When you walk, only your feet touch the earth with a firm grip. But you do not carry the earth with your feet when you walk.

There is a path of Truth. On both sides of the path are found the trees, shrubs and creepers bearing flowers and fruit of attractive hue. They are the numberless glittering hypnotic attractions of the world. They are the flower gardens and orchards of Illusion (Maya) which attract man with the hypnotic fascination and lead him astray and deprive him of True Wisdom (Arivu). The glittering fruits of the joys of Illusion (Maya) fall on both sides of the path. This is the world of the senses.

Between the two sections, full of the hypnotic attractions of Illusion (Maya), runs the path of Truth, the road of Wisdom (Arivu). When travelling along the path of Truth, one should use his faculty of Divine Wisdom (Pahuth-Arivu) and analyse the nature of the flowers and fruits on the sides of the path and come to the conclusion that they are the seductive fruits of Illusion. (Maya). He should switch on the light of Radiance of his Divine Luminous Wisdom (Perr-Arivu) and get into the middle of the path of Truth, and proceed beyond.

When you walk, your feet press the ground and move on. But you do not carry the ground with you. In the same way, when you travel along the path of Truth, guided by the light of the Radiance of Divine Luminous Wisdom (Perr-Arivu), you need not carry with you the glittering hypnotic fruits of Illusion (Maya) which you see on both sides of the path.

The Eastern Philosophies, Mythology, Legends and Methods of Meditation you spoke of, or the Western Philosophies and Methods of Meditation are all like the shrubs you see on both sides of the path. You will not achieve any result by following these Philosophies or Methods of Meditation.

The faith of the East is based on the five elements of Earth, Fire, Water, Air and Ether. They observe these five elements carefully. As a result of their observation, thoughts arise in their mind; the mind concentrates on these thoughts; the concentration on these thoughts become an obsession; the obsession becomes a dream; the dream becomes an impression on the mind; the impression in the mind is transformed into a physical vision; the physical vision becomes a mental vision. The mental vision creates beautiful painting and statues; the sixty-four arts lead to the creation of various types of beautiful statues; these statues become the gods of the elements; the statues give rise to soul-stirring devotional songs in which the five elements gambol; the devotional songs give rise to classical music, vocal and instrumental; the music produced by the veena, the drum, the cymbals, in various ragas are appreciated by the sense world; the rhythm of the music gives rise to dances to suite the rhythm; the dances please the eyes and the music the ears; this rouses the senses and leads to sensual pleasures. It is to this state that faith and religion has degenerated in the East today.

The religion and faith of the West is the spectacular advancement of science, the joy derived from Darkness (Agnana) and economic freedom. They develop these, dedicating to them their body, wealth and spirit.

Some enjoy music and dancing, others enjoy doing research work in various fields of science. Through these two you cannot gain spiritual freedom and bliss of knowing and reaching God. They only lead to the never-ending cycle of birth and death.

But, if man wants to get Liberation for his Soul (Atma), the Radiance of Divine Luminous Wisdom (Perr-Arivu) should shine brilliantly within him. The darkness of the mind is Poignana or False Wisdom. The beauty of False Wisdom (Poignana) is Ignorance (Agnana). The beauty of Ignorance (Agnana) is science (Vingnana). The end of science is destruction. The

True Wisdom that arises in the wake of destruction is the True Gnosis (Meignana).

The powers of the one hundred and fifty million manifestations and the four hundred billion hypnotic attractions of Illusion (Maya) found in the attractive and seductive side of the path of Truth, appear to be the Faith and Religion of the West.

So said His Holiness Guru Bawa to Miss Suzanne Matthews.

126.   **At 9:00 A.M. or 10/11/70**

Mr. Nizam asked His Holiness Guru Bawa, "The sufferings arising from the evil actions of a father do not end with his life. The wife and children also continue to suffer for his evil acts. Why should they suffer when they did not commit those evil acts?"

His Holiness replied: Look at the tree. When you cut it down, do not think that the tree has wholly disappeared. Its roots are spread out in all directions in the earth. It is with its roots that the tree keeps its hold on the earth. You have removed the trunk of the tree. But the roots with which it keeps its hold to the earth are still there. Only when you have removed all the roots from the earth can you say that the tree has been fully removed.

A person thrives on prohibited food and takes alcoholic drinks. The resulting characteristics of his blood, his servility to the senses, his faith in demons projected by the five elements, and the mood and state of mind of the parents at the time of union, are all imprinted in the foetus growing in the womb of the mother. The semen of the father becomes the skeleton, and the ovum of the mother becomes the muscles and skin of the child in the womb. Because his body forms from part of the father and part of the mother, the father's sins are also attached to him. The characteristics and diseases of the parents are latent in him. He cannot say that he has completely annihilated with his intelligence what he inherited from his father. It will be analogous to a person saying that he has completely removed the tree by merely cutting down and removing the trunk of the tree.

In the same way, as the roots of the tree have to be completely removed from the earth before one can say that he has removed the tree, one has to make use of the services of a Guru to remove with Wisdom (Arivu) all the inherited tendencies embedded in him when he was an embryo. All his blood attachments will have to be removed with the help of the Guru. Only then can he be free from the suffering caused by the evil actions of his father.

God (Allah) should not be blamed. One has to reap the fruit of his own actions. Since the son was formed out of this person's body, what this person suffers as a result of his evil actions has to be suffered by his son, his grandson, and so on, as long as this blood affinity, this blood relationship is not removed with the help of the Guru.

127.   **At 12:00 Noon on 10/11/70**

His Holiness told those gathered in the Ashram:

The life of the weak-minded, the life of the hunter who cannot aim properly, the life of the cripple who has no crutches and a government which is partial, will not produce any useful result.

The life of a person devoid of Forbearance and Patience, the prayer of a person who does not have a contented mind, the devotion to God of a person who does not adopt Divine Qualities, and the Wisdom (Gnana) of a person devoid of True Wisdom, will destroy the Truth of God.

128. At 6:25 P.M. on 10/12/70

Miss Suzanne Matthews, the American Lady, came to the Ashram for the second time and requested His Holiness Guru Bawa to explain certain things.

She said, "When we are leading our lives as members of a family, we have to come in contact with our relatives in the course of our duties to earn our livelihood. It is stated that the seeker after Truth should give up all attachments to wife, children, relatives, etc., and give up what the mind desires. Will your Holiness explain in detail?"

His Holiness replied: There is a knife. A person uses that knife to cut a thing. It is the knife which cuts. But did the knife derive any profit by cutting? Did it undergo any experience in doing so? No, it did not. The profit and the experience goes to the person who uses the knife for cutting. But the knife does its duty.

In the same way, the contacts you make in your family life, the attachments you develop, are all the requirements of your senses. These requirements originate from your senses. These are not needed by your Wisdom (Arivu) and your Soul (Atma). The knife did not get any profit or experience by the duty of cutting which it performed. The man who used the knife gained the experience and profited. In the same way, the contacts you make as a result of the requirements of the senses give satisfaction only to the senses. They are of no use to your Wisdom (Arivu) or Soul (Atma). Wisdom (Arivu) does not require the earnings of the physical body. You must use the physical body under the guidance of Wisdom (Arivu). The Soul (Atma) derives no benefit from the things that concern the physical body. You should understand this.

She asked, "How can we escape from the clutches of the senses?"

His Holiness replied: Sugar causes change in sourness. In the same way, the senses can be changed by Wisdom (Arivu). In the same way as sourness is removed by sugar, the influence of the senses can be removed by Wisdom (Arivu). Raw fruit is sour. After it matures the sourness disappears and only sweetness remains. When it is fully ripe there is no sourness but only sweetness in the fruit. In the same way, when the senses of a man merge in Wisdom (Arivu), the nectar of Divine Grace gives permanent sweetness to him. This is called Divine Luminous Wisdom (Perr-Arivu).

Miss Suzanne Matthews asks further, "What is really man's duty? I would like to have a correct interpretation."

His Holiness Guru Bawa replied: You are living in a town. The town is in imminent danger. It has become necessary for you to escape to the next town. There is a sea between your town and the next town. You have to get hold of a boat or ship and sail across the sea to the next town. You have no time to think of your house and your property at this time of grave danger. All your attention is devoted to escaping from that town, somehow or other, leaving behind your house and your property to fate.

The physical body in which you dwell cannot indicate to you when death will overtake it. It swerves between the two extremes of joy and sorrow. The body gets fatigued. The limbs become powerless at the approach of death. Before the great calamity of death overtakes your body, you should leave it and get into the boat of Wisdom (Arivu), sail across the sea of Ignorance (Agnana) and settle on the shore of True Knowledge (Meignana). You should do this with the same speed with which you will get into the boat and escape from the city which is doomed to destruction. Only then will you obtain Spiritual Liberation in this birth itself. Otherwise, you, your Wisdom (Arivu), and your Soul (Atma) will be destroyed. As a result, you have to take several births and meet with spiritual loss. It would be better for you to understand this and act accordingly. This is man's duty, his inescapable duty.

Suzanne Matthews asked, "What is the state beyond joy and sorrow, pleasure and pain? Please explain."

His Holiness replied: To prepare tea you first boil cold water. You put tea in the boiling water. Then you strain it and add sugar. When the sugar is dissolved, it becomes palatable sweet tea. If you take the cold water, it will be cool and refreshing. On the other hand, there will be dangerous germs in it. They may cause disease and suffering. So, there is joy and sorrow in the cold water. The hot water has its characteristics. But, it can also scald your hands. So, it also can cause joy as well as sorrow. Take the hot tea. Now, the tea has its qualities. It is a tonic and tones up the nerves. But, at the same time it has a bitter taste. So, it also causes joy and sorrow. But once you put sugar into the tea, its bitter taste disappears. It becomes a sweet drink and one does not mind even the heat. In this state of the sweetness of the tea, one does not think of the joy or sorrow caused by its tonic effect or bitter taste. One only enjoys the taste of the tea to which sugar has been added.

In the same way, when the mind disappears within Wisdom (Arivu), there is no joy or sorrow. Just as the attributes of the tea which cause joy and sorrow disappeared when sugar was added, the states of joy and sorrow caused by the senses disappear when mind disappears and Wisdom (Arivu) holds sway. In this state one only feels the Taste of God which is free from joy and sorrow. This is the transcedent state beyond the state of joy and sorrow, pleasure and pain. But, as long as one's senses do not disappear within the fold of Wisdom (Arivu), one will continue to feel joy and sorrow, pleasure and pain.

When one desires to protect his landed property, his mind becomes subject to a lot of pain. He will have problem after problem to solve. In the earth there are four billion hypnotic fascinations. If he starts to protect them, these hypnotic fascinations of Illusion (Maya) will create one problem after another. There will be no end to problems. A man will not be able to find a solution to the problem of his birth. Even if he takes four hundred billion births, he will not be able to solve these problems.

Miss Suzanne Matthews intervenes and says that people have landed property as it offers a state of security to them.

His Holiness replied: If you possess land, there will be also a nail that causes wounds in your mind. I have two or three pieces of land. I am undergoing a lot of difficulties due to them.

Look at the monkey. It will jump wherever it likes, run and play. It will be up to various types of antics. The mind is like the monkey. As long as the mind of a man if freely active, he will always have problems. If the mind disappears within Wisdom (Arivu), it will be the state of Man-God (Manu Eesan). It is in that state that Wisdom (Arivu) will appear.

Miss Suzanne Matthews stated that only very few people in the world can reach that state.

His Holiness replied that it was so. There are millions of human beings. But there is only one God. He rules over the eighteen thousand worlds. He is the Ultimate Unique One. Man-god (Manu Eesan) is the God of the World. It is very difficult to become Man-God (Manu Eesan). Only very few reach that state of Perfect Man. If one succeeds in reaching that state, then God and Soul (Atma) become One. God will become the Soul (Atma) and the Soul (Atma) will become the body of God. Both will stay in one place. This is a wonderful mystery.

Unless we reach this state of perfection we will never succeed in seeing God even if we search for Him in all the directions. If you want to see God, you should give up all the attachments to the world of Illusion (Maya) described earlier. Mind must disappear; craving should be destroyed; you must get out of the state of stupor caused by Illusion (Maya); you should develop the extra-mundane faculty of Wisdom (Arivu); the Wisdom (Arivu) should mature and shine in Resplendence; then only can you see That One Ultimate Reality. To show you the way, you need the help of an authentic Guru of True Knowledge (Meignana Guru); such a Guru is found very rarely in this world.

Therefore, you should remove the darkness of your mind with your Wisdom (Arivu), avoid the seductive fruits handing on both sides of the path of Truth and walk straight along the centre of the road. At the end of that road Wisdom (Arivu) will take you to the Guru.

Ants lay a large number of eggs. They move in large numbers. If you throw a piece of burning charcoal, they know not what to do. They get burnt up. The remaining ants disperse on all sides. In the same manner, there are several crores of human beings in the world. If you drop the latest nuclear bomb on them, the bomb discovered by man will destroy all men. In the same manner if the Creator looks at them with anger they will all be destroyed like the ants. He can create. He can destroy. However populated a nation may be, if it does not get God's Love and Compassion, it cannot thrive. If God looks at that nation in anger, all of them will get burnt up and destroyed.

Miss Suzanne Matthews said, "These human beings have been born in such large numbers. God must have had some purpose in creating them."

His Holiness replied: God has also created the bacteria in our body with some purpose. If you understand the suffering and pain caused by these bacteria, you will understand what I told you earlier. Bacteria were also created by God, as were these human beings. Human beings who are not devoted to God, who do not adopt His Divine Qualities, are similar to the bacteria in the body. These bacteria in the body and the attachments of the body cause immense suffering to the Wisdom (Arivu) of man. In the same way, the created beings who do not realise the Truth, cause suffering and pain to the Love and Compassion of Truth. There is no use in talking about these two. You should understand it with your Wisdom (Arivu).

Miss Suzanne Matthews asked, "Human society exists because of the ties of family, the institution of husband, wife, children, etc. Is that not so?"

His Holiness replied: It rains. The rain water stagnates in low ground. It fills up the pits. But, it does not rain for the purpose of filling low ground and pits and flowing beyond. It rains on its own. The rain water fills up low ground and pits. It runs down from high ground and flows down into streams. It will stay where it should stay. It flows where it should flow.

In the same way, God is the Creator of all beings. It is His duty to feed and protect and save his created beings. He is Eternal; He sees everything; it is His duty to create, protect and save. You cannot perform His duty. It is due to ignorance that you think that you can protect and save your wife, children, property, freedom, caste, creed, etc. When your body itself is not permanent, what is the guarantee that you will be able to protect others? You should reflect a little on this aspect.

We, the created beings, allow our mind to follow the path of the senses, and meet with joy and sorrow in the same way as the rain water runs over the ground and fills up pits and hollows. When the pits are full of rain water, the crabs and frogs wallow in the pits thinking that the water there will be permanent and that the pit of water is theirs. They do not think that they will be in danger when the water dries up.

In the same way, the senses of men fall in the sea of hypnotic sex, thinking that it is permenent and it belongs to them. The very place which brought them into the world sucks their life-blood and brings a state of torpor to their limbs and causes death. They do not know this. When they lose their stamina and become a skeleton, their egoism, attachments, creed, caste and intellectual power will disappear. If you reflect a little on this, you will understand.

Those of you who do not reflect on these aspects, wrack your brain with such questions. Finally you become the victim of Death. If you reflect a little on all these things, you will understand.

129. At 7:30 P.M. on 10/15/70

His Holiness Guru Bawa addressed those gathered in the Ashram as follows:

Children! I will relate to you a story. Please listen and reflect on it. In the West there lived a black man who had a very good physique and was very strong. He had obtained the world championship in boxing and wrestling on several occasions. His name became a household word. His photos were found in houses in various parts of the world.

A European lady read a lot of literature about him and also witnessed his boxing. She came to the conclusion that he was a great hero and brought a copy of his photo and hung it in her bedroom. She and her husband used to discuss him often. In the course of time she conceived and gave birth to a child. The child looked like a black child. When the husband saw the shape and color of the child, he suspected that his wife must have had illicit sexual relationship with that famous black man and that the child was born to the black man. He thought this because the child's colour and shape were not like him. As a result, there were frequent quarrels between the husband and wife.

He stopped looking at the child. He also stopped speaking to his wife with love and affection. He scolded her, saying, "You were intimate with the black man. That is why you have given birth to a black child." She replied, "I have taken only you as my partner in life. I have not been intimate with anyone else. I swear in the name of God." He did not accept her oath. The more he looked at the child, the more suspicious he became. He was unable to calm his mind. He cried over the disgrace that had befallen him. Finally, he filed a case in a Court of Law for divorce.

When the case was taken up in court, the wife swore in Court that she was faithful to her husband. The Judge asked her to produce the child in Court. The child was produced in Court. The child did not look like either of the parents. It looked like the black man. The Judge reflected a little and said, "I accept your oath that you were always faithful to your husband. But anyone may suspect that the child is not born to you two because of its colour and shape. Did you, in your childhood, love any boy like this child? Did you have a person like the child as your childhood companion or friend? Did a person like this child study in your class at school and become your school friend? Or, in your travels in the lands of black people, did a face like this get impressed in your mind?" She replied that she did not have such friends or companions and that she did not get impressed in her mind a black face similar to that of the child during her travels in the lands of black people.

Then the Judge asked her whether she had any photos in her bedroom. She replied that there were two pictures in her house. One was a picture showing the gods. The other was a photo of the black wrestler which was hung in the bedroom. The Judge asked her to bring both the pictures. When the photo and picture were brought, the Judge found that the child was like the face of the black wrestler in the photo. The Judge asked her whether she had ever met the black wrestler personally and talked to him. She replied that she had never met and talked with him. The Judge asked her whether the photo was hung on the wall at the foot of the bed, at the head of the bed or on the sides. She replied that it was hung on the wall at the foot of the bed.

Then the Judge said, "At the time of copulation, there was the impression in her mind that the black man in the photo was a great hero. Further, her eyes also were gazing at the photo at the time instead of looking at the face of the husband. That is the reason why the child was born like the black man in the photo." The Judge gave the verdict that the child was born to the husband, and advised the couple not to keep that photo in their bedroom. He suggested that they keep their own beautiful photos in the bedroom, and sent them away.

Children! Many people keep beautiful statues in the bedroom or other parts of the house. Some keep beautiful pictures. Since they see these statues and pictures often, their eyes and minds and thoughts are always directed towards them whether they like it or not. As a result, these statues and pictures capture a definite place in their minds. Different statues and pictures remind the mind of their characteristics which get imprinted in their subconscious mind. So, at the time of conception, their shape, colour and characteristics are impressed in the embryo. In the growing foetus, in addition to the physical characteristics and colour, the mental characteristics and conduct and predilictions of the characters indicated by the statues and pictures will also get imprinted. When this foetus matures and is born, the child will look like these statues and pictures and also develop their characteristics and mental set-up.

But, instead of admiring these beautiful statues and pictures of the

189

sensual world, if the husband and wife always think of the nature and characteristics of That Ultimate One whose Effulgence pervades everywhere, and if their mind is saturated with the Divine Characteristics of God, the children born to them will become Gnanis (Gnostics), rulers or great men. The type of children born to a person depends on his or her mental state.

Let us consider the case of a beggar. He gets up at two or three o'clock in the night and goes to the bazaar to beg. He roams all over, sings and assumes several poses to make the people feel pity on him and give him some coins. He begs like this till sunset and goes home to his wife and children with whatever he has received that day by begging. His mind is worried as to what his wife will think, whether she will be satisfied with the money he obtained by begging that day. He calls his wife and gives her the money. Being fatigued, he lies down on the ground.

The wife tells him, "What? From dawn till night you have been out. The children have been crying with hunger. I shed tears on seeing their suffering, but you brought only twenty-five cents, which is not enough to buy rice to prepare liquid rice for even a single meal. What am I to do?" She cried. The beggar replied, "What can I do? Am I to steal? I went to every house and pleaded and begged. With the quantity you can buy, you may prepare liquid rice and give it to the children." He was dejected. He was tired. He continued to lie on the floor. She took the money and bought half a measure of rice and a little salt. She boiled it and prepared liquid rice and gave it to the children who were starving. Then she took a mug of liquid rice to her husband and woke him up. She asked him to take it and then sleep.

In a dejected mood he said, "What food? What water? When God has put us in this position, what is the need for food for me? Give the liquid boiled rice to the children. You may also drink it and go to sleep. God has no eyes. The world does not understand the Truth. The minor gods and goddesses have no compassion. People have no mercy in this world. Drink the boiled rice water and sleep."

When his wife heard him speaking in this way, she replied, "Why are you blaming God, the people and the world? It is a disgrace for a man to beg. It is still worse for such a man to marry and have children. God has given you eyes, ears, a nose, a mouth, legs and hands. He has given you a tongue with which to speak. He has given you Wisdom. He has given you physical strength. Is it not a disgrace for you to cringe before people and beg, when you can use your physical body and earn an honest living? Is it not a shame for a man of Wisdom to blame God? When He created you, He did not give you any physical defect. It is because of the degradation of your Wisdom, as a result of your deciding to earn your living by begging, that you dare to blame God. God created the fowl. He created the world where the fowl can search for its food. God has given you a beautiful body and has given you the faculty of discerning between the good and the bad in order for you to live in this world. If you analyse the world with your analytical mind and do your duty, you will not think of begging. Now, take this boiled rice water and sleep."

He replied, "What you say is correct. But you would know the real state of affairs if you wandered in the town and got tired. When one is hungry he forgets everything else. He cannot use his Wisdom. I am thinking of what my fate will be tomorrow. You are speaking Wisdom (Gnana)." She said, "Forget the advice I gave you! Now, take this boiled rice water." He took the bowl of boiled rice water. Lying down without washing his hands, he drank it and cleaned his hands by rubbing them against his clothes. Then, he went to sleep. She asked him to lie on a gunny bag. He refused and slept on the ground. She also laid down and slept by his side. While he was sleeping his mind was troubled about the next day; "What am I to do tomorrow? Where am I to go? How am I to live my life?"

Even though his mind was worried about the morrow, his desire for sex roused him. Almost as a reflex action, he had sex with his wife who was lying by his side.

As a result his wife conceived. The embryo developed with the same attitudes which the man held at the time of conjugation. His thoughts were about poverty, that he had nothing, that what he had was not enough, of dejectedness, of concern about tomorrow and of how he could earn the next day's living. After it was born, the child developed the same characteristics as the father, only to a greater degree. The child had a greater feeling of poverty and went to a larger number of houses to beg than had the father.

The same is the case of the usurer. His business is to increase his wealth by lending money at a higher rate of interest. After concluding the business for the day, he comes home in a happy mood. He and his wife apply scent to their bodies, chew betel and have a discussion about their wealth and income. They talk about the tens of thousands of dollars in their safe. In a happy mood they have sex. The wife conceives. The child born to them develops the same characteristics as his father. This child when it grows up, loans out a larger amount of money on interest and annexes a greater amount of wealth and is very happy in doing so.

The same is the story of the ruler. He has sex with his queen when his mind is bent on conquering the neighbouring state. The child born to them actually conquers that neighboring state.

The image which fascinated their minds is impressed in the foetus. Therefore, one's mind should reflect fullness and contentment. If the parents feel contented with what God has given them, the children will also be contented. If, in the mind, this fullness is impressed, there will be no want. The child will adopt the qualities of God. It will be full of Patience, Forbearance, Serenity, Love and Compassion.

Therefore, when the fault is in himself, man should not blame God for his misfortunes. He has lost his fullness of mind, his heritage. He is discontented and greedy. He puts the blame on God, who is Plentitude itself. God is the photographer, man is the actor. The actor cannot blame the photographer for mistakes in his acting which are shown in the film.

A man writes a play and sends it to the printer for printing. The printer publishes it as a book. In writing the play it is as though the playright has to read his play and act out the various parts. Pleasure and pain, joy and sorrow have to be shown in the acting. He cannot act the parts of characters which give pleasure and joy only and request the printer to act the parts of characters who suffer pain and sorrow. It is wrong. He will say, "You acted. I printed what you acted. It is for you to act both parts of pleasure and pain." The playright has to show how both parts have to be acted. It is not the duty of the printer to act. Man should understand this with his analytical mind. He has to sincerely act his part in this birth on the state of the world and fully complete the drama of life. He who does this is really a wise man. A man who is born as a Man (Insan) should know this. So said His Holiness Guru Bawa.

Dr. Selvaratnam asked, "People say that the mind should be still. Please explain this."

His Holiness replied: It is enough if you make the mind perfect and full. If your Heart (Qalb) has reached a state of fullness and perfection, the mind is said to be in a state of stillness.

130. **At 8:30 P.M. on 10/15/70**

His Holiness Guru Bawa tells Mr. Nadarajah, D.R.O.:

Child! There lived a carpenter. He had a son. The carpenter's daily earnings were three rupees. With that he had to support his family.

His son wanted to go to the West to qualify as an engineer. He pressed his father repeatedly to allow him to go. At last the father agreed. He gave him two thousand rupees and sent him to the West. When he went to the West, he found that they were teaching him what his father had taught him at home. All that he learned was what his father had done at home, and what he had taught him. But the father continued to send him two thousand rupees every month. After completing his studies, the son returned home with his certificate that he had qualified as an engineer. The father asked the son, "You went to the West to qualify as an engineer. What are the subjects you studied there?" The son replied, "In the West I did what you did here and what you taught me here. After wasting all this money, I brought this certificate, a piece of paper."

The father was surprised. He exclaimed, "Is this all you studied in the West where you went to qualify as an engineer? Is it for this purpose I sent you two thousand rupees a month? Without all this expenditure, you could have learned all this work here and also earned money. For all the money I have spent, you have only brought a piece of paper called a Certificate!" The father felt very sad.

In the same manner, a person who is born as a human being feels sad like this carpenter, who realised he had been wasting his money in sending his son to the West to qualify as an engineer, without coming to know the place of his birth and the place of birth of his parents, the experience they had and the work they did. If he clearly understands these things, undergoes these experiences, finds out with his analytical mind what is good and what is bad, and understands the nature of his body and the elements it is composed of, it will give him greatness in this birth. Instead, if he studies theology like the carpenter's son who studied engineering in the West, what he will get will be a certificate and a name to qualify him to have locked hair, moustache and beard. If they study about God like this, they will lose their spiritual heritage just as the carpenter's son lost the money. He will also lose the nobility of his position in this birth. In addition, he will become subject to several births. Instead, if he will study the nature of his body, control his mind, his five senses and the force of the five elements out of which his body is made, he will get the Divine Qualities of God.

At this juncture Dr. Selvaratnam interposed, "Your Holiness! Somehow or other we have been born in this world at this time. Let us act our part on the stage of the world and depart."

His Holiness said: Child! A Divinely Wise Man (Gnani) was doing penance on the slope of a mountain. A hunter came that way with hunting dogs to hunt deer, sambhur and other animals. After hunting these animals he went away with his dogs. A bitch got lost. It ran here and there following the scent of human feet and finally came to the place where the Divinely Wise Man (Gnani) was doing penance. It lay down some distance away from him.

A python came there to seize this bitch. The bitch barked on seeing it. The Divinely Wise Man (Gnani) opened his eyes to find out why the bitch was barking. He saw the python approaching the bitch to seize it. So, he turned the bitch into a fox, as the fox is capable of killing the python. So, the fox killed the python. The Divinely Wise Man (Gnani) closed his eyes and went into Meditation.

Bears like to eat foxes. So, a bear approached the fox from the forest. The fox used all its wiles to escape. But, the bear was intent on seizing it. So, the fox started howling in fear. The Divinely Wise Man (Gnani) opened his eyes to find out why the fox was howling. On seeing that the fox was howling because it was unable to fight with the bear and overcome it, he turned it into a tigress. The tigress jumped on the bear and tore it into pieces. The Divinely Wise Man (Gnani) closed his eyes and went into Meditation.

After some time, a tiger came from the forest to attack the tigress. The tigress was unable to fight it. On seeing this, the Divinely Wise Man (Hnani) turned it into a Bengal tiger. The Bengal tiger leaped on the tiger and fought with it and chased it away.

A rhinocerus came from the forest to attack the Bengal tiger. The Bengal tiger leaped and roared. The Divinely Wise Man (Gnani) turned it into a lion. The lion leaped on the rhinocerus and killed it and ate its liver. The bitch now lay there as a lion.

It thought thus: "It is due to this Holy Man that I am a lion today. I am the ruler of the forest as king of the beasts. But, if one day the Holy Man becomes angry with me, he may turn me back into a bitch. I must wait for an opportunity and kill him. If I do so, I can continue to live as a lion." So, it was waiting for and opportunity to kill the Holy Man.

When the Divinely Wise Man (Gnani) was in Meditation, the lion stretched its legs and moved its body in readiness to leap on the Divinely Wise Man's (Gnani's) head. When the Divinely Wise Man (Gnani) moved his body a little, it gave up its attempt and kept quiet. It tried like this for many days. The Divinely Wise Man (Gnani) knew what was in the mind of the bitch which he had turned into a lion. One day he sat still in Meditation without moving his body to find out what the lion would actually do. The lion, which was behind the Divinely Wise Man (Gnani) bent its body, stretched its legs and got ready to leap on him.

The Divinely Wise Man (Gnani) looked in the front and in the back with his Gnostic Eye to watch its movements. The lion raised its tail, stretched its legs and crouched to leap on him. The Divinely Wise Man (Gnani) opened his eyes and told it, "Former bitch! Why are you trying to do this wicked deed?" The lion immmediately became the former bitch, and sat down wagging its tail.

There are such people in this world. Their actions are like that of the bitch. Man has been created by God to become Man-God (Manu-Eesan). Even if his parents forget him, God does not forget him. God shows Compassion to him, gives him food even when he is in danger, shares his joys and sorrows, stays with him and gives him food day and night, protects him and saves him. God takes the form of Love and protects him. He remains within him as Wisdom (Arivu) within Wisdom (Arivu).

But when man gets material comforts in the world, he forgets God, and tries to kill Him within his heart like the bitch which was turned into a lion by the Divingly Wise Man (Gnani) and who then tried to kill him. Man thinks he is the master of the world and tries to control it, thinking that he can kill God and live forever. God, who has bestowed on man whatever he wants, makes him subject to Hell and several births, when man becomes wicked.

Therefore, children! You should not attempt to kill Truth, Justice, Forbearance, Patience, Compassion, Human Nature, Wisdom (Arivu) that is the birthright of man, and God Who dwells in your Heart (Qalb). You should develop the Divine Qualities of Compassion, and grow in God's Grace, and live within His Divine Love. As Wisdom (Arivu) within Wisdom (Arivu) you should merge within Him. If you do so, you will rule both the worlds, as King of Wisdom (Gnana), as the Judge of Truth, as the Friend of God and as the lover of people who love you.

131.   ## At 9:10 P.M. on 10/16/70

Dr. Selvaratnam asked His Holiness Guru Bawa, "Your Holiness! Is it not possible for a person, through his own efforts using his Wisdom (Arivu), to remove his desires and other evil qualities arising from the darkness of Illusion (Maya) and reach God?"

His Holiness replied: Children! If you plant a rare and valuable fruit tree which will one day bear fruit of exquisite taste and colour, you have to irrigate it. That is not enough. You also have to apply proper manure and fertilizer. You have to prevent people from cutting and destroying that tree. That is not enough. When it spreads out its branches and flowers, you have to apply more manure, and keep watch day and night to prevent anyone from plucking the flowers. When the young fruit comes forth you have to employ a watcher to prevent people and animals from plucking the young fruit. If the tree is in an open space, you have to protect it by erecting a fence around it. It is not enough. All the fruit will not mature at the same time. Some will mature early. Some may be half ripe. Some may be unripe. You will have to employ a person to pluck the fruit who can distinguish between the ripe fruit and unripe fruit. The fruit should be plucked carefully and not allowed to be damaged by falling on the ground. It should be given to the persons who desire it. If you employ an inexperienced person, he will use a stick and knock down the unripe fruits and cause them to rot. A person who knows the art of preventing the fruit from decaying is also needed. A person who can grade the fruit and find out which are good and which are bad, and fix prices accordingly and sell them is needed. Persons who know the taste of the fruit, who will buy the fruit, again and again, are also needed.

Dear child! God is One. A real Gnana Guru (Wise Guru) who knows God's powers and your mental powers, who can preach to you and initiate

194

you accordingly, control your five elements, drive away hypnotic fascinations of the five senses, explain the nature of reality and show the Unique One to you, is needed. Otherwise, you will meet with situations where you will have to succumb to the forcible currents of your mind, the desires created by your senses, the plays of the five elements, the joys of mental visions, and the dances that attract the eyes and the manifestations projected within you by the changes in powers of the four hundred billion hypnotic luminosities within your body. In such situations, whatever method you may adopt, you will not be able to see Him and His truth. In that state, you will enter these hypnotic manifestations and lose your five senses and the six states of Divine Wisdom and become subject to several births. Nowehere can you learn a trade without a Guru. Therefore, Wisdom (Gnana) without a Guru will be like crops without water. Such crops will never grow and yield a harvest. You should understand this well.

132.   ### At 9:20 A.M. on 11/15/70

His Holiness Guru Bawa addressed Dr. Selvaratnam and said:

Child! There are various types of created beings in this world. Among the human beings there are various types. I, the most insignificant and useless of all human beings, am of a peculiar type. The ways and speech of others appear to be wrong to me. My words appear to be wrong to the world. There are diverse types of persons in the world. For example, there are the Hindus and the Muslims. The Hindus call me a crafty Muslim. The Muslims call me a false Hindu Swami.

One set of people say, "He is attacking our religions (Vedas), our castes and our philosophies (Vedantes). He says that all the Gods which appear before us are visions, not real. We should not allow him to live. He should be killed."

Another set of people say, "He is damaging our Holy Scriptures. He is destroying our jobs. He is destroying our methods of Worship. He says, Know yourself, Know your Creator and Pray (Unnai Arinthu, Andavani Arinthu Vananku). But they misinterpret the word 'Arinthu', meaning know, as 'Atinthu', meaning cut. How can people cut themselves and then pray? How can one cut himself and cut God and pray? This fellow is an imposter. The world has gone bad because of him. We have lost the respect of the people. Our learning has become useless. He does not give honour to our learning. Only if he does, can we prosper. God! We beseech you to cause his death."

Others say, "In this vast Universe, it is said that there is only one God. How can He rule this world? How can we see Him? The God we see with our eyes as Astral bodies, as gold, as property, He hates. He wants us to investigate God who is in an Unknowable Place. What our Religion (Veda) and Philosophy (Vedanta) show as God we are able to see. This man wants us to see something which cannot be seen. Why does he do all these wicked things? After finishing our work, we can bathe and go to the temple and pray and tell him our difficulties and return home. The God he speaks of cannot be seen even if we die. He is an imposter. Why is God keeping him alive still? God! Cause him to die." Thus both parties pray to God and wish in their minds that I should die.

Child! One party calls me a Muslim imposter. The other calls me a Hindu imposter.

All their scholarship has only brought them to this state. Ancient Hindu Myths (Puranas) speak of Desire (Karu Mal) and Mind (Thiru Mal). Both started on a voyage of discovery to see the head and feet of God. Desire (Karumul) groped its way down into the earth, into the nether world. Mind (Thirumal) went up to the worlds above. They did not see God anywhere. They felt tired and came back to the original place from where they started. Mind (Thirumal) asked Desire (Karumal) whether he saw God in the nether world. Desire (Karumal) replied in the negative. Mind (Thirumal) said that he could not see him in the upper worlds. Both came to the conclusion that there is no God but ourselves. We create; we protect; we destroy; we are gods. So they decided to assume the role of gods. They created visions of the mind and physical visions. They created manifestations which appear with forms. They created statues to represent them. The Mind (Thirumal) and Desire (Karumal) created four hundred billion manifestations of hypnotic fascination. They further created the mythological poems of exquisite beauty and rhythm (Puranas) from the mental visions; they have created characters to suit the scenes, composed suitable songs and created exquisite dances. They have created the sixty-four arts (Kalas) of the ninety-six attributes or states of man; the eighteen ancient myths (Puranas) the ten manifestations which are actually the manifestations of the ten sins (the five elements and the five senses). They have created innumerable devotional songs to suit each of these manifestations and have devised numberless methods of worship. The senses composed songs and poems on all these aspects of the sense-world. The mind was hypnotized by these.

It is this spiritual state about which they have written in books. In a state of hypnotic torpor caused by the darkness of Illusion (Maya), their intelligence and Wisdom enters a state of degradation. They commit the six sinful acts of desire, hatred, miserliness, vanity, lust and jealousy under the influence of Egoism (Anawan), Action (Karma), and Illusion (Maya), and religious fanaticism. They get illusory success in the world and have removed the Liberation of the Soul from birth and prevented man from becoming Man-God (Manu Eesan) in this birth itself.

Child! I have not studied the methods of obtaining material success in this world. In the middle of my physical body, which is like a cage, within my Heart (Qalb) there is That One Who is a Mystery within a Mystery, Wisdom (Arivu) within Wisdom (Arivu), Wonder of Wonders, Truth of Truths, Light within Light; That which is Eternal. I have studied the nature of everything from That Unique One.

If the two sections of people I referred to want to know That One, they should use the eye of Wisdom (Arivu) and look within their own Self and know where the Indestructible Place is, and come to understand That which is within. They will be able to study and know what I have studied, they will know the difference between what I have said and what they have said, and come to know what Truth is.

But, if they see only with their physical eyes, what I have said will appear to be wrong to them. I have placed my experience in my physical cage and analysed it. Then I have placed the characteristics of the physical cage in my intelligence and weighed it. What the intelligence assessed I put on the intellect and weighed it; what the intellect assessed I analysed with Wisdom (Arivu). The conclusions of Wisdom (Arivu), I placed on Divine

Wisdom (Pahuth-Arivu) and analysed and rejected book learning and the physical body as of no consequence and took only the Truth, and placed the Truth in Divine Luminous Wisdom (Perr-Arivu) and experienced the nature of Truth. All other attributes about God I examined with the eye of Wisdom (Arivu) and rejected them as wrong.

But, dear child! You might have seen and wondered at the vision created by book learning, the jungle seen by the senses, and the kingdom ruled by the mind, and enjoyed these visions. What I have learned from my experience may appear to be strange and unacceptable to you. You may consider them to be foolish. The people who come to see me may say, "Man, man! Why all these antics? You are born as man; why did you become such a useless man?" I may be a strange sight to them.

If you give up all these things, come to know the Truth, reflect with your Wisdom (Arivu), analyse with your Divine Wisdom (Pahuth-Arivu) and understand with your Divine Luminous Wisdom (Perr-Arivu) and look with intent gaze within your Heart (Qalb), your Wisdom (Arivu) will be able to see That Perfection of Beauty, the mysteries of His Beauty and lose itself in It. Then the senses will die. There will be an end to the cycle of birth. The 96 types of obsession will disappear. When these obsessions disappear, the devotee of Wisdom (Arivu) will be understood. When that is understood, you will see the Plenitude. If you see that Fullness, you will reach That Perfect Unique One. Child! To unravel that mystery is why we were born in this world.

That which mind and desire were unable to find, Wisdom (Arivu) was able to search and find. Wisdom (Arivu) was able to find That One which is Wisdom (Arivu) within Wisdom (Arivu) and in the inner space it stood in ecstacy and disappeared in It. Wisdom (Arivu) appeared originally from It. Later, Wisdom (Arivu) disappeared in It. It is That Unique One which we came into this world to know. We came to this world to reach That State. You should understand this. You will never be able to see God with mind and desire. You will only see what mind has created. When everything else was discarded by Wisdom (Arivu), it found only God. That which is Wisdom (Arivu) within Wisdom (Arivu) can only be seen by Wisdom (Arivu).

His Holiness further continued: Child! I will elaborate on what I told you by giving you an example. In the Muslim (Furkan) religion, the Messenger of God (Rasool) is the Prophet (Nabi) of God in the previous world, in this world and in the next, and he is the final Prophet (Nabi) of God. The Quran came down to him in the Voice of God (Allah). It is the Holy Scripture (Thiru Maria) in the fourth religion. In the same way as the Hindus and Muslims rejected me, the world rejected the Prophet. They expelled him from his birthplace. As a result, as indicated in the Quran, several wars took place. This is described in the books on his life.

One day, he and his disciples lay in an open space avoiding their enemies. When he was in that state, God gave him, through the Angel Gabriel, a sword to enable him to win the battle. He kept the sword by his side and lay down in Meditation. Others were also sleeping there.

One of his enemies came there quietly, took that sword in his hand, woke up the Messenger (Rasool) and said, "Don't shout! I am going to cut you down with this sword. You have said that God is in an Unknowable Place. Request Him to protect you now!" The Messenger (Rasool or Sal) replied to him, "He will come now." The enemy raised the sword to cut him. But his hands shivered and lost the grip and the sword fell down on the earth. The Messenger of God (Rasool or Sal) took that sword in his hand.

The idols of three thousand higher gods and the idols of three hundred and thirty million smaller gods, whom the enemy worshipped, were kept in the Temple (Ka'aba) in Mecca. The Messenger of God (Rasool) kept the sword in his hand and told his enemy who earlier attempted to cut him, "I want to cut you now. Request your gods to come and protect you." His gods did not come to protect him. The Messenger of God (Rasool or Sal) placed the sword on his neck. His enemy touched the Messenger of God's (Rasool's) legs and said, "You are my refuge. Do not cut me."

Then the Messenger of God (Rasool) said, "Brother, let go of my legs. You are my brother. You and I were born to the same father. There is no enmity between us. You touched my legs and sought me as your refuge. It was for that purpose that we were fighting. I am telling you that God is in the Unknowable Place. I seek His protection and help. But you were relying on the gods you are keeping in the temple at Mecca. You were seeking their help. The fight is between this ignorance of yours and my Wisdom (Arivu). You and I are not enemies. Only Truth and Falsehood are fighting. You gave up your ignorance and requested me to save you. It is the faculty of Wisdom (Arivu) that made you do so.

"When you took the sword to kill me you told me to request my God, Who is in the Unknowable Place, to protect me. I told you that He would come. At that moment, the sword fell down from your hands. I took the sword which fell down and said, 'I want to cut you. Request the gods you were worshipping to come and protect you.' You took hold of my legs and sought protection. So, the battle is between Truth, which is God, and the gods of ignorance, created by the mind. The battle is between ignorance and Wisdom (Arivu), not between you and me", said the Holy Prophet of Islam.

"Truth, which is God, protected me. Falsehood, the god which you made and placed in the temple and worshipped, deserted you in your hour of need. You have to protect that god from being stolen by thieves. But when death overtakes you, it will not protect you. That is why the battle is between Truth, which is Wisdom (Arivu), and ignorance which made you love and pay devotion to the thing which was unable to protect you. There is no fight between you and me. You should understand That Unique God which protects you. You should know that God rules you within and without. If you become true to God, God will come and help you when you are in danger.

"God, Who Creates, Protects and Saves you, is very much nearer to you than your own soul. It is very easy to tell Him your difficulties. There is no need for a wireless to do that. He understands and sees through your wish. He shows His Compassion according to your wish. Because of your state of ignorance, you do not know where He is. He is in an Unknowable Place. But, He who is Wisdom (Arivu) within Wisdom (Arivu) is within you. If Divine Wisdom (Pahuth-Arivu) emerges in you, you will see Him in it. That is not far away. There is a great distance between your ignorance and God. But he is not far from your Wisdom (Arivu). The fight is between the ignorance that misguides you and brings you to a state of degradation, and

Wisdom (Arivu). If ignorance and misguided knowledge dies in you, you and I and God will be in the same place. You sought the help of your gods, and then sought refuge at my feet. The fight is between your earlier ignorance and later Wisdom (Arivu)."

When he heard that he said, "Messenger of God (Rasool), forgive me! Please initiate me into the Truth and teach me the Holy Recitation of Faith (Kalima) of Truth." The Messenger of God (Rasool) taught him the Holy Recitation of Faith (Kalima) of Truth. I have given you in a few words what is written in the Islamic (Furkan) Religion.

Now the sword means the sword of Faith, Determination, Certitude and Sanctity. If that sword is taken up by people who are full of ignorance and falsehood, they will shiver and will not be able to use it. They will fall down, not being able to bear God, who is Truth. Only those who have that Faith, Determination and Certitude will be able to bear God. It is that sword of Faith, Determination and Certitude which can bear God which was given by Gabriel to the Messenger of God (Rasool). It is with the sword of Faith, Determination and Certitude that one can cut asunder the torpor caused by the benumbing influence of the darkness and ignorance and wrong knowledge. Without it, this will not ever be possible. Please understand this well. Human beings are all the children of the same parents. God is one. There is no fight among them. The enemy to humanity is ignorance. The fight is between ignorance and Wisdom (Arivu). The fight is between the darkness of Illusion (Maya) and the Light of Truth. Therefore, there is actually no emnity among men. There is this torpor caused by obsession. There are ninety-six obsessions. You can cure these obsessions only with the medicine of Wisdom (Arivu). It is not possible to cure man of these obsessions with any other remedy. So said His Holiness Guru Bawa to Dr. Selvaratnam.

133.   **At 8:10 P.M. on 11/22/70**

Dr. Selvaratnam requested His Holiness to explain the meaning of the words, "Nirveeka Katpa Samathi."

His Holiness explained as follows: 'Nirva' means 'Niramayam'. 'Nira' means the place where the senses, the elements, body consciousness and connected factors were destroyed completely in man. 'Niramayam' means Soul (Atma), which has become fully purified and reached a state of sanctity without equal, and gets fertilized in His Effulgence.

'Samathi' means this: Within the womb of the Grace of God, Wisdom (Arivu) appears as an embryo and grows and takes full shape and grows within His Law of Truth, Equality and Peace and comes out of the womb and appears. This birth of Wisdom (Arivu) is 'Samathi'. The state of steadiness in which the Soul (Atma) has obtained the right of closest relationship with God is 'Samathi'. Soul (Atma) has become God (Athi). It was conceived in His nature; it took shape in His Love, reached its full stature in His Grace, began to spread its Radiance in His Justice, and merged within His Truth. It appeared within His Patience and Forbearance, reached fullness within His Plenitude, and merged within His Eternity, disappeared within Him, spread its Radiance and merged within the Effulgence of God. This state is 'Samathi'. It is a state where That One has become That Unique One. That is God (Athi) and Brillance (Jothi). Children! You should understand this with your True Wisdom.

Some people wear the ochre robe, grow locked hair, apply ash on the body, stage the drama of the mind within the physical cage, allow the mind to dance, the senses to sing, the elements to play, chase away the Truth, perform the penance of selfishness and self-agrandisement, allow their egoism to grow, wear the jewels of external show, increase their vanity, sit cross-legged and show that they are 'Samathi' in the presence of people. But when people are not there, they open their eyes, incant magic words (mantras) and conduct ceremonies to please their mind. A Man-God (Manu Eesan) with Divine Wisdom (Pahuth-Arivu) will not accept this as 'Samathi', my child! But the ways of the world are diverse. There are various types of created beings. There are many types among beings born with the human face. Their devotion and worship is limited to the world of the five elements and the five senses. You should understand this well.

134.   **At 8:40 P.M. on 11/22/70**

His Holiness tells Peter:
    Lack of Wisdom (Ariveenam) is the shadow of Wisdom (Arivu). Ignorance (Agnana) is the shadow of Lack of Wisdom (Ariveenam). Illusion (Maya) is the shadow of Ignorance (Agnana). Hypnotic torpor (Mayakkam), which makes one succumb to the attractions of the sense-world, is the shadow of Illusion (Maya). Darkness of Ignorance is the shadow of hypnotic torpor (Mayakkam). The cycle of birth is the shadow of the Darkness of Ignorance. The end of the cycle of birth is Hell. You should understand this.
    The essence of Wisdom (Arivu) is Light (Oli). The essence of Light (Oli) is Grace (Arul). The essence of Grace (Arul) is Divine Luminous Wisdom (Perr-Arivu). The essence of Divine Luminous Wisdom (Perr-Arivu) is Light of God (Noor). The essence of Light of God (Noor) is God.
    The man who desired and followed the path mentioned earlier will, of his own seeking, get several births. If a man understands the nature of the path explained later, he will cut the cycle of birth and reach the state of Fullness and avoid future births. You should understand both these roads.

135.   **At 9:00 P.M. on 11/22/70**

His Holiness Guru Bawa tells Mrs. Sivamany Thambish:
    Daughter! I will give you an illustration. When a cow is grazing, another cow goes and licks it. As a result of the feeling of joy caused by licking, it stops grazing.
    A cow was grazing. A cow from behind started licking it. The cow which was grazing stopped grazing and stood still as it enjoyed the licking. The sun went down. The cow did not graze because of the licking. The herdsman drove the cow home to the pen and closed the pen. The cow which did not graze because it paid attention to the licking became hungry and thirsty in the night.
    We have come into this world to stay for a few days. We have to gather what is necessary within this short period. If we fail to do so, we will meet with death in the same way as the cow felt hunger in the night. We will become subject to rebirth.
    Sivamany! You gave up household life and came here in search of God. But when your friend Thavam comes here, she spends the time talking with you of worldly matters and you listen like the cow which paid

200

attention to the licking by the other cow without grazing. As a result, you may meet with hunger and death like the cow. Therefore, you, Sivamany and Thavamany, should seek the Guru, accept his precepts, understand what he teaches and attempt to escape Death that awaits you both. It is better to do this. But instead of trying to achieve spiritual greatness with the knowledge about Divine Wisdom (Gnanam), both of you are using your friendship to lower your spiritual state, like the cow licking the cow that is grazing and preventing it from grazing. Try to adopt the attributes and characteristics of God. That will give greatness to both of you.

136.   **At 6:20 P.M. on 11/24/70**

Mr. Nadarajag, D.R.O., told His Holiness, "An Astrologer has predicted that a world war will start on the 4th of December, but it will not be this year or next year. Will your Holiness explain the implications of this prediction?"

His Holiness Guru replied: Brother! There is a thing called a horoscope. But it does not suit Wisdom (Arivu). Horoscopes will agree with only Earth, Fire, Water, Air and Ether. But horoscopes will not suit the faculties of Perception or Feeling (Unarvu), Awareness or Cognition (Unarchi), Practical Understanding or Knowledge (Madthi), Wisdom (Arivu), and Divine Luminous Wisdom (Perr-Arivu).

The horoscope is for the body, not for the Grace of God. Everything comes within the control of Divine Grace. The twelve signs of the zodiac fall under the four categories of Earth, Fire, Water and Air. With the aid of these you can predict the state of the physical body. But you can't predict the actions of the Soul (Atma). Only a Gnostic (Gnani) is qualified to speak about the Soul (Atma). The horoscope can predict the state of the physical body of only Ignorant Souls (Agnanis). But these predictions will not hold good for people with Wisdom (Arivu) or knowledge (Gnanis). It is where Earth, Fire, Water, and Air disappear that the light of Wisdom (Arivu) appears. As long as one is controlled by the four elements of Earth, Fire, Water and Air, then egoism, sex, jealousy, Illusion (Maya) and the hypnotic torpor caused by Illusion (Maya) will exist. These effects are indicated in the horoscope. But horoscopes will not suit a person in a state of Divine Wisdom (Gnana). As far as Wisdom (Arivu) and Truth are concerned, horoscopes are useless.

Child! Horoscopes are interpreted for the use of the five senses and the mind. Horoscopes do not agree and are opposite to the Truth of Wisdom (Arivu). Horoscopes will not apply to persons who are not liable to take future births. If one comes to know the Radiance of the Soul (Atma Jothi), he will have transcended the physical and sense-world, lost body-consciousness and be able to reverse the world of Truth, the eighteen thousand worlds, and the world of Grace and Divine Wisdom (Gnana).

The horoscope only covers the physical world of illusion (Maya). If you submit yourself to a belief in horoscopes, you will be traversing only the physical world and the sense world. You cannot go beyond. Believing horoscopes will not allow you to traverse the world of Truth and Divine Grace and Divine Wisdom (Gnana).

137.   **At 11:25 A.M. on 12/30/70**

Mr. Harischandra who came from Badulla told His Holiness Guru Bawa: "I came to learn from you how to succeed in Yoga by controlling and stilling the mind. I tried for a year to study and understand the method. I did not succeed. I request Your Holiness to explain the method to me."

His Holiness asked Mr. Harischandra whether he was trying to know about the method of reaching God or whether he was trying to know the method of succeeding in Yoga. Mr. Harischandra replied that, "He was trying to know the method to reach God."

His Holiness told him: One cannot reach God through Yoga and that Divine Wisdom (Gnana) is beyond Yoga.

Mr. Harischandra asked His Holiness, "How can one achieve Divine Wisdom (Gnana)?"

His Holiness tells him: It is through the knowledge of the beauty of God's nature and characteristics that one can achieve Divine Wisdom (Gnana). It is Wisdom (Arivu) which should reach God. There are four steps in spiritual development, i.e., Sariyai, Kiriyai, Yogam and Gnanam.

Siriyai: When a man is at this step the mind brings all it sees in the world and all the events that take place in the world and keeps them in its store house.

Kiriyai: When a man is at this step, he comes to a definite conclusion that what the mind brought and stores is liable to destruction, and that there must be One Indestructible Eternal Thing. The man develops one-pointed steadiness in his conviction about That One Indestructible Thing and arms himself with the weapons of Faith, Determination and Certitude to prevent himself from being destroyed by any other weapon.

Yogam: What one has conjured in his mind, he sees in his dreams; what he sees in his dreams, he sees in his physical vision; what he sees in his physical vision, he sees with his mind. These mental visions create four hundred billion hypnotic fascinations, demons, spirits of darkness, false projections of Illusion (Maya) which pose as divine powers; exhilaration in the attractions of Illusion (Maya); statues; idols; arts; sexual joys; and the sorrows arising from sex, lust, and the alluring attractions of beautiful seductive damsels. All these dreams and recollections and visions of the myriads of projections of the five senses, and the five elements are recorded in the mind. The mind traverses the same world as the world of senses, enjoys the scenes and is in a state of exhilaration. This is Yogam. This state will show the place of origin as the place of joy. That state will only point out this joy. Within this house is the physical body; if one gets what the senses point out, one gets joy. If he fails, he meets with sorrow. This is Yogam.

Gnanam: What the eyes consider to be joy, Intellect (Puththi) should place within Wisdom (Arivu). When Wisdom (Arivu) adopts the nature and characteristics of God, it will get the Beauty of God. In that Divine Beauty it will appear in the form of Divine Grace. When Wisdom (Arivu) appears in that state, all that Intellect (Puththi) brought and placed within Wisdom (Arivu) will be burnt by the fire of Truth in the Radiance of Wisdom (Arivu). If any Thing cannot be burnt by the fire of Wisdom (Arivu), Wisdom (Arivu) should come to the conclusion that this Thing is God.

Whatever mind brings should be driven away with the faculty of Wisdom (Arivu). When Wisdom (Arivu) continues to reject everything which the mind brings, the mind will become tired and dejected and stop functioning. It is when the mind comes to this state of fatigue that God's

202

Grace will appear. Within God's Grace will appear Divine Luminous Wisdom (Perr-Arivu). The Effulgence (Jothi), the Ultimate Primal Unique One (Athi Param) which remains forever in fullness as Wisdom (Arivu) within Divine Luminous Wisdom (Perr-Arivu) is God. The above is the path of Divine Radiant Wisdom (Gnanam) that leads to the stillness of the mind.

But the other three steps mentioned earlier will not enable one to go beyond the world of the senses and the world of Illusion (Maya). They will keep one within the world of senses and the world of Illusion (Maya). But Wisdom (Arivu) will enable one to traverse the world of Grace. You should understand this well.

Mr. Harischandra asked His Holiness, "When we follow the path of Divine Radiant Wisdom (Gnanam) can we attend to our day-to-day duties?"

His Holiness replied: Yes, you can. This is the duty you have to do, because you are born into the world. It is a Divine Injunction that you should realise God through Wisdom (Arivu). This will explain to you the cause of birth and death. I have been explaining to you the glory of the nature of Wisdom (Arivu). It is to know That Unique One that we came into this world. This is the fundamental injunction of God. This gives man the Glory of understanding his birthright. While you are performing your daily chores, do not fail to develop in this birth itself, Divine Grace, Contentment, Patience, Forbearance and Peace of Mind. Do all your work adopting God's Divine Qualities and Characteristics. Follow the path that will help you to know who you are, Do not lose in this birth your birthright, your right to reach the fullness of your Soul and reach God.

138.   **At 7:55 P.M. on 2/6/71**

An illustration:

An ass carries loads of articles. It will carry any number of bags placed on its back. Because it has craving, it accepts more and more loads on its back without any feeling of weight. It thinks that all the loads belong to it.

In the same way, there are human beings who are really asses. These are two-legged asses. Like the ass, he also loads on his back all that his five senses bring in as a result of his attachment to the world. There is no place where he can take and store these loads. He is unable to find a place to sleep as a free man, freed from the weight of all these loads. He keeps half the loads within the house and half outside. He is the watcher for the loads inside as well as outside. He cannot enjoy sleep in the day time or at night. There is no end to the work he does. Therefore, there is no rest to his mind. His desires have not subsided.

The ass's milk will putrify in one and three-fourths hours. Only a person who is suffering from madness is given ass's milk as medicine. To this human ass, full of Ignorance (Agnana), the milk of the ass, which had carried the load of several births, should be given. This milk which causes hypnotic torpor and degradation will make him take thirty five million births and finally become a worm in Hell and become food for Hell.

The milk of the ass, which carries attachment and the ten sins on its back, can only be given to the ass full of Ignorance (Agnana). This milk is not suitable for Man-God (Manu-Eesan) or the Wisdom (Arivu) of Man-God (Manu-Eesan). The Man-God (Manu-Eesan) should be given the

203

milk of the Grace of the Primal Unique Effulgence (Athi Param Jothi), which is full of Compassion, Love, Charity, Pity, Patience, Forbearance, Tranquility, Contentment, and other Divine Qualities, but at the same time, free from the attachment of the ten sins, from any particular nature or characteristics, from race or religions, from foolishness and ignorance, from birth and death, from joy and sorrow, from wife and children, from world and mind, from desire and hypnotic torpor of Illusion (Maya), from body and elements, selfishness and vanity, jealousy and egoism. It is that milk which will elevate his Wisdom (Arivu) and Soul (Atma). This is the milk that Man-God (Manu-Eesan), the Perfect Man (Insan Kamil) will drink with relish.

An authentic Gnostic Guru (Meignana Guru) will note carefully to which of these two sections of mankind the people who come to him belong, and give them the milk that is suitable according to their need.

There are four-legged asses. Their braying is repulsive. Also, there are these two-legged asses with human shape. These are more dangerous than the four-legged asses. Even if it takes tens of millions of births, the repulsive braying of the two-legged ass will not come to an end. Its desire will not subside. Its hypnotic torpor (Mayakkam) will not come to an end. Its mind will not get fatigued. Its nature will not change. Whatever number of births it will take, its senses and elements will never rest in one place and sleep. Therefore, the two-legged ass is more dangerous than the four-legged ass. The milk of ignorance and hypnotic torpor caused by the senses and the elements secreted by the two-legged ass is also dangerous, because it springs from Hell. Along with it come germs of several births. It putrefies when it comes in contact with the air of the senses.

You must understand the nature of the two types of asses. You must find out which obsession the two-legged ass is suffering from and give it the milk of the four-legged asses. For the obsession caused by the hypnotic torpor of the senses in the two-legged asses, you should give the milk of the two-legged ass. Whatever is given to it, this two-legged ass will never be cured of its obsession. It will get sixty-four types of obsessions. If they are cured, it will get four thousand, four hundred and forty-eight types of obsessions. If they are cured, it will get one hundred and five million obsessions. If they are cured, it will get the obsessions of four hundred billion hypnotic projections which twinkle in the darkness of Illusion (Maya).

Therefore, if you waste your time with these asses, you will be treating them for their never ending obsessions and your life will be wasted. You should not attempt to treat this ass. You should avoid getting the obsessions yourself. I have told you earlier of the milk that is suitable to you and your devotees of God. Do not waste your time with these asses who are obsessed with their senses. It is dangerous to do so. You should escape from them.

So said the True Gnostic Guru (Meignana Guru) to the Guru whose Wisdom (Arivu) is developing and to the disciples whose Wisdom (Arivu) will be developing.

139.   **At 8:15 P.M. on 2/6/71**

Child! I will explain to you how disease is caused to man.

I am speaking of the disease of hypnotic torpor (Mayakkam), which appears in birth. The disease is caused by Earth, Fire, Water, Air and Ether. Ether is mainly the poisonous colours of green and blue. These five are considered by Intellect (Puththi) to be five Angels (Devas), five elements and five senses. Among the five elements, the Earth is named 'Parasakti', 'Poomadevi', or Illusory Power (Maya Sakti) and the power that covers it is called 'Sivam', 'Parapathy', or 'Paramasivam' by Intellect (Puththi) on the first level. On the second level Fire is called 'Agni Deva', and the flame that shines over it is called 'Swala Devi'. Air is called 'Vayu Bagavan' and the five senses which hover over air are called 'Devi' and Illusion (Maya). The senses over which the mind traverses are called Mother. The eldest of the seventy crores of monkeys born to 'Vayu Bagavan' and 'Anjana Devi' is called 'Anjaneyan'. Since the desire of the mind never ends, it is called 'Siranjeevi', i.e., Eternal. What the mind takes, nurses and shows in exaggerated proportions is called 'Visvarupu', i.e., the appearance or form of the Universe.

The sky appearing in the inner mind of the person under the hypnotic influence of Illusion (Maya) shows seven colours like blue, green, etc. It shows itself as the senses, religions, light, twinkling lights, thunder, lightening, rain, hypnotic torpor, smoke, currents of air, and many other forms. It shows the nature of the poisonous characteristics of the seven evil desires (Nafs), called 'Neelan', and appears as space, darkness and light. This state is the shape and body of the senses, the elements, the embryo and the foetus.

Each of the things described above create numberless thoughts and characteristics. All these create innumerable projections of hypnotic fascination. They, in turn, cause the degradation of Wisdom (Ariveenam). This degraded state of Wisdom (Ariveenam) causes endless desires. Desires cause several births. These births create various physical forms. These forms create various diseases. These diseases create numberless mind-monkeys. They, in turn, have created forests, which cannot be crossed by flying over them or cutting a way through them. In these forests are cruel animals which prey on one another. These animals have created the diseases of hunger, disease, old age and death. These four diseases have created the power of the four hunderd billion (lakhs of crores) of hypnotic fascinations projected by Illusion (Maya).

That Power (Sakti) has caused ignorance. Ignorance causes jealousy. Jealousy causes vanity. Vanity causes joy and sorrow. Joy and sorrow causes selfishness. Selfishness has created creeds. Creeds have created projections of the mind. They create mental visions and physical visions. Physical visions lead to sexual joy of the spiritually degraded person. The sexual pleasure has led to the creation of sixty-four arts (Kalas). The arts have created music and songs. They have led to Ignorance (Agnana). Ignorance (Agnana) has led to Science (Vingnana). Science (Vingnana) leads to destruction in the end. Destruction creates endless births. The human shape and other shapes are the forms made of the elements affected by the diseases of the senses.

If a Guru is to treat people affected by these numberless diseases, he has to use five methods of treatment, i.e., 1. Medicine, 2. Magic words (Mantras), 3. Sagacity (Tantra), 4. Wisdom (Arivu), and 5. Grace (Arul).

1. Medicine: The Guru who gives treatment to the Soul (Atma) must first find out what category of disease he is suffering from and then start

treatment. If he is suffering from the diseases of the senses and egoism, he should be given the medicine of the hypnotic facinations of Illusion (Maya). When he is in a state of torpor caused by these fascinations, the Guru should escape from him.

2. Magic Words (Mantra): If he is suffering from the ghosts of birth, the projections of the monkey-mind, the Guru should incant the five letters of the Intellect (Puththi) and tell him, "This is good for the five senses. But this is of no use for the sixth faculty of Wisdom (Arivu). This will not save you from the danger of rebirth. This medicine is good only for the sixty-four poisonous plays which originate from your obsession, caused by the hypnotic attractions of Illusion (Maya." The Guru then gives that medicine of Intellect (Puththi) to him and escapes from him.

3. Sagacity (Tantra): All the above-mentioned diseases inherent in the body are born to the mind and 'Anjana Devi' in the form of a mind-monkey. It takes illusory forms of Illusion (Maya) and gambols in the forest of the mind. It sees in that forest innumerable fruits, such as attachment, lust, hatred, miserliness, desire, jealousy, egoism, Action (Karma), Illusion (Maya), earth, fire, water, air, space and four hundred billion hypnotic projections of Illusion (Maya). The monkey will leap from tree to tree and try to pluck these illusory fruits. Since these trees had been created by the illusory power of Illusion (Maya), the fruit will be out of the reach of the hands of the mind-monkey, whatever number of times it may leap. They appear to be fruit to the eyes of the mind-monkey. But when it thinks it has plucked the fruit and examines it in its hands, it does not find the fruit in its hands. The monkey goes round and round the forest and leaps again and again and finally becomes senseless. This is the fate of the mind-monkey, whose desire for the illusory fruit has become an obsession.

The Guru will find out what type of obsession the monkey is suffering from and call 'Anjana Devi', the Illusion (Maya), who gave birth to the monkey and tell her, "Your son is senseless. He was madly after the illusory fruit you created in the jungle. Since he could not succeed in getting the fruit, his mind had become deranged and he is senseless. Only you can cure him. Since you educated the mind-monkey, which you gave birth to, you have the remedy for his malady. You may give it to him." The Guru will hand him over to Illusion (Maya) and escape from the seventy crores of monkey tricks.

That mind-monkey will obtain the boon of existence without an end and cover the Universe with its body. 'Anjana Devi' shows the indication of the mind-monkey as the basis of light reading 'Anjanam': She reads the horoscope of the mind-monkey. Therefore, the Guru should tell her, "You can read the horoscope of the notorious mind-monkey to whom you gave birth. You may explain his future to him and calm him by reading his horoscope", and escape.

4. Wisdom (Arivu): If a person is suffering from the disease of Lack of Wisdom (Ariveenam) the Guru must tell him, "The eighteen maladies of Hunger, Disease, Old Age, Death, Egoism, Action (Karma), Illusion (Maya), Craving, Anger, Miserliness, Lust, Vanity, Jealousy, Earth, Fire, Water, Air and Space have entered your system in the form of eighteen mythological lyrics and modified your Wisdom (Arivu) and caused the disease of wrong and misguided Wisdom (Ariveenam) of the mundane level

which will lead to spiritual degradation.

"If you are to be cured of this disease, you should develop the qualities of the fourteen worlds of Divine Compassion, Love, Forgiveness, Charity, Pity, Patience, Forbearance, Tranquility, Contentment, Complete Surrender to the Will of God, Love for other Beings in the same measure as Love towards one's own Self, Faith, Justice and Truth, and sit on the Throne of the Radiance of Wisdom (Arivu) in the Court of Justice of God, and take the medicine of the Resplendence of Divine Luminous Wisdom (Perr-Arivu). If you do so, all the earlier mentioned diseases caused by succumbing to the hypnotic projections of Illusion (Maya) will run away from you. Their conspiracy against your attainment of the fruit of your birth will become ineffective. You will progress spiritually. Your Lord will join you. If He merges within you, you will not be subject to your Practical Understanding or Knowledge (Madthi). You will not have the destiny of births and deaths. Here is the medicine. Take it. Understand well who you are and Who your Lord is. Note carefully where the fruit of Gnosis (Gnana) is. Search and find it." Saying so, the Guru will adminster the medicine of Wisdom (Arivu) to him, speak to him with Love and take his leave and go further away.

5. Grace (Arul): If the above patient gets clarity of mind, gets cured of the diseases, understands God and comes back to the Guru, the Guru will place a drop of Grace (Arul), the honey of Divine Wisdom (Gnana), on his tongue and make him taste its sweetness and show him the mysteries of the Saviour, the Unique One, Who dwells within that sweetness, feed him with His Secret, imprint on his head the State of God, free from Joy and Sorrow, and make him drink the honey of Divine Grace of Wisdom (Arivu) to make him live forever free from birth or death and shine in that world, this world and the other world as the Resplendence of Divine Wisdom (Gnana Jothi) and as the Resplendence that gives Radiant Bliss to the Soul (Atma Ananth Jothi).

The Guru should understand the meaning of the five magic words (Mantras) referred to above, from the Wisdom of the Wisdom (Arivu) of Gnostics (Gnanis), from the words of Love, from Compassion, from the Form of God, from the Beauty of God's qualities, from the Fullness of Forbearance, from the Grace of God's Patience, from the Nobility of His Justice, from the Verdict of Mature Truth and from the ever-full reservoir of God's Treasury and administer the suitable magic words (Mantra). If he uses the wrong method or magic words (Mantra), he will become the victim of one of these five types. The Guru whose Wisdom (Arivu) is developing and the disciples who are learning about Wisdom (Arivu) should understand this well. So said His Holiness Guru Bawa.

140.   **At 9:10 A.M. on 2/7/71**

Child! Listen to an illustration.

If the thief is within the house, you cannot call him a thief. If you feel that he is the thief and tell him so and punish him, he will continue to try to steal, only more secretly and more carefully. But if you make him the watcher of the house and give due respect and responsibility to him and tell him, "You should keep watch within the house and outside the house and see that these articles are not stolen", then thefts will come to a stop. He will have no time to go outside, into the village and steal. Also, he will not steal in the house. As a result, his evil nature will diminish and he will remain as a watcher in the house.

In the same way, the thieves, called elements and the senses, steal and spend uselessly the Good and the Truth within the house of human personality and take the Truth of God surreptitiously without, hide it and bury it. If the Light of Wisdom (Arivu) employs the five senses as watchers on all the four sides of the Heart's (Qalb's) house, they will not be able to destroy Truth that is within that house. They will not be able to hide Truth that is without. By not employing them as watchers, it will not be possible to destroy the house built of the five elements and the thieves who steal the things within. It will not be possible to destroy the four hundred thousand crores of commanders of troops born of the elements and the senses. If we chase them away, we have to fight with them. Therefore, we have to use our Wisdom (Arivu) to control the senses and employ them as watchers of our house to prevent them from stealthily entering our heart. Since the mind-monkey has obtained eternal life, it cannot be destroyed. If it is brought under control and given a job suitable to it, it will spend its time doing it. That is the best way to protect the Divine Treasure in the Heart. So said His Holiness Guru Bawa to those gathered in the Ashram.

141.   **At 6:10 P.M. on 2/8/71**

Child! Listen to an illustration.

The fox howls to entice the crabs to come out of their holes toward it. The crab thinks that it can escape if it gets inside its hole. The fox cannot get into the water and catch the crab. Its idea is to catch the crab when it comes to the small dam.

In the same manner, Wisdom (Arivu) howls, "Hoo! Hoo!", like the fox to entice the degraded senses of man which are grazing in the dark field of the hypnotic state of torpor called Darkness (Agnana). When the elements and the senses are grazing on the crop of Darkness (Agnana), man gets the diseases of poverty, sickness, joy and sorrow, trials and tribulations and losses. In this state, man's senses and Intellect (Puththi) are in a desperate state, not knowing what to do. At that time Wisdom (Arivu) howls. Just as the crabs got inside the holes in the dam to save themselves on hearing the howling of the fox, the senses get inside the Heart thinking that they are in danger. The fox allows its tail to get into the hole. When the crabs get hold of the fox's tail, thinking that it is their food, the fox draws its tail out and seizes the crabs which have got hold of its tail and eats them. In the same way, Wisdom (Arivu) will kill the senses. When the senses have been killed, Wisdom (Arivu) will become Resplendent. The Resplendence of the Soul (Atma Jothi) will merge with Wisdom (Arivu) and then merge with God Who is Wisdom (Arivu) within Wisdom (Arivu). So says the Guru to the disciple.

142.   **At 8:00 P.M. on 2/8/71**

Mr. Wijeyasuriya, Assistant Commissioner of Excise, asked His Holiness Guru Bawa, "What is the meaning of the word 'Duty'? What is one's duty?"

His Holiness replied: Craving or desire is hypnotic fascination (Mayakkam) of Illusion (Maya) which leads to spiritual degradation. Duty

208

is the path along which Wisdom (Arivu) travels. There are various types of duties. In the constitution of the body there are four hundred billion duties. All are called duty. The chief duty a man has to perform is to do what God does. To do good to others without developing attachment to them or expecting reward from them, is duty. To do a good turn expecting God to reward us with Heaven or give us comforts of life is not duty. To do whatever you do, without expecting any personal benefit in any form whatsoever, is duty. All other duties are caused by the hypnotic torpor (Mayakkam) of Darkness (Agnana). They cannot be called Duty.

143.   **At 8:10 P.M. on 2/8/71**

Mr. Wijeysauriya, Assistant Commissioner of Excise, asked His Holiness, "How can one obtain Divine Wisdom (Gnana) in a second?"

His Holiness Guru Bawa replied: If you pour water on a piece of burning charcoal, the colour and nature of the fire disappears and the characteristics of the firewood also disppears. It becomes a piece of black charcoal without any heat or glow.

In the same manner, if the natural characteristics of the five senses and the natural characteristics of the body have been burnt up by the fire of Wisdom (Arivu), immediately that Wisdom (Arivu) becomes Divine Wisdom (Gnanam), as God exists as Wisdom (Arivu) within Wisdom (Arivu). In the same manner as the piece of burning charcoal is transformed when water is poured on it, the colour of bodily craving and the plays of hypnotic torpor (Mayakkam), caused by the senses and the elements, are transformed on the emergence of the Resplendence of Wisdom (Arivu). Man then has reached God. When mind is dead, only God remains. God is He. He is God. You can reach this state in a second or in a moment.

On the threshold of death, how quickly man leaves behind his body and the senses and faces Yemen, the Angel in charge of Death. With the same speed, if man will give up the senses and body-consciousness and look at God, God will look at him and both will merge. This is Divine Wisdom (Gnanam). God and Man will merge within a second of Man's giving up the sense world and body-consciousness.

144.   **At 8:15 P.M. on 2/8/71**

Children! I will give you an illustration. Listen to it.

A cultivator plants the seedlings of some type of crop. Later he applies fertilizer near the roots. The soil absorbs the fertilizer. Only the soil and the plants are seen. The fertilizer is not visible. The plant absorbs the essence of the fertilizer and grows. Therefore, the soil has a relationship with the fertilizer. The relationship extends to the plants also.

If you do your duty with a motive of selfishness and find yourself in a state of suffering due to illness or misfortune, you will feel badly if your children and relations fail to visit you and do not speak words of solace to you.

Just as the essence of fertilizer is absorbed by the plants, the essence of attachment to wife, children, and property has been absorbed by you as the motive force in performing your duty, so that when you meet with misfortune you will be affected by sorrow. To do your duty with an impartial eye on the world and without any motive of personal benefit, is

Duty. If attachments are there, actions (Karma) will follow you. Therefore, that cannot be called Duty. To do anything without selfish motives and without expecting personal benefit, is Duty. So said His Holiness Guru Bawa to his disciples.

145. At 8:30 P.M. on 2/8/71

Child! A word of explanation:

There are two worlds in which created beings live. One is the world of Darkness (Agnana). The other is the world of Truth (Meignana). The world of Darkness (Agnana) is illusory. The world of Truth (Meignana) is the Real world. God, who moves in the world of Truth (Meignana) dwells in the world of Truth. He does not dwell in the illusory world. He does not have two worlds. Because we have a wife, children and property, we have two worlds. If a man moves only in the one True world, he will not meet with death. If he lives in two worlds, he will have births and deaths. Child, you should understand the nature of both these worlds. If you live in the world of Truth, you have no birth or death. In the world of Truth, God lives forever. You will never meet with destruction. So said His Holiness Guru Bawa.

146. At 8:50 P.M. on 2/8/71

Children! Listen to an illustration.

A person who has developed Wisdom (Arivu), Divine Wisdom (Pahuth Arivu), and Divine Luminous Wisdom (Perr-Arivu), to enable him to understand the nature of the illusory world and the world of Truth; who has the 'Arivu' to distinguish between Truth and falsehood, the Real and the Evanescent; who is able to know That Reality which is in the innermost recesses of his Heart; who has completely surrendered himself to His Creator and has become His Slave (Abd); who has become the Representative of God on Earth; who has made himself fit to merge with God and hold communion with Him, is the noblest and rarest of God's Creation. He alone can be called Man.

All the worlds will take refuge with him. He will be the King of the Worlds. God (Allah) will be the Emperor of these Kings. Only a person who has acquired this greatness can be called Man. He will be able to know the nature of the lower seven worlds through his Wisdom (Arivu) and reject them. He will be able to ascend the upper seven heavens of Perception (Unarvu); Cognition (Unarchi); Lower Mind, Intellect (Puththi); Practical Understanding, Knowledge (Madthi); Wisdom, Conscience within Reason (Arivu); Divine Wisdom, Intuitive Spiritual Wisdom in Association with Purity of Heart (Pahuth-Arivu); and Divine Luminous Wisdom (Perr-Arivu), and understand their nature.

But, Man who is meant to obtain such a heritage as his birthright, has entered the false world of the senses, lost his Arivu, succumbed to the influences of the senses, and tries to read his horoscope by studying the signs of the zodiac. There are twelve signs in the zodiac. They are: the ram, bull, crab, lion, balance, scorpion, virgin, etc. Such people use these signs of the zodiac to fortell the good and evil, the joys and sorrows, the life and death of Man.

When you analyse their actions with Wisdom (Arivu), these people can be considered to be of lower intelligence than the ram, the lion, the bull, the crab, etc. Man, who is the rarest and noblest of created beings, appears to act as if his intelligence is less than that of the bull, the crab or the goat. He goes about singing the effect of the signs of the zodiac.

The body is made up of five essences which are indicated by five letters. In Arabic, the letters are: 'Aliph', 'Lam', 'Meem', 'Hey', and 'Dhal'. In Tamil, the five letters are: 'Na', 'Ma', 'Si', 'Va', 'Ya'. These five letters indicate the five elements of Earth, Fire, Water, Air and Ether. The five letters are also called 'Panchadcharam'. 'Panchadcharam' means body. The horoscope is for the body. The body is made of the essence of the five elements of Earth, Fire, Water, Air and Ether. The body is the Almanac (Panchankam). The horoscope (Sathagam) and Numerology (Aroodam) are used by men to predict the events that will happen to the body. The horoscope is based on the twenty-seven stars. The twenty-seven stars indicate the night of the Lunar Month. The twenty-eighth night, is the night of the New Moon. The completely dark night indicates the conception of man as a result of the succumbing of the parents to the dark hypnotic influence of Illusion (Maya). It is the night that indicates the night of degradation of Knowledge (Madthi), resulting in the formation of the body with the five letters (indicating the essence of the five elements) and the five senses.

To give shape to the senses, the twenty-eight stars were divided into the twelve signs of the zodiac. The Almanac (Panchankam) was created to indicate the period of the senses. The body is made of the five letters. The twelve openings of the body are the twelve signs of the zodiac. Without analysing these twelve signs of the zodiac with the faculty of Wisdom (Arivu), you are trying to use them to read your horoscope. So, your intelligence is less than that of the ram, the bull, the lion, the crab, etc. This will destroy the fruit of your birth, this wrong and misguided wisdom of the sense world. Get out of this darkness of misguided wisdom (Ariveenam). If you look within your own self with Wisdom (Arivu), you will become the King who can rule the whole universe and all beings created in it.

The twelve openings of the body are:

1. Look with your faculty of Wisdom (Arivu) at the nature of the anus. It is the opening ruled by egoism.

2. Through the genitals you came into this world. Water, Fire, Earth, Air and the five colours ooze out of this opening of Hell. Know well that this is the door of Hell that made you then and makes you now, and in the future succumb to the hypnotic fascination of sex and makes you dance to its tune.

3. This is the navel to which the umbilical cord was attached when you were in the womb. It is the door of poison which indicates the treacherous nature of satan (Ibiliesan), who means one thing and tells another thing. When man was created, satan (Ibiliesan) behaved in a treacherous manner, having succumbed to the influence of darkness.

4. This is the mouth, the door of the tongue, which speaks good and evil, activated by the one hundred five million powers of Illusion (Maya).

5-.6 The two nostrils are the openings through which the sun and the moon move about. You should understand the nature of these two arts (Kalais): Art of the Moon (Chandra Kalai) and Art of the Sun (Sooriya Kalai).

7-8. The two eyes which shine are the sun and the moon.

9-10. The two ears through which man hears the sounds of the power of Illusion (Maya) in this world and the resonant voice of God.

11. The eleventh is the Gnostic Eye on the forehead (Kursh). This eye helps one to analyse with Divine Wisdom (Pahuth-Arivu) and find out the real and the transient world.

12. The Throne of God on the top of the head (Arsh).

These twelve openings are the twelve signs of the zodiac in the body, which is actually a cage-like fortress. Man must understand the nature of these twelve signs of the zodiac (Rasees) and the nature of the cage-like fortress; reign within this fortress as the King of all beings in the Universe, as the deputy of God, the Primal Unique Effulgence (Athi-Param Jothi); hold communion with God; converse with Him; and merge in Him. He should know about good and evil, about creation and preservation. Man must merge in God and God in Man. Then he must perform conscientiously the duty given by God. Only such a person is Man-God (Manu-Eesan) or Perfect Man (Insan Kamil).

Without knowing this, by adopting the characteristics of the twelve signs of the zodiac formed by the five letters, by adopting the nature of the bull, the lion, the ram, the scorpion, etc., and by consulting astrology, one cannot become Man. He will be liable to be born as beings of a level lower than animals. Finally he will become the food of Hell. He cannot become Man-God (Manu-Eesan).

You should understand well all these things I have told you. You should understand the nature of the fortress and its mysteries, the nature of the Real World in which you and God will merge and move about. You should know the Truth that dwells in that Real World. Within that Truth, you should shine as Wisdom (Arivu) and read the Wisdom (Arivu) that is within Wisdom (Arivu). If you achieve that state, what sorrow is there for you in this world? What joy is there in this world? What birth is there for you? What death is there for you? There will be none. So said the Truly Wise Guru (Meignana Guru).

147.   **At 9:40 P.M. on 2/8/71**

Dr. Selvaratnam asked His Holiness Guru Bawa; "Swami! People speak of Fate (Vithi). Please explain."

His Holiness Guru Bawa explained: Many people with human faces say God has inscribed our Fate on our head. What is written is bound to happen. In the world of Wisdom (Arivu) and Truth, it is not so. You should analyse every event with Divine Wisdom (Pahuth-Arivu). You should remove the darkness of Ignorance in the forest of Illusion (Maya) with the Resplendence (Jothi) of Wisdom (Arivu). You should drive away the projections of Illusion (Maya) and the satanic animals of the projections of Illusion (Maya) with the Resplendence (Jothi) of Wisdom (Arivu). When you are doing so, if you come to a stage where even the Resplendence (Jothi) of Wisdom (Arivu). When you are doing so, if you come to a stage where even the Resplendence (Jothi) of Wisdom (Arivu) is unable to prevent an event, and you fall down senseless saying, 'It is Your Will', that is what is called Fate.

Till you come to that extreme limit, there is a place for the Light of Wisdom (Arivu). Otherwise, if you say that every event is due to Fate, as

God has ordained everything long ago, there would have been no need for people like me, the one hundred and twenty-four thousand Prophets (Nabis), Saints (Olis), Messengers (Thoothars), and Divinely Wise Men (Gnanis) to have come into this world to proclaim the name and Truth of God, and explain these things. No occasion would have arisen for this. God would not have told them, 'Go and explain these things to your followers.' Where Wisdom (Arivu) fails, only this is Fate. Only then can you call it the work of God. You cannot attribute all other events to Fate (Vithi). You should understand this well.

148.   **At 12:10 P.M. on 2/12/71**

Sathu Sinnathurai asked His Holiness Guru Bawa, "Swami! Illusion (Maya) falls into two categories, Pure Illusion (Maya) and Impure Illusion (Maya). How can one escape from it?"

His Holiness Guru Bawa replied: Child! There are no two categories of Illusion called Pure and Impure Illusion (Maya). Illusion (Maya) is one. Once you look below it is impure. When you look above it causes a state of torpor caused by hypnotic fascination (Mayakkam). You look above. You are in a state of hypnosis (Mayakkam). When you get free from this state of hypnotic torpor caused by Illusion (Maya) you have no death. In that state, you can see God.

The skin and the hair of the bull protect that animal from wind and rain. The skin is thick. The bull relies on that skin for protection from the wind and dew. Look here! Man uses that skin for making slippers, sandals, and other footwear. The skin which was covering the bull is now below man's feet.

In the same manner, what your mind, the senses, and the projections from the elements considered to be necessary for the protection of your life, you should use as footwear under your feet, and walk. Just as the skin of the bull is used for footwear, you should turn the darkness of Illusion (Maya) in your mind into slippers and put them under your feet and walk. If you want to prevent the thorns of the thorn bushes, in the dark forest of the hypnotic fascinations of the world, from pricking your feet, you should use the darkness of your attachment to the joys and sorrows of the world, which the senses bring to your mind, as the slippers for your feet of Wisdom (Arivu) to walk on. Then, only, you can escape from the destruction of your birthright as Man.

But, you are keeping your attachment to your house, property, and relations (e.g., wife and children), as your protection. It is these attachments which, without your own knowledge, suck from you the Truth and the benefits which you are entitled to as Man. But if you use as footwear for your feet of Wisdom (Arivu) all that the senses bring into your mind, they will not be able to suck away your rare and noble birth as Man. They will not be able to make you liable for taking future births. The thorns which grow in the dark forest where the senses and the projections of the elements live, cannot injure your feet. You should understand this well, Child Sinnathurai!

Sathu Sinnathurai said, "Father, the thorns of attachment to the world are pricking me. Please remove these thorns from me, and save me."

His Holiness replied: Only if there is room in your Heart (Ullam) will

213

these thorns enter. If there is no room in your Heart for them, they will not prick you. Even if there is a space equal to that of the point of a needle, the weapon thrown by the hunter will pierce it. As long as the world is within you, the thorns will pierce you. If the world is not within you, the thorns will not pierce you. Therefore, you should protect your Heart (Ullam) with Wisdom (Arivu).

Child! From the time of our birth, till we go out of this world, there is only one path. On both sides of this path are dark forests with tall trees, shrubs, and thorns. In these forests live satanic animals, poisonous creatures, and demons. There are numberless animals who always do harm. When you proceed along the road, whirlwinds, gales, dry winds, cold winds, fire winds, northeast monsoon winds, north-westerly winds, south-easterly winds, winds of hypnotic torpor, winds of Illusion (Maya) and innumerable types of winds like these will blow on you from the forests on both sides. Since there are forests on both sides of the road, the force of the winds will be felt strongly on the path. When on this road, you will be assailed by these winds and animals on all sides. If you proceed without swerving, courageously and straight along the path with Faith, Determination and Certitude and are guided by your faculties of Perception (Unarvu); Cognition (Unarchi); Lower Mind, Intellect (Puththi); Practical Understanding, Knowledge (Madthi); Wisdom, Conscience within Reason (Arivu); Divine Wisdom, Intuitive Spiritual Wisdom in Association with Purity of Heart (Pahuth-Arivu); and Divine Luminous Wisdom (Perr-Arivu), they will not be able to do any harm to you. You can cross the forest of birth, and forest of death, and join the ever-wakeful Light of Wisdom (Arivu) and reach the limitless plain, where there is no night or day. In that void you will see That which is Plentitude or Fullness. If you see It, you will not have want. You will reach Fullness or Perfection.

Therefore, when these winds blow, do not become senseless. Do not allow your mind to waver. Do not be afraid of the animals. Do not tarry on the path in hypnotic torpor! Do not lose heart. Go forward with determination and reach That Fullness or Plentitude. This is the path that will prevent you from taking future births. This is the only advice that will help you to go along the path of life, and reach your Destination. Understand this well.

149. At 6:10 P.M. on 2/13/71

Children! A small explanation:

When the infant after birth is taken by the mother and breast fed, it embraces the mother's breasts with its hands. When the infant is taken up and placed close to the face, it embraces the mother's neck with both its hands. When the child grows up and starts running, it embraces the mother's feet with both hands. After a few years, when it is able to walk and run freely, it embraces the mother below the waist with both its hands. When he has grown up and completed his education and obtained a job, he again embraces a woman by thowing his hands round her below her waist. Only on the day the man gives up this habit of embracing will he become God-Man (Manu-Eesan). When the animal-man (Neesan) has given up the body consciousness and the world, he becomes Adam (Sivan). Ponder a little over this.

214

At 6:30 P.M. on 2/13/71

An illustration:

A Guru was teaching astronomy to his disciple. When he was teaching he made use of a Murunga (drumstick) tree, and its branches, to show the disciple the positions of the various stars. "Look at that branch. Look at that leaf at the end of the branch. From there look beyond at the sky. There you see a star. That star is called so and so." Thus he used the Murunga tree, its branches and leaves as a medium to teach the disciple the positions of the various stars. After completing his study of astronomy, the disciple took leave of the Guru and embarked on a ship to return to his country.

The travellers on the ship asked him where he was coming from. He replied that he was returning home after studying astronomy from his Guru.

When the ship was sailing, the sky became dark. There was lightening and thunder. One of the travellers in the ship asked him, "The sky is becoming dark. The stars are twinkling unsteadily. What is the reason? Is it going to rain?" He looked at the sky and said, "The sky is becoming dark. The stars are twinkling unsteadily. But I am unable to answer your question because the Murunga tree is not here. Only under the Murunga tree can I note the position of the stars and reply to your question."

This illustration suits us also. I am a Swami. You and many other disciples study Wisdom (Gnana) only when you are in the Ashram. When you go out of the Ashram, the state of the learning of Wisdom (Gnana) of the disciples, our state of Wisdom (Gnana) and the teachings of the Guru are like that of the disciple who was unable to answer the question of the traveller on the ship in the absence of the Murunga tree. You say 'The Guru is not here to give the meaning of what we studied.' You will be able to understand the nature of God only when He appears before you. If the Guru is not with you, your state is like that of the disciple who wanted the Murunga tree. You should ponder over this.

151. ## At 6:50 P.M. on 2/13/71

Please listen to a small discourse.

A disciple should give up all thoughts about the world and sit in silence in front of his Guru. He should sit with decorum and due respect to the Guru. To obtain the fruit you want from the Guru, you should sit in front of the Guru with a one-pointed mind. It is through that one-pointedness of the mind that you can obtain that Light. Otherwise, like the traffic policeman at the junction, the Guru will show his hands and send him away along the way suitable to his ideas, actions and predilictions. If one is a true disciple, the form of the Guru should appear in his heart naturally. It will not do if the disciple grows a beard, wears ochre cloth, and covers his head with a a cloth like the Guru. When his ego has been destroyed, God will remain God. One can grow a beard, wear ochre cloth, grow long nails, and apply holy ash (Tilak) on the forehead, and put on a show. But, he must keep in his Heart the characteristics of God and the characteristics and teachings of the Guru, and create the Guru's form in his Heart, and preserve it without allowing it to be destroyed. Only then, Wisdom (Arivu) will become Resplendent according to the Guru's initiation and teaching. Children! You can actually reach the God of Truth. Otherwise, you will never reach God. It will end like the story of the disciple who needed the presence of the Murunga (Drumstick) tree to read the position of the stars. So said His Holiness Guru Bawa to his disciples.

152.   **At 7:20 P.M. on 2/13/71**

Mr. Wijesuriya, Assistant Commissioner of Excise, asked His Holiness Guru Bawa, "In every religion a particular method is prescribed for reaching God. Can't one reach God by worshipping God as prescribed in a particular religion?"

His Holiness replied: God is beyond the pale of race and religion. God is beyond the furthermost limits of Religion (Veda) and Philosophy (Vedanta). He is not within the restriction of any particular religion. We cannot see Him by staying within the limitations imposed by a particular religion. If one goes beyond and outside the formal religions of the world, only, then, can one see God. When you go beyond all these restrictions, you will reach the Unique One that pervades everywhere. God is That which has no night or day; That which has no birth or death; That which has no end or destruction; That which has no blemish; That which is Plentitude; That which is Perfection embracing the whole Universe; That which is the Inner Effulgence (Jothi); That which has the form of Soul (Atma); That which is Wisdom (Arivu) with Wisdom (Arivu). Race and religion cannot go beyond the limits of Human Intelligence (Puththi). These were created by man. Only in the place where Wisdom (Arivu) has emerged in Resplendence can the way to pray to God be told. What is worship? Who worships whom? Who worships? Who receives that worship? Who accepts that worship? One must know all these things. What is Worship (Vanakkam)? What is Meditation (Thiyanam)? It is not bringing the palms of both the hands together. You must yearn for Him with all your Heart and worship with the hands. When your Heart and Soul are not in unison at the time you worship, it is not worship. What springs from your Heart is Meditation (Thiyanam). What you do with your body is Worship (Vanakkam). You must understand this.

153.   **At 6:05 P.M. on 2/14/71**

Mr. Wijesuriya, Assistant Commissioner of Excise, asked His Holiness Guru Bawa, "Can a person worship a symbol and get out of darkness into light? Or should he fix a mental target and pray?"

His Holiness replied: How can you fix a target to reach a person who is within you and without? There is an Arabic expression 'La Ilaha Il Allahoo'. It means 'There is nothing but God. Thou art God (Allah).' This is called Remembrance (Dikr). This is Meditation (Thiyanam). We breathe out 21,621 times a day. We breathe in 21,621 times a day. When you breathe out and breathe in with the meaning of the Arabic expression clearly impressed in your mind, with the 43, 000 odd breaths in and out, His name is expressed deeply from your Heart. This breathing is Remembrance and Meditation (Dikr-Thiyanam). The breath that goes out through the left nostril is Art of the Moon (Chandra Kalai). You must open all the pores of your skin and tissues and express the word through your out-going breath. All the one hundred and five million hairs on the body must express the words.

The breath 'La Ilaha' should mingle with the Soul (Atma) and Wisdom (Arivu) and go out of the left nostril with feeling and awareness. You should get a feeling in the body similar to the feeling you get when an ant moves over your foot.

The breath 'Il Allahoo' that comes in from outside through the right nostril should go in and settle in your Heart. In that place you don't exist. Only Wisdom (Arivu), Soul (Atma) and God exist. You and all the worlds cease to exist. When you do Meditation (Thiyanam) like this, you do not exist. You are dead. You are God (Allah). In that place there is no point or target. You are the target. Who did Meditation (Thiyanam)? God did Meditation (Thiyanam). To whom was the Meditation (Thiyanam) performed? He meditated on Himself.

Mr. Wijesuriya asked, "By following this method can we get that Divine Luminous Wisdom (Perr-Arivu)?"

His Holiness replied: When you have become He, how can you fail to get Divine Luminous Wisdom (Perr-Arivu)?

Mr. Wijesuriya asked, "If that is so, can't we reach that state by doing this type of Meditation (Thiyanam) a few hours each day?"

His Holiness replied: That will not produce the desired result. This is like school lessons with promotion from one class to another class. If you proceed like that, it will be too late to pass the final examination. There will be no time. You should not allow time to be wasted. I am not explaining some state which cannot be reached. One can reach that state.

I will relate to you a story. In a town a King ruled. He had a Minister. Several Kings paid tribute to him regularly. One day the King inquired from his Minister whether all the Kings under him had paid the tributes. The Minister told him the name of a King who had not paid tribute. Immediately the King went out with his troops to that Kingdom to capture it. There was a fight between both the armies. At the end of the battle on that day, the battefield was full of corpses.

There was bright moonlight. The King and his Minister said, "The troops have all been destroyed. What shall we do? Let us go round the battlefield and examine the position." So, both went to the battlefield.

At that time a large number of vultures flew there in a flock, sat on every corpse and examined it and finally went to a corpse in a corner of the battlefield. All the vultures ate that corpse. When the King saw this he asked his Minister the reason. The Minister replied, "Great King (Maharajah)! My grandfather had a book. I read in that book that vultures are very fond of corpses of human beings. Only if these are not available they will eat the dead bodies of goats, asses and bulls." The King asked, "How did these vultures come to the conclusion that he is the only human being (Man) who died in the battlefield today?" The Minister answered, "The vulture has two white wings. They look at the bodies throught the two white wings and find out who is really Man and eat his corpse."

Then the king killed one of the vultures and cut off its two white wings and looked at all the corpses through the wings. All the corpses appeared to be like dead bodies of various types of animals except for the body which the vultures were feeding on. The King became surprised and looked at the Minister through the feathers. He appeared to be a black monkey.

Then the Minister looked at the King through the feathers. The King appeared to be a small monkey.

The King said, "We should rule the forest. But we have come to rule the Country. It is very difficult to be born as Man. Man is endowed with the beauty of God. We are monkeys. We should do penance to change our monkey characteristics and become Men by developing human qualities. Only a Man should rule this Kingdom. The only Man that lived we have killed. He was the only Man who was fit to rule this Kingdom." After saying this, the King went to the King of the neighbouring Kingdom and told him, "You may rule this Kingdom. We want to go to the forest to do penance to be born as Men." Then they went to the forest to do penance.

Like them, if you also look at your wives, children, relations, father, mother, etc., through the feathers of the vulture, you will know their real shape or form. When we understand what they really are, only then will we be able to give up our attachment to them, and proceed on our journey towards God.

Mr. Wijesuriya asked, "If we come to that high state only we can find out these things. We do not possess the wings of the vulture to look through."

His Holiness replied: Child! The two wings are Divine Wisdom (Pahuth-Arivu) and Divine Luminous Wisdom (Perr-Arivu). If you look with these two eyes of Divine Wisdom (Pahuth-Arivu) and Divine Luminous Wisdom (Perr-Arivu), you will be able to know the flocks of crows and host of demons projected by the five elements who have come to this market (i.e., world). If we understand their real nature, only then can we proceed further on our spiritual journey. A person may say often 'I want to fall into the well. I want to fall into the well.' But if he accidentally falls into the well and struggles for his life and somehow or other manages to escape, he will always be afraid of the well.

So, if a Man looks at the crowds that come to market with the eyes of Divine Wisdom (Pahuth-Arivu) and Divine Luminous Wisdom (Perr-Arivu) and understands their nature by experience, he will not again waste his time with them. He will proceed further away from them towards God.

154.   **At 6:55 P.M. on 2/14/71**

An illustration:

After crossing the sea in a ship and reaching the port of destination, you have to leave behind the ship, the chair in the ship you used, and the pole around which you held your hands firmly to keep yourself steady, and go away. You can't carry the pole, the chair and the ship with you and go to your destination.

In the same way, if you want to achieve Widsom (Gnana), you cannot achieve Wisdom (Gnana) when you carry in your mind your wife, children, house, property, attachments, friendships, etc. It is not possible. If you cast away all things from your mind and go alone, you can achieve Wisdom (Gnana).

155.   **At 10:40 A.M. on 2/15/71**

Children! An illustration:

It does not matter to the world whether a miser is alive or dead. It does not matter to the world whether the poisonous nux vomica tree flowers or

218

bears fruit. In the same manner, a person who does not have Feelings, Awareness, Wisdom (Arivu), Compassion, Divine Qualities, who does not treat other beings as he treats his own self, one who does not extend Friendship and Equality to all beings, is of no use. It does not matter whether he is alive or dead. He, the miser, and poisonus nux vomica tree, fall in the same category.

156. **At 8:10 P.M. on 2/15/71**

When you go out in the open, you take an umbrella with you. Wind and rain strike you from all sides. Your whole attention is on the umbrella. You are fully bent on preventing the opened umbrella from being broken and torn by the force of the wind. In such a situation, you will hold the umbrella with both your hands and press it against your head and try your best to prevent it from being broken, over-turned and torn.

When you go out you carry an umbrella for protection. In the same manner, if you bring with you what is called religion by this world, when you come to the Guru to learn Wisdom (Arivu) and pay off your debts of birth, you will not be able to take the teachings of your Guru into your heart, because your heart is full of the teachings of what the world calls religion. There will be no room in your heart to take and preserve your Guru's teachings. Since the Guru's teachings will have to remain outside the heart, it cannot be retained by you. It will go out of you. The moment you go away from the Guru, his teachings also will go out of your mind. Therefore, you will not feel the effect of the Guru's teachings.

When it rains, the power of the atom is in the rain drops. When it falls directly on the earth, the earth will absorb this atomic power and allow only pure water to flow out or fill a pond or tank. If the rain falls directly on plants, the plants will absorb this atomic power and grow luxuriantly.

In the same manner, if you keep in your mind what you learn from books in this world, then when words of Divine Grace come out of the Guru's mouth, you will try to interpret them according to your book knowledge. It will be like the stagnating rain water after the earth had absorbed all the atomic power in the rain drops. Therefore, you must come with an open heart to the Guru. You should receive the words of the Guru with an open heart, without any barrier of thought, of book knowledge, of prejudice or of preconceived notions. If you receive the words of the Guru with a curtain before your heart, the power of his words of Grace, their essence, their magnetism will all be deflected, and your heart will only receive mere words. But if you receive these words of Grace with an open heart, the words will be absorbed by your heart with all its Divine Force, Magnetism and Power. As a result, you will progress very fast on the path leading towards God just as the plants will grow luxuriantly when the rain falls directly on them. Children! You should understand this well.

So said His Holiness Guru Bawa to his diciples.

157. **At 8:35 P.M. on 2/15/71**

His Holiness Guru Bawa told his disciples: In a branch of the Drumstick (Murungo) tree, there can be one hundred to two hundred flowers. At least there will be twenty-five flowers. But, out of all these flowers, only two or three drumsticks will develop.

In the same manner, among the crores and crores of human beings created by God, only one or two will have the real Wisdom of Man. Only he will be able to understand what is good and what is evil, what is merit and what is sin, by analysing everything with his faculty of Divine Wisdom (Pahuth-Arivu). All others will have the carnivorous instinct of thriving at the expense of others. They will think only of their hunger and their needs and not the hunger and needs of others. Children! You should understand this well.

158.   At 8:55 P.M. on 2/15/71

An Illustration:

The woodpecker pecks on the trunks of dead trees and makes a hole inside it and builds a nest for itself. In the same manner, in the body of a person in a state of degradation, in whom the faculties of Perception (Unarvu), Cognition (Unarchi), Intellect (Puththi), Practical Understanding (Madthi), Wisdom (Arivu), Divine Wisdom (Pahuth-Arivu) and Divine Luminous Wisdom (Perr-Arivu) have dried up, the woodpeckers of the five great sins, the six sinful actions, the sixty-four arts, the thirty-two attributes of the elements, the poisonous diseases of the 4,448 tissues will make holes and build nests and live within. When these live within him, his life as Man, the rarest of creations, will dry up day by day and decay and his physical cage will fall down in the same way as the tree in which the woodpecker pecked and made holes. As a result, he will become subject to many births and finally become the guest of Hell. If man will make use of the seven faculties of Perception (Unarvu), Cognition (Unarchi), Intellect (Puththi), Practical Understanding (Madthi), Wisdom (Arivu), Divine Wisdom (Pahuth-Arivu) and Divine Luminous Wisdom (Perr-Arivu) and keep his tree of life alive, these evil woodpeckers will not be able to make holes in his heart and live there.

159.   At 9:10 P.M. on 2/15/71

Children! An illustration:

The crab has ten legs including the two claws in front. It uses all these ten legs and moves about in a staggering manner. It walks on the eight legs, but primarily uses the two legs in the front to catch its food. It cannot catch its prey with the other eight legs. It has to use these two legs like hands to seize its food. If it did not have these two legs (claws), it would be difficult for it to quickly seize its food and put it in its mouth. In the same manner, man will not be able to seize the world and keep it in his heart if he did not have the hands of craving and state of degradation of his Spiritual Wisdom. Cast these two away from you by using your faculty of Wisdom (Arivu).

160.   At 9:20 P.M. on 2/15/71

An illustration:

One who has set out on the venture to know the Truth, should control the currents of his five senses and the five elements. Senses and Truth live in the same place, the Heart (Qalb or Ullam). When the projection of the five elements and the five senses are removed from the Heart, he will be able to see the Truth in the Heart. That Truth is hidden by the darkness caused by the senses and the elements. When the darkness disappears, the

Truth of Wisdom (Arivu) will become Resplendent.

161.   **At 6:55 P.M. on 2/16/71**

An Explanation of the terms "Fish and Flesh:"

Attachment, friendship, wife, children, vanity, titles, worldly glory and property are all fish which swim and gambol in the sea of mind, the sea of Illusion (Maya). They swim in the sea of mind and pick up the refuse and the maggots of Action (Karma) for the benefit of persons mentioned earlier. They are the Intellect (Puththi) born of the parents, Craving and Lust. In the natural sea you will not find such terrible creatures and fishes which commit murder and sin. They are the fishes that occur in nature.

But these other fish change their nature and swim artificially. These are the fishes of the treacherous and terrible Intellect (Puththi) of craving which sacrifice Truth, Good, Justice, Patience, Tranquility, Duty and such other good qualities, as the food for the fish of Hypnosis (Mayakkam). But the natural fish are not like the other fish. They have no faculty of Divine Wisdom (Pahuth-Arivu). So they feed on one another and live. But this other fish eats this Rare and Noble Life itself. Out of these two types of fish, it is the fish which lives in the sea of mind and seizes the other person's heart and consumes it which is the most cruel fish.

Regarding Flesh: When one body consumes another body, it is consumption of flesh. One who consumes and tastes the blood of another consumes flesh, i.e., one who exploits the labour of another person and lives on it is consuming flesh. One who understands this state and avoids this situation with his Wisdom (Arivu) and burns up this state, is Man-God (Manu-Eesan). He is the real Vegetarian (Saivite). Abstinence from eating the flesh of four-legged animals is not Vegetarianism (Saivam). Only one who does not kill the body and feeling of other beings is a Vegetarian (Saivite). This should be understood clearly.

162.   **At 7:35 P.M. on 2/16/71**

His Holiness Guru Bawa told his disciples:

When you sow paddy (rice), weeds will also germinate with the paddy. This is natural. Only the person who removes the weeds completely will get a good yield of paddy.

Man's body has been created out of the five elements of Earth, Fire, Water, Air and Ether. The physical form of these elements supports his Spiritual Body. Within his Astral body, the eighteen thousand worlds are found. If he sows the paddy of good actions in the field of the Spiritual Body, the weeds of the darkness of Illusion (Maya), Hypnosis (Mayakkam), Misguided Wisdom (Ariveenam), Ignorance, Envy, Treachery, Egoism, Action (Karma), the grass of Action (Karma) arising from the senses, and ten and a half crores of other types of grass will germinate within the paddy crop of Goodness and Wisdom (Arivu).

These weeds and grass of Action (Karma) should be completely weeded out. Then, only, will he become Man-God (Manu-Eesan) or Perfect Man (Insan Kamil). It is only after these weeds and grass have been uprooted and removed completely that the crop of Grace arising from the rays of the Good can thrive. This crop can be harvested and used for the benefit of all beings created by God. Otherwise, just as the paddy in the unweeded field will be smothered and destroyed by the weeds, his Good and Wisdom

(Arivu) will be smothered and killed by Actions (Karma). One should understand this and remove the grass of Actions (Karma), which cause rebirths, with your Wisdom (Arivu).

163. ## At 8:20 P.M. on 2/17/71

Mr. Wijesuriya, Assistant Commissioner of Excise, asked His Holiness Guru Bawa, "Swami! We are living in the world guided by the senses. But, if we live with Faith in God, can't we reach God?"

His Holiness replied: If a gold sovereign has fallen into the pit of Hell, can it be taken out? Will Hell give due honour and respect to the gold which has fallen into it? Can people make use of the gold sovereign which has fallen into the pit of Hell? Will such gold have any value? Will it get the honour due to gold?

If man lives with the body of the elements in the world of senses, and leads a life guided by the senses, the elements and the senses will fly out of the heart, full of Illusion (Maya), with limitless speed round the world and within a second bring many visions and scenes and fill up his heart with them. Then they will remind Intellect (Puththi) about these. They will tell the Intellect (Puththi) 'That is available there. That is available here. We should go there. That is like that. This is like this. Buy that and give. Buy this and give.' When the Intellect (Puththi) descends to a state of hypnotic torpor and degradation as a result of this, how can this man evaluate the worth of the heritage meant for human life?

How can one who has not obtained the dignity of human life and Wisdom (Arivu) ever reach God? Only Wisdom (Arivu) will enable a man to reach the greatness of human existence. Wisdom (Arivu) that man is entitled to, will enable the noble qualities of humanity, the nobility of human action and the beauty of God to become Resplendent; only then will he be able to reach God. Otherwise, he cannot.

On the other hand, if he lives in the form of the five senses, and continues to feed the elements, he can only end in death and reach the limits of many rebirths. He cannot reach God.

164. ## At 8:40 P.M. on 2/17/71

His Holiness Guru Bawa gives an illustration to Mr. Nadarajah, D.R.O.

Though the wind blows in the open plain at the speed of one hundred and forty to one hundred and fifty miles per hour, one cannot see it. But if there is a tree in the plain, the power and force of that wind can be seen when it strikes against the tree. At that moment, if the tree shows its power, strength, and courage, the wind will break its branches and uproot it. If the tree, on knowing the strength and force of the wind, bends its branches in the direction towards which the wind is blowing, the wind will go beyond without damaging the tree. The branches will come back to their original position.

In the same way, the four hundred billion hypnotic projections of Illusion (Maya) will assail you with the speed of that wind and the speed of the mind. At that moment if you, with your determination and Wisdom (Arivu), appear to bend slightly with the aid of your Wisdom (Arivu), like the bending branches of the tree, they will pass you and go beyond. All your sufferings will disappear. You will stay where you are. If you bend completely to the sufferings, you will die. If you oppose it firmly you also will die. If the tree shows its egoism against the wind, it will be broken by the force of the wind. In the same manner, if you show egoism your life will be destroyed by them. So you have to escape by yielding slightly with the use of Wisdom (Arivu).

In life, there is one Hypnosis (Mayakkam), one night and one day. You should understand all these three periods of time, and yield with your Wisdom (Arivu). You came into existence in Hypnosis (Mayakkam), lived in the night and came to an end in day time. It is good if life is adjusted on the basis of this knowledge and understanding. Whatever medicine is given when a man is senseless, he will not know it. In the darkness, whatever light with whatever candle power you may use, the darkness cannot be totally removed. But in day time, light is not necessary. You can see everything with the Light of God. If Wisdom (Arivu) is used at the proper time, one can reach God. If you learn and practice Wisdom (Arivu) the suffering of the mind can be removed.

165.   **At 9:05 P.M. on 2/17/71**

His Holiness told his disciples:

Children! Unless there is a tree, there will be no fruit. A disciple should remain with his Guru for twelve years, adopt his qualities, use the Guru's Wisdom (Arivu) as his Wisdom (Arivu), consider the Guru's beauty as his beauty, and live with discipline and good conduct. If he does so, the Guru will be able to pluck the fruit of Divine Grace and Wisdom (Arivu) from the disciple and feed him. Studying methods of obtaining Divine Wisdom without a Guru, is like trying to pluck the fruit when there is no tree.

166.   **At 9:10 P.M. on 2/17/71**

There is a Tamil saying, "Manthiram Kaal, Mathi Mukhaal, Thanthirame Perithu." The meaning of the saying is this.

'Manthiram Kaal': We were born out of Manthiram, the five letters. This represents only one-fourth unit.

'Mathi Mukhaal': We are to assess our life, to assess the aim and end of life and act accordingly. This represents three-fourths unit.

'Thanthirame Perithu': (Than-Tharam) One is to know his own state, his own Destiny, his birth and death. To know all these things is a full unit. It is big.

167.   **At 7:20 P.M. on 2/18/71**

His Holiness Guru Bawa told his disciples: I will relate to you a story.

Children! Please listen. A Swami was doing penance on the bank of a river. It was the custom of the passers-by to leave milk, fruit and food near him for his use. The Swami used to eat those foods. Boys used to graze their cows nearby. A poor boy who used to graze cows there, saw this and thought, "Why should I work hard and graze the cows? If I also become a Swami, I will get my food where I stay." So he went to the Swami and begged him to teach him what the Swami himself had learned. The Swami did not give him any reply. He went on asking like this for six months. But the Swami did not tell him anything.

One day he went to a sand bank in the middle of the river, sat there and started doing penance repeating the words, "What is good for him is good

223

tor me." The Swami also was doing penance. As usual the Swami got milk, fruit and food. When the Swami ate the food, the essence of that food got into the boy's body as his sustenance. In this way, both were doing penance.

One day it rained very heavily, and there was a flood. The flood carried the Swami into the mid-stream of the river. But the floods did not do anything to the boy. Even then the boy continued to repeat the words, "What is good for him is good for me." Adam (Eeswaran) and Eve (Eeswary) appeared before him and asked him what he wanted. The boy said, "What is good for him is good for me." Adam (Eeswaran) told him, "He is dead. Do you also want to die?" Even then the boy said "What is good for him is good for me." Adam (Eeswaran) told him, "He has become subject to many births. Do you also want to become subject to similar births?" The boy replied, "What is good for him is good for me." Adam (Eeswaran) told him, "Because he did not explain to you this Truth of Wisdom (Gnana), and was protecting his body and his food, I destroyed him. He has become subject to many births. He did not teach you as you desired. All the merit of his penance has come to you. You have obtained the love of God. What do you want?" He requested Adam (Eeswaran) to bring the Swami back to life. Adam (Eeswaran) brought the Swami back to life and gave the boy all the boons he wanted.

The Swami, whose life had been restored, woke up and fell at the feet of the boy and said, "Because of the mistake I committed, I have become subject to several births. You should be my Guru. My former life was destroyed. I am now a child. You should by my Guru and teach me the Truth."

A disciple should be like this boy. Whether the Guru is good or bad, whether he is right or wrong, the disciple should have Faith and Determination in the belief that what is good for the Guru is good for him. Only if the disciple is in that state can he reach God. Once you have accepted a Guru, you should place your body, Soul, and property at the disposal of the Guru and you should maintain the Faith and Determination which the disciple had in the story. Children! You should understand this well and act accordingly.

168.   **At 7:50 P.M. on 3/2/71**

An explanation:

If you want to sow a seed, you should sow it within its viable period. If you sow it after that period, the seed will not germinate, as the embryo would have died. After that period, the seed can be used only as food grain.

In the same way, within a proper period, if one searches for a Guru and finds him and gets his services, he will be able to know the purpose of his life. He will be able to reach God.

If one fails to get a Guru within the proper period, he will become subject to many births, just as the seed beyond the period of viability has to be used as food. Children! You should know this well.

169.   **At 8:15 P.M. on 3/2/71**

An illustration:

If you fix the microphone and the tape on the tape-recorder and switch on the power supply to make the tape move and speak into the microphone, your voice with all its modulation will be faithfully recorded on the tape. If the tape is played back, you will hear a faithful reproduction of your voice.

Like the tape recorder, the disciple should record faithfully in his Heart all the teachings of the Guru. When the Guru taps the disciples's Heart, the voice and teachings of the Guru should rise from the disciple. Such a disciple is the best disciple. But, instead, if he records in his heart the voices of the outside world, such as the cawing of the crow, the twittering of the birds and other sounds, when the Guru taps his heart, only the noise of the world will come out. Such a person is not a suitable disciple to the Guru. He is not a disciple who can study the Truth, put an end to his cycle of births and attain Wisdom (Gnana). He will be immersed in Darkness (Agnana), get entangled in the meshes of the net of misguided Wisdom (Ariveeman), lead a life of intellectual degradation, be immersed in the sea of attachments, become subject to selfishness and consider himself to be a great man. When he is in that state, Guru, Truth and Wisdom (Arivu) will not become Resplendent within him. If he is a real disciple, he would not record the noises of the world and his own opinions in his Heart. He should record only the teachings of the Guru and keep them within his Heart. If he does so, he will become the king of Grace and Wisdom in both worlds. He will be the disciple who will be able to get Liberation of his Soul from bondage to the world at the hands of the Guru and reach Heaven. You should understand this.

It is not enough for the disciple to live with the Guru in his Ashram. What the disciple should do is to dwell within the Guru. The world the disciple sees and observes should be the Heart of the Guru. Then, only, will the Guru be able to point out to him all the places he visits. The Guru will show him Heaven, Hell, the world of Spirits (Devas) and so on. He will point out the heavenly personages and explain to him who they are. But you are speaking in a different tone. You do not know what the Guru is. You do not know what Wisdom (Gnana) is. You do not know what service to the Guru means. You simply say that you are disciples. A disciple must merge within the Guru. Remember this!

170.   **At 7:05 P.M. on 3/4/71**

Craving or desire arose from hypnosis (mayakkam). Hypnosis (mayakkam) brought forth misguided wisdom (ariveenam). Misguided wisdom (ariveenam) gave rise to ignorance. Ignorance gave rise to egoism. Egoism gave rise to vanity. Vanity gave rise to sectional religious fanaticism. This gave rise to foolishness. Foolishness brought about caste. Castes brought about discrimination and divisiveness. The divisive force of caste gave rise to falsehood. Falsehood gave rise to intoxicants. Intoxicants gave rise to lust. Lust gave rise to theft. Theft led to murder. Murder led to sin. Sin gave birth to ignorance (agnana). Ignorance (agnana) gave birth to science (vignana). Science (vignana) gave rise to false wisdom (agnana). False wisdom (agnana) led to several births. Births gave rise to endless suffering. Suffering led to death. Several deaths led to several births. Several births gave rise to cruel hell. Cruel hell gave rise to numberless poisonous creatures. The poisonous creatures ate him. Finally the foolish ignorant man ended as a worm.

The end of desire showed the nature of the Light of Truth. That Light showed the nature of Wisdom (Arivu). Wisdom (Arivu) showed the Fullness of Perfection. That Fullness showed That which is Eternal. The Eternal showed the final state of beings. That State showed the Judgment Day. Divine Luminous Wisdom (Perr-Arivu) showed who the Judge is. That showed the Omnipresent God (Ehamparam), and His All-Pervading Resonance.

In this way, Wisdom (Arivu) and ignorance, Truth and falsehood, night and day, and other states arose from some other state which caused them. If you understand well the nature of these chain reactions in the spiritual field, annihilate completely all that arose from craving, and take what arose from emergent Spiritual Wisdom (Arivu) and analyze all facets clearly, you can understand your secret, God's Mystery and the mystery of your birth.

Now, look at the created beings like the bull, ram, dog, fox, tiger and lion. One is the prey of another. The senses also prey on one another. To gratify the desire created by the senses, man commits all sorts of sins. He hurts the minds of other people. He kills other beings to satisfy his palate. Only when men get out of the grip of the senses, which cause them to do harm to serve their ends, will men be able to reach God. In nature, one thing becomes the victim of another. We have referred to the animals. Look at the earth. It grows consuming whatever falls within its grip. Look at water. It dissolves or causes decay of anything that comes within its grip. Look at the air. It also causes destruction. It also consumes whatever it comes into contact with in some way or other. Even mountains consume things and also cause destruction in various ways. Trees are like that. Plants and crops are like that. All these consume other things for their physical development. Only when that physical body is destroyed, can one experience the fullness of God. That is, one must make the body dead to the world of senses. One must lose body-consciousness.

'Saivam' means 'Ultimate in Purity'. The body, which is impure, is not 'Saivam'. So the body must become dead in the spiritual sense. One must give up killing and eating the flesh of animals or birds or other beings that one has killed. In nature, one thing consumes another. One animal uses another animal as food. One animal may use another animal's body to satisfy its carnal desires. It may use the body of another for its benefit. It may use the body to show off or attract. But in man, only if the elements and the senses which form the body die, will his Spiritual Wisdom (Arivu) become purified. When that purified and sanctified state has been reached by man's Wisdom (Arivu) he will be able to obtain God's Grace. Know this well. So said His Holiness Guru Bawa to his disciples.

171.   **At 10:20 A.M. on 3/5/71**

His Holiness tells his disciples: Please listen to a small discourse. I will describe to you the history of the infant.

The father's body becomes strong and virile. The virility gives rise to the sexual urge. This gives rise to a desire for sexual union. This makes man lose his self control and succumb to the hypnotic fascination of the attraction projected by Illusion (Maya) in the form of his wife. This results in sexual union where man loses his self. This culminates in sexual pleasure. His desire results in the ejection of his blood in the form of semen and sperm from which the embryo takes shape after fertilization with the ovum of the mother. The embryo absorbs the mother's tissues, blood, and essence of her body, and develops. Finally it comes out as an infant into this world through a detestable place. Then it gets hold of the mother's breasts with both hands, and sucks her milk in gulps, and along with it the essence of the air, the essence of the earth, the essence of the sex urge, the essence of sex, joy, etc. After sucking all these things, the infant asks, "Is there anything which has escaped me?"

Later as the infant grows up, he wounds the minds and feelings of others, and sucks, as it were, their mind. He goes on sucking and destroying Divine Laws, Divine Grace, Love, Liberality, Charity, Pity, Tranquility, Peace, and other Divine Characteristics and hides them within his misguided Wisdom (Ariveenam), or degraded state of worldly wisdom. Only if he gives up this state of degradation (Ariveenam) will he be able to reach God. He should not cause pain of mind to others.

He drinks blood, which even ghosts will not drink. The earth will not accept blood. Because blood was formed in darkness, it will automatically become dark and decompose. He grows on craving, sexual urge, lust, sexual joy, and misguided Wisdom (Ariveenam). He should avoid these things.

When you look within you, you will find that you are a 'Neesan', i.e., a person full of satanic qualities. You are full of hypnotic torpor caused by your state of degradation of Wisdom brought about by the influence of Illusion (Maya). Darkness fills up everything. Grace also pervades everywhere. When Man's Heart (Qalb) becomes brimful of God's Grace, he becomes Man-God (Manu-Eesan). When his Heart is full of darkness he becomes satan (Manu-Neesan), i.e., the most degraded among human beings. If you analyze the nature of both with your Divine Wisdom (Pahuth-Arivu) you will know the difference between the characteristics of Manu-Eesan and Manu-Neesan, i.e., the difference between man as man ought to be and satan.

172.   **At 8:40 A.M. on 3/6/71**

Child! Listen to an illustration.

Look at the margosa tree and the sandalwood tree. Even long after they have died, even after the roots are decayed, even after they have completely disintegrated within the earth, their inherent qualities will remain with them. Even if you burn the logs of these trees after a long period of years, the bitter taste of the margosa and the sweet scent of the sandalwood will be there till they are turned into ashes.

In the same manner, the characteristics of the parents get embedded in the embryo which develops later and is born as an infant and grows up into manhood. These inherited characteristics which are latent in Man are called in Tamil 'Vaasanaamalam'. Man may, with his Wisdom (Arivu), continue to remove these inherited characteristics. But when he meets with joy or sorrow, these inherited characteristics become apparent in the same way as the bitter taste of margosa will show itself, even if the log is burnt after a very long period, and the sweet scent of the sandalwood will reveal itself even if the sandalwood is rubbed against a stone after a long period.

Man can get rid of his inherited characteristics (Vaasanaamalam) only if he keeps himself in a state of discipline under the ken of a Guru and gets a place in a niche in the Guru's Heart. The fire of Wisdom (Arivu) emanating from the Guru has the power to remove the inherited characteristics and inborn nature. The taste of the margosa can be removed only by burning the log to ashes. The scent of the sandalwood can be taken out by destroying the sandalwood by causing friction with a stone. But the Guru will be able to burn the inherited characteristics and inborn nature of man without actually burning his body or destroying it by friction. The Guru can do it with his look and with his will. If one submits himself to the will of the Guru, the Guru can remove his inherited bad characteristics and inborn satanic nature. Otherwise, he will not be able to get rid of these. What pain or pleasure he undergoes, or trials and tribulations or sorrow he meets with, he should bear all these with equanimity and patience and keep himself under the discipline and supervision of the Guru. If a disciple does so he will be able to remove the odour of rebirth from his self. So said His Holiness Guru Bawa to a disciple of his.

173.   **At 9:55 A.M. on 3/6/71**

An illustration:

Look at the plantain tree. When the plantain sucker is planted, it grows up. From its tuberous root, a large number of plantain suckers come up. But that plantain tree and the suckers are bound to be destroyed. Still the plantain tree thinks, "There is none like me. I am a big personage." It exhibits its leaves and tender shoots with pride and grows luxuriantly and brings forth a large bunch of plantain fruit. Man looks at the bunch with relish. The world is attracted by its beauty. The plantain tree exhibits its true nature. The bunch of fruit matures and ripens. Both the tree and the bunch, (the mother and the daughter) are cut and killed by man. The plantain tree knows this by its instinct. The young plantain suckers also know the fate of their mother. But, still they do not stop growing. They follow the footsteps of the mother tree while pondering over the fate that awaits them. Finally, they meet with death.

But, when a good event like marriage occurs, men bless, saying, "May you prosper like the plantain trees!" But within a year, all the prosperity disappears. Foolish man blesses that the other people should get prosperity which actually is impermanent. There are a large number of people in this world with such foolish mentality. Without reflecting even a little they bless a person thus. But the plantain tree dies within six months of the appearance of suckers round it. Within one year of the plantain tree getting suckers all round it, in the height of its beauty, it is killed and destroyed by man for the sake of its bunch of mature plantain fruit. Like the plantain tree, man expands his desire of evanescent sexual pleasure and enlarges his circle with wife and children and supports them. When he is engaged in this, the darkness of misguided Wisdom (Agnana), lust, hypnotic torpor of Illusion (Maya), desire for intoxicants, adultery, theft, murder and falsehood and other evil tendencies develop and multiply in him and reach maturity. They, in turn, try to kill the Truth and Wisdom (Arivu) in him.

In that state, when he joins with the darkness of Ignorance (Agnana) without thinking of the purpose of his existence and sets out to wage a war with Truth, Truth addresses him and says, "Is it you who is trying to destroy me? Look here!" Immediately he loses his life in the same way as the vain plantain tree bearing its bunch of ripe fruit is destroyed. In the same way as the sucker of the plantain tree meets with death after growing up, his descendants also follow his footsteps and die.

When man considers these evanescent material possessions as real profit and says with arrogance, "Look at me! There is none who is equal to me.

Look at my wife! Look at my children! Look at my royal state! Read my poems! Listen to my music and my songs! Think of my glory!'', and exhibits his own greatness and glory, the demons projected from the darkness of hypnotic torpor of Illusion (Maya) will consume his life as a delicacy in the same way as man consumes the ripe fruit of the plantain tree with relish after cutting it down. You should know this well. Man was born the rarest and noblest of creation. The aim of human life and existence is to know one's own self. But instead he exaggerates his notion of his own greatness and inflates his ego. As a result, he is destroyed like the plantain tree. His glory is like the glory of the plantain trees. Just as we bless a person saying, ''May you prosper like the plantain trees'', Ignorance (Agnana), the dark Illusion (Maya), blesses his existence.

Therefore, you should know this well. You should eat the blissful fruit with the exquisite taste of Wisdom (Arivu), the Everlasting, the Eternal Fruit. So said His Holiness Guru Bawa to his disciples.

174.   **At 7:20 A.M. on 3/7/71**

The True Gnostic Guru (Meignana Guru) tells a disciple who has reached a state of maturity:

Son! You should note a few facts. Man has been created by God as the noblest and rarest of created beings, as the friend of God, as the treasury of God's Grace. God is man's treasury. Man is capable of merging with God, and dispensing His Grace. Such is the noble heritage meant for man. That Rare and Noble Unique One has created man. He Protects, Succors and gives Salvation to him. God has given into the charge of man His Divine Laws and Thoughts, His Wealth of Grace, material wealth, His Soul's (Atmic) Wealth, and the whole Universe. But crores and crores of men have squandered and wasted this Wealth and have succumbed to the hypnotic projections arising from the darkness of illusion (maya) and entered into a state of hypnotic torpor. They lie in a state of illusory sleep caused by the degradation of their Wisdom. When they awake from this hypnotic sleep, their eyes see everywhere the world of illusion (maya), the movement of the mind, demons and elements, inherited characteristics, the three moods of apathy, (ragas, thamas, and sathvic), the six evils of craving, hatred, miserliness, vanity, lust and envy, the all-powerful mind, the four hundred billion (lakhs of crores) of hypnotic projections of illusion (maya), the state of torpor caused by the darkness of the eighteen thousand worlds, the women of illusion (maya) women with satanic qualities, women of beauty, women visualized by visions of the mind or conjured up by visions of the physical eyes, women of craving, seductive women, women of shadow, women of darkness, women of arrogance, women of hatred, women of the mind who explain the privilege of taking ten and a half crores of births, women of evil conduct, etc.

When their eyes meet these forms, these people will run after them and get hold of them as their ''Goddesses of death''. In that state, four hundred billion (lakhs of crores) of ''Goddesses of death'' appear in their visions. These men will make idols for them and bend before them and request them to give them remedies for their sorrows. These men will create ten and a half crores of 'priests' to explain to them the significance of the forms of the idols which originated in their minds. There are priests to cater to every event from conception to internment after death. There will be priests to guide them after rebirth till they are born as worms and go to Hell. There are ten and a

229

half crores of priests for the ten and a half crores of births. There will be priests to show the physical visions and mental visions. These priests or 'gurus' appear in the world in sixteen groups. To the mental vision there will be ten and a half crores of 'gurus'. For the physical vision, the 'gurus' are so numerous that they cannot be counted.

They will consider all creations of God such as animals, reptiles, birds, snakes, centipedes, asses, horses, elephants, lions, dogs, foxes, creations of God which can speak, creations of God which cannot speak, earth, sky, stars, sun, moon, gold, silver, fire, water, air, etc., as gods who demand sacrifice. They will look at them, worship them, do penance before them, and try to get boons from them.

Intoxicants, lust, theft, murder, falsehood, envy, treachery, gambling, creeds, castes, divisiveness, egoism, hastiness, vanity, arrogance, possessiveness such as 'mine' and yours, paradoxes caused by degradation of wisdom, etc., are the manifestations of the 'grace' of these 'gods and goddesses'. The priests of these 'gods' are also experts along these lines. These things are the gifts they bestow on the 'devotees'. These gifts the 'devotees' get and enjoy number in the crores and crores. Also, so numerous are these 'gurus' that they number in the crores and crores. The visions conjured up by their minds and eyes are these things. People with such temperaments follow 'gurus' with similar characteristics.

If you try to draw these 'devotees' who follow these 'priests' towards you, and try to preach to them, you will be in danger. You must consider all these things carefully before you select people to teach the Truth. You should be God's Treasure. God should be your Treasure. Therefore, you should understand all these things and preach, as you are a Noble and Rare Creation. Otherwise, you may bring discredit to yourself and the rare and great Treasure of God's Grace. You should know this clearly.

You may keep a dog locked in a room, protect it from the world, feed it on the food of Grace without giving it flesh or fish. One day when you bring it out of the room to show the world, it will use its instinct of smell and without your knowledge run out, eat human excreta and return. Even though you have kept it away from the influence of the world for such a long period, it will eat excreta the moment it is taken out of the room. You should know that human excreta is like sugar to the dog.

A 'dog' like this lives in man. It has succumbed to the hypnotic attractions of the darkness of Ignorance (Agnana) and entered into a state of degradation. However long you may keep this 'dog' under your custody, feeding it with the wealth of God, it will start eating the excreta of the darkness of Ignorance (Agnana) the moment it gets out of your custody. You should understand this.

You must find out whether visions of the mind and physical visions and the senses are hiding anywhere in their hearts, and give the Grace of God to them only if these are not lurking in their heart. Otherwise, it will cause distress to Truth and Resplendent Divine Wisdom. You should understand this and use the Truth.

There are people with human faces in whose hearts lurk the nature of the dog referred to. They change their colour like the chameleon. You should know this.

175. **At 10:25 A.M. on 6/23/71**

An illustration:

Bugs and lice thrive in dirt. They cannot thrive in a clean place. They breed only in dirty places. When they appear, it is their nature to suck blood. After sucking the blood, they bring out this blood as eggs and breed. A bug will hatch one hundred to two hundred eggs. A louse will breed fifty lice.

In the same manner, the illusions of Illusion (Maya) arise from an impure mind. The hypnotic fascination for the attractions of Illusion (Maya) makes man survey the world, pick up Ignorance (Agnana) and feed on this dirt like the bug which sucks blood. When the dirty food reaches maturity in its body, it gives rise to ten and a half crores of births.

The degradation of man originates from the impure state of the mind which allows Illusion (Maya) to breed in it. You should know this.

When you know that bugs breed in dirt and suck blood, you use the proper insecticide to kill the bugs. In the same way, you should kill the Illusion (Maya) which breeds in your Heart with Wisdom (Arivu) and keep your Heart and your body clean. So said His Holiness Guru Bawa to his disciples.

176. **At 10:50 A.M. on 6/23/71**

Child! An explanation:

The seven lower aspects of the self (Nafs) which affect man are: (1) the mother's characteristics, (2) the father's characteristics, (3) the characteristics of earth, (4) the characteristics of fire, (5) the characteristics of water, (6) the characterisitcs of air, and (7) the characteristics of ether. He is born with these seven types of evil tendencies or characteristics, which were embedded in him when he was an embryo. Fire has the characteristics of burning everything it meets. Water will erode everything. Wind will carry with it everything it meets. Earth will retain all dirt and bad odours. Ether will keep within it the seven colours and lights, Each has its own particular characteristics.

Earth will say, "There is none equal to me!" Wind will say, "There is none equal to me!" Water will say, "There is none equal to me!" Fire will say, "There is none like me!" Ether will say, "None have colours like me!" So each says, "I am the greatest!" In addition to these are the characteristics of Illusion (Maya) pervading the 18,000 worlds which have been inherited from the parents. They were embedded in the embryo before he was born. Therefore, his existence is full of bitterness. His body is bitter.

Look at the mango fruit. When the flowers appear, there is the odour of milk. When the fruit is formed, the young fruit is bitter and also exudes sap (milky material). When the fruit is a little mature, it has the additional characteristic of astringency. When it has matured a little more, the additional characteristic of sourness is there. When it has matured fully, there will be the additional characteristic of sweetness. When it is fully ripe, only sweetness remains.

In the same way, man comes into this world with bitterness. When he goes to a Guru; surrenders himself to the Guru; keeps in his heart the Guru's teachings, words, actions, characteristics, etc.; puts them into practice; and adopts His qualities, he will be able to see the Honey of Truth, like the mango which becomes fully sweet in the end. At that stage the seven lower aspects of the self (Nafs) will disappear; he will get out of the chain reaction of Action (Karma); he will free himself from rebirth; he will become the Honey of God. All Saints (Awlias), Prophets (Nabis) and Heavenly Beings (Devas) will like that Honey.

If man does not become the Honey of Divine Grace in the same way as the mango fruit got into a state of sweetness, he will not be able to free himself from the cycle of births. He will not be able to get rid of the seven lower characteristics (Nafs). You should understand this and progress quickly towards the goal of Spiritual Perfection. So said His Holiness Guru Bawa to his disciple.

177.   **At 10:30 A.M. on 3/5/70**

A disciple inquires from His Holiness Guru Bawa: "My Guru! From the time of his birth, as he tries to follow the path to attain Gnanam (Divine Luminous Wisdom), one man sees or tries to see God with form. Another type of man seeks and finds a Guru and follows his teachings to attain Gnanam or Divine Luminous Wisdom. After a man attains Divine Wisdom, how will he come to understand the implications of these two stages or paths? After he reaches the Guru, which method should he follow to reach the highest Spotlessly Pure State?"

His Holiness Guru Bawa replies:

My child! You have mixed up the mystery of life and the Mystery of God. I will describe to you the paths man follows from the time of conception in the mother's womb. Please reflect on this.

After conception the foetus takes shape and ends in the form within the womb. I will describe it in terms of Arabic letters. The body was first in the form of a Ray. Then it became a Nokkat, a point or dot. The point became a Sukkoon, a circle. From the circle a straight extension developed, it became a Meem. Meem then became an Alif. When the Alif turned upwards, it became Lam. Then it bent down a little and became a second Meem which supports the Sukkoon or circle. When Meem and Alif turn, they become Hey, the face. Then it makes a curve and becomes Dhal. When Dhal and Hey face each other, the head, the face, and the legs are formed. The circle in Hey and the shape of Dhal join and form the Onkara shape. In this shape the child in the womb looks at the heart with folded arms. In that state it looks at the Ruh (the Soul) and God within the heart and meditates.

When the child is in this state of meditation, it sees within its heart the past, the present, and the future. It sees the explanations of these events. It sees the history of mankind. It is merged with God and it is in a state of meditation by itself. It remains in the 'shape' of divinity and meditates on God and sees within itself the eighteen thousand universes, the fifteen worlds, the four hundred lakhs of crores of hypnotic projections of maya (illusion), the aeons and the various events that pertain to each aeon. It understands all languages. At the end of its period of meditation in its house, the womb of the mother, it comes out into the world to find out the secrets in this world of maya. When the child comes out into this world, it starts crying 'Ah! Ooh!' as it inhales a different air, feels a different temperature, and sees a different earth.

People (who appear to it as examples or exhibits of the world) take it, wash it, clean it, and keep it in a place, thereby showing to it within a minute what sorrow and joy is. They call it child, infant, and so forth. The child will not be able to hear what they say for forty days after its birth. Although its eyesight falls on these people, it cannot recognize the shapes for forty days. During these first forty days of its existence on earth, the infant reflects on the scenes it saw when it was within the mother's womb. The infant meditates on it when it closes its eyes and reflects on it when it opens its eyes. In its sleep and during waking hours it sees the scenes it saw in the womb, and it laughs and cries according to the effect of the scenes it saw. In the same way as it sucked the nourishment from the mother when it was in the womb, it sucks nourishment from the mother in its sleep as well as during waking hours.

After sixty days of its existence on earth, the infant considers what it sees on earth to be examples of what it saw earlier when it was in the womb. Then it sees what it considers to be the examples of father and mother. It sees other illustrations of the scenes it saw earlier.

After one hundred and twenty days of its existence on earth, it is able to recognize its father and mother on earth by their facial features. Although it recognizes them, it thinks of the shape of the mother and father and other shapes that it saw and talked with in silence in various languages when it was within the womb. When it sees the earthly example of what it saw when it was within the womb, it breaks its silence and speaks in various languages 'Aah! Ooh!', and so forth.

After one hundred and fifty days of its existence on earth, it is able to recognize the taste of milk, sugar, sweets, and so on. Whatever it may discover in this material world, it does not forget what it saw and spoke during the period when it was in the womb; and it talks in the same way in various languages with the people whom it considers as examples of what it saw in the womb.

At the end of two hundred and forty days of its existence on earth, it becomes acclimatized to the six foot high human shape. When the air of the earth oozes through it in full force, it attempts to stand up and walk a step or two. Even in that stage, when it sees on earth the illustrations of what it saw when it was within the womb, the infant speaks the language that it used while within the womb.

When it has completed two hundred and seventy days on earth, it imitates the posture of its father at the time the parents co-habitated in order to create the infant from the essence of earth, fire, water, air, and ether. The infant treats the earth as the mother. It uses the two legs and two hands as four legs and it moves about. It still remembers and speaks the languages it used inside the womb.

When it has completed two hundred and eighty-nine days on earth, the body of the infant is attracted by the diversity of relationships, by the diversity of mental attitudes, and by its own ties caused by the five elements of earth, fire, water, air, and ether—just as a piece of iron is attracted by the magnet. When the infant is lifted by the hands of the parents and others in the world and fondled, the mother and the infant are drawn towards one another like the iron and the magnet, thus resulting in close family ties. The people show the child various objects and teach it the language they speak to indicate those objects. When it picks up these new words the child does not

233

forget its own language or the languages it knew when it was in the womb. People impress on the child's mind new words for the scenes it saw in its mental visions when these visions are actually seen by the child as physical visions.

By the time the child is three years old, the people of the world make firmly rooted in its mind the scenes that it sees, the examples that it uses as illustrations, and the words that are used to indicate them. The child gradually forgets its earlier experiences and the languages it knew when it was within the mother's womb. The child impresses all the objects that it sees, in the film of its mind.

The child grows into a youth under the guidance of the people of the world who help to firmly impress the objects of the world as real objects in his mind. When the physical visions have become mental visions, the mental visions cause his physical activities.

By the time his wisdom becomes steady, he has become a youth. Four hundred lakhs of crores of beautiful hypnotic projections of maya and the objects illustrating them enter his mind and come out as mental visions. Craving, sexual urge, hypnotic torpor, and the darkness of ignorance—all these enter his mind. If his mind is inclined toward particular forms or aspects of illusion, they appear to him in dreams or in meditation or in sleep. Cinema pictures can be shown only in a dark place. Only in a dark place will the pictures on the screen appear brightly. In a brilliantly lit place the pictures cannot be seen on the screen. So it is, that in the darkness of his mind the person sees all the beauty of the forms of the projections of the elements and enjoys their sight.

In this state he thinks he has seen God. He worships these forces of illusion seen in the darkness of his mind. In the darkness of his mind, in his degraded state of wisdom, he sees the four hundred lakhs of crores of hypnotic projections: gold, silver, earth, sky, eyes, light, gems, various forms of beauty, various forms of joys, and innumerable mental visions such as these. He sees in his mental visions the forms of various deities, such as Siva, Iswara, Iswary, Amman; various beautiful forms of gems, lights, stars, crescents, the sun, and so on. He thinks he has seen God and His Power in various forms. He gives various names to them, extols their glory, worships them, and becomes their devotee. What he sees with his physical eyes is impressed in his mind. He gains experience of desires in mental visions obtained by the so-called four steps in spiritual development: sharihai, kirihai, yogam, and gnanam of the lower order. When he meditates with this state of mind, he sees lights, the colors of various gems in the mind and in dreams. He sees mountains, seas, plateaus, caves, and darkness. When he sees the visions of various colors, he thinks that he has seen God in his dreams. His mind convinces him that he has become a real devotee of God.

When he is finally convinced of this, he goes on strengthening his hold on these mental and physical visions. Then he develops the desire to fly through the sky, to go to heaven and to the abode of the angels. When his mind is in this state, the elements and the senses hypnotize him and carry him to the sky. He sees in his mental visions that he is flying over mountains and seas. He sees the demons fighting with the projections of the elements. He sees that he is crossing the oceans. According to his desires, he will be carried all over the world of mental and physical visions by the elements which will finally disappear in his body. In his mental visions he will feel convinced that he has visited heaven and the abode of the angels.

He will feel that he has flown in the sky without wings, that he has flown in chariots without a chariot, that he has fought wars without wars, that he has made weapons without actual weapons. In daytime he is in darkness. In nighttime he is in daylight. Thus he dreams in the darkness of degraded wisdom and considers these dreams to be Gnanam (Divine Luminous Wisdom). He feels elated over these dreams and sings about them. During his sleep in the darkness of degraded wisdom he sees innumerable physical and mental visions. He loses Pahuth Arivu (Divine Analytic Wisdom) and falls into the hell of sexual joy and perishes. All that he sees he records as his mental visions. Then he looks at these mental visions through his senses and enjoys them. The words of people like this are accepted by the world as Gnanam (Divine Luminous Wisdom).

You should reflect upon these things. The visions you saw until now were shadows, forms, ethereal forms, examples, dreams, memory, the world, maya, illusion, the mind, colors, and mayic forces. You have been seeing the physical visions and mental visions of the fifteen worlds and the four hundred lakhs of crores of worlds of maya.

When you were in your mother's womb, these things were not in your mind. In silence you saw God and meditated on Him. You should now give up all these mental and physical visions and return to that pure state in which you were when you were within your mother's womb. At the time of creation, when you appeared from the Primal Unique One, in what state were you? If you assume that state and see God, you will find that within that state the physical and mental visions do not exist.

In that State, He will be the Grand Vision of Divine Luminous Wisdom. It is that Beauty of Divine Luminous Wisdom within Divine Luminous Wisdom which pervades everywhere. It has no form. It has no shape. It has no color. It has no end. It is indestructible. It has no blemish. It is Limitless. It is Omnipresent. It is the Beginning. It is the Beginningless. It is Everlasting. It is It. You are within It. Everything is within you. In that State 'you' have nothing. You have become He. That Beauty is Gnanam, Divine Luminous Wisdom.

What you saw in the world are illusory visions which arose from maya. They were physical and mental visions, the illusive forms of the senses and the elements. You worship these forms as various colors and shapes. The ones who impressed these forms in your mind are called maya. It is these mayic forces which prepare these physical visions and create mental visions. Like the chameleon, they show the five senses and the five elements in the form of illusion in various colors, to suit your wavering degraded state of wisdom. If you succumb to the changing colors of this chameleon, maya, you will not be able to see God who has no color or form. To see Him you must seek a Guru who has overcome these mental and physical visions. With his help you must learn the limits of physical and mental visions and go beyond and merge with That which has no form, that Primal Unique One. If you do so, you would have achieved the ultimate purpose of your existence on earth.

So said His Holiness Guru Bawa to his disciples.

178.   **At 4:40 P.M. on 4/5/70**

When a crab is fertilized, the eggs hatch within the crab's body. Within the body of the mother hundreds of newly hatched crabs feed on her fat, liver, and heart. With their claws they will tear out all the tissues in the organs of the mother crab and feed on them. When all the food essence in the mother crab has been sucked out, the mother crab will become unconscious and the hard shell of the crab will break open and the young crabs will crawl out. In this process the mother crab dies.

There are a large number of human beings who have the characteristics of the crab. They do not realize that all human beings are descended from the same original parents, that they are all brothers. They do not realize that there is only One God for all mankind. They have succumbed to the evil characteristics of maya (illusion), under the influence of which they have succumbed to the divisive forces of religious fanaticism and race. Religious fanaticism and racial hatred grow in their mind like the young crabs within the mother crab's body.

The young crabs after coming out of the eggs stay within the mother crab's body for twenty-one days, feed on her fat, liver, and so forth, and finally bring about her death. In the same manner, within the first twenty-one years of his existence on earth, man grows under the love and affection of the parents, kills his Divine Wisdom and Truth, and removes from his mind the fact that there is only One God and that all men are brothers. He falls victim to the senses and considers men to be different according to race and religion. He tries to rule the world with his egoism. The progeny of the senses bring about his destruction.

This crowd of human beings who are like the crabs appear in the world, get destroyed, appear in the world again and get destroyed, and thus continue this process. They try to develop after destroying the heart of man and consuming it. They do not realize that they are themselves liable to destruction. The crab, in the process of its emergence from the mother's body, kills her and tries to live. The crab-like man kills the Truth of God in his heart and tries to live. You should note the crab-like crowds who are in a degraded state of wisdom. You should avoid the company of this group and live with God in your heart.

So said His Holiness Guru Bawa to his disciples.

179.   **At 5:05 P.M. on 4/5/70**

Child! Please listen to an illustration:

Snakes live in holes. When they come out of the holes and move about, if they see anything moving, they will run back into the hole. If you catch hold of the snake which has entered half-way into the hole and, with the intention of removing its poisonous fangs and training it, try to pull it out, it will not be possible to pull the snake out. The snake will hold its breath and spread its body and hold onto the hole with all its strength. When it is in that state, even an elephant cannot pull it out. If you pull it with great strength, the portion of the snake in your hand may snap and you may fall down. The snake will escape inside the hole. It will cover the broken part of its body with dust and heal the wound. Then it will lie in wait for you and when you go there later, it will bite you.

There are human beings like the snakes, who have entered the dark holes of hypnotic maya or illusion in their degraded state of wisdom. If you try to pull out such a human snake from his hole with your Wisdom in order to remove his poisonous fangs of illusory mayic action and train him to follow the path of Truth, you will not succeed. He will not come out of the hole. Even if you pull with the strength of one thousand elephants, you will not be able to pull him out. He will hold his breath and cling onto the hole with all the strength of the senses, the elements, and the six evil actions, and the power of the four hundred billion hypnotic projections of illusion. If you pull with all your might, this human snake will snap in two. You will get only the portion you were holding onto. You will not get the whole human snake. The other portion will remain in the hole. These are people like some of the disciples here. Even if the Guru has pulled them half out of maya, the other half will still be in illusion.

Those who are half in the hole of illusion will cure their wound by applying the dust of hypnotic projections of illusion and they will wait for an opportunity to do harm to the Guru who removed them half-way from illusion and who tried to remove their poisonous characteristics. Therefore, even if you succeed in pulling such human snakes fully from the hole of illusion, you should remove their poisonous fangs, their poisonous characteristics, by teaching them carefully with your Divine Wisdom.

Though you may not be afraid of snakes, you should be careful about these human snakes. They have the matured poison of the six sinful actions. In their tongues and in their hearts they have four hundred billion types of poison. You should understand the nature of these human snakes and teach them with care. Do not think that because you have the snapped half of the human snake in your hand that he has fully come out of the hole of agnanam (ignorance). You must remember that the other half is still in the hole of maya (illusion). If you teach the Truth to him without knowing this, it will be like throwing a stone at a rocky hill. The stone may reflect back and destroy your Gnostic Eye, the Eye of your Soul. Know this well and teach Gnanam. Evil actions originate from the place where evil characteristics originate. That is the place where the actions of the projections of the elements originate. When one has entered that place, it is not possible to pull him out.

So said the Guru to his disciples.

180.   **At 8:20 P.M. on 5/5/70**

Dr. Selvaratnam addresses His Holiness Guru Bawa: "We are listening to your illustrations regularly. Yet our mind has not become still or one-pointed. A gnostic, Marcus Aurelius, has also commented on this state. Our state is like the suffering undergone by a person who has been stabbed with a knife. It will be of great help if Your Holiness will show us some 'Sathanai' or method to enable us to get out of this state of pain." His Holiness Guru Bawa replies:

The method of 'meditation' you want me to show you is not the correct method. It will only lead to death. When you try to meditate for a second, the senses will bring the work of five seconds and keep them in your mind. Therefore, how can you do real meditation for even a second? When you try to do meditation for two seconds, the senses will bring into your mind enough work for a thousand seconds and show them to you as mental visions. Then how can you still the mind? No one in the world has stilled the mind. No one has been able to still the mind and meditate. He has not done meditation. He has only done something that leads to death.

You should know one thing. There is an iron safe. You cannot keep all types of things there. You keep only gold, diamonds, and various types of gems in it and lock it up. A man might bring iron, paper, cotton, food, lead, and machinery in a ship. The goods may weigh eighty thousand or ninety thousand tons. He gets them unloaded. He cannot bring them and keep them in his iron safe. He has to sell them and keep only the realized cash or gold in the safe. The iron safe will not take in the goods imported in the ship. It accomodated only the value of the goods.

Your physical body, the gross components of which are earth, fire, water, and air, is like a ship sailing on the sea of mind, which is maya or illusion. It carries as its cargo the fourteen thousand worlds and all the goods in them, the four hundred billion hypnotic projections, all the scenes and visions, darkness, light, hypnotic torpor, intoxicants, miserliness, envy, deceit, egoism, demonic qualities, vanity, poverty, lust, theft, murder, falsehood, death, and so on. You cannot keep all this cargo in the iron safe of your heart. You must dispose of all these things in the proper markets and keep only the realized value in the iron safe of your heart.

It is for the purpose of realizing the value of your cargo that you have to go and meet a Guru or Spiritual Master. You should carefully keep the Diamonds that he gives you in the iron safe of your heart. The heart is the proper place for keeping these Diamonds. It is not the proper place for keeping the cargo. Fill up the iron safe of your heart with the Diamonds which the Guru will give you. You may do business with these Diamonds. If you do so within the iron safe of your heart, you will be able to see God, His Grace, and His Wealth, you and me, Truth, Good, and the nature of evil—everything. You will see those who meditate, those who worship, those who follow special methods of meditation, and those who suffer. You will see yoga and Gnanam, Grace and Spiritual Wealth, joy and sorrow, heaven and hell, the earth, the other worlds, hypnotic torpor caused by the attractions of maya or illusion itself, birth and death, gold, women, property, caste, race, creed, poverty and wealth, degradation and sublimity. You will see the worship and the worshipped, the Soul, Divine Wisdom, Light, Divine Luminous Wisdom. You will see all these things there. You will see the destructible and the Indestructible. You will see the Ultimate Unique One. You will see all these within the iron safe of your heart. Again and again you can see all these mysteries.

In that State the Person who studies and the Person who teaches will be God. The Person who assesses the wealth and the Person who lays the wealth will be He. He will be the Seller and the Buyer. He will wear the Diamonds. He will feel joy in wearing them. He will be the Person who will explain the immense value of the Diamonds.

In that State you do not exist. Only God exists. You should understand this.

To see Him, there is no need for any special methods of meditation. Surrender yourself to Him. Lean on Him and look at Him. Then you will realize this Mystery.

181.   **At 9:05 P.M. on 5/5/70**

Child! A word of explanation:

Forget your body consciousness. The world is a vast void. God is the Light. Know that Light.

Children! Who is to meditate on whom? Who is man? Who is God? Where is man? Where is God? Who is to use special methods of meditation? To meditate on whom?

Children! Only God can meditate on Himself. Man, in his degraded state, cannot meditate on God because God is One. This man is another. There are innumerable hunters and wild animals within this man. God is unique. He is alone. He is not prepared to fight with this man who is accompanied by this army. God has no weapons. When man goes with his army to fight with Him, He disappears. This man is in the shape of darkness. God is Light. When darkness covers the Light, the Light disappears. When this man gets rid of this darkness and stands without any weapon, he becomes Manu Eesan, Man-God. Then this Manu Eesan is one with God. In that State he is not ordinary man. In that State man has no weapons. God also is in a weaponless State. He should worship Him. He is He. In that state the Soul is the body of Arivu (Divine Wisdom). The Heart of the Soul is the Resplendence of Perr Arivu (Divine Luminous Wisdom). The Soul of that Resplendence is God.

In this State who is to worship whom? Who is God? Who is this Man? When Man has merged in God and God has merged in Man, when he has become He, he is worshipping Him. For this, why do you want sathannai or a method and the resulting pain or death? Know this well.

Earth, fire, water, air, and ether are merged in the earth itself. This earth is merged in the mind. The mind has within it four hundred billion hypnotic projections and innumerable things. This mixture of the mind is merged in the Soul. The Soul is merged in Pahuth Arivu (Divine Wisdom), which is merged in Perr Arivu (Divine Luminous Wisdom). Perr Arivu is merged in the Effulgence of the Primal Unique One. You should understand this well. You should find Divine Wisdom where your Soul merges. Where the Divine Wisdom merges, you will see that Resplendence of Light merge. If you merge and disappear, then 'you' and 'I' do not exist; only God exists.

So said the Guru to his disciples.

182.   **At 9:25 P.M. on 5/5/70**

Child! Please listen to an illustration.

A drama is being staged. A large number of people go to see the drama. Vocal musicians, drummers, violinists, flutists, persons who want to see the women acting in the drama, those who are interested in the acting, those who want to know what type of drama it is, those who want to hear the music all go to that theatre. Scholars, gnanis, gnostics, yogis, sithars, people who have achieved control over the forces of nature, muktars, those who have obtained liberation, and others also may go to that theatre. Each man has his own predilections, his own interests.

When they see the drama, each will observe only the particular aspect that he is interested in. One who is interested in love will be concentrating his attention on the beauty of the actress. The drummer will concentrate his attention on how the drums are being played. Those who are interested in vocal music will concentrate their attention on the singing. Those who are interested in dancing will concentrate their attention on the dances. The violinists will listen carefully to the tunes played on the violin. Each will concentrate on that particular aspect in the drama in which he is interested. Each spectator will be an expert in a different line. He will concentrate only on that aspect in the drama. They will not concentrate their attention on those aspects of the drama in which they are not personally interested. There will be none who have come there to see the drama as a whole entity. Everyone will judge the drama from the aspect in which he is interested. A poet will judge from the manner in which poems were presented on the stage. The Gnani or man of Divine Luminous Wisdom, however, will consider every aspect of the drama to refer to God, the Primal Unique One—the movements of the legs, hands, eyes, the songs, the dialogue, and the story.

In the stage of the world, people in search of a Guru and God go to see holy men and Gnanis. They also judge the Gnani according to their own state of wisdom and interest, like the people who judged the drama. In the drama the actors acted like the characters whose part they played. But these people reveal what they have in them. They will not be able to reveal what is not in them.

But only that Unique One is within the Gnani, the man of Divine Luminous Wisdom. The Gnani will consider every sound or song he hears to have its source in God. This is the difference between the Gnani and others in the stage of the world. The Gnani will look into the entire history and hand over everything to the Creator of that history. But the man of agnana or ignorance will only act his individual part on the stage of the world, take several births, and continue to act his special part. You should understand this.

If one knows his self, he has no time to waste with others. When one has decided to check his own self and find out his blemishes and remove them, he will have no time to find out the blemishes of other people. One who has decided to find out the faults of others will have no time to discover his own faults. Why should we follow this wicked path of finding out the faults of others? It is high time you start reforming your own self and proceed on your spiritual journey. That is the Divine Path that will lead you to your Eternal House. Look at the seat of the Guru within you. Search within it for the Sublime Fullness. That is the House of Liberation that you should attain during your existence on earth.

So said His Holiness Guru Bawa to his disciples.

183.   **At 6:35 P.M. on 6/5/70**

Please reflect on this interesting aspect.

In this world there are innumerable varieties of trees, shrubs, creepers, grass, and so forth which bring forth flowers. Only at the time the flowers open will you be able to distinguish the scents of the various types of flowers.

Among human beings there are various types. They all have human faces. The mind of man, the lotus of the human heart, has innumerable things within it. It has within it their peculiar characteristics and scents. Within those characteristics it has innumerable hypnotic projections, physical visions, and mental visions. All things are registered in the mental visions. Men turn these mental visions into physical visions. These are turned into physical forms with the five elements of earth, fire, water, air, and ether, and they are also turned into astral forms. These are kept as examples or illustrations of their physical visions. These examples are then considered to be basic things. These basic things are then turned into saktis, forces or energies. Those saktis are kept in the intelligence. Then man pays his devotion to his intelligence. Thus man worships and pays devotion to objects of illustration or examples, he does penance before them, and asks for boons.

From what station did he worship? With what did he worship? With

240

what purpose did he worship? What did he worship? Before whom did he do penance? From what did he ask boons?

The nature and fragrance of his worship and meditation depends on the answer to the above questions. Accordingly, he attains suitable characteristics and results. He gets appropriate births and deaths. Whatever race he may belong to, whatever religions he may belong to, whatever language he may speak, if the fragrance emanating from the flower of his heart is one that attracts Divine Wisdom—one that does not cause hypnotic torpor of the fascination of maya or illusion to the mind and wisdom of man—that fragrance will attract God.

All types of flowers will not emanate the fragrance of the jasmine and mullai flowers. Man does not like the scent of all types of flowers. He wears only flowers the fragrance of which is pleasing to his mind. In the same manner there are crores of types of human beings. They worship visions of the mind and visions of the eyes. Their piety is like the flowers whose scent man does not appreciate. So God will not accept the scent of the flower of their heart because it is repellent to Him. Man likes and wears a flower whose fragrance pleases and calms his mind. If man develops God's Characteristics, and if the lotus of his heart which grows on those Characteristics blossoms in Love and Compassion and opens the petals of Perr Arivu (Divine Luminous Wisdom), the Fragrance of Grace will emanate from it. God, who is Infinite Beauty, likes that Fragrance. So he will wear that Flower. If man's piety flowers with that Fragrance only, God will accept his piety and devotion in the same way as man plucks and wears the flower whose scent pleases him. If man gets this Natural Flower to open and spread out its natural fragrance of Grace and offers this Flower to God, that Flower will have the Characteristics and Fragrance of God. The man who worships God in that manner and offers the flower of his heart with God's Characteristics is one who has reached the crown of existence, understood the glory of human heritage, and attracted the attention and Love of God. He is Manu-Eesan, Man-God, among human beings. Such a person is the rarest and noblest among men.

All other types of worship will be worship of the hypnotic projections in his mind. He will be worshipping those various hypnotic projections of illusion and asking boons from them. The result will be that his heart will attain the characteristics of the elements and emanate the scent of the hypnotic torpor caused by the attractions of illusion, just as the various flowers in the world emanate various types of scents. You should understand this.

Therefore, it is best for your existence on earth to know your self, know your Lord, forget your self, get rid of the earth and all material things connected with it, give up all visions of the physical eyes, lose your self, see the Unique One, and merge within It.

So said His Holiness Guru Bawa to his disciple.

184. **At 8:20 P.M. on 6/5/70**

Child! Please listen to an illustration.

Look at the iguana. It feeds on insects, worms, ants, and termites. It goes to the holes where ants and termites live and extends as much of its tongue as possible into the hole. The insects, worms, ants, and termites in the hole will bite its tongue thinking that it is good food for them. The iguana will patiently bear all the pain till a large number of ants and termites have got hold of its tongue. Then, all of a sudden it will withdraw the tongue into its mouth and consume all the ants, then extend its tongue again into the hole. The ants and termites in the hole will swarm on the tongue and bite it thinking that it is good food for them. The iguana will withdraw its tongue into its mouth all of a sudden and consume them. It will repeat this process again and again.

There are crores and crores of human beings who go along the dark path of maya and agnanam or ignorance, following the senses and the projections of the elements. Like the iguana which extends its tongue into the holes, these people extend their tongue of degraded wisdom into the holes of birth for food. The hypnotic torpor caused by the darkness of ignorance goes in search of food within the seventy thousand veils of illusion, within the ten and a half crores of holes which cause reactions. The tongue of degraded wisdom extended into the holes of illusion will be bitten by the demonic projections of ignorance, intoxicants, theft, murder, lust, hatred, miserliness, craving, egoism, envy, ghosts, the four hundred billion hypnotic projections of illusion, and other essences. These men withdraw their tongues of degraded wisdom and consume the above things like the iguana which withdraws its tongue from the hole and consumes the ants, termites, and so forth. All these poisonous essences, the hordes of projections of the elements, and the four hundred billion hypnotic projections of illusion which they took into themselves with their tongues of degraded wisdom as their food will remain within them and slowly consume them.

But a man of Divine Wisdom will keep away from these holes of dark maya. If you teach the Truth to a person who comes to you escaping from the holes of maya, you will be proceeding on the path of Fullness to reach that Sublime One.

185.   **At 8:35 P.M. on 6/5/70**

Child! Please listen to an illustration.

Look at the vulture as an example. The food it relishes most is the dead body of man. If that is not available, then under the compulsion of hunger it eats the dead bodies of bulls and sheep.

There are seventy-three groups of human beings. Among them there are human beings who are liable to take ten and a half crores of births. Among these human beings there may be a very few men with real human qualities. The vulture will search for the body of such a man and eat it. If a thousand people died in a battle, through their wings the vultures will examine all the bodies and find out the body of the man who had all the human qualities within him and who always acted as a human being should. Only the body of such a man will they eat with relish. And only if the body of such a man is not available, will they eat the bodies of other men under the compulsion of hunger. Suppose there are ten thousand dead bodies in the battlefield, and a thousand vultures come there—all of them will examine with both their wings each of the thousand corpses. If they find out only the body of one man who had really lived like man, all of them will eat the body of only that man with relish.

People with all types of shapes and all types of characteristics come to a Guru or Spiritual Master. The Guru has two wings. One is Pahuth Arivu (Divine Wisdom), the other is Perr Arivu (Divine Luminous Wisdom). Just as the vulture examined the dead bodies of human beings with both its wings and discovered the bodies of men who had the real characteristics of men, the

Guru also will examine all the people who come to him with his wings of Pahuth Arivu and Perr Arivu and find out their real nature. He will be able to find out whether the inner nature of the person who comes to him is that of an ass or a mynah, a hawk, a crow, a crocodile, a buffalo, a monkey, a horse, an elephant, or whatever. He will get into the mind of every one and find out his history—the nature of his birth, his thoughts, his predilections, and inclinations. He will discard those with animal qualities. He will discover the person who has real human qualities and whose actions are really human. The Guru will sit within this person's spiritual heart which has six angles. He will embrace him with Love and with Divine Wisdom. Just as the vulture enjoys the taste of the body of real men, the Guru will enjoy the characteristics and Divine Wisdom of such a real man and will decide to merge his Divine Luminous Wisdom with the Divine Wisdom of that man.

You should search for a Guru who has this ability and surrender yourself to him. Your heart and his Heart should merge and become resplendent and resonate and spread the Radiance everywhere.

So said the Gnana Guru to a disciple of his.

186.   At 9:10 A.M. on 7/5/70

Child! Please listen to an illustration!

Look at the crane. If the crane is to catch the fish in the pond or stream, it should stand motionless in such a way that its shadow does not fall in the water. Only if it is able to do so will it be able to catch fish. If the shadow of the crane falls clearly in the water, the fish will run away. The crane will not be able to catch fish.

Man is larger than the entire universe. This man who is potentially capable of ruling the whole universe will be able to achieve his object of realizing God only if he remains still and shadowless like the heron—if he removes from himself the shadow of the mind, the shadow of the lower self, the shadow of egoism, and the shadow of the senses. If the heron has to exercise so much self-control to catch such an insignificant thing as a fish, what amount of self-control and self-effacement should man adopt to reach God who rules the universe?

The beetle has shadow. The worm has shadow. The ant has shadow. Every article in the world has shadow. If man is to reach God, he should not have even an atom of the shadow of the mind and the shadow of the lower self. The Soul has no shadow. God has no shadow. If man is to merge with God, he should remove from himself the four hundred billion hypnotic projections of maya (illusion) and become shadowless. If he attempts to see God without removing the shadows of the four hundred billion hypnotic projections of maya, he will not be able to reach God. You should understand this clearly.

So said His Holiness Guru Bawa to his disciples.

187.   At 9:40 A.M. on 7/5/70

Child! Please listen to an illustration.

A man brings up a dog as his pet. He feeds it with tasty food. If one day he places before it a food it likes best and then tries to remove it—thinking 'It is my dog, I brought it up'—the dog will bite its master.

God has created many beautiful beings and given them intelligence and wisdom suitable to them. He has created man as the noblest and the most intelligent of all created beings. He has endowed him with Pahuth Arivu (Divine Wisdom), Love, and Compassion. He feeds him and protects him with His Grace. Even if the parents forget him, God does not forget him. He protects and succours him day and night, in sleep and in the state of wakefulness, in joy and in sorrow.

In spite of all this, man who is the noblest of God's creations has forgotten God. He has lost Compassion, Forbearance, and the Resplendence of Perr Arivu (Divine Luminous Wisdom). He has sunk into the degradation of carnal pleasures generated by the hypnotic attractions of the darkness of maya (illusion). He is struggling in the deep pit of sex, the experience of hell, thinking that it is real comfort. When he is in that state of hypnotic torpor, unable to get out of that deep pit of hell, if God or His Representative the Guru renders him necessary help to save him from that pit and gives him the rope of Arivu (Wisdom) and tells him, "O Man! Get hold of this rope and come up," and pulls him up with Wisdom and seats him in the throne of Pahuth Arivu (Divine Wisdom) and says to him, "What amount of suffering did you undergo by falling into this deep pit? Forget it! Here is the Blissful Honey of Grace. Here is God's Fruit of Grace. Eat! There is no food sweeter than this," and if He places the Fruit before him, man will take a piece or two into his mouth and spit it out as if it were salt or tamarind. Like the dog he will bite God and the Guru with his mouth of degraded wisdom. He will scold, "Where is God? Where is the Guru?" Again he will fall into the pit of sex. There are men with such a degraded state of wisdom. You must understand this well and preach Truth.

So said the Guru to the disciples.

188.   **At 10:35 A.M. on 7/5/70**

Child! Please listen to an illustration.

Look at the egg. After fertilization it remains in the womb of the hen for a certain period and then comes out of the orifice in the hen. When it comes out, the shell is soft. As soon as the egg comes out of the hen, the air and heat of the atmosphere and the heat of the five senses of the hen make the shell rigid. Is it possible to send this rigid egg back into the hen through the orifice through which it came out?

In the Beginningless Beginning the Soul of Man shone as an infinitesimal Radiance, like an atom within an atom, of a Ray of God's Grace. This Radiance, the Soul, came into the cage of the five elements, the physical body. Within the fertilized ovum, which is made of the essence of flesh, bones, blood, lymph, fire, and heat arising from the five elements of earth, fire, water, air, and ether, the Soul enters as a Ray. With the motive power of the Soul full of Grace, the fertilized ovum develops shape. It straightens, bends, rolls, and turns, and after the normal period it finds its way into the world through the gate of birth.

Once the baby has come out into the world, it is affected by the air of the hypnotic torpor of the darkness of the world, by the wind of the ties of blood, by the wind of murder, by the wind of poisonous egoistic characteristics, by the wind of the divisive forces of 'I' and 'you', by the winds of the ten and a half crores of births, by the winds of desire, joy, sorrow, laughter, and beauty generated by the four hundred billion hypnotic projections of maya or illusion and by the visions of maya. As a result the body of man becomes rigid, like the egg which comes out of the hen. He is unable to go back to his place of origin through the gate of birth. He is unable to go there through Divine Wisdom because he has closed the Gate of Divine Wisdom by submitting himself to the influence of craving, blood ties, gold, property, wife, child, disease, birth, death, and so forth. He becomes rigid and old under the hypnotic torpor caused by the darkness of the four hundred billion worlds. Therefore, he will not be able to go to his place of origin. He will not be able to reach God who is his Source.

If the rigid egg is allowed to stand in vinegar for some time, it can be squeezed through an even smaller opening than the one through which it came out of the hen. In the same manner, if an authentic Gnana Guru is to make the man who has become rigid under the influence of maya, as indicated earlier, pliable and fit to go back to his place of Origin, he has to soak him in the Essence of Grace, the Resplendence of Perr Arivu (Divine Luminous Wisdom), and remove from him all his rigid nature. He should turn him into the State in which he originally was, bury him within Perr Arivu, and make It travel at a speed of a Ray faster than that of the mind, and turn that Ray into an unatom, and bury that Effulgence which is an unatom in that Effulgence which is an unatom. Only a Gnana Guru who has that capacity can do this. The Guru can do this if the man is of a certain state of rigidity. If the man has become too rigid, if his heart has become harder than stone or steel, if he has become darker than maya, if he has fallen into the ultimate state of degradation, it is not possible for even a Gnana Guru to redeem him.

So said Guru Bawa to his disciples.

189.   **At 12:20 P.M. on 7/5/70**

Child! Please listen to an illustration.

There is a bird called iuvachi. The male and the female birds live together. To protect the eggs and hatch them, they build a nest out of clay on the high branches of trees, inaccessible to animals and snakes. When the nest of clay is half built, the male bird urges the female to lie in it and lay the eggs. When the female bird has laid one or two eggs, the male bird completes the nest of clay, covering the female bird and allowing only its beak to appear outside the cage-like nest of clay. Then the male bird regularly feeds the female bird.

When the eggs are hatched and the sound of the young birds is heard, the male bird will demolish the part of the nest around the beak of the female bird in order to enable the female bird to come out of the nest. Then after the female bird comes out of the nest, the male bird will remain and protect the young birds. The female bird will bring food and feed the male bird and the young birds. After seven days, both the male and the female birds will go out in search of food and feed the young birds. When the young birds are old enough, the parents teach them to fly, show them their food and how to catch their food. When the young birds become fit to fly and find their food and feed themselves, the parent birds will leave them and live separately.

Man is engaged in the life of this material world in the same manner. He is leading his life on two levels, at the Soul level and at the worldly level. When the Soul and the body or illusion are together, during certain periods they lay the eggs of craving, desire, and lust. These eggs are covered with the nest of illusion, and the body is fed with the six evil actions of craving, hatred, miserliness, vanity, lust, and envy. When the eggs of craving, desire, and lust are hatched, they are fed with the food of lust, theft, murder and falsehood. Then they are shown how to fly in the realms of the mind, and they feed on the visions of the four hundred billion hypnotic projections of illusion. Under the influence of illusion, the Soul of man allows the mind to live freely feeding on them.

But a man with Wisdom will analyze everything with Pahuth Arivu (Divine Wisdom), saying thus: "What a fix I am in. I am covered up within a house built of illusion. I have accepted only those things, such as wife, children, and relations, which will finally destroy me. There is danger to my Divine Wisdom and Truth from these things." Then his Divine Wisdom, the Truth, and the Soul will give up the attachment to maya and run and fall within the house of Divine Wisdom of the Guru. Then the Guru will embrace the Truth, cover him with the Resplendence of Divine Wisdom, protect him and feed him with the honey and fruit of Divine Grace, and allow the disciple to develop. When the Guru hears the Voice of Divine Wisdom of Grace of the disciple hidden within him, he will take him out and show him the characteristics of Compassion and his own Wealth of Divine Grace, the Fruit of Patience, the Honey of Love, the Fruits of the Heart, the Tastes of Forbearance, the Rights of Peace, the Fullness of the Unique One, and the All-Pervading Effulgence. He will give him training in all these aspects and allow him to go free in the world, just as the bird trains the young ones and allows them to live on their own.

A person who thus sought refuge within the Guru and gained strength and certitude is the real disciple. He who has adopted those characteristics will win the love of the Guru. He will be able to fly in all the eighteen thousand worlds, move within and without, and be the repository of the Grace and Wealth of God. Reflect on this. You should strive to attain this State.

Truth, the disciple—and Resplendence, the Guru, are like two mouths of the same personality. The words of the disciple and the words of the Guru will come out of the same mouth, the Mouth of God. Since the disciple and the Guru have merged in God, their words will be the words coming from God.

So says the real Gnana Guru.

190.   **At 3:40 P.M. on 7/5/70**

Child! Please listen to an illustration.

This is referred to in the scriptures of several religions. In Hindu scriptures it may be found that Lord Siva is said to wear the snake as an ornament around his neck. In several Arabic mythological stories a lot has been written extolling the snake. There are several types of snakes. In Hindu mythology it is stated that the cobra is worn by Lord Siva around his neck. In Arabic mythology also you find similar stories.

In the beginning the snake had one thousand legs. It did not have poisonous fangs. It emanated from its body the scents of thousands of types of flowers. When a light fell on it, all the colors that are in the sun appeared on the body of the snake. God kept this beautiful snake on the northern gate of heaven as a guard. God had kept angels and the peacock as guards at the other gates of heaven. The angels liked the beauty and scent of the snake and used to wear it around their necks, waists, or hands like ornaments whenever they wished to do so.

In the meantime God wanted to create mankind. For this purpose, from the earth He created Atham (Iswaran) and Hawwal (Iswary), or Adam and Eve. The leader of the angels in heaven became jealous of Atham, the Primal Man. He wanted to bring Atham under his influence. He thought of helping Atham if Atham obeyed him. He decided to do all possible harm to Atham if Atham was placed above him.

One day God Almighty called all the angels and dwellers in heaven and ordered them to stand behind Atham and worship Him (God). The leader of the angels said to God, "You have created Atham out of earth and the five senses. You created me out of fire. I am not prepared to worship You while standing behind him. I know how to worship You."

God told him, "I have created Atham as the commander of all my creations and as the original father of mankind. He knows My secrets. I know his secrets. Man will know what the heavenly beings do not know. Stand behind him and worship Me." Because he was jealous of Atham, he stood there without worshipping God. So God called him satan or Malkoon (one who follows the wrong path) and ordered him to go to hell.

He replied, "I am prepared to go to hell, but please grant me a boon—that I should be the enemy of Adam and his progeny. I should be able to move within and outside of them. I should be invisible to them. By worshipping You they will try to reach a high state. Please grant me the power to lead them astray and bring them under my influence. I will make them join me."

God replied, "Those who follow you will never follow Me. Those who worship Me will never follow you. If you waste your time on those who worship Me, you will meet with disgrace in the end and go away." God cursed him and threw him onto the earth. Along with him, his one thousand followers were thrown from heaven to the earth.

God kept Adam and Eve in heaven and got the angels to guard them. Satan went quietly up to the seventh heaven to tempt Adam and Eve. He deceived the peacock guarding the heaven within its mouth. He told lies to cheat the peacock and the snake. He told them, "I have found a herb on earth which will make a person indestructible forever. If you also get it, you too can live forever. It is available within heaven also. If you take me inside heaven, I will take that herb and give it to you." By speaking to them thus, he deceived them.

Since the snake carried satan inside its mouth, the treachery and envy of satan became the poison and the poisonous fangs inside the mouth of the snake. Since Adam and Eve were led astray by satan, they were also thrown out of heaven along with the peacock and the snake. God removed the one thousand legs of the snake and the exquisite scents coming from its body. God told the snake, "From today, Adam's children will be your enemies. You will be their enemy. Wherever they see your progeny, they will kill them. You will move on your belly and eat dust and drink the air and live in holes." The evil nature, envy, and treachery of satan became the poison in the snake. When the poisonous snake bites man, he will die.

In the same manner, man also has sixteen poisonous teeth. In a way, man also has four poisonous fangs—treachery, envy, anger, and egoism. Each of these teeth has seventy thousand types of poison. If a man bites a person with these poisonous fangs, he may die. Just as in the beginning the snake had the characteristics and scents of flowers, in the beginning man had Divine

247

Characteristics and the scent of Divine Grace so much so that his glory was sung by the eighteen thousand outer worlds and the four hundred billion inner worlds. Just as the snake lost its original characteristics, man also lost his original Divine Characteristics and Divine Grace as a result of treachery, envy, anger, and egoism. One is a snake that moves on its belly. The other is a snake that walks with its legs.

When a snake comes to bite, if one boldly kicks its body, its poison will enter its own body and kill it. Also, when it thunders the snake dies because the poison gets absorbed in its body as a result of the shock. In the same manner, if the human snakes try to do harm with their poisonous characteristics to men and women of noble character, chaste women, men of Divine Luminous Wisdom, and those who have overcome the forces of nature, these human snakes will die as a result of the effect of their poisonous nature on themselves when the Radiance and the Resonance of Divine Wisdom comes into contact with them.

Human beings should avoid these poisonous characteristics. Just as the snake in the beginning had the scents of flowers emanating from its body, we have the scent of Divine Grace. If we adopt God's Characteristics to preserve within us the scent of Divine Grace, we need not be afraid of the poison of snakes which crawl on their belly nor of the poison of the human snakes. These poisons cannot do any harm to us.

SECTION III

LETTERS OF THE
GURU'S CHILDREN

Beauty was not beautiful
All love soon tired
Movement became motionless
as every action—every breath
pleaded in a darkness with no bounds
Hidden by confusion my heart waited
its wakefulness soon wearied
by the world's confrontation
When the birth of direction cried
the true meaning was found
Blessed with a beginning
that has no end
Life with my Father
towards heavenly ground.

Carol Bogosian
1 Ponalyn Lane
Berwyn, Pennsylvania

* * *

I can't remember not believing in God, but I certainly was not searching for Him. Coming from a sheltered Christian southern background, I had never heard of most things, and certainly had never heard the word "Guru". Of these things, I also had no intellectual knowledge, whatsoever. So what happened was both self-revealing—and in the light of my former life, totally inexplicable.

Life here in the world was always an unhappiness. As I grew older and saw more, life became worse instead of better, mostly due to an innate and incredible lack of judgement. There was always present a feeling of separation, of loneliness, that caused pain. It never ceased. But I never connected this feeling with God. I thought it was due to lack of love from the world.

It was in this setting, that, one day when I was twenty-three—and I still don't know why, the most incredible thing happened. I was alone, standing still in a detached mood. Things became visually very clear. Then everything seemed to be made up of dark colored dots, all in silence. Then it all disappeared. Everything. No sight, no sound, no smell, no touch, no body, nothing. Then through another kind of sight, seen as if looking at a movie, scenes appeared. It turned out that whatever was wished to be seen could be seen. Things in back of me, things miles away, whatever occurred to one to see, appeared.

At some point, there began an awareness of a "silent" voice explaining what was taking place. As the voice spoke, whatever it said became actuality. If it said something, that was what existed at that moment. Nothing else was, except the voice and the state that it explained. It was speaking very quickly, and many things simply can not be remembered.

But this much was very clear. It said: "There is no time or space. They are One." And then—they were. Then it said,
"THERE IS ONLY ONE"
What came with this statement simply cannot be described. It is not of

language or concepts. All took place on an experiential level. Only this can be said about it:

There is One Thing, with all Knowledge, Who is Perfection, Who has the quality of Absolute Love, with a Compassion beyond earthly conception, with a Wisdom capable of creating and sustaining every existing thing that there is in all the universe. It has no form whatsoever, yet all forms come from it. It is all there is, nothing else exists. This world we live in is a total lie. It can disappear in a split of a second, if this One does not cause it to be here. It is not possible to describe this One.

To live on this earth without knowing this Presence is to be in a prison that causes anguish; it is death and it is hell. Nothing else is Beautiful, nothing else is satisfying, nothing else can give Peace. Nothing else can give Love. The voice said one more thing. After "THERE IS ONLY ONE", came "AND I AM THAT". After that nothing is remembered. The next thing "I" knew, I was again aware of the world of form and was filled with an intoxication of immense joy.

As time went by it became covered over by the problems the world and ourselves give us. But from that moment on, something inside cried, "Please come! Please come!" After that the world was a very empty place. I still did stupid things. I still do. And I knew that I did not understand what had been experienced, but I did at some point realize that I had to find my Guru. I cried for release and I cried for my Guru.

The quality of that One is Compassion. After eight years, my Guru came. In the same way that That One cannot be described, He cannot either. He is the Same. The only "difference" is that He appears to have a form (But I remember what can happen to form). He is That. It is His Own. It is His Love. He has come from that One because we needed Him, because He *is* Love, is Compassion. The Trust His coming fulfills is what He is.

Since the time that I have spent with the Guru, I have noticed that the arrogance that was in me is lessening day by day. The quality of my life has improved greatly. Many burdens have been taken from me. Still, to an extent, this ego, with its myriad evil qualities, separates me from Him and causes pain. I pray that in the Light of His Infinite Wisdom and Love that I can get out of the limitations and confinement of my present form, and that the senses and the mind and desire will go and there will only be the Beauty He is, the Love He is, the One He is.

There is One thing that is the Truth. There is One God. And everything that happens by His Will is Perfect. The Wisdom of His Loving, Perfect, Complete, Compassionate Grace is the Limitless Wealth. That Wisdom is the Love of God, His most generous Wealth to souls and lives. I see in Him those characteristics, that Love and that Perfection. He is the Meignana Guru. I had had written contact with Him for two years and have now been directly with Him for six months.

I have seen in Him the Beauties that I had expressed previously and the problems of my mind continue to be alleviated. I pray that all my brothers and sisters should similarly seek and find the True Guru and obtain clarity. There are many, many gurus in the world, but what is best is to find the True Guru. May God protect and sustain all of us.

Ameen
Carolyn (secretary)

250

We wrote to a Guru and then he came.
Who is this Guru? Guru Bawa is his name.
After seeing this prince of a Human at first sight,
A peace came over all, in his path,
With the smile of father angel covering his face.
He took us into his heart, and all my brothers
and sisters that came after, he put in the same
place.

Being with him day after day, and the love
in his heart, a voice that gladdens our very souls,
with eyes that "God" had given in the very best
of care.

Look at a baby you'll see the same there.
With wisdom so deep and yet so profound
even children listen and hang onto each sound.
Taking from the four religions the truth and the
good of them all
How do I know? Well I have been in three
and my brothers and sisters more, yet we
sit at his feet his Love in us all, and for the
first time we know what a family is for.
With a father like ours only the scriptures
can tell a wee bit about, but
Because of Man's ego interference, Man
has kept the truth out

Do we love our father?
Just ask any one of his children, then look
into their smiles.
        You'll see! You will see his Love, com-
passion, and an air of delight, a smile greater
than joy. The fact is it can not be explained.
        Yet with our father you are unable to
get too far out of line, even in your most
secret place, he will know and if you but look
you will see his face
        If you are right our father will smile
but if you wrong he will look at you straight
then the feeling of guilt will fill your heart,
Then our father will explain wisdom to you, then
give you a new start.
With compassion as big as his ocean of love
with understanding larger than the universe, you
are welcomed in his heart as you were at first
        Is our father a prophet? we feel his is
much greater than that.
Yet he said he is nothing. Only "God" is greater
than that
What is his name? you may ask

Guru Bawa is the name his children call
with the deepest love, honor, and respect, but
feel in our hearts his name is far greater than
that.
What does our father teach us?
about "God"; there is nothing more
and how to reach him; that's what this life is for
Not like pie in the sky or something after death
our father saved me from death, when angel Israel
came.
Our father tells how to save the soul and this is
our goal.
Many questions are asked, some by professors, some
by fools,
yet unlettered is he, answers them all; some with
his voice and sometimes in your heart.
The words may come from the prophets beyond,
but you'll get the answer
This you may rest assured

To make us MAN "God" is our father's duty
on earth. We are trying, striving, working at it
each day. Our father keeps close check that we
don't go astray.
If we are sick our father is our doctor, too.
His name just has to be much more than Guru
Mohammed, Jesus, Moses and Gabriel our
father knows well, Adam and Noah, Abraham too
and many more—each and all of them answer his
call
His children bear witness to this and much more.
Our father came to this land and only a few knew he
came, but this is the way a "true son of 'God' "
came
OH yes in time man's ego will distort the words
as only man can.
But "God" smiled on us—we get them first hand
One of the beautiful things about truth
it stands on its own.
If I am so small that behind a crumb
a million ants can't find
I will still be much too big to see "God"
this life Time
Because of so many brothers and sisters, we
can never say, "He's mine.",
this is just a little about our father, a gnana Guru
All praise be to God our father
for our father, the Gnana Guru

"Kjaja 'Muhaiyadeen'
(Robert F. Demby)

our father does not keep anything, he even gave
me his name

I had gone through a very unhappy childhood and on to being a young woman, and still I was having a very difficult time. The many illnesses that overtook my body caused me much suffering and pain. Much of my young adult life was spent in and out of one hospital or another. Expenses became great and still I was not well.

My parents and guardians stressing to me in my childhood a teaching religious background, I turned to the church for help in hope that I would learn spiritual teachings. I wanted to find God, for I felt that the answer was there in the finding and knowing of God. Instead of finding out where God is I learned more about the world. In the church I did not find spiritualism. What I found was Socialism, Politics and Religion. The church ran the whole gamut of the world. This became an addition, I then had not only physical illness but also the mental anguish.

I left the place, the city of my birth, and came to Philadelphia. I brought with me all my despair. Thinking that I could break my ties with friends and family, I wanted to start a new life. In my childhood, I spent many vacationing times with my grandfather, and he would tell me about having a spiritual life. Remembering the things that my grandfather said to me when I was nine years of age, I longed for a spiritual teacher, a true spiritual Guru.

In my ignorance and desperation it was then I tried to pray, pleading to God for help. No one I knew or met tried to aid me in any way. It was then that I met Robert Demby and became his wife. That was the year of 1960. We sat before our Guru as He explained my past and I understood. Our Guru knew me then but I knew Him not, and how can I say who He is. I only know that my prayer was answered.

Not knowing at the time that I had been joined in marriage by our Guru, not knowing that I had a Guru I continued my search for a spiritual teacher. My husband enrolled me in a number of schools so that I might learn. I put much effort in my studies. I studied Yoga, Metaphysics, Occultism and Hypnosis. My life became a daily ritual.

I then became an instructor of Yoga classes and instructed hundreds and hundreds of people in a period of six years. I had been well trained in Hatha, Raja, Gnana, Bhakti, etc., and was being a successful teacher, yet I still longed for a true Guru.

Three years ago another Guru came to Philadelphia and I became his follower. I thought surely I will become egoless now, go to God and Converse with Him. This did not take place. This Guru could not teach me how to be egoless nor was he in a state of being egoless. This Guru lived in our home with as many of his followers as he chose to bring with him, as he collected people along the way. This Guru initiated and gave me a mantra to chant. I still could not rid myself of the evil qualities within that every person carries from the influence of the five elements. One day the one who was my so-called Guru at the time, requested of me two knives and he took them with him to a graveyard and performed a ritual. When he returned, giving back to me those two knives, I placed them in the room that had been set aside as a shrine where we could go to worship. This room had been decorated with Buddha statues and things of similar nature.

My mind became very strong and powerful and I performed in ways that I **could not** explain nor **understand**. Somehow my thoughts of God were still there and I felt as though something was wrong. It was not power that I was after. I wanted to merge with God. I continued constant chanting of the mantra that I had been given and more and more power came.

Once more unhappiness crept back into my life. Still following my daily ritual I'd go to that room I called a shrine. Attempting to meditate I soared through space; the universe. Flying higher and higher than ever before, yet I could not sever those magnetic forces that kept me from going and merging with God. I sat there totally flustered and cried, tears would come from my eyes and there would be sobs that would shake my whole body. I'd hear the words that came from my mouth. The sound ringing out saying My God, My God, help me.

I had been used, I had become possessed. Those knives had been used to cut up the bodies of graveyard corpses. I had been possessed by demonic spirits and my so-called Guru. My mind grew stronger and as power increased my physical body became weaker and weaker. Each day I lived in fear that my life would end and I had not gone to Him, "He" our God. (One "God")—ALLAH—

Oct. 11, 1971

The arrival of our Guru: He had come in the person of His Holiness Muhammad Muhaiyaddeen Guru Bawa.

We waited at the exit door of International Customs incoming flights of the B.O.A.C. airlines, Philadelphia International Airport. Some traveller asked me if someone special, some very important person was coming. We were all waiting with garlands and other floral arrangements. There were moving cameras in readiness for pictures. My reply: Yes! Our Guru. Guru Bawa! As He entered a peacefulness filled the place. I could hear the voice of onlookers say: Who is He?, Who is He? It is now April of 1972 and people are still saying, Who is He?

I write this meaning no disrespect to Our Guru.

A confrontation with His Holiness Guru Bawa.

Guru Bawa drove out of my body those evil spirits and my so-called Guru. My body was weak. The heart was slowly failing me, it was threatening to stop. The kidneys would not function properly, the spleen enlarged and bile was constantly spilling over into the stomach. I could not eat and my bones were deteriorating. His Holiness viewed my case and saw all that had taken place. He told me all that had happened and I knew it was true. I knew, because it happened to me.

The days that followed, His Holiness proceeded to remove the demons from me. Though I wanted to be rid of those demonic forces my ego struggled to hang on.

I sat there in total desperation, feeling that my questions were being misconstrued. The words that came from my mouth were translated and directed back at me. They came to my ears and fell on my face like the blows of a thousand fists, that carried the sting of being hit with a thousand weights. Ringing out in my head were thoughts. I was quite aware. Like a bomb that had exploded in my mind, I could only think how can this be: it seemed like to me, that in a split second that my Guru had mitigated His abode. The kind face I had seen changed and the warm brown eyes that I thought I was learning to know seemed to gleam down on me like a burning blazing flame. My mind and body just sat there feeling like a seared and crumpling mass that any minute would be an ash. I got a feeling that He could destroy my entire state of being. The thought that came to my mind was like the loudest of speaking voices I could imagine, that said My God! What is this. What is going on. Till this day I have not completely recovered from that awesome experience. He freed me from the giant of satanic forces.

Even now as my body is still recovering from its physical damage. Guru Bawa, The unselfish One, The Selfless One suffers my fatigue and my pain. With a kind look, a loving heart He caresses my cheek with His healing hands and says Pula (child) you rest, eat and become strong.

      All Thanks to God.
    Guru Bawa will not accept any
    thank you from me.
    We still ask, Who is He?
    Who is He?
  Little by little
His Holiness lets me merge with him
as he goes to converse with God.
    Fraction of a Fraction
    He lets me see.
He purifies my heart to take me to Thee
    Yet we ask, Who is He?
    Who is He?
      In as much as Guru Bawa spreads God's
      message for free, without a paid fee
      He also passed this name on to me.

"Khadiijra"
Virginia Gibbs Demby
328 S. 45th Street
Philadelphia, Penna.
19104

Down through the annals of time, mankind has sought to explain and understand the mysteries of the Universe, God and himself. In awe, with wonder, man seeks to unravel the knots which encase his questions. He wants to be *vis-a-vis* (face to face) with the answers. Oh! to Know, with Wisdom, the Truth to questions such as: From Whence did man originate? Who is Man? Where is man going? Thus, the following words, which are now being imprinted on paper, are made in Faith, with certain Beliefs and Convictions.

The mystery behind the Universe, since the beginningless beginning, is none other than God. Man originated from God. Therefore, man is in God and God is in man. The Soul is the Essence of God in man. Man has the capacity, during this lifetime, to return to God, from Whence he originated, if he so chooses. This is what Life is all about and this is what man must be about, i.e., returning to God.

The one, who is the author of this book, *The Divine Luminous Wisdom that Dispels the Darkness,* God-Man: Man-God, is: One who is about God's Mission; One who discourses and expounds on such questions; One who speaks and lives Truth; One who possesses Wisdom; One who Knows from Whence he originated; One who Knows who he is and One who knows God.

This one is Shaikh Muhaiyadeen, Guru Bawa. He has come to Philadelphia, from Ceylon, and is now dwelling among us and sharing with us. However, as a 'seeker' after Truth, who has been in his physical presence since November of 1971, words seem completely inadequate to express the deep inner feelings of the heart. There is certainly present within the inner recesses of this 'seeker's' heart an abundance of Gratitude and Thanksgiving for the opportunity of this meaningful experience. One is also indebted to the translators who are so willing to share their time and talents.

As a Westerner one is greatly tempted to want to evaluate and analyse one's stage of consciousness and spiritual advancement. But, one knows to do this is to continue to play the games of the mind and intellect and desire and illusion. Thus, for one on the spiritual pilgrimage, who does not possess Wisdom within Wisdom, there is no yardstick with which to judge or measure one's level. The important issue does not seem to be where one is, but rather, where one is headed. To assess would only tend to depress one and cause one to lose Faith and look elsewhere for an easier and shorter way, though one knows there is no easy way, or else to falsely build the ego, which must be lost in order to 'arrive'. Since the potential to 'arrive' is internal, it becomes a matter of externalizing the internal that is Eternal. The Light on the Path which Bawa, the Compassionate Father, has provided has been appreciated and accepted with awe and in gratitude.

One of the meaningful experiences during this time with Bawa, for this 'seeker', has been that of the recognition of the importance and value of being in the physical presence of a True Guru, a Teacher of Truth and Wisdom, and a Compassionate Guide.

He, as a Guru who dispels the darkness fulfills for those in his presence a triple role, i.e., as Teacher, as Prophetic Preacher and as a Pastor (Healer). In his illustrations, which he so aptly expounds, he is able to capture the needs of those present and Teaches in the style of oral tradition. Through his discourses, which he so eloquently delivers, he Prophetically

Preaches the Word with Fervor, Conviction and Authority. In personal situations, he Ministers to the vast spectrum of the needs of individuals in a Pastoral way, showing forth his bounty of Love, Compassion and Understanding. He teaches the Words of Divine Truth and Wisdom. He speaks the Words of Divine Truth and Wisdom. He lives the Words of Divine Truth and Wisdom. Because he knows Divine Luminous Wisdom, he radiates it to all who enter his presence.

A second meaningful experience during this time with Bawa, for this 'seeker', has been the stark and constant confrontation with the Reality of those things which must be 'rooted' out of one's life. In their place must be 'nurtured' the Divine Qualities, Attributes, Virtures and Truths of God, which must transform and shine in Radiant Splendor in one's life. It is so easy and natural for one to become a slave to one's physical senses.

One gets caught and engulfed in the fire of the 'triple-flame' of egoism, evil actions and illusion. One tends to value everything only in reference to one's own selfish interest. One builds up one's self importance and becomes arrogant, conceited and proud. The things which one knows one should not do, one falls prey to doing. One loses sight of the Real, deceives one's self with false impressions, images and visions, all for the sake of one's own glorification and self preservation.

Every association with Bawa causes this 'seeker' to come face to face with those evil characteristics, desires and defense mechanisms that must be totally 'rooted' up, sacrificed and burned at the Altar of God's Grace, Love and Compassion. The desires of the flesh and mind must pass, though the process is often slow.

All doubts, disbelief and lack of commitment must unquestionably give way, in Absolute Surrender, to Unswerving Faith, Belief, Conviction, Certitude and Determination that the Only Reality in the Universe is God. All hatred, enmity, malice, animosity and hostility shown to God's created beings must be dissolved by Love and Harmony. All hastiness, impatience, quickness of temper, jealousy, suspicion, covetousness and condemnation exemplified in one's life must be overcome by Patience, Trust, Tolerance and Forgiveness. All agitation, anger, resentment, violence, indulgence and anxiety must be overthrown by Calmness, Peacefulness, Self-Control, Forbearance and Tranquility. All cruelty, harshness, brutality, relentlessness and vengeance must be negated by Compassion, Pity, Charity, Kindness and Mercy. All traces of ego, pride, vanity, arrogance and selfishness must be devoured by Humility and Selflessness. All injustice, unfairness and falsehood must be overpowered by Justice and Truthfulness.

To show Love and Compassionate concern to those who persecute, abuse, assault, injure, torture and hurt one can only be done with the assistance of the Grace of God. It is God's Wisdom that comes to fruition in one's Soul that releases us from the bondage of darkness and ignorance.

To be in the presence of Bawa, whose very being manifests these virtues, one so desperately needs, is in itself a humiliating and penetrating experience.

A third meaningful experience during this time with Bawa, for this 'seeker', has been the challenge of attempting the discipline of sitting in silence and patiently listening. One has endless questions one would like to ask Bawa. However, from this experience one slowly comes to see a little more clearly, though still 'through a glass, darkly', the folly of the academic game of endlessly raising questions. For this listening in silence and reflecting is beyond words and their multi-meanings. It is rather a time for inward cleansing and understanding when one attempts to atune the Soul to the vibrations of Wisdom, Peace and Harmony of the Universal Soul.

The silence seems to prepare one for the absorption of Grace, the purification of the Soul and the cessation of human desires so that the Light of the Soul might appear. The time spent reflecting seems to 'silently whisper' to one that the 'pent-up' possibilities of the deeper capacities of the Soul can be set free when Divine Luminous Wisdom is allowed to escape the darkened veil of self to 'The Self'.

This 'seeker' is constantly aware of being confronted by mistakes, shortcomings and the endless cycle of falling away from the Good that one has been taught. But, also present, is the expectation of someday actions being in Harmony with Words and Truths. There is difficulty in the attainment of the goal of Spiritual Liberation. However, this 'seeker' is very appreciative of the encouragement Bawa provides to continue the pilgrimage. May what has been learned and experienced someday burn out that which must be removed so that one may express in the life one lives the Gratitude and Thanksgiving that is present in the heart because of these experiences and many others.

Thank you, Bawa: for quickening my sleeping soul; for arousing and softening my heart from its state of slumber; for helping to pluck out and destroy life's weeds; for assisting in planting and watering the dry places; for seeking to illuminate the darkened spots; and for patiently waiting, teaching and being. For Truly,

"The Light that shows us our sins
is the Light that heals us."

A 'seeker' after Truth
Elizabeth W. Fenske
3310 Baring Street
Philadelphia, Penna.
19104

* * *

For most people in the world life is a process of continuous flux and change. We see and experience life from different vantage points. Even to see a rose from different perspectives will give one different pictures of that rose. And our inner feelings and awareness cause us to respond differently to situations, to people and to ideas, depending on how we "feel". But deep inside of us there is an urging which pushes us to explore that we might find "firm and unchanging ground" on which to stand. We carry on our explorations in such a way that we are taken to hundreds of places to sample feelings, ideas, relationships, etc. We visit many places; we experience through our senses and mind a fantastic array of sights, sounds, feels, smells and tastes. None of these experiences is really the experience that satisfies. None of them brings us to that solid and unchanging ground for which we are looking. These experiences only incite us to ask for more and more.

Within, one knows that this is not the answer. Within, there is the still small voice that, on occasion, breaks through the sounds and the activity of the earthquake, wind and fire. It is a voice which can only speak when there is quiet for it speaks from the Soul. For a moment one listens and then the bombardment from the worlds of sense and ego obliterate the voice. But—there has been the experience of hearing the voice. And that can not be taken away. It is a voice that gives assurance that all things are not passing, that there is stability, that Love is indeed more potent than hate, that Trust is stronger than fear, that there is Bread for life which takes away the hunger and longing of the Soul. It is the voice which tells us what life is really all about. It is the voice which brings healing and wholeness to lives that are torn and broken.

I ask myself why can I not experience that PRESENCE with great frequency and intensity. I question why must life be as a great sage once said, "For now we see in a mirror darkly, but then face to face. Now I know in part, then I shall understand fully." And the small voice reminds me that I cannot accept more than I can carry. I must learn to be patient. But patience is difficult. It is painful. For in waiting and in being tempered I am again and again distracted by the things of this world and by an imagination which is like some wild, untrained creature. Again and again, I experience that emptiness—that "dark night of the Soul." It is my fault, for in my impatience I flee from Him—who is the "Rock of my Soul." It is I who flees from MY GOD, my Lord, and my Father. What I forget is that I can not escape from Him, for where I go He goes with me. He is always nearer to me than my very self. And yet, I keep forgetting it.

Through all this experience of moving along the pathways of life with its anxieties, its failures, its heartaches, there is assurance in the words of Jesus, the Christ, "Ask, and it will be given you; seek and you will find it; knock and it will be opened to you." There is an orderly plan in the universe. One aspect of it is that what a man asks for in Faith, this he will receive. There are many today who fervently ask our God to come and show them a pathway through the maze of this world.

There was such a group who cried out from Philadelphia, that city called out to be the "City of Brotherly Love". In response to that cry, God responded. Bawa came to dwell among us. He came to teach us and to minister to our needs in this time of great uncertainty. Through his sensitivity, his love, his understanding, his giving and sharing of himself we have been awakened, supported, strengthened, directed and redirected in our pilgrimages. Bawa has been and is truly a father to his children. Through his imparting of Love and Grace to us, we are experiencing a change in our lives. This time it is not the feeling that change is all about us and that there is no solid ground on which we can stand. Rather, Bawa is helping us to find in ourselves, in our Souls, that solid ground which is nearer to us than our very selves. Little by little we are changing in a way that we are more sure of that Reality. Little by little Bawa is helping us to know that aspect of God which dwells within every Human Heart.

For his coming, we offer the only words we can,
LET US REJOICE AND THANK GOD!!!

Paul Fenske
3310 Baring Street
Philadelphia, Penna.
19104

April 10, 1972

For as long as I can remember I looked for a way to find God. I went to Churches, but He wasn't there. I read books and studied yoga, I walked in the woods and stood on mountain tops, still I did not see Him. I asked the wise men and teachers I met if they knew God, but by their actions, I knew they hadn't found Him either. I received "Knowledge" from a Guru, who I thought might know Him, but he only showed me that I must continue my search.

On January 6, 1972, two friends and I were invited to come and listen to a discourse given by His Holiness Shaikh Muhaiyadeen Guru Bawa, and there my search ended. I had at last come into the Presence of that Radiant Light of Wisdom, the Perfect Guru, One who Truly Knew God, One who was for me the Living Example of the Perfect Father, the Perfect Human Being. He had come to Philadelphia from Ceylon to teach my Brothers and Sisters and me how to develop the Wisdom within each one of us to become True Human Beings and to become One with God.

How fortunate I am to sit at the Feet of this Perfection called Guru Bawa and learn from Him all the wonderful Truths He has to Teach. I know Beauty by His Beauty and music by the sound of His voice. He teaches me Love by Loving. He teaches me Compassion by His Compassion to all Beings, regardless of races or religions. My Father teaches me Patience by His Patience with us, and Honesty by His Honesty. I learn Tolerance by His Tolerance and Kindness by His Kindness. My Father Guru Bawa teaches me to be respectful to others and not Judge them, no matter what I think, because I can't know their hearts, only God can. He teaches that it is I who must correct and restrain myself, I who must be dutiful, I who must be without anger and prejudices, without doubt and suspicion, I who must have the Faith and Forbearance, Determination and Certitude if I am to see God. All these Truths, my Father, Guru Bawa, teaches me.

He has given me life and sight. He has brought me a peace unlike any I had ever experienced before. He has given me food unlike any I had ever tasted before in the form of Divine Wisdom. I want only to be able to live in that Wisdom and have all of those Divine Qualities that are God's so I can become One with God.

I pray that with Your help, my Father I many develop those qualities and become that True Human Being.

Most Respectfully,
Your Loving and Grateful Child

Jean Gilbert
702 Pine Street
Philadelphia, Pennsylvania 19106

Imagine, if you will, a child who has been born blind. No one has ever placed a flower in his hand. So he has never seen, smelled, touched nor even tasted a flower.

Now imagine that a few kindly friends read some of the finest poems about flowers to the child. Others patiently explain the meaning of the poems in great detail. Some, with a more scientific background, fill the child with every botanical detail known about these specimens of nature.

With all of this, how much does the child know about the true nature of flowers? This is how much I knew about the true nature of the human being and his relationship to God prior to meeting His Holiness, Guru Bawa.

Oh, the great and religious fervor of the poets, scholars and philosophers and the patient explanations of pious teachers and earnest scientists enabled me to imagine all sorts of things about man and God. Finally, though, I despaired of finding God in words. They simply would not lead me to the direct experience of God.

So I began a search that I hoped would lead me to that experience. I looked for God in nature itself. More than ever, I became filled with a hunger to find He who had created all that I saw. One brisk morning, standing on a rock and watching the sun rise over the Atlantic Ocean, my consciousness swelled. I could feel the sun hurtling through space and the planet earth revolving. If such a wonderful thing could happen, truly, this must be the way to find God. So, religiously, I continued to watch sunrises and sunsets and observe all growing things. I had many beautiful experiences. I learned much. But I never found God.

I am too conscious of self, I thought. I reasoned that since the closest I had come to an abandonment of self was in sexual union, perhaps that was the way. So I sought help to overcome any of my emotional distortions about sex. I learned the arts of physical love making. I studied biology, psychology and bio-energetics. I studied Tantra Yoga. And, indeed, my sexual experiences grew in intensity. But I did not find God.

I experimented with drugs. And in drug induced states, I gave up my attachments—even the attachment to my body. I had what I believed were truly mystical experiences. But when the drug wore off, my attachments returned—and I had not found God.

So I practiced Yoga and studied Zen. I meditated morning and night. I sought and received what was called "knowledge" from a so-called "perfect master". I saw what I was told was the light of God and heard what I was told was the sound of His Universal Presence. And, for a while, I believed. I thought of God and talked of God constantly.

But somewhere, inside, there was a gnawing doubt. I wondered if I still was only imagining God? Could this new awareness be some kind of magic—an esoteric part of nature beyond previous experience—but not God Himself? Could I hope for no more than a light and sound show—perhaps, like the rest of nature, produced by God—but not the direct experience of the Divine Producer?

My spiritual thirst was not quenched. It had been hinted—even promised—in all that I had studied and experienced, that a more direct contact/merger/union with God was possible.

I was no longer satisfied to see the shadows of God, hear the echoes of His sound or feel His presence outside of myself. I was like a hungry man who had been given a taste of food but had been unable to swallow. All that I had experienced only intensified my hunger to know God.

But by this time, I was beginning to realise two things. First, if God is in all of nature—both obvious and esoteric—He is certainly within the human being. So the best way to experience God must be to experience Him within myself.

But I also realised that if I was ever to find God within this ocean of intellect, desire and ego with which I identified, I would need an expert guide. I would need the help of one who had gone completely beyond intellect, desire, ego, or even inspired imagination. I would need the help of one who did not depend on the magic of sunrises, sex, drugs or powerful meditations.

I sought the help of one for whom union with God was as effortless as the union of an unborn child with its mother. For such a person, God would be his thought before he thought, his words before he spoke, his actions before he moved.

Not surprisingly, I despaired of ever finding such a teacher. Then I met His Holiness, Guru Bawa. And, little by little, as I sat at his feet and listened to him speak and gazed at his beauty, I began to understand the nature of the inner search for God.

The Light of God I seek is not the light I can see with my eyes—open or closed. It is the light that emanates from me. It is the light that God placed in me and every human being as the birthright of the human being. It is the light I was burying under all my intellectual knowledge and the magic of my sensational experiences. It is that light which, because it is without shadow or form, is the only way to merge with the shadowless, formless, effulgent Light of God.

I began to understand—just a little—the real meaning of the words, "If I am here, God is not. If God is here, I am not."

Most important, because I had found a true Guru, one who truly performed God's work, I gained three invaluable tools to aid me in my search.

Now, through the living example of Guru Bawa, I have absolute Faith that God exists.

Through the experience of myself, inspired by His Holiness, I have absolute Certainty that God exists within me.

Finally, through the Grace of the gifts of Faith and Certitude, I have gained an indestructible Determination to merge with God.

At last my true search has begun. And the time it will take is no longer relevant. Because the major victory has already been won. Doubt and despair have been destroyed.

This book contains grains of the power that destroyed my doubt and despair. They are the words of Guru Bawa—answers to questions put to him by some of his thousands of children.

But the original power was more than words. The original power contained his love which is the manifestation of Divine Love. The original power contained his Grace which is a manifestation of Divine Grace. The original power contained his wisdom to see into the heart of the particular child who asked each question.

Still, the wisdom of Guru Bawa is a manifestation of the Divine Wisdom. And it is Guru Bawa who asked, in his wisdom, that this book be

262

published for all of those children who have not yet had the opportunity to sit at his feet. In his wisdom, he has asked that this book be published for all of those who came to him with full cups and, therefore, were unable to hold his gifts in their too full containers.

So this book in his gift. And within it, I am sure, is God's prayer that you begin the search that will return you to Him. If, as you read it, you can empty yourself of intellectual theories, binding attachments to the desires of the world and unyielding identification with the magic of sensation, then it will be a gift you can not only taste, but swallow.

I am impelled, therefore, to share with you, that gift of insight His Holiness, Guru Bawa, shares with every child who comes to him.

La i la ha: nothing is real but God.
Il a la hu: only God is God.

Mitch Gilbert
209 S. Catherine Street
Philadelphia, Penna. 19147

*   *   *

Guru Bawa

His Holiness, is old and wise but yet,
young and childlike. He speaks the truth
and his love flows with understanding.

He dispels the darkness with his luminous wisdom
and lightens my heart. He makes me feel holy
and peaceful.

I thank almighty GOD for blessing me
with his Divine Messenger.

Joe Golden

*   *   *

I wasn't looking for a guru, but that ineffable something which resides deep within me, deeper than the "I" can see, that something was restless and searching. That searching, that insatiable drive was answered by Guru Bawa. It's funny; He lives so close by and yet I just discovered he was there.

Barbara Goodman

263

Praise to Allah and Guru Bawa Who are as close as the Light to Its Brightness

Words are referential; they are not the things themselves to which they refer. For this reason I feel at a loss to describe Who and Where Guru Bawa is. But to try means to say He is one with The One which is everywhere and no where (now here) which is beyond form and formless and which is within each of us as a doorway to Itself. Guru Bawa is also that doorway.

I have attempted to find The Source through various forms of ego annihilation. Whether it's been communal living, music (the metaphor that fools), sex (the ego destroyer that destroys to feed itself) on and on . . . I have found that instead of gaining liberation I have gained attachment to new forms. I haven't given up these activities, but have learned their nature and place.

Probably the best of these dangerously entrapping forms has been political involvement, for it can include a love of that which holds us as one family. For me, it also included a rage against those material forces and desires which separate and oppress parts of our family.

One cannot reach Knowledge, Everyman, God-Man carrying any baggage of rage. One cannot reach Mt. Meru's summit carrying any baggage at all.

This includes the baggage of the mind. Drugs like LSD and grass spun me into beautiful adventures and movies in my mind that only showed me my own mind. "So what. Yeah, that too." Many times they gave me the experience of knowing without knowledge. Worse, they led me to associate higher states with physical stimulants.

The highest states don't even have physical correlates. This is something one can feel immediately in Guru Bawa's presence. His body is so obviously a metaphor for something beyond the physical it stuns.

To be with Guru Bawa one must be in the present. The closer one gets to Him the closer one gets to the Now. Moments of closeness are moments that move towards the experience of infinite time. He is totally Here and Now.

He is an image of the potentiality of man merging with God, Everything, The Present Formless Source (semantics, semantics!) that extends far beyond the mind's conceptual horizons. To merge with This requires unending love, love beyond the mind and the self, love beyond place and time. He is an image of that Love.

Somehow He has been a mirror for the worst in me. Desires, motivations and verbal muddleness which I had thought had disappeared years ago have now become clearly present and I can deal with them more squarely.

One cannot go too far to be with one who speaks Truth. Beware of those who garb themselves in spirituality, yoga, shmoga, and religions. When one speaks with Wisdom one does speak of God, even without mentioning His Name, for God is Truth.

There are many we can learn from, Guru Bawa teaches to look at all hearts equally and carefully with love; there are a few teachers of wisdom, consider yourself blessed if you meet one; there is only one Guru Bawa.

Jon Granoff

AHAM MUHAIYADEEN

I
was a larvae.
I
feasted on leaves.
l-e-a-f after l-e-a-f
tasting each one in sight
My body grew HUGE
also My APPETITE.

this larvae then saw a butterfly

gliding and soaring grace in the sky

spreading the essence in sun-light bliss
this larvae now seeks its chrysalis.

Dick Hayne
929 S. 46th Street
Philadelphia, Penna.
19143

*   *   *

Guru Bawa's presence in Philadelphia was made known to me by my
brother, when he invited me in January to visit him in order to meet a
Guru who never ate. I had just become conscious of a spiritual reality
through several books which I had read in the preceding months, and was
eager to meet a Guru with such powers, yet at first I was not impressed by
His Holiness. In Cambridge I had been working zealously in radical
politics, and was only interested in an intellectual approach to God, one
which I might synthesize with revolutionary economic, political, and social
theory. As Guru Bawa is extremely humble and informal in manner, and
would speak of (seemingly) simple parables rather than Eastern philosophy, I was unable to appreciate who He was, and found fault with those
concepts which I judged did not reflect omniscient wisdom.

My criticizing, despite my brother's counsel, continued during subsequent visits to interfere with my perception and understanding of the
Guru, and served to perpetuate my preconceived ideas and prevent the
revision of my beliefs. At the same time, however, I felt a strong desire to
return to Philadelphia whenever I was in Cambridge, and noted the
unfavorable contrast between my politically-active friends and the
lightness of the varied types of people at the Fellowship.

Then two remarkable instances occurred in March which helped resolve
my doubts and made me realize that my sole purpose should be to remain
with the Guru to incorporate His divine wisdom. One Thursday, I called
several people who would be driving to Philadelphia for the weekend, but
all of those rides were full and I was resigned to remaining in Cambridge

until the following week. The next morning, as I was hanging pictures of Guru Bawa in my apartment and recalling the pleasure of seeing Him, the phone rang. It was a call about one of the previously unavailable rides which was leaving in fifteen minutes, now with room for another passenger. It was also a ride in a private airplane. This coincidence recurred two weeks later when a friend invited me to go to a farm in Vermont for the weekend. As I had just returned from Philadelphia the day before and had not been to Vermont for more than a year, I agreed to go, and we were walking out to his car when the phone rang. It was a friend calling to tell me that she would be driving to Philadelphia the next day, although, as she told me later, she had not intended to call when she did.

It now seems impossible that despite daily proof of His Holiness, such as the ability to exist without food, knowledge available unrestricted by boundaries of space or past or future time, an egoless teaching transcending systems and affirming the unity in all creation, that I required a personal invitation to accept Him. Perhaps some who now think as I did may give up the vain attempt of organizing all knowledge within the mind, and will not wait for a personal experience before accepting Guru Bawa as One who knows God.

Roger Hayne
929 S. 46th Street
Philadelphia, Penna.
19143

136 Radnor Street
Bryn Mawr, Pennsylvania

April, 1972

A mystery has materialized in our midst here in Philadelphia known as His Holiness, Guru Bawa. In the few months that He has been with us, hundreds of people, each according to his needs, his faith, and his hopes, have experienced Him in a personal and unique way. He has come as the "Complete Physician" to dispel binding ignorance, to shatter the illusions which blind us, to heal our ills, both mental and physical, to end our enslavement to worldly ambitions and desires, and to join us as one family in the service of God. What has been accomplished towards these ends, including the preparation and publication of this book, in such a short time, surpasses all mortal understanding.

To be counted among the beneficiaries of this experience has meant more than ever this one heart could express. It is my fervent hope that all who read this book and these letters will begin to share with us this path of Wisdom so beautifully set before us by our unfathomable, loving Father, Guru Bawa.

Jeanne C. Hockenberry

* * *

After being in Guru Bawa's presence each day for about three weeks, I experienced a change, an awakening in me. I experienced God. Mohammed was beginning to read about man, listing the qualities of a true human being. I could feel these qualities within me.

As he read each one off I could feel them stronger within me until my body was trembling with each word. The words kept coming, reverberating inside me and tears were pouring from my eyes. I could feel happiness and purity inside me.

I looked around the room at the people assembled there and saw love on their faces.

My weeping intensified as the pains and joy of realizing the qualities of a true human wracked my body. Bawa reached out and comforted me and I kissed his hand.

As I began to settle down a ray of light entered the room and pierced my heart with a burning intensity. I felt as though a hole was being burned through my chest. I knew there was nothing stronger than that ray.

I felt my heart, my Guru felt his, I knew that he knew.

Charles Hurwitz
Secretary, Guru Bawa
Fellowship, U.S.A.

My parents are the cause that brought me to find the truth of Almighty Allah. They told me when I was a small child that Allah exists in every thing, in every place, every where. There is no place where He doesn't exist, even in my heart, even in me, in the whole universe. Through that teaching, I had a feeling to search for Allah.

Then onwards I was searching to find a true gnostic guru. I met many gurus and priests who came to my parents' house and lived with us. The question I asked them was, "Where is Allah? He is in me and in all; can you tell me and guide me in the right path?" Then they said to me, "Do your prayer and do the right thing and when you grow up, you will come to know." But I was not satisfied. From then onwards I even travelled to India in search of a true gnostic Guru and stayed three months in many parts of India: Nagoor, Madras, Bombay, Ajmir, Agra and Malabar; in all those places I went searching. And even in all those places I never saw a real gnostic guru to teach me the true Path of Allah.

Then I came to know a guru named Kirinda and I was learning with him for a few years, but still I was not satisfied. Still I did not get the answer to "Where is Allah and the truth?"

One day, one of my cousins telephoned me and asked me to come to his house saying, "There is a Holy Man at my place. Please come, as you were searching for a Holy Man." Then we all went at once to see Him. He was seated on a bed. All the others were seated around Him. I kissed His hand and gave salaams and sat among the others and we had a little discussion. We asked Him to come to our house and He accepted and said, "I will come to your house, my children." And His Holiness Guru Bawa came to our house. After that He used to give us spiritual guidance and teaching daily, and He would say, "The reason that I have come to teach the truth of Allah is your parents' wishes."

Then one day He told all of us that He was going to give us a prayer. When all of us went near Him, He gave us, one by one, the prayer, and blessed us. When He called me to bless me and give the prayer, I had a shivering and my heart vibrated and opened out, and I saw the Divine Light in Him. I was intoxicated. I cannot explain the delight; it cannot be expressed. Never have I had a feeling like I had that day when I saw the Divine Light in Him and knew that He was the real gnostic guru that I had been searching for.

From that time onwards I have surrendered my whole being. There is nothing existing in the eighteen thousand universes here and hereafter but Allah alone, and His Holiness is the gnostic guru to guide me to the right path. The teaching He has taught me for these eight years is in me and I can't express in writing what I have in my heart. This is the experience I have found out in my lifetime. I have surrendered to my Guru and become a servant to Him. His Holiness even gave me a name: Gnaniar (gnostic).

From your obedient,
selfless, disciple,

Gnaniar Noorul Kareema
74 Park Street
Colombo 2, Ceylon

There was no way for me to preconceive Guru Bawa or what he was to give me when I entered a humble row house on the night of January 18, 1972. It was a house devoid of anything of beauty in the material sense, but already for me there was a feeling of contentment in that place, and an appreciation of the qualities of goodness in many of the people who had come to hear Guru Bawa.

At the appointed time, he came down the steps smiling. His warmth and Beauty touched every one. His hands were clasped over his heart as he made his way to a wide chair, sat down and folded his legs under him in the graceful style of the Middle East. I felt my heart begin to beat rapidly. After some moments of supplication to God he began his discourse. While he was giving the awesome account of the interaction of God and man, great waves of heat were travelling from the base of my spine to my head and it seemed that the magnetic vibration might become too powerful. I was soaked with perspiration. Here at last, was someone who would help me weave the pieces of life's tapestry that I already had, into one great fabric. Bawa's Light would be the tool for the work.

So, as the chick inside the egg responds to the hen, I continued to respond to the vibration of Guru Bawa. And with the aid of his love and compassion and concentration, I chipped away at my shell in an effort to be with him and the truth.

Then one day at the end of March, it seemed to me that because of the nearness, every day, of those Divine characteristics embodied in Bawa, I finally understood the One from Whom I had come. With this realization the shell was gone, and the exquisite warmth of His Grace could be felt without obstacle. From all the work had come this perfect joy, knowing that goodness, kindness and understanding everywhere are God's gifts to us. And God is in His gift. That if I am loving to others and serve them, that there too, will be God's Light. And as I grow in this understanding, so, too, will God's Light grow. And this consciousness which is more real than anything else, came to me because of the presence of God's precious messenger, Guru Bawa.

From the depths of my joyful heart,

Sonia Leon Klein
1309 Andover Road
Philadelphia, Penna. 19151

*   *   *

He came,
i saw,
i understood.

Alan Kurlansky

My Brothers and Sisters,

It has been such a short time since I met my Guru Bawa in His physical form, but each time I am with Him I am reminded that many times in my life I have felt His presence and known His tender Love and Compassion.

My experiences have been small, but I have felt the boundless ocean of Love He has for all His children.

His Holiness teaches not only in words, but in His total Compassion and Understanding for all who come to Him.

He has taught us that God's Love for each one of us is eternal. No matter how often we forget Him He never for a moment forgets us. And if we would know God within us we must bring God within us by practicing His virtues. We must try to show His Love, His Patience, His Compassion and His Forgiveness to whomever we meet. He cannot exist outside of us. God is alive within each of us or we are dead to Him.

He teaches that the Wisdom of God, which is the soul, overcomes the ignorance of the mind and dispels the illusion of separateness.

I do not have the eyes to see nor the wisdom to know who Guru Bawa is. But when He speaks my heart is made light and His Wisdom flows as if from some eternal spring deep within His Heart. The nectar from the spring is cool and sweet. From this spring we, His children, take whatever measure we can carry and we drink slowly for we are young and weak.

His radiance lights a fire in our hearts and guides us through the darkness . . . . until we are home.

> He has taught us that God is everything
> There is nothing but God
> He is my Father — i am His child.

Kelly
3310 Baring Street
Philadelphia, Penna.
19104

* * *

I had come with a small vessel to measure
and analyze; and now find myself swimming in
the sweet sea of His Divine Grace.

John Love

When I was a child . . . . . Actually, I don't remember too much of it, kind of blocked out as a bad memory. Never seemed to be able to get along "socially" very well. Affinity for animals, "They'll accept you for what you are, respond to kindness, no talking, games, they don't care what you look like." School goes by in a blur. "Daydreaming" never quite understanding what was happening. "Church people and other people all around fighting and criticizing, nothing like the Christ they professed to follow, doing it for an occupation and didn't seem to know God at all. If God is in this church, if this is the way religious people are, prefer to ignore." Eventually to marijuana, hashish, 'tripping' scene-looking for something, nothing to lose. Friends, laughter, play, good times, turn to disillusionment, fear. Absurdity of it all very evident. All complete insanity. "Nothing is real, nothing matters, even love is just a game, people are as absurd as their surroundings." Then into yoga, meditation. Calm quiet people, no need to talk, try and forget yourself. Begin to become aware of 'something there'. People speaking of "God", contented, loving people. Turns to head games, "psychic phenomenom", astrology, magical swamis and more insanity. Then one night to see Guru Bawa. "I wonder what this swami is like, maybe he'll tell me about my past lives, or give me some new meditation technique . . . . . "

Very beautiful little man with sparkling eyes and shining face comes down the stairs. Feelings of real peace, love. He talks of "My God". Of being a true human being. Not philosophical concepts, He's speaking to you from the depths of his loving heart. Truth! Hearing the first real true things I'd ever heard, though it seemed I'd heard them all before. Left feeling light in head and warm in heart. Return soon. "Guru Bawa is the father of our souls", says someone. Yes, he truly is your father, you know it in your heart.

Love God, He'll take care of you. La-illaha-il-Allah-hu There is nothing but God, only God is real. Truth of this is becoming more real all the time. Learning how to become a good child to my most loving, kind, compassionate, wise, graceful father. How wonderful to recognize your original father and mother and be going home to be with them.

All thanks and praise to "Andavane"
for the love, understanding,
and many blessings he is forever
showering on all His children.

Lovi

It was eight years ago, deeply entrenched in a world I had created, a world I had believed was right, that I met His Holiness. The first meeting, the first glance when His Brilliant Eyes met my eyes, it annihilated the world I had created and the world I had always believed in. My whole destiny was changed. This was the beginning of a new world to me. This was the moment of annihilation of falsehood and the moment of appearance of The Reality. There was no turning back for me. My soul and my wisdom continues to bathe in The Reality and hopefully will continue in this state till it finally vanishes within The Reality. What is This Reality? This Reality is none other than "Guru Bawa" disguised in a human form.

Who is "Guru Bawa"? How can I ever know Him? What is His relationship to my soul and my wisdom? I have not found the answers to these questions. How can this limited 'I' ever find the answers? As much as how can I ever know the number of grains of sand on this earth or the drops of water that form the ocean. It is a futile quest to find out who "Guru Bawa" is. I may well ask who God is. Perhaps the answer lies there.

When I know what I am; What is my soul; What is my wisdom; What is God. And when I know the answers to these, still I am not sure whether I will ever know what "Guru Bawa" is. My wisdom proclaims He is the Primal Soul, He is the Awwal Qutb, He is the Nur Muhammed, He is Allah. He is all these Appelations. But what is the Primary Soul, What is the Awwal Qutb, What is Nur Muhammed, What is Allah, What are these Appelations?

All I know is "Guru Bawa" alone exists and none else exists. I do not exist. He alone exists and I exist in Him and He exists in me. This is all I know. And all I need know is He.

What I see with my external vision and perceive in my mind is the most beautiful of human forms, with a radiant countenance. I kneel in supplication before Him and pay my obeisance to Him.

What I see with my wisdom is the dazzling Nur of Wisdom, the Essence of The Truth, The Divine Knowledge, The Divine Grace, The Divine Beauty, The Divine Love and The Divine Compassion and the exuberant Divine Patience and Forbearance. I see no form. I see the formless.

Now Who is "Guru Bawa"? Is He what the eyes see and the mind perceives? or is He the Incomprehensible, the Inexplicable, the Incomparable, the all-Encompassing, The Creator, The Nourisher, The Sustainer and all that my Wisdom comprehends and much more!

I live unfortunately in this state of duality of mind and my wisdom. Who can remove this veil of duality? Who can annihilate my mind? Certainly not I. It has to be He, it has to be "Guru Bawa". When the veil of duality is torn asunder by the Beauty of His Grace, that will be the end of the 'I'. Then I am no more. I am He. I am "Guru Bawa", and what I see is He, what I feel is He, what I smell is He, what I speak is He, what I know is He. Everything is He. He is "Guru Bawa".

OH! How my heart yearns for this state of Unity! which was once mine and now temporarily separated.

His slave.
Ajwad Macan-Markar.
139 Turret Road
Colombo 7, Ceylon

Whatever I did or said my mind was not satisfied until I met His Holiness Guru Bawa who became my Sheikh and everything I valued most. This happened eight years ago. My heart was turbulent, discontented and constantly dissatisfied until the moment I saw my Guru and felt the impact of His Truth within the innermost sanctum of my heart. I felt a marvelous change in me almost instantaneously and the peace, tranquility and the contentment which followed it.

As a child I always loved the poor, the humble, and the meek. And my heart would bleed for them with love and compassion. But when I met my Guru I found that His Love and Kindness exceeded the dimensions of the oceans and He gave His Love and Compassion to everyone, rich or poor, black or white, Hindu or Moslem, Jew or Christian, Buddhist or Pagan, without any discrimination. His act of Love and Compassion to all beings alike made my heart melt and tears to roll down.

From the day I met my Guru my only intention in my thoughts and in my dreams was to consume His Divine attributes of Love and Compassion. My whole idea is to obey without question whatever my Guru commands me, and follow His preachings to the letter. This makes my mind peaceful and happy. In all my problems I exercise the patience my Guru has taught me and place my entire Trust on Him. And I find that all my problems melt away under His Divine Grace. In this way I have found the solution to all my worries and troubles.

I always like to sit in the presence of my Guru and absorb from His Wisdom and Truth. And feel His Divine vibrations. When I first met my Guru I was only able to understand a little of the Tamil language. I was always hoping that I could know enough of the language in order to read and understand His Magnus Opus, "The Voice of Allah". But I did not know how to read nor did I know even the Tamil alphabet. I approached my Guru with tears rolling down my cheeks and told Him of my difficulty. He smiled and touched my head and said, "My child, from now onwards you will be able to read this book fluently and understand the discourses!" And from that day I was able to do exactly what my Guru told me. I always read this Book whenever He is in Jaffna and I feel His immediate presence then.

My constant wish and prayer to Almighty Allah is to be close to my Guru so that I can always serve Him with the little needs He requires. I have surrendered my soul, my body and everything I had held dear to me to my Guru, even the children. Since I have done this I have found myself lighter and the children are better and wiser.

Now I have found my eternal peace and tranquility and my solace. I now await the day that my soul and my wisdom will be merged in His Perfection and Grace.

His humble disciple (Pulle).
Ameenathu-Zoharia. Macan-Marker.
139 Turret Road
Colombo 7, Ceylon

When you find the True Guru
you have found the Truth of God.

There has been no Guru other than the Guru named Qutb Mohideen which means the life of the Truth. This Guru has appeared in the world 11 times, with 11 different names, and in 11 different places. Now this Guru has appeared for the eleventh time in some way. This Guru could be 150 years or more. God has given Them His Grace and His Wealth. From time to time, the Guru Mohideen has come to teach the Truth of God to people, who in their own different ways are in search of, and thirst for the Truth of God. The teacher comes by the commandment of God to teach His Truth to His creatures.

My mother used to talk to me about the story of this Qutb Mohideen from the time I was eight years old. In my own way, I was in search of the Guru Qutb Mohideen. I loved Them with my whole heart. I have never loved anyone like I love Allah, the Rasool, and Qutb Mohideen. When my mother told me the story of the life of Qutb, it was as sweet as honey, and I drank it. I was so much in love with Their story. I kept saying in my heart, 'I will one day search for the Guru. It must be Qutb Mohideen.'

When I was fifteen, my mother asked me if I would like to become the disciple of her guru. I said, "I am young! When I get older, I will find the Guru." I can still remember from the age of fifteen, whenever I was in any trouble, or sad, in my own way, I would appeal to God through the Qutb Mohideen. I always succeeded. I knew then that the Qutb Mohideen was alive within my heart although to the world They had come and gone many years ago.

I can remember my mother used to go to a place called Jeelani, in the jungles of Ceylon. When I was old enough to understand, I made up my mind to go to Jeelani. I went with many of my relatives. The place was heaven for me because of my love for the Qutb. I recited only the name of Qutb when I was there. One day when I was there, I had gone to the pond to take ablutions for my prayers. While at the pond, my mind thought, why there were no fish in the water and only frogs and crabs. I said, "O Qutb Mohideen, O God, why is it like this?" Then to my surprise, I saw three goldfish in the pond. The others who were there saw the fish also and they said, "O God, what a miracle this is! We have been here for ten years and we never saw fish in the pond." My mind was bewildered, my faith was saying, 'God is great, Alhamdulillah, all praise to God who is the Creator. He can create in a second, and He can destroy too!' This I know because of my love for my Qutb, and this made my faith in God firm without any doubt.

Some time later when I had transfixed my love, my concentration, and my intention upon Them, one day my cousin telephoned me and said that the Guru whom I was looking for was visiting him and to come and visit him. When I met this Guru, whose name was Guru Bawa Mohideen, I invited Him to come to my house. He said, "You my child have been appealing to me for a long time and I will come to your house."

The next day we met the Guru when he was healing sombody from a very serious illness and after having observed this, we brought the Guru to my house. He arrived in our house about six o'clock that evening. Starting from about seven that evening, he talked and talked to us about God and were so involved in what he was saying that we did not move from the about Truth for a long time. My relatives and I who were listening to him room until we realized with a shock that it was seven o'clock in the morning. The people who came with the Guru Bawa Mohideen said that they had to take him back so that He can rest and that they will bring him back again.

Another very important thing happened that day. Several years ago I had gone to a Light Teller who told me that there were three evil charms in my house and if I paid her some money, she would undo the charms. I felt that it was not a good idea and within my heart I said that I have faith in God and prayed for the Qutb Mohideen to come and remove the charms. Now when Guru Bawa Mohideen was leaving the house, He said, "Child, there are three charms in your house and I will trample on them." Before He left, He trampled in three places with His feet. Then I knew that at long last I had found the one and only true Guru. He is my Qutb Mohideen whom I have loved from the very beginning, whom I had searched for in my heart from my childhood. With my belief, my faith, and my determination, I had found my true Guru by the help of God. That was the first step. The second step is to give up my physical vision and to control my mind and my desire with the zikr. La ilaha illallahu; There is nothing but God and only God is God.

From that day onward, I loved to be with Guru Bawa Mohideen and to listen to His sayings and discourses. They give peace to my heart. His face changes from moment to moment according to what He is saying at that time. His face shines. When He speaks, His words pierce through the heart and get firmly lodged within. I had seen fifteen or sixteen gurus before I saw His Holiness Guru Bawa Mohideen. But never before had I experienced this piercing strength of the words. The words of my parents got deeply imprinted within my heart when I was young and after that, it was what this Guru Bawa Mohideen taught me that entered within the inner recesses of my heart. And this is not just for me. Whoever asks whatever question of the Guru, I have heard Him explain so that they will realize with their wisdom.

Whenever we are with our Sheikh, Guru Bawa Mohideen, our qalbs are full and we see His Rahmath (Grace). Allah, Nur, and Qutb all appear as One. When He sings, it melts the heart and it flows like water. It enters one's consciousness. Whether one knows the language or doesn't know the language, the sound goes within and explains.

I've had several misfortunes. I have been afflicted by several fatal illnesses that even doctors could not cure. In those instances, even before I wished it, the Guru has come to me and cured me, regardless of whether I was at home or in the hospital, whether it was during the day or during the night. Even though He is 250 miles away, when He is needed, He comes as if He were just a mile or two away. He is with us in happiness and in sadness. When there is sadness and when we think about Him, He comes and relieves us of the pain. My personal experience in this regard is indescribable: The lessons we have learned for our life and the help that we have received. When we cry, He cries. When we smile, He smiles. He is the form of compassion. He is full of the qualities of God. It is because of this that I recognize Him as the Qutb, as the Sheikh, as one imbued with Qutubiyath. Knowing this most definitely and certainly, I have found and arrived at the feet of the Guru that my parents taught me about. My only prayer is that my brothers and sisters may find what I found.

Through my Guru Bawa Mohideen, I have come to understand the path of God and the meaning of what was written by the prophets, the saints, and in the four religions: Know thyself and you will know God.

April 14, 1972

His humble disciple,
Noorul Ameena Macan-Marker
32, Galle Face Cottage,
Sir Mohamed Macan Marker Mawatha
Colombo — 3,
Ceylon

* * *

For about 8 years before His Holiness came I had been searching. Searching for what I was never really sure, but this painful and incessant searching, this lack of fulfilment, was one of my very few certainties. This search led me through school, therapists, drugs, travel, gurus, jobs, girl friends, diversions, philosophies, etc., ad nauseum. Not until 3 years ago did it become clear that I was searching for God, but even that realization did not make my pathway any more direct. Tortuously I wandered from guru to guru, from mantra to yoga to meditation to ashram to monastery, never finding fulfilment, never sure if I was at fault through being unable to surrender, or whether I just had not yet found "my guru". I despaired of any solution.

Then in January 1972 I was on the verge of traveling once again, this time to New Mexico, to try yet another pathway. I saw a poster for Guru Bawa, but dismissed it, saying, "Not another guru. I'd o.d.'ing (overdosing) on gurus." I had seen so many, and none had the answer for me. Then, in the way God seems to sometimes work, through coincidence, thru the selfless devotion of His seekers, a new friend told me he was going to meet Bawa, and invited me to come with him.

Since that time it seems as if nothing in me has changed, and yet everything has changed. The certitude and determination and faith in God, which I never before had, have now, only now, just begun to take root within me. I did not experience any sudden transformations, no visions or flashes, telling me Guru Bawa is to be my guru. Yet from the first night I saw him, heard his speech, and received his blessing, I have sat with him every day and every night. I did not know why I was doing this. That was three months ago.

There is no certain moment, no special time when I realized I had accepted Guru Bawa and had decided to give myself to Him. Yet every time I asked for help He gave to me — help for my body, advice for my emotional problems, and wisdom to quench my thirst for God. He has fulfilled me, in a way that I have never, absolutely never, experienced before. Who other than a true instrument of God could quench the thirst to know Him?

The path now for me, a path clear where once there was only darkness, is surrender — surrender of my ego, my mind, my desires, my visions of this world. All my obsessions — with happiness, with a girl friend, with nature, with creativity, all these must go. There is left only one obsession, the obsession for God. And for the cure of this obsession I come to His Holiness Guru Bawa. I pray that through His Grace I may leave all else and come, finally, home to Him.

Please, please, please forgive me.
How can an ignorant person praise the sun?
My eyes cannot see, I cannot hear, taste, or
touch
The sun that arises in the East this day.
He but smiled, and we came to be.
He planted us, and we germinate.
He waters us, and we gracefully grow.

What is the place whence we came?
Who is our Father, where is our station?
We came from the light, and grow towards the sun:
Bright, bright without fault,
Cloudless, but always raining,
Raining little atoms of light,
Tiny, invisible particles, they
Blind our eyes, stun our ears.
Dumbfounded, we wait,
Awaiting more light.

Open, open, open,
Empty-full, empty-full, empty-full,
Gone, gone, gone.
Alone.
How can I? How could I?
He alone is.

Carl Marcus
254 S. 46th Street
Philadelphia, Penna.
19139

I find it very difficult to write about my experience with His Holiness. In one sense I could write for a million years about each moment I have spent with Him. Because everytime His glance falls on me, every time His words reach my ears, I feel my consciousness being stretched back to a period that I do not quite comprehend, long before I was born, and stretched forward to a time so far ahead in the future that I cannot see where it ends. And it seems like, from the time I met Him in 1964 to the present time, there have been millions of such moments, each of which can only be described in terms of millions of years. These moments of infinity are experienced by something within me which is not an aspect of my physical senses but bears some kind of mysterious relationship to it. It is a mystery, very similar to the mystery of the awareness of infinity within the confines of simple moments.

There are no ways of describing those moments. They are ecstatic experiences which can only be felt or understood, not explained. However, it would not be an exaggeration to say that those moments have been the greatest, the most worthwhile moments of my life up to now. Those brief moments that I spend with Bawanga make life worth living.

Mohamed Mauroof
254 S. 46th Street
Philadelphia, Pennsylvania
19139

* * *

I was hesitant in writing this little note for fear of doing His Holiness Guru Bawa an injustice.

I truly know that Guru Bawa is a true Gnostic Gnana Guru because of the way in which he has lifted, and is lifting, the veils of darkness from my eyes. And the way in which He has satisfied my life-long hunger and thirst.

Before meeting Bawa, I used books for my guru – I got absolutely nowhere. I sat in front of Bawa one night and knew that I had finally found The True Guru, the Guru of all Gurus, and that I could really begin The Real Search for God.

After searching around the world, both physically and vicariously, I found the True Guru in my own "backyard".

I don't have too many words, just Thanks to Allah, Thanks to Allah for sending us Guru Bawa.

Striving to become Egoless,

Jehora (Charlotte Miles)
6155 N. 17th Street
Philadelphia, Penna. 19141

Many experiences in life had prepared me and that which is within me for the experience of finding a true Teacher or Guru. When I was about three years old, my father, upon seeing me behave in an incorrect manner, said to me, "Why are you behaving that way? You know the difference between right and wrong." The words came as a shock to me because although I didn't have all the knowledge that grownups had, I realized with my full consciousness at that time that something within me knew with the utmost exactitude what was the difference between right and wrong.

Despite the warnings of this inner voice, I gradually tasted and involved myself with most of the evils of this world. As a child I occasionally lied and stole and was disrespectful to those who were wiser than I. In college I learned the "pleasures" of intoxication and sex. In the Army I learned how to kill although thanks to the protection of God I never had to kill or fight in a war. During this time I also worked at many occupations and what I learned in each of these was that whatever a man does, his ego makes him believe that that occupation and his involvement in it are the most important things in the world and that his way is the only true path toward self-perfection. But I also noticed that ways of life perished, but the world didn't come to an end; and people died, but the world didn't stop nor, for the most part, did more than two or three people remember those who had died two years later. So although these occupations or paths in life may help an individual perfect himself in regard to an occupation or his self-esteem, neither the occupations nor the individuals with their self-esteem seemed permanent; all died or changed into something else.

During the many years that I had been learning about these worldly things I also held within me a belief that God existed and had created us and everything else that existed. My religious experience as a child had been to go to church and to hear preachers and Sunday school teachers preaching things which were sometimes contradictory; things which they seemed to have memorized but not fully to have understood. They, while preaching good conduct, continued to show anger, falsehood, pride, avarice, lust, racism, and egoism. I also noticed that even those who regularly attended church still continued to exhibit the above evil traits and that when they tried to eradicate those evil traits through their religious practices, they were almost always unsuccessful. To follow in the footsteps of such preachers and practitioners of religion seemed hopeless. The topic of only one sermon stuck with me. The sermon concerned the word "straightway" in the Gospel of Mark. No matter whom Jesus called to follow him, they were said to have "straightway" dropped whatever they were doing and followed Jesus. What a phenomenal power of truth and righteousness Jesus must have had, what enormous trust and faith he must have been able to instill to be able to induce even two men who had been fishermen all their lives to drop their occupations and all that was familiar to them and follow him in a moment.

Involvement with various occupations and modes of living taught me many things, although for some mysterious reason other people involved in the same occupations learned entirely different things. Almost always when I was working, studying, drinking, making love, and so on, the real "I" felt separate somehow from what the body was doing, almost as if my body were performing the task while that part of me which was the real

"I" was looking on and evaluating the body's performance. Thus I learned that the pleasures of physical love soon passed and usually left tiredness and disillusionment and sometimes other difficulties. Being an archeologist taught that all bodies of people and all civilizations perish and are consumed by the earth and the sea. Being a cook taught that different flavors and heat must be mixed with the greatest care if a satisfactory taste is to result. Being a ranch hand taught that fresh air, clean work, and good diet were not a cure for disease, old age, and death. And the ranch owner once said that it is never wise to try to return to earthly experiences one has already left. Being a salesman taught the nature of the techniques of guile, deceit, emotional appeal, and how to make people desire things they didn't need, and other aspects of evil ascribed in most religions to Satan. Being a printer taught that those who are in haste and try to rush things cause anger and ill feeling. Being an oil drilling specialist taught how loss of temper and impatience could in a single instance cost a company thousands of dollars, an individual his job, and through an accident cost a person's life. Being a soldier taught that it is impossible to turn sheep into lions or lions into sheep, and that it is almost impossible to turn a mule into anything; and that a human being can at times act like all of these. Being a research assistant and studying chemistry taught that almost all of science is based on egoism and vanity, and that a scientist formulates his theories either to be able to sell a project or idea or to gain a reputation for himself as an expert on an obscure or currently popular topic, then arranges his mode of finding information and the information itself in order to prove he is right and his pet theory is true. During this curious procedure he unabashedly steals ideas and secrets from others and claims them as his own. Having in such a way construed the truth to prove his theory, he, often unconsciously and with frequent declamations that he is being purely objective, deceives himself into actually believing what he has found is the truth, and sells himself or his pet theory for money. Being a research assistant and studying chemistry taught that science is the epitome of egoism and deception. Being a social worker taught that all therapy, including the deepest psychotherapy, only looks at the surface of man, and that no medical treatment can cure a person who wishes to be ill. The roots of problems which afflict man seemed unknown to psychiatrist and social scientist alike, and they seemed only to be fixing a band-aid on a scratch on the finger of their patients while a cancer unknown to these "helpers" ate away their patients' hearts. It also taught that those who help in such professions seem to suffer the same diseases as their patients and because they never cure themselves eventually die from the cumulative effects of their own illnesses combined with those illnesses which they have succeeded in transferring from their patients to themselves. Working for a large corporation taught that it is easy to rise to top management if one ignores his conscience and is willing to exploit others, lie, and steal while still paying obeisance to selected superiors and inflating their feeling of self-importance. Being a musician taught that no matter how long one practiced to perfect one of the arts and crafts in this world, one can never reach perfection or find real peace in what he is doing. Also, an elderly musician once said, "No matter how much we kid ourselves that we are special, we're all doing pretty much the same thing, and we all end up the same way." Being a cab driver taught that taking the shortest route to one's destination earns the largest tip or reward.

During this time, although I believed in a Creator, I had no definite conscious belief that man was any different from the animals. Although I had been learning since the age of twelve when something had told me to learn as much about the world as possible, I knew that I was still in a state of ignorance. I also knew that I had many noxious habits, attitudes, and mannerisms which remained with me however hard I tried to eradicate them. Reading religious books taught that one needed a Teacher or Guru to achieve Divine Consciousness and to eradicate the evil actions, thoughts, and desires, but all preachers, "gurus", and self-styled "prophets" that I encountered or read about had the same vanity, egoism, lust, miserliness, anger, and arrogance that I was trying to clear from myself. How could they help if they suffered the same illnesses? Also, they always seemed to have memorized what "someone else" said was the truth, and somewhere along the line when the evil qualities above manifested themselves, the smell of hypocrisy was easy to discern.

About three weeks previous to my meeting Guru Bawa my wife had visited him and returned to say that she felt that everything he said had seemed the truth and that she could detect no hypocrisy in his actions. Knowing from past experience that my wife was perceptive in separating truth from falsehood, I resolved to visit this apparent sage to find if, at last, I could find a true Guru. During the three weeks that intervened between my wife's report and my first evening in front of Guru Bawa, I readied myself by attempting to bring my body and mental state through good diet and exercise and exclusion of sights, sounds or thoughts, that were evil to a point where nothing physical and nothing impure or false within or without would influence my perception or judgement as to whether he was a true Guru. This decision, my wisdom told me, would be one between a possiblity of finding a way to God, or a possibility of continued disillusionment with what seemed an endless search which without my finding who I was, why I was on this Earth, or what the meaning was of what was happening in this world, would lead eventually to death.

But then on January 20, 1972 through the Grace of God, the wonder of which is beyond all comprehension, I first visited Guru Bawa. As he talked, the words seemed to spring from his mouth like the clear pure water flows endlessly from an artesian well. The force of His very words as they struck the consciousness within me caused my body temperature to rise, but although I felt as if I had a fever, there was no discomfort. During the first two nights, despite the awesome force of a presence which seemed so full of love, compassion, truth, and wisdom, I searched to see if I could discern even one shred of hypocrisy or worldly attribute. That nose which I had sharpened by a lifetime of smelling out falsehood told me without any doubt at the end of the second day that I had at last, by the Grace of God, found the True Guru. At the end of that day I straightway accepted Bawa as my Guru without reservation, suspicion or doubt. At the end of the third day 95% of the evil attributes that I had spent a lifetime trying to eradicate, dropped off me as does the skin of the chrysalis of an insect when it emerges into adulthood. In three days 95% of the vanity, arrogance, anger, lust, miserliness, happiness, sorrow, egoism, untruthfulness, desire, impatience, and attractions to the material world dropped from me almost without effort, such was the force of the Guru. At last I had found that Tree the fruits from which satisfied all hunger and desire and could cure disease, aging and death. In three days I had learned that the way to become One with God was to follow His guidance: always without fail to do what the Conscience within says is right, never to do what is wrong, and always without swerving an atom to act with the 3,000 Divine Attributes of God, loving all living beings equally and placing them all before myself. From that day on there existed only my Duty to God: to follow explicitly His commands and those of Guru Bawa; to rid myself of all desires for worldly things seen by my eyes and the mental visions and distractions of the mind; to scrub all dirt and that which belongs to the Earth from the lens of the flashlight of my Soul so that when the current of Divine Luminous Wisdom is connected, God's Light can shine through my Soul, its force undiminished by any cloudiness of egoism on the lens. In this way, my Soul, merged with God, might administer God's Light to all living beings as does the Guru.

On subsequent days I felt my body becoming lighter. Frequently as I sat before Guru Bawa my entire body vibrated, shivered, and heated up as the Truth flowed from Him and struck my Soul. When I heard His description of the Creation of the Universe, the utter beauty and Truth of it caused the tears to pour from my eyes. Nothing from science or religion could have done this. Then Bawa showed me how He had cared for my family for three generations and that my Soul had been lodged in my body in response to a prayer of my father that he be given a son who was responsible. Indeed, I realized that I had heard my father use the name "Bawa" in my youth many times, but I had never known the significance of this. With this also I realized that I had never been alone in this world as I had thought, and that all the occupations and experiences I have had, and the lessons I have learned had all come from Guru Bawa even before my mind knew he existed. Surely, none of us blind creatures can comprehend the Compassion and Grace of God.

We are none of us alone for God has sent His Truth, manifested in the form of Faith, Certitude, and Conviction. The Wisdom of God, resonating with God's three thousand Divine Qualities flows from Him with the intensity of seven hundred million Suns, burns out evil, and unites with our Soul. The Soul and the Wisdom unite with this Truth, and these Three merge with the Noor or the Divine Effulgence of God. This Effulgence merges with God and All are One. Nothing exists but the One God. His creations will all perish. Other than God all is ignorance, falsehood, and darkness. It is the birthright of one born as a True Human Being to become One with God. God's Truth is among us. Let us straightway claim our birthright, become One with God, and accomplish our *real* Duty.

If anything I have written is
false, may God forgive me.

Dick Miller
1937 Chestnut Street
Philadelphia, Pennsylvania
19103

Guru Bawa came as Truth. His staff,
named Wisdom, touched the heart
and woke the gently sleeping seed
of Love and Wonder in each child.
This Trust He took, and with one smile
Brought all, so subtly to His fold
For God, Mysterious, Endless Light.

He called, we came, and gave our heart
to Him, the Perfect Endless One,
He moved His lips and like the wind
blew Faith to spread the spore of Truth.
There blossomed forth a gushing spring
of freshest water, ceaseless Bliss.

With Wisdom, Love and Vigilance
He placed the bud of Purest Good,
the Pearl of Grace, God's greatest wealth
into the longing, searching heart
and lit the torch of Certitude
to walk the long and dangerous path.

We are His Children, now, as then,
Each golden heart has joined the force
of Light, Eternity and Love
with Darkness gone, no more to come.
We give Him back the spark of life
The Soul, it's His, the journey's right.
Perfection knows no end.

> In Praise of Him,
> Myrna Elaine Miller

283

In attempting to describe to others how I feel about Guru Bawa and what meeting him has meant to me, some descriptive words do come – effulgent wisdom, all encompassing awareness, all-loving divine grace, abundancy, ray of Light. However, I always feel I haven't really expressed how I feel. For how can I describe this truly holy man, this beacon of divine Light; how can I describe God. So, instead, I usually relate some of my experiences, hold out my hand, and say come with me. Come and hear, and see, and be for yourself. For I have come to learn that each person receives according to his own particular needs – feels, sees, reacts from who he is.

When I first met His Holiness, I was a little nervous – comfortable, yet nervous. How do I greet a Guru, what do I say, what do I do? I knew little of these matters and still do. But, more important, I know now God is with me. I entered the room where Guru Bawa was, turned around, saw his face, those radiant eyes and nodded – a kind of bow and also recognition. As Bawa smiled and nodded in return, this simple act impressed my awareness and I became aware of a bond – a bond I am just beginning to fathom. I had postponed coming to see and hear Bawa for what seemed an eternity, about a week, for I felt I had obligations and commitments to complete and I felt once I came I would become intensely involved. I guess the bond was there long before I had any awareness.

I know now that Bawa is with me. All those obligations, commitments, duties, everything is more understandable, more easily handled or completed so very much more wisely – with more awareness now that His Holiness is helping me on my road to wisdom. I used to be fearful of many things, particularly being alone or loneliness, and had many questions with inadequate answers. Now the appropriate answers are beginning to come and there is little fear. I still question, I still am a little lonely in the physical world, but I'm just not that fearful or that lonely for God is with me.

Shortly after meeting Guru Bawa I was very upset about something I had done. I came to His Holiness seeking understanding and was forgiven for five sins. In my lack of awareness, faith, and understanding, I felt Bawa didn't know what was troubling me for I hadn't said the problem in his presence. In the next week, until I could speak with him, I talked and cried to Bawa the problem while not in his presence. Once again, Bawa tried to tell me he knew but I still didn't hear. Finally, when I told Bawa, face to face, he shook his head lovingly, smiled, and reminded me that I had already been forgiven – that it was time to understand and let go – now it was time to come to God. I had had the need to say the words, I had had the attachment. Bawa had known long before I had even intentionally spoken to him in my thoughts. Now I know he is with me.

I also know I stumble and fall; I feel the road ahead is long; I have no idea where all of this will lead me in the external world. But, I thank the Supreme Light for blessing us by sending Guru Bawa and I pray that someday I can attain wisdom, awareness and understanding with my true Guru.

Your learning and loving child,
Barbara G. Marmon

Time and moments of questions have slowly
transformed into gentle waves of continuity.
Faith the sustainer. Bawa the Protector. God
the Creator. The heart rejoices at the return —
such a festive spring!

To approach such brilliance has resulted
in so much cleansing. The ego abhors its
strength. The desires fall short. The mind
submits. The eyes are amazed.

January '72 climaxed the return of a
heritage — Light. The form was complete. The
source One. The moment fulfilling and the metamorphosis continued its slow but constant movement.

Seeing its splendor, the recognition was
instant — such welcome! And the healing was both
from within and without — such health!

His hand was placed within my head — Guidance.
His heart within mine — Wisdom. And now the within
is within — Wholeness; without, a moment of
gratitude.

Mark Ostrander
254 S. 46th Street
Philadelphia, Penna.
19139

* * *

Experiencing Guru Bawa has been like letting myself be exposed to a
great Light/Magnate. The Light gradually probes into my deepest and
darkest recesses, flushes things to the surface, and focuses on them an
acute awareness in an attempt to oust whatever needs to go. The Magnate
works from without and within. From without there is the pull to merge
with Bawa, to trust and surrender to him completely. From within there is
the pull to let go (of the self — ego — mind) and to merge with the SELF,
to experience the outer and inner (all) as One. And all the while "I" am
resisting as hard as I can resist — holding desperately on to the "known",
fearing a further plunge into darkness which must eventually become
LIGHT.

There are all sorts of games — like my mind rejecting what it *thinks* it
heard Bawa say, and thus bringing in doubt. There is the wild wild game of
the ego trying so very hard to let go and merge — and then scampering off
with glee once it's been found out, leaving behind only the pain (ego) of
having been duped again. But beyond the games is the ever present inner
KNOWING which pulls onward and inward. There is no turning back.

June Ridgway
5225 Germantown Avenue
Philadelphia, Penna. 19144

When I first came into Guru Bawa's room, there seemed to be no floor, and the television was on. There were people smoking cigarettes and talking. Some were watching television, some were not. It wasn't until I was well inside the room that I realized that this was a bedroom, and there was a bed in the bedroom and there was someone sleeping in the bed. The bed was a very usual, yet unusual bed. It had a blue dust ruffle and a green velvet quilt which was pulled up to the chin of the most beautiful face. There was something about the face that was very special, that radiated a very unique quality, the face and right hand that was curved softly, like a child's hand curves in a deep, peaceful sleep.

I was astounded that these people were here in the room, smoking, talking, watching television, and walking around in the presence of this man whose sleeping face radiated the Light of all the lights in the universe. Yet, it did not seem as if He slept. It seemed more as if He were in another plane, in some kind of meditation, there was that kind of stillness about Him.

The beauty of His face awed me. The incongruity of the noise and the television and the smoke made me feel as if He weren't there at all. My next thought was that He must be there because He was the One I had come to see – the Guru. I sat down next to the closet, alone, incredibly alone within the motion of feelings and emotions about the quiet presence of His utterly still face.

When I look at Guru Bawa, His physical form is so *defined,* so clear. The other physical forms that my eyes see are undefined and they somehow seem to be fuzzy and to blend into one another; other physical forms are in pastel, mixed colors. His form is in clear, primary colors. The color of His skin is like no other color I have ever experienced. His physical form is so extremely defined, that it loses all definition. His form is so clear that He is formless. His color is so beautiful that He is colorless. The clarity of His face does not exist in this world that we ordinarily experience.

When Guru Bawa taught us to breathe with the Kalima, the First recitation of Faith, "La illaha illallahu, Muhammadu Rasoolula," and when it was translated into English as, "Nothing exists but God. Only God is God. The Divine Face and the Beauty of the inner self is the true Messenger of God", I realized I had seen this Face, Guru Bawa's face many times before I had come into His room.

Last summer, before I met Guru Bawa, in a very small open space, a small green insect about a half inch long suddenly and gently appeared on the top of my left hand. I admired this small being's beautiful green color, the color was so perfectly green in the sunlight that it contained all colors.

I lifted my hand and this lovely green insect closer to me and held it at the level of my eyes. I examined it closely. I looked at its head. I saw its very big eyes. My attention wandered to the area under its eyes. Like a picture coming into focus, there was a face under his eyes – a truly human face full of compassion and joy. I looked more closely and the face became more and more beautiful, more and more glowing with a soft, clear light.

The face smiled the most beautiful smile I had ever seen. The smile was so beautiful that I could feel it, I could feel the warmth of it, the love, the radiance that came from that smile, the light that came from that face was so overwhelming that tears came from my eyes. I was filled to overflowing with this smile, with this light.

The face had some kind of small, soft, clear voice, but I couldn't hear what it was saying because the beauty of the face overwhelmed all sound. I looked at that beauty for a long time, but my attention wandered, and this beautiful green being disappeared as suddenly as it had appeared.

And when I was a tiny child, I saw God as a face. The One who is God, the Light of the un-atom within the within of the atom, the One who is Jesus and Moses and Mohammed, the One who has taught the Buddha, the One who has taught us everything we know, is our Father, Guru Bawa, is the only father I have ever known. As a tiny child, when I was old enough to be lonely for a Father, I used to pray to my God to bring me a Father. I never dreamed of the depth, of the vast extent to which He would answer my small prayer.

Guru Bawa, who is the Qutub, the Noor, who is Divine Luminous Wisdom calls us His "funny family", His children. He scolds us when we have been foolish and near danger, He wipes our tears away when we cry, He laughs with us, He tells us stories and secrets, and sometimes He sings us to sleep; He covers us when we sleep, He awakens us from bad dreams, He heals us, He teaches us, He feeds us, He takes care of us and He always loves us. He is our Father.

In His presence, all His children love each other, because of the love they have for their Father.

Guru Bawa often speaks of mankind as having One Father, as all of us being the children of One Father. That is what being in His room is. The variety of people who come to Guru Bawa is amazing; there are young people, old people, happy people, unhappy people, Christians, Jews, Hindus, Buddhists, Zen people, Yoga people, Sufis, people of all nationalities, races, creeds, people of all kinds, and He loves all of us, He fills all of us with His Beauty and Wisdom, He loves all of us, He is a Father to all. In His Presence we are truly the children of One Father.

I love You, Father, with my entire being, and I pray that Your children may always be in Your Presence, that we may someday come to a realization of who we are, and through knowing who we are — to know You.

Your child,
Crisi

Crisi Rudnicki
335 Hillside Road
King of Prussia, Pa.
19046

This experience with Shaikh Muhaiyudeen, or Guru Bawa, is being written at His request. Trying to express with words something as intricate as an inner-awareness is impossible. Any amount of words could never make it clear to anyone. More than likely, it will generate misunderstanding. It is something that transcends words or any other form of human expression, except for love.

I came to Guru Bawa with the prayer that perhaps He would be the one I had been searching for in the deepest recesses of my heart. That He would be the one who could faultlessly direct me to God and end my confused wanderings. That He would be the one who could fill the bottomless pit of my hungry soul, not for only one day, but for an eternity.

It has been ten days since His rain of Grace fell and found its way beneath the rock between me and God. And like a wild seed, I have split this rock. Now, like any other young plant in the sustaining radiance of His Light, I begin to grow. I must withstand the elemental forces that would overcome me so that my flowers will return the fragrance to Him. And with water from the Divine Spring and the Gentleness and Love of the Holy Gardener, my Guru, I shall bear fruit worthy to be placed on the alter of His Heart.

William D. Rutledge

* * *

When I first heard about Guru Bawa, I thought that he might be an interesting person to see and hear. But after seeing him that first time, I was drawn to hear him more and more, as I realized that I had finally found a human being who could relieve the intensity of the questions that had for a long time been troubling me: How can I live in this world and be with God? Who or what *is* God? What am I to do with my life? What is a spiritual life, and how can I know that I am growing spiritually?

Guru Bawa has shown me the meanings of these questions, and continues to show me how I might lose my self and grow in wisdom and love. My sometimes painful search for a true guide along the Path has ended; although I may not always know what is happening in me or to me, I have placed my life and growth in his hands, in his heart. Through him, I have finally understood that to seek God is to seek to be a perfect human being, and having given myself over to Guru Bawa's care, I can at last be sure that I am growing in that direction.

His loving child,
Anne Stokes

* * *

INDEX

293

297

301

305

Other Books by M. R. Bawa Muhaiyaddeen ﴿رَضِیَ﴾

Truth & Light: brief explanations

Songs of God's Grace

Wisdom of the Divine (Vols. 1–6)

The Guidebook to the True Secret of the Heart (Vols. 1, 2)

God, His Prophets and His Children

Four Steps to Pure *Iman*

The Wisdom of Man

A Book of God's Love

My Love You My Children: 101 Stories for Children of All Ages

Come to the Secret Garden: Sufi Tales of Wisdom

The Golden Words of a Sufi Sheikh

The Tasty, Economical Cookbook (Vols. 1, 2)

Sheikh and Disciple

Maya Veeram or The Forces of Illusion

Asmā'ul-Husnā: The 99 Beautiful Names of Allah

A Mystical Journey

Questions of Life—Answers of Wisdom (Vols. 1, 2)

Treasures of the Heart: Sufi Stories for Young Children

To Die Before Death: The Sufi Way of Life

A Song of Muhammad ﴿صَلَّ﴾

Hajj: The Inner Pilgrimage

The Triple Flame: The Inner Secrets of Sufism

The Resonance of Allah: Resplendent Explanations Arising from
    the *Nūr, Allāh's* Wisdom of Grace

Enough for a Million Years

Why Can't I See the Angels: Children's Questions to a Sufi Saint

The Tree That Fell to the West: Autobiography of a Sufi

Islam and World Peace: Explanations of a Sufi, revised edition

Booklets

Gems of Wisdom series:

Vol. 1: The Value of Good Qualities

Vol. 2: Beyond Mind and Desire

Vol. 3: The Innermost Heart

Vol. 4: Come to Prayer

Pamphlets

A Contemporary Sufi Speaks:

To Teenagers and Parents

On the Signs of Destruction

On Peace of Mind

On the True Meaning of Sufism

On Unity: The Legacy of the Prophets

The Meaning of Fellowship

Mind, Desire, and the Billboards of the World

Foreign Language Publications:

Ein Zeitgenössischer Sufi Spricht über Inneren Frieden
(A Contemporary Sufi Speaks on Peace of Mind—German translation)

Deux Discours tirés du Livre L'Islam et la Paix Mondiale: Explications d'un Soufi (Two Discourses from the Book, Islam and World Peace: Explanations of a Sufi—French translation)

¿Quién es Dios? Una explicación por el Sheikh Sufi (Who is God? An Explanation by the Sufi Sheikh—Spanish translation)

For free catalog or book information call:

(888) 786-1786 (toll-free in USA) or (215) 879-8604

or fax: (215) 879-6307

or e-mail: info@bmf.org

Web Address: http://www.bmf.org

About The Bawa Muhaiyaddeen Fellowship

Muhammad Raheem Bawa Muhaiyaddeen ☙, a Sufi mystic from Sri Lanka, was a man of extraordinary wisdom and compassion. For over seventy years he shared his knowledge and experience with people of every race and religion and from all walks of life.

The central branch of The Bawa Muhaiyaddeen Fellowship is in Philadelphia, Pennsylvania, which was M. R. Bawa Muhaiyaddeen's home when he lived in the United States before his passing in December, 1986. The Fellowship continues to serve as a meeting house, as a reservoir of people and materials for everyone who is interested in his teachings.

The Mosque of Shaikh M. R. Bawa Muhaiyaddeen is located on the same property; here the five daily prayers and Friday congregational prayers are observed. An hour west of the Fellowship is the *Mazār*, the tomb of M. R. Bawa Muhaiyaddeen ☙ which is open daily between sunrise and sunset.

For further information write or phone:

The Bawa Muhaiyaddeen Fellowship
5820 Overbrook Avenue
Philadelphia, Pennsylvania 19131
Telephone: (215) 879-6300
E-mail Address: info@bmf.org
Web Address: http://www.bmf.org

If you would like to visit the Fellowship, or to obtain a schedule of current events, branch locations and meetings, please write, phone or e-mail Attn: Visitor Information.

21636518R00194

Made in the USA
San Bernardino, CA
29 May 2015